MUGHAL ADMINISTRATION IN DECCAN UNDER AURANGZEB [1659-1707]

ZAKIR HUSAIN
M.A., M Phil (Alig.) Ph.D. (IGNOU)

GYAN

Published by

Gyan Publishing House
5, Ansari Road
Daryaganj, New Delhi-110002
Phone: 011-47034999, 9811692060
E-mail: books@gyanbooks.com

Distribution Network
gyanbooks.com
India, USA, Canada, UK, Australia, France

ISBN: 978-81-212-6474-7 (HB)

Reprint in India, 2024
First Published, 2022

Printed at: Gyan Press, Delhi.

Mughal Administration in Deccan Under Aurangzeb (AD. 1659-1707)
Author: Dr. Zakir Husain

DEDICATED TO MY REVERED PARENTS

LATE MRS. MARYAM

&

LATE MR. NASRUDDIN

رب ارحمهما كما ربياني صغيرا

O Lord, Show mercy on my parents as they have nourished me when I was young.

– Surah Isra ch. 17 verse 24

Contents

Preface

The Deccan has been an extremely crucial part of the Mughal Empire which began to be annexed and incorporated into Mughal imperial dominions from Akbar in AD 1601 and completed by Aurangzeb in AD 1706 after his last battle against Wakinkira. Aurangzeb held the Viceroyalty of the Deccan twice since December AD 1635 to August AD 1644 and AD 1652 to AD 1659 ending with his accession as Emperor both of which have been carefully analysed and commented upon.

However, when Aurangzeb became the Emperor of Mughal India in 1659 then the Deccan began to be dealt with like other provinces almost till the first half of his reign from AD 1659 to AD 1682 for a period of 24 years as Prince Muḥammad Mu'azzam remained the Viceroy during 1st to 2nd R.Y., 6th to 7th R.Y. and 10th to 13th RY; Shāista Khān from 3rd to 5th R.Y., Mirza Rāja Jai Singh from 8th to 9th R.Y., Bahadur Khān Koka from 14th to 19th and 24th R.Y., Diler Khān in 20th R.Y. and Prince Shāh 'Ālam from 21th to 23rd R.Y. of the four provinces of the Deccan namely, Khandesh, Berar, Aurangabad and Bidar. The Deccan viceroyalty in the last years of Shah Jahan, the Deccan provinces, AD 1659-1682, army organisation and deployment in the Deccan and the revenue and financial administration have also been carefully dealt with. But the situation dramatically changed when Aurangzeb following the conclusion of the Rajput campaign moved south with his entire court, household and the large Imperial army to Aurangabad in pursuit of Prince Akbar, who had taken refuge at the court of Shambhājī, son of Shivajī, which served the headquarters for the Mughal Viceroy. Aurangzeb's march to south for expansion is very much obvious as he had annexed Bijapur and Golconda in AD 1686-87 and Maratha Kingdom by 1689 besides conquering the major Maratha strong hold of Jinji in 1698 during the late seventeenth century.

In the second phase expansion of the Mughal Empire in the Deccan [1682-1707] has been explained in detail where territorial expansion and creation of new *subas* of Bijapur and Golconda has been elaborated systematically along with the conquest of the Maratha Kingdon in AD 1689 whereafter subsequently annexing Jinji in AD 1698. The administrative problems of the newly conquered areas were dealt with properly where assignments in the newly conquered areas were though taken care of yet were done in a few cases only to keep areas in *Khalisa* to meet the future plans of financing the Deccan.

As far as the provincial administration is concerned the emperor surved literally as Viceroy to cope with the financial difficulties which naturally pressurised the resources that effected the situation in *paibaqi*. The way as their occurred low income from the *jagir* assignments as similarly *faujdari* rights and jurisdictions have been discussed systematically. Special light has been thrown on the local administration and the maintenance of the military contingent has been highlighted. Not only role of *Názims* and *faujdárs* has been shown but also other *ṣūba* officials like *bak͟hshis*, *faujdars*, *qiládars*, *thanadars*, *qazis*, *ṣadrs* and *muhtasibs* have been clarified unambigiously.

As fas as land revenue and taxes are concerned the problems of revenue collection have been discussed where not only the geographical surveys of the *pargana* Ādilābād its means of irrigation, taxation and settlement with conclusion have been elaborated side by side explaining in details of the *jizya* already discussed by Satish Chandra in his well known article in *JESHO* of 1959 has been illuciated.

The question of *jagir* crisis, *paibaqi* and *khalisa* and income from *jagir* assignments has been discussed while the great famine and the role of the Mug͟hal administration has been explained in brief.

The four appendices are too significant as these throw light on the viceroyalty of Aurangzeb in the four *ṣūbas* of the Deccan from December 1035 to August 1644, besides giving full Persian photographic text translation and annotation of Aurangzeb's *farman* of 1665 to Mirza Raja Jai Singh in detail. A *farman* of Aurangzeb to Muhammad Azam Shah concerning Raja Ram is equally important. Thereafter statistics of *pargana* Ādilābād have been given as the purpose of this book is an understanding and comprehension of the 'Mughal Administration of the Deccan under Aurangzeb [1659-1707]' which has been divided into two parts from 1652 to 1681 and 1682 to 1707 till his death, including expansion in Deccan as it does cover provincial administration, land revenue and *jizya*, problems of the *zamīndārs*, question of *jāgīr* crisis, the great famine and Mughal administration along with appendices, preface, glossary and select bibliography.

I am highly thankful to my supervisor the late Prof. M. Athar Ali, who was kind enough in explaining numerous difficult passages in my research work. My special thanks are due to my revered teacher Prof. Irfan Habib, Professor Emeritus, Aligarh Muslim University, who has rigorously scrutinised most of the chapters. He has been generous enough with his precious time as and when I approached him. I am extremely grateful to my supervisor Prof. Abha Singh of IGNOU, New Delhi who has helped me in many ways specially by offering constructive criticism of my work. My friend Prof. S.Z.H. Jafari, Department of History, University of Delhi, has been instrumental in pursing my research and making it possible to get it press ready for which I am highly thankful to him. I am also thankful to my colleague Ms N.S. Alam for her help in several ways. I am also thankful to Dr. Faizan Ahmad Azmi who has been kind enough in getting it submitted as well as to Mr. Zahid of the National Archives, New Delhi who has excellently typed the draft.

In the last but not the least I should express my deep sense of gratitude to my late parents Mrs. Maryam and Mr Nasruddin whose constant encouragement and warm and good wishes had always been a great source of inspiration to me. My daughter Mrs. Asma Shaheen, sons Mohd. Iqbal and Mohd. Tariq together with my wife Halima Begum have patiently waited for the result of my researches for which I owe much gratitude to them. Along along with my grand-daughters namely Amina Iqbal,Anam Tariq Aiman Traiq and my grandson Ammar Iqbal Sallamaho.

Date 15th Safar, AH 1444 **Zakir Husain**

13th Sept. AD 2022

New Delhi

Introduction

While this book was written as a doctoral thesis, in the middle of 2014-15, the purpose was to check and prove the hypotheses that held the field at that time, like Jadunath Sarkar in his magisterial book, *A History of Aurangzeb* where Sarkar turned from a sympathetic biographer in volume one to a strict critic in the subsequent volumes, saw Aurangzeb's religious bias, and an increasing lack of balance in its pursuit, created a 'Hindu Reaction', whose base consequences his own undoubted ability and strong will could stem.[1] SR Sharma, in his *Religious Policy of the Mughal Emperors*, underlined the same argument, furnishing substantiation from qualitative data which suggested a decline of the Hindu component in the Mughal nobility.[2] Interestingly, Faruki, in his *Aurangzeb and His Times*, answers Sarkar, essentially transferring the allegation from Aurangzeb to *shariat*.[3] Whereas historians like I.H. Qureshi accept the Sarkar-Sharma hypothesis of a decline in the position of Hindu nobility, and acclaimed this as an achievement rather than a lapse on the part of Aurangzeb. With this controversy dominating the academic space, it seemed best for me to go to the evidence with an open mind and make a detailed survey of the Mughal nobility and trace the changes in its composition based on the *mansabs*, or numerical ranks held, making for the purpose as comprehensive a scrutiny of contemporary evidence as possible. The scrutiny was partly qualitative, partly quantitative. The evidence assembled did not in any sense exonerate Aurangzeb, but Athar Ali thinks it did set different limits within which the Emperor's personal preferences and decisions had impact; and it suggested a number of age factors, besides the one of religious bias, that seemed to lie behind changes in the composition and conduct of the nobility.

Other questions to which I was obviously responding were emulated by Satish Chandra (*Introduction to Parties and Politics at the Mughal Court*, 1707-40, Aligarh, 1959) and Irfan Habib (*Agrarian System of Mughal India*, 1556-1707, Bombay, 1963). Continuing in the tradition of Ibn Hasan and Saran, they argued that the Mughal Empire was a centralised and fairly

1. Jadu Nath Sarkar, *A History of Aurangzib,* 5 vols, Calcutta, 1912-30.
2. S.R. Sharma, *The Religious Policy of the Mughal Emperors,* Oxford, 1940; 2nd edn., Bombay.
3. M. Faruki, *Aurangzeb and His Times,* Bombay, 1935.

systematised polity; but going further, Satish Chandra implicitly, and Irfan Habib explicitly, identified another one, sharing in political dominance, which, in contrast to the nobility, generally segmented and localised, namely that of the *zamīndārs*. Irfan Habib suggested that the relationship between the two classes was one of adjustment and contradiction, and that the vicissitudes of this relation that explained much of internal Mughal history. This became necessary to explore the extent of *zamīndār* penetration of the Mughal nobility and test the thesis of increasing exploitation and the postulation of an agrarian crisis. Qualitative evidence overshadowed the quantitative; and if Athar Ali's preferences went against Bernier's picture of a nobility driven by its members' instability of fortune to reckless self-defeating exploitation of the peasantry, that was a preference that was stated necessarily with much caution and circumspection.

In 1966, from the publication of M. Athar Ali's *The Mughal Nobility under Aurangzeb*, some fifty six years have passed and during these years much has been written on Mughal history and some new questions have been asked. Were Athar Ali to sit down to write his book now, his text would doubtless be different from that pictured in 1966; he would clearly have been obliged to find space for interesting views published since that time, and also invoke the aid of such new evidence unearthed.

The popular enterprise is to cut to size the pre-modern Indian scene, especially in its imperial incarnations. The theory of the contemporary scene, with its rituals and symbols, originating in social anthropology and with particular reference to Africa south of the Sahara was applied to early medieval South India by Burton Stein, out in challenging the view of the Chola Empire as a centralised entity.[1] G. Awasthy and Romila Thapar have applied it to the Mauryan Empire;[2] With Frank Perlin and Andre Wink in the van, the Mughal Empire has come under scrutiny from those who intuitively feel that a powerful state could not have existed in India before the English *sahibs* arrived.

Parallel to the above, C.A. Bayly put forward the captivating hypothesis that the decline of the Mughal Empire was a positive phenomenon, since it released the innovative enterprise of local or regional 'corporate groups'. Such groups won the collaboration of the English East India Company, so that the early British rule was really a continuation, and not a supplanting, of the preceding Indian regimes. Chetan Singh has pushed back the existence

1. Burton Stein, *Peasant State and Society in Medieval South India*, Delhi, 1980.
2. Fussman, '*Central and Provincial Administration in Ancient India: The Problem of the Mauryan Empire', Indian Historical Review,* Vol. Nos. 1-2, 1987-88; Romila Thapar, *The Mauryas Revisited,* Centre for Studies in Social Sciences, Calcutta, 1984, pp. 1-23.

of such regional elites already within seventeenth century Mughal Empire, and Muzaffar Alam has endorsed the Bayly thesis in seeing positive features in both the seventeenth-century Empire and its shrinking successor states of the next century.

On the very impressionistic foundations on which this theory rests, Athar Ali has written elsewhere; and he takes the liberty of referring the reader to two of his papers, one of which deals with the question of regional affinities of the Mughal nobility, that could well have been included as an appendix to the present edition, while the other takes up the issue of the 'personality' of the eighteenth century.[1] Athar Ali would endorse J.F. Richards's sagacious statement that 'the reality' of 'Mughal centralized power' is one matter, whether 'this was good or bad' is quite a different one.[2]

On the issue of centralisation Athar Ali has not seriously felt that a change in the position adopted in his book is called for. Rather, on both the *mansab* and *jagir* systems, detailed studies have reinforced the basic view, even when calling for certain modifications in the picture he had presented in the first edition.

On the numbers and composition of the *mansabdars* constituting the class whose higher ranks formed the Mughal nobility (*umara*), Athar Ali has been collecting further material in connection with his project of presenting a comprehensive chronological list of all imperial awards of ranks, appointments, titles and *jagirs* in the Mughal Empire gathered from the sources and archives. Volume One of this work has appeared as *Apparatus of Empire*, Oxford University Press, Delhi, 1985. This volume set out the list for the period 1574-1658, and in the introduction Athar Ali presented numerical data, based on the details assembled, which may now be compared with similar data that appeared in the first edition of his book.

The argument that there had been a tendency to expand the numbers of *mansabs* and *mansabdars* (1st ed., p. 9), is supported by the new figures given in the *Apparatus*, pp. xiii-xvi. The total *mansabs* of those holding 1,000 *zat* increased from 163,000 (*zat*) in 1595-96 to 629,500 *zat* and 499,450 *sawar* in 1657, on the eve of Aurangzeb's accession (p. xiv). In his first two years (A.H. 1037 and 1038), Shah Jahan granted net enhancements of 48,900 *zat* and 45,650 *sawar* (p. xiv), figures that are slightly divergent

1. M. Athar Ali, 'The Mughal Polity ... A Critique of "Revisionist" Approaches,' *Modern Asian Studies,* vol. 27, University of Cambridge, 1993; 'Recent Theories of the Indian Eighteenth Century', Indian Historical Review, Vol. XIII, Delhi, 1986.
2. John F. Richards, *New Cambridge History of India,* I, 5, *The Mughal Empire,* Cambridge, 1993.

from those in the 1st ed., p. 10 (43,500 *zat* and 44,420 *sawar*), but bear out the fact that in his first two years, Aurangzeb was obliged to grant more *mansabs* (89,000 *zat*, 54,000 *sawar*) than his predecessor. For decades (based on lunar years) one can present the picture as follows:

NET PROMOTIONS

		Zat	*Sawar*
Shah Jahan	1st decade	100	90,385
	2nd decade	-5.050	130,215
	3rd decade	97,100	68,470
Aurangzeb	1st decade	73,700	103,950[8]

These figures depict that despite some effort to restrain enhancement of ranks, Aurangzeb's awards of *mansabs* over the whole first decade were considerable, though largely in line with Shah Jahan's rather generous awards in his third decade. The inherent tendency in Mughal administration to enhance *mansab* ranks, with consequent possible pressure on resources, is thus manifest.

On the ethnic composition of the nobility under Aurangzeb Athar Ali is not aware of any substantive questioning of the data presented in his first edition. Certain figures for the earlier period given in that edition should, however, be modified or reinforced on the basis of the more comprehensive survey of the sources in the *Apparatus*. His revised finding is that in Shah Jahan's 30th regal year (1656-57), there were 53 Turanis of 1,000 as against 67 in 1658-78; and 75 Iranis in 1656-57, as against 67. Thus, the advance in the position of the Iranis in the last phase of Aurangzeb's reign, in relation to the Turanis, when compared under the position in Shah Jahan's time is especially marked. The figures have made some gains. As 16 among 248 nobles of 1,000 and a fraction above 6 per cent during the period corresponding figure was 43 out of 486. The Indian Muslims' share remained practically per cent in 1656-57; they were, at 65, some 13.4 per cent during the period 1658-79. The Rajputs constituted at 46 nearly above in 1656-57, a share higher than 18.5 per cent for the period 1658-78; the decline in Rajput influence, despite the high ranks of Jai Singh and Jaswant Singh, was thus perceptible even in the first phase of Aurangzeb's reign. As against this, the Marathas, constitute over 2.5 per cent in 1656-57, accounted for 5 per cent in the period of 1658-78. The Hindus, as a whole, numbered 56, i.e. 22.4 per cent in 1656-57, and 21.6 per cent during the period 1658-78, so that the several things in their strength were insignificant.

If the foreigners and their descendants (Iranis and Turanis) are to be juxtaposed to the rest, the foreigners comprised over 51.5 per cent of the nobles of 1,000 *zat* and above in 1656-57 and practically the same.

From 1590 onwards the Mughal Empire had been almost continuously involved in military operations against the Deccan states. Except for an interruption of twenty years after the settlement of 1636, all peace treaties had been in the pact of ceasefire arrangements, which both sides were prepared to break whenever an opportunity presented itself. In this the Deccan presented a sharp contrast to Northern India, where Mughal conquests had been as expeditiously consolidated as they were made. There were surely geographical reasons – as the hills there made transport difficult and enabled great fortresses to be built – which may be held partly responsible for the slowness of the Mughal progress in the Deccan.

There were also additional reasons and one of them was the peculiar attitude which the Mughal nobles had towards the questions of the annexation of the Deccan. Explaining why the Mughals had failed to annex Bijapur, Bernier declares that this was because the generals set against it "conduct every operation with langour, and avail themselves of any pretext for the prolongation of war which is alike the source of their emolument and dignity. It is become a proverbial saying that the Deccan is the bread and support of the soldiers of Hindustan."[1] Fryer repeats the same statement calling "Deccan, the Bread of the military men."[2]

Support is lent to these general statements by individual incidents during the reign of Jahangir, Abdul Rahim Khan-i Khanan is said to have been taxed by Raja Man Singh Kachwaha for his dilatory way in conducting operations. The Khan-i Khanan retorted that the result of Man Singh's own success in Bengal was that he had been deprived of his command there; if he (Khan-i Khanan) also succeeded in the Deccan, he too would have to go.[3] Similarly, in the times of Aurangzeb, when Namdar Khan urged Shaista Khan to make a direct attack on Shivaji, the shrewd noble replied that if the Deccan campaign was so quickly concluded, an attack on Qandhar would be ordered; and if that too succeeded, the contingents would be disbanded.[4]

It was not, thus, the deliberate design of the Mughal officers that prolonged the war in the Deccan. The problem of supporting the war through the resources of occupied Deccan only was always there. Owing to the ravages of war, the Deccan had suffered heavily and its resources

1. Figures for the first decade of Aurangzeb's reign calculated from the table 'Net total ranks granted' on p. 10 of the first edition.
2. Bernier, pp. 196-97.
3. Fryer, II, p. 51. See also Manucci, III, p. 271.
4. *Dilkusha*, f. 123a.

were diminishing, as is emphasised again and again in the letters written by Aurangzeb himself when he was the Viceroy of the Deccan for the second time. Mughal nobles who were posted in the Deccan found it much difficult to maintain their request to *subadars* agents and were not militarily superior to their Deccan agents.[1]

In such circumstances, it was inevitable that cases of collusion between commanders and the Deccanis should be frequently reported. Jahangir, the Khan-i Khanan, and later on Khan-i Jahan Lodi, that has been suspected of accepting bribes from Ahmadnagar for the favour of ceding some territory. In the earlier part of Aurangzeb's reign a large number of officers from Prince Shah Alam downwards were deployed to have been opposed to a forward policy in the Deccan. In 1663 Aurangzeb charged Shah Alam with culpable negligence in defeating the Marathas, and he was replaced by Jai Singh as Viceroy of the Deccan. In 1667 on the recommendation of Prince Shah Alam and Jaswant Singh, Shivaji was pardoned and his son Shambhaji was given the rank of 5,000/5,000; Shivaji was also permitted to conquer as much Bijapur territory as his resources permitted, or else, he was to confine himself to his own territory and act according to the advice of the *subadar* of Deccan.[2] There were differences between Dilir Khan, on the one hand and Prince Shah Alam and Jaswant Singh on the other, when Shah Alam was *subadar* of the Deccan in 1668, because the prince and the *subadar* were slackening in punishing the Marathas.[3] In A.H. 1095 (1682-83) it was alleged that Shah Alam, Saiyid Abdullah Khan, Maumin Khan, Najam Khan Sani and Sadiq Khan were in secret alliance with the king of Bijapur. Aurangzeb strictly reprimanded the Prince, arrested Sayid A'bdullah and dismissed the others.[4] Later on Aurangzeb again had to reprimand Shah Alam, along with Bahadur Khan Kokaltash, for adopting a mild attitude towards Abul Hasan, the ruler of Golkunda. Shah Alam informed Ibrahim Khan, the commander of the army of Golkunda, that owing to the mild attitude adopted by Shah Alam towards Abul Hasan he had been sharply censured by the Emperor.[5] In 1685 Shah Alam was arrested on the charge of being in secret alliance with Qutb Shah and of being friendly with Shambhaji.[6]

Bahadur Khan (or Khan-i Jahan Bahadur Zafar Jang Kokaltash),

1. *Ibid,* f. 123a; *English Factories,* 1665-1667, p. 152.
2. *Adab-i Alamgiri,* ff. 25b, 27a-b.
3. *Dilkusha,* f. 35a-35b.
4. *Dilkusha,* ff. 34b-35a; Shah Alam was opposed to the forward policy of Dilir Khan in the Deccan directed against Bijapur (*Fatuhat-i Alamgiri,* f. 59a).
5. Mamuri, 168b-169a; Khafi Khan, II, pp. 320-21; *Fatuhat-i Alamgiri,* f. 100b; *Ma'asir-i Alamgiri,* pp. 293-94.
6. Mamuri, f. 165a-b; Khafi Khan, II, pp. 300-301.

who had for a time been the premier noble of Aurangzeb, was repeatedly suspected of being friendly with the Deccan powers. He was appointed Viceroy of the Deccan in 1672. Dilir Khan, a Mughal noble and Abul Hasan of Bijapur. It appears that Aurangzeb was not prepared to control such large forces to the Deccan as Jai Singh demanded, no approval of the recruitment and promotions of the Deccanis which Singh recommended for sowing dissensions among the Adil Shahis.[1]

There were naturally objections to Jai Singh's plan from who did not believe in an aggressive policy. It is true that the Mughals had started giving *mansabs* to the Marathas since the time of Jahangir. But to ask for co-operation from Shivaji, who maintained for all practical purposes a separate centre for his political power, was another matter Jai Singh's predecessor in the Deccan, Shaista Khan, had been so hostile to the Marathas that he never employed them either as cavalrymen or foot-troopers.[2] The test came when Shivaji appeared at Agra for grant of a suitable *mansab*. A number of nobles led by Jaswant Singh (who dismissed Shivaji as a "petty bumia"), Jafar Khan and Rā'd Andaz Khan were opposed to any concessions to Shivaji, while Jai Singh's policy was backed up by Amin Khan, Saiyid Murtaza Khan and A'qil Khan.[3] The Emperor seems to have remained undecided with the unfortunate result that Shivaji was neither crushed nor coneiated.

Thus, neither the policy of Jai Singh nor that of his critics prevailed. Whether by design or by force of circumstances, Aurangzeb waged a simultaneous struggle against all the three Deccan Powers – the Marathas, Bijapur and Golkunda. This was a forward policy with almost no qualifications. But it required a tremendous military effort, which exhausted the Mughal Empire, and once it had been undertaken, neither the Deccan nor the Mughal Empire could have been the same again.

THE DECCAN PROBLEM AND THE MUGHAL NOBILITY (1689-1707)

From 1682 to his death in 1707, for over 25 years, Aurangzeb remained in the Deccan. During the first phase of this period, he seemed to

1. Mamuri, f. 171a-b; Khafi Khan, II, pp. 330-34; *Dilkusha,* 93b-94a; *Fatuhat-i Alamgiri, Ma'asir-i Alamgiri,* pp. 294-95; Manucci, II, pp. 302-4.
2. For a definite account of Jai Singh's plan, see Sarkar, IV, 120-21, which is based largely on *Haft Anjuman.* See also *Alamgir Nama*, p. 913; *Dilkusha*, f. 28b; Khafi Khan, II, p. 184. For Aurangzeb's disapproval of the recruitment of the Deccanis, see *Dilkusha*, f. 31b. On 29th Ziqada, 8th R.Y. Aurangzeb told Jai Singh that the Deccanis could not be trusted in their word and deeds.(*Jaipur Documents*, No. 98, p. 184); *Nigar Nama-i Munshi*, p. 121.
3. Mamuri, f. 130a.

have succeeded in smashing all the three centres of political power in the Deccan. Bijapur fell in 1686, Golkunda in 1687, and in 1689, Shambhaji, the Maratha ruler, was captured and executed. It soon became clear, however, that the Marathas would continue the struggle despite their lack of an effective centre. While Mughal armies marched into the Carnatik in pursuit of Rajaram, the Maratha chiefs organised raids all over the Deccan from their innumerable hill-fortresses. Aurangzeb stuck to his resolve of wiping out all political opposition in the Deccan with a will that never slackened. Committing a very large part of his military resources to the task, he declared the war against the Marathas be a *jihad* (1699). He hoped that this, together with his own presence in the Deccan, would deter any open opposition among his officers to the Deccan war.[1] But the commitment of the immense Mughal military resources in the Deccan on the one hand and the prospects of a long drawn-out war, the outcome of which remained uncertain on the other, created a profound political crisis to which the nobles did not remain indifferent. Doubtless different nobles viewed the Deccan involvement in different ways. To the nobles of the old families – the *khanazads* – the influx of the Deccanis into the Mughal nobility was anathema and they longed for the restoration of their previous dominating position.[2] To others, who were actually fighting in the Deccan, the never-ending war against the elusive Marathas appeared to be futile, many of them desired an agreement with the Marathas so that both parties may live peacefully in the Deccan or in the alternative, they wanted the Emperor to return to North India with his chief officers while leaving his subordinates to carry on a desultory warfare. The historian Bhimsen, an officer of Dalpat Rao Bundela, is a good representative of the opinion favouring a settlement. He was deeply impressed by the desolation which the war had caused in the Deccan, the way in which the Marathas lived on plunder and the extent to which the Mughal military organisation had deteriorated.[3] He was extremely critical of Aurangzeb's strategy. The whole country was being lost and the people were being plundered by the enemy, but the Emperor was concerned only with capturing the Maratha forts (*qala-giri*).[4] Even Asad Khan, the Emperor's *wazir*, believing that no settlement with the Marathas was possible as long as the personal prestige of the Emperor was involved, once ventured to suggest that the Emperor should leave the Deccan since all the objects for which he had come had

1. Mamuri, f. 196a; Khafi Khan, II, p. 478-80.
2. See Chapter I.
3. *Dilkusha*, ff. 138b-140a. For the miserable condition of the imperial army in the Deccan, see *Waqa'-i Niamat Khan Ali*, pp. 15, 117.
4. *Ibid.* f. 146a.

been achieved, but he only got a severe reproof from the Emperor,[1] as Muhammad Murād Khan also notes like the Deccan campaign.

Some nobles were personally anxious to leave the Deccan and return to North India. Bahramand Khan offered a lakh of rupees to the Emperor for permission to go to Delhi for one year.[2] The majority, however, sought safety in half-hearted obedience to the imperial command or in secret understanding with the Marathas. Aurangzeb, it has been said, declared that he had to remain in the Deccan personally, for otherwise his nobles would not carry out his orders.[3] His complaint that his officers needed reminders to act according to his orders is preserved in *Akhbarat*.[4] Bhimsen says that Mughal officers often found private deals with the Marathas more profitable than resisting them.[5] Manucci also makes the same statement and cites the example of Daud Khan Panni who had a secret agreement with the Marathas.[6] The Deccani nobles were actually most unstable in their loyalties. In 1689 the Haiderabad nobles, who had recently been taken into Mughal service, caused great damage to the imperial cause by breaking into an open rebellion. In 1691 when Zulfiqar Khan was besieging Jinji, the Deccani noble accompanying him deserted to Rajaram.[7] Writing in the late seventeenth century, Bhimsen says that large numbers of the *mansabdars* of the country (Deccan) were deserting to the Marathas.[8]

In such a situation suspicions and intrigues at the Court and mutual jealousies among the nobles naturally found free play, Aurangzeb himself told Muhammad Murad Khan that he was aware of the exceptional courage in battle shown by him, but some of the nobles did not wish it to be brought to the notice of the Emperor.[9] Tarbiyat Khan was jealous of Muhammad Murad Khan, while a number of leading nobles were jealous of Fathullah Khan.[10] Aurangzeb could not give due promotion to Muqarrab Khan, the captor of Shambhaji, owing to the jealousy of other nobles.[11] There was

1. I'nayatullah Khan, *Aḥkam-i Alamgiri*, f. 25b-26a.
2. *Akhbarat*, 28 Shaban, 43 R.Y. For the indolence, dilatory tactics and cowardice of the Mughal nobles in the Deccan, see *Waqa-i Niamat* Khan *Ali*, p. 142.
3. *Dilkusha*, f. 140a-b.
4. Manucci, IV, pp. 98, 228-9.
5. Sarkar, V, p. 68.
6. *Dilkusha*, f. 99b.
7. Ibid., f. 140a. An interesting study of one of such deserters, Rahim Dad Khan, has been made by Prof. S.R. Phadke, *Proceedings of Indian History Congress*, Aligarh Session, 1960, pp. 259-60.
8. Mamuri, f. 145a-b. There was rivalry between Muhammad Murad and Shuja'at Khan; *Ibid*, ff. 197b-198b).
9. Khafi Khan, II, pp. 488-89.
10. *Ibid.*, pp. 391-92; Mamuri, f. 181a.
11. *Ma'asir-i Alamgiri*, p. 356.

keen rivalry between Saiyid Lashkar Khan, son of Saiyid Khan-i Jahān Barha, on the one hand and Zulfiqar Khan Nusrat Jang on the other.[1]

In 1686 when Aurangzeb was besieging Golkunda, some nobles out of jealousy alleged that Saf Shikan Khan, son of Qiwamuddin Khan, was not pressing the siege vigorously, Aurangzeb thereupon dismissed him and confiscated his property. But when it was established that the allegations were false, Aurangzeb restored Saf Shikan Khan to his former post and *mansab*.[2] In 1699 when Iradat Khan was transferred to the contingent of Tarbiyat Khan, he petitioned to the Emperor that he was prepared to undertake any assignment given by the Emperor but was not prepared to work with Tarbiyat Khan.[3]

Such instances of rivalry and jealousy among the nobles during the Deccan Wars could be multiplied,[4] but those given above should suffice to reveal their nature.

In this situation, the formation of cliques and factions pulling in different directions was inevitable. Since there was a growing doubt about the success of the Mughal cause as a whole, the nobles naturally started looking to their own personal interests. "Nothing", observed Manucci in 1700, "can be more surprising than the way things go in the Mughal Empire. The king, the princes, the governors and the generals have each their own lines of policy, calculated for securing success to their designs."[5]

Two important groups among the greatest nobles arose, which typified the new factionalism, which may be loosely designated as Irani and Turani. Between the nobles of these two races there had been an ancient rivalry, as we have seen. In Aurangzeb's last years the leading Irani nobles were Asad Khan and his son, Zulfiqar Khan and the leading Turani nobles, Ghaziuddin Khan Feroz Jang ad his son, Chin Qilich Khan.

The character of the two groups, and the careers of the leading figures of each, have been carefully analysed by Satish Chandra in his *Parties and Politics at the Mughal Court*, 1707-1740. As pointed out by him, the first

1. Khafi Khan, II. p. 359; Mamuri, f. 175b.
2. Rivalry between Saf Shikan Khan and Feroz Jang (*Ma'asir-i Alamgiri*, p. 290); Jealousy between Ali Mardan Khan and Zulfiqar Khan (Manucci, III, p. 273); Khudaband Khan refused to cooperate with Zulfiqar in 1702 in crushing the Marathas because he was jealous of Zulfiqar (*Dilkusha*, f. 137a). For the jealousy between the *Khanazads* on the one hand, and the Deccani nobles who were new entrants in the Mughal service on the other, see Mamuri, f. 181a; Khafi Khan, II, pp. 391-92.
3. *Parties and Politics*, p. 9.
4. *Dilkusha*, ff. 162a, 172b; *Azam al Harb*, pp. 188-92; Khafi Khan, II, p. 572.
5. This aroused Aurangzeb's displeasure (*Ma'asir-i Alamgiri*, pp. 391-2).

group was "essentially a family-cum-personal group and was held together by family loyalties, and the personal relations of its adherents with Zulfiqar Khan.[1] Besides Asad Khan and Zulfiqar Khan, Daud Khān Panni, Dalpat Rao Bundela and Ram Singh Haṛa could be considered members of this group. Their combined *mansabs* at Aurangzeb's death amounted to 25,000 *zat* and 23,500 *sawar*:

Asad Khan	7,000/7,000
Zulfiqar Khan	6,000/6,000
Dāud Khān Panni	6,000/6,000
Dalpat Bundela	3,000/3,000
Ram Singh Hara	3,000/1,500
	25,000/23,500

Ghaziuddin Khān Firoz Jang's group was a "racial-cum family group" inasmuch as all its important adherents were Turanis.[2] The combined *mansabs* came to 20,000 *zat*/15,600 *sawars*.

Ghāziuddin Khan Firoz Jang	7,000/7,000
Chin Qilich Khān	5,000/5,000
Muhammad Amin Khān	4,000/1,500
Ḥamid Khān	2,500/1,500
Raḥimuddin Khan	1,500/600
	20,000/15,600

An important element common to both groups in the time of Aurangzeb was their deep involvement in the Deccan. Both Zulfiqar Khan and Ghaziuddin Khan had a long record of military service in the Ḍeccan and were certainly his leading generals. Their interest in the Deccan was revealed by their extreme reluctance to accompany Prince Azam to the North after Aurangzeb's death.[3]

But it appears that within the Deccan the two groups were protagonists of different policies. Asad Khān and Zulfiqar Khan believed – gradually came to believe – in the necessity of placating the Marathas and saving Mughal authority in the Deccan through a settlement with them. In 1698 Zulfiqar Khan captured Jinji, but Rajaram escaped or was allowed to escape.[4] Only a year earlier Zulfiqar had forwarded a proposal from Rājarām for a settlement to Aurangzeb, but Aurangzeb was not prepared to entertain it.[5] In 1705 when Aurangzeb was hard pressed at Wakinkera, Zulfiqar was summoned along with his officers. The arrival of Zulfiqar Khan changed the situation and the fort fell after a short time. Aurangzeb,

1. *Dilkusha*, f. 122a-b.
2. *Ibid.*, f. 153a.
3. *Dilkusha*, ff. 154-55b; *Ma'asir-i Alamgiri*, p. 511; Manucci, III, pp. 498-99.
4. *Raqaim-i Karaim*, f. 23b; *Dilkusha*, f. 98a.
5. *Dilkusha*, ff. 154b-55b.

however, suspected that it was due to Zulfiqar Khan and Rao Dalpat's intrigues that the Maratha forces escaped unhurt.[1] Later on when Aurangzeb wanted to sow dissension among the Marathas, he handed over Shahu to Zulfiqar Khan to enable him negotiate with the Maratha *sardars*.[2] Shahu was also given the rank of 7,000/7,000 and the title of Raja.[3] Zulfiqar Khan wrote conciliatory letters to the Maratha *sardars* and asked them to join Shahu, but there was no positive response on their part.[4] Zulfiqar Khan's attempt at placating the Marathas was also noted by a French observer, Francois Martin, who thought that he was seeking to strengthen himself by this alliance.[5]

Daud Khan Panni, a bosom friend of Zulfiqar Khan, had s secret agreement with the Marathas and did not try to crush them when he was governor of Carnatik in 1705.[6]

In contrast with the attempt at a negotiated settlement with the Marathas repeatedly made by Zulfiqar Khan, Ghaziuddin Khan Firoz, the king adopted a firm and uncompromising attitude towards them. Yet he was reputed to be harbouring ambitions, which were not entirely in conformity with the spirit of loyalty. Isar Das describes an incident which shows that Ghaziuddin Khan was thinking of becoming independent after Aurangzeb, and he might have hoped to carve out a kingdom in the Deccan for himself on the basis of his military successes. It was believed that Aurangzeb had begun to suspect him, and Isar Das goes so far as to allege that Ghāziuddin Khan's blindness had been thought about by a physician sent by Aurangzeb.[7]

The jealousies, rivalries and factionalism within the nobility, which these two groups reveal, give an indication of the serious political crisis that the Mughal Empire would have to face in the future. Aurangzeb's policy might have succeeded – though even this is doubtful – if the majority of his officers had brought loyalty and a singleness of aim and purpose to their task. But their factionalism, while it deprived Aurangzeb precisely of this support, also reflected in a great measure a grievous lack of confidence

1. Quoted by Sarkar, *History of Aurangzeb*, V, p. 101.
2. William Irvine, *The Army of the Indian Mughals: Its Organisation and Administration*, reprint, Delhi, 1962, p. 105. Irvine seems himself to fall with this opinion and calls the matchlock a cumbrous and probably ineffective weapon... left mainly for the infantry' (p. 91).
3. *Bernier's Travels*, A. Constable (tr.), V.A. Smith (ed.), London, 1916, p. 48.
4. S.N. Sen, *Indian Travels of Thevenol and Careri*, Delhi, 1949, p. 242.
5. Niccolao Manucci, *Storia do Mogor*, tr. W. Irvine, London, 1907-8, I. p. 140.
6. Iqtidar Alam Khan, 'Socio-Political Implications of the Dissemination of Handguns in Mughal India' (Mohammad Habib Memorial Vol., forthcoming)
7. Cf. W.H. Moreland, Rank (*Mansab*) in the Mughal State Service', JRAS, 1936, pp. 641-65.

in the Emperor and the Imperial policy on the part of the great nobles. It is significant that the group led by Ghaziuddin Khan, while it ostensibly supported the Deccan policy of Aurangzeb, also visualised its eventual failure, and thus led to the creation of an independent principality in the Deccan under his son.

At that moment Athar Ali was engaged in compiling the massive data on all rank-awards in appointments from the historical works and documents of Aurangzeb's reign, and he expected from that work this deficiency could be partly rectified, enabling us to speak with greater confidence in our absolute figures as well. But at that moment, he was unable to present the figures that could hopefully emerge in Apparatus, II, though the work was in an advanced stage of that almost was completed.

The total figures of 575 holders of 1,000 *zat* and above for the period 1679-1707, that is an undercount, do suggest a notable increase in the *mansabs* over the earlier period, 1658-78, where the corresponding figure is 486, though undoubtedly the earlier period is shorter. But one must set the increase in aggregate pay-claims against the additional revenue resources of the territories annexed during the period in the Deccan. With appropriate manipulation of *jamadami* (assessed revenue) and assignment of month-ratios to individual nobles for setting their military obligations, the basic schedules and rules could have continued without much modification. Rather surprisingly, the increase in numbers of ranks was not anywhere near the scale witnessed between 1595 and 1656-57, an increase of 4.2 times (ranks of 500 *zat* and above), and totally out of proportion with the actual addition of territory within that period. One can only hold that Aurangzeb did his best to hold back the pressures for higher *mansabs* with greater vigour than his predecessors were able to do. He could, therefore, in large measure, avoid the formal pay-deflation by which his predecessors had countered the rank inflation. The consequential changes in the required size of military contingents could also be avoided.

It is less easy to see how the *mansab* rules could be made to accommodate the changing needs of military organisation. They were originally made when mounted archers were the mainstay of the Mughal army. Irvine actually noted that the matchlock "up to the middle of the 18th century was looked on with less favour than the bow and arrow which still held their ground."[1] Even so it cannot be imagined that all musketeers were in the direct employ of the Emperor and that no noble was expected to maintain them as part of his obligatory military contingent. It is not yet clear how the musketeers were adjusted against the bow-bearing cavalry in

1. Muzaffar Alam, *The Crisis of Empire in Mughal North India: Awadh and Punjab, 1707-48*, Delhi, 1986, p. 5.

the prescribed rules. It seems, indeed, that the rules contemplated an army mainly of cavalry, where the breeds of horses and the rider's skill with the bow were the main considerations. In 1666, observers like Bernier thought that the advantage still lay with such troops. 'It cannot be denied that the cavalry of this country manoeuvre with much ease, and discharge their arrows with astonishing quickness, a horseman shooting six times, before a musketeer can fire twice.'[1]

In 1695 Careri, speaking of the army of 'the Great Mogul', says, 'most of the soldiers have bows and arrows,[2] while Manucci (c. 1700) notes that the Mahomedan great men pride themselves much upon their good shooting with bow and arrow', practising the art 'many times a day'.[3]

While it may be conceded that by mid-seventeenth century mounted archers could still prevail against infantry carrying heavy, cumbersome muskets, it is unlikely that by 1700 this remained the case. As Iqtidar Alam Khan has pointed out, the diffusion of the manufacture and use of muskets was causing anxiety to the Mughal administration in the time of Aurangzeb.[4] If so, the very rigidity of the *mansab* regulations worked against the formation of a kind of army (preferably, a directly paid standing army, and not one raised through contract farms, as was the Mughal army),[5] in which the arms of musketeers and artillery were given their due. In such circumstances two things could happen: The Mughal army could become increasingly obsolete; and, with this obsolescence, the entire structure of *dagh-tas'hiha* (verification) could lose its relevance. This is an aspect which Athar Ali entirely overlooked in the first edition. In 1996 AD edition he pinpointed it, because it seemed to him that the purely military factors in the decline of the Mughal Empire need to be given adequate attention.

On the features of the *jagir* system under Aurangzeb as described by him in Chapter III of this book, no major disagreement has appeared in the published work. It is true that Muzaffar Alam has casually contested the finding, based on extensive material cited in Athar Ali's text (pp. 78-9, 92-4), that *jagir* transfers not only continued till the end of Aurangzeb's reign, but, if anything, tended to become more frequent. He tells us, on the other hand, that such transfer, encountering resistance from nobles 'was

1. Richards, *Mughal Administration in Golkunda*, Oxford, 1975, pp. 158, 308-9.
2 Alam, *Crisis of Empire*, p. 7. Incidentally, none of the proponents of the jagir crisis has argued that it was confined only to the Deccan, 'a deficit area'!
3. J.F. Richards, *Mughal Administration in Golconda*, pp. 160-1. Read 'Khalisa Sharifa' for 'Khalisa Sharif' in the heading of col. 1.
4. Cf. W.H. Moreland, *Relations of Golconda*, London, 1931.
5. The document is published in Selected Documents of Aurangzeb's Reign, Yusuf Husain Khan (ed.), Haiderabad, 1959, pp, 233-5.

left unimplemented in a number of cases in the 17th century'.[1] Since he does not provide reference to a single such case, or to any contemporary statement of such failure to implement *jagir* transfer orders during the period before 1707, one is at a loss to understand the basis for so confident an assertion made by him.

More substantive is J.F. Richards's questioning of Athar Ali's thesis of a 'crisis in the *jagirdari* system' in the last years of Aurangzeb. It is worth noting that he at least originally confined his doubts to the situation in the annexed kingdom of Golkunda, becoming the province of Haiderabad upon annexation (1687).[2] Such are the attractions of a new faith, that Muzaffar Alam, without any further evidence, supposes the theory of *jagir* crisis to have been refuted ('demolished') by Richards for the whole of the Deccan.[3] It is, however, important to realise that Richards' doubts were based entirely on one document, which gives only the specifications of the area held in *khalisa* and *paibaqi* (lands temporarily held by the Treasury prior to assignment in *jagir*) and does not mention *jagirs* at all, if one goes by Richards' own tabular analysis of it.[4] It is apparently a paper compiled immediately upon conquest. Since the Qutb-Shahi Kingdom had a system of revenue farms (*ijara*) rather than *jagir* assignments,[5] it would be natural to expect that the Mughal government would first have a statement of fiscal resources compiled, with *paibaqi* possibly representing the pool out of which *jagirs* would be assigned to nobles posted there; and *khalisa* would, for the moment, be a very large area, pending decision as to what would in due course be retained out of it. The exceptional nature of the situation and untypicality of the document (no *jagirs*, only *khalisa* and *paibaqi*) is borne upon us when we compare it with another statement, giving the breakdown of the assignments of the Karnatak portion (19 *sarkars*) of the *suba* of Haiderabad in AH 1117/1706. All figures are in rupees and annas, representing the fixed assessment (*jama'i muqarrari*). Its information may be tabulated as follows:

---

1. See Bernier, p. 341. The formal general order, however, came later in 1672-73 (*Mirat-i Ahmadi*, I, p. 288).
2. Bayly, *Rulers, Townsmen and Bazars: North Indian Society in the Age of British Expansion, 1770-1870*, pp. 164-70.
3. *The Crisis of Empire in Mughal North India*, Delhi, 1986, pp. 39-42. On p. 318, Alam takes *ijara* to be one of the main indicators of the 18th century endeavour to make use of possibilities of growth within existing social structures. On p. 42 he invents a term, *baqqaliat* (translated by him as shopkeeping), not found in his source (Khafi Khan, II, 902 or anywhere else). The translation too is wrong: *baqqal* was the Indo-Persian term for a *banya*, not green-grocer or shopkeeper.
4. 'Portfolio Capitalists and the Political Economy of Early Modern India', *Indian Economic and Social History Review*, vol. xxv. no. 4, 1988, pp. 401-24.
5. Royal Asiatic Society (London) MS, *Akhbarat*, A 193, 197.

A.	Khalisa sharifa	990,679.14
	That includes territory in control of polygars	138,427.13
	Peshkash (Tribute)	23,000.00
		161,427.13
B.	(With) *Jagirdars*	6,080,125.10
	(Includes) *Qiladars*	1,177,688.70
	Dāud Khan	557,651.12
	Bahādur Khān	176,538.40
	Abdun Nabi	143,444.12
	Sa'adullah Khan	15,591.70
	Roshan Beg Khan	8,346.00
	Troops (*ahsham*)	1,994,173.30
	Service staff	6,816.5 ½
	Miscellaneous	2,013,875.7 ½
C.	*Inam*, etc.	28,223.4 ½
	Includes *Inam*	25,610.4 ½
	Cash-grants	2,613.0
D.	Temporary levies (*sih-bandi*) accompanying *Amirul Umara*, etc. (Jama' assigned to levy under each officer separately stated)	5,249,305.0
E.	*Paibaqi*	3,291,863.5 ¼
	Area under Polygars	2,629,216.4
	Balance	662,647.1 ½
	Total[1]	**15,640,202.8**

Although there are presumably some misreadings or misprints in the published document yet the totals being not exactly consistent with the detailed figures in some cases, still the thrust of the contents is obvious. Interestingly, the *khalisa sharifa* accounts for barely 6 per cent of the *jama'*. The *paibaqi* amounted to 20 per cent of the *jama'*, but of this the bulk was really in the hands of Polygars, so that only a small balance of a little above 4 per cent of the *jama'* remained effectively available for assignment in *jagir* for revenue-extracting purposes. If the entire phenomenon of the *jagir* crisis is to be judged on the basis of just a single document or a pair, one may argue that here, by 1706, we have good testimony for the intense pressure for *jagirs*, which contemporaries were speaking of. But clearly, the question is not one to be settled by stray documents; and I am not convinced that contemporary 'qualitative' depictions of the phenomenon must necessarily be disbelieved.

1. Blochet Suppl. Pers. 482, f. 12a. [in 1650 AD]

While re-reading Athar Ali's Chapter IV, I would continue to argue (as on pp. 98-9) that there could be a connection between Shah Jahan's death (1666), signifying the removal of a possible replacement, and the rather meagre results in the net of Aurangzeb's feverishly active military policy pursued until then, on the one hand, and the purposeful enforcement of a policy of religious discrimination which began thereafter, on the other. But perhaps Athar Ali's original text is far too confident in making it appear that Aurangzeb's turn towards an active religious policy could thus be 'rationally' explained. This Athar Ali may say was not even his intention. I did not intend to exclude Aurangzeb's own strong grounding in orthodox Islam. His attitude before 1666 was already different from that of Shah Jahan, as manifested in his withdrawal of a number of cash and land grants to Hindus during the early years of his reign.[1] Shah Jahan's death and the lack of military success can only be seen as circumstances which drew Aurangzeb more towards the strengthening of a policy already embryonically present.

Had Athar Ali's book in its 1966 garb been published today, then surely some reviewer would have expressed his astonishment that on so crucial a theme as revenue-farming (*ijara*), Athar Ali should have devoted barely one and a half pages (pp. 83-4), and that too in connection with the administration of *jagirs*. With C.A. Bayly's *Rulers, Townsmen and Bazars*, published in 1983, 'revenue-farming' has indeed aggressively moved to the centre stage of Mughal and late-Mughal history as a leading institution of 'warrior entrepreneur(ship)', a channel serving equally well for ensuring smoother cash flows and better local collaboration.[2] What in the seventeenth and eighteenth centuries was regarded as an evil feature, contributing to over-taxation and 'rack-renting', has come to be regarded, post-Bayly, as an innovative institution of great vigour. Thus Muzaffar Alam, deprecating the earlier view of the institution, champions the cause of the Sayyid brothers' protege Ratan Chand, a major practitioner of revenue-farming in the reign of Farrukh Siyar (1713-19).[3] The keystone to the whole arch of the new doctrine has now been doubtless laid by the identification of revenue-farming with a portfolio capitalism by Subrahmaniam and C.A. Bayly.[4]

1. Yusuf Mirak, *Mazhar-i Shahjahani*, ed. Sayyid Husamuddin Rashidi, Hyderabad (Sind), 1962, pp. 52-3.
2. Irfan Habib, *Agrarian System of Mughal India*, Bombay, 1963, pp. 317-51.
3. Athar Ali's reservations appear on p. 92 of the first edition of his *Mughal Nobility*. Similar doubts are now recorded by J.F. Richards in *Mughal Empire*, Cambridge, 1993, pp. 291-2.
4. Shireen Moosvi in *Studies in History*, I (i), New Series.

The present is unable to share in the euphoria over the discovery of new virtues in the old virus of farming. Revenue-farming existed at all levels of Mughal administration in the seventeenth century; but, so long as the empire functioned as a centralised apparatus, it was kept under control. In December 1702-January 1703, Prince A'zam, Governor of Gujarat, considered the farming out of the *sarkar* of Sorath (or/and its *faujdari*). He had two offers: Muhammad Beg Khan, offering to maintain the entire local levies (*sih-bandis*) and pay Rs 3 lakhs, guaranteed by a reliable banker (*sahukar*), and Safdar Khan Babi offering Rs 2½ lakhs, presumably on the same conditions. But the prince rejected both bids for the express reason that he could not assign duties in his own establishment (*sarkar-i 'ali*) to imperial officers (*banda-hā-i pādshāhi*).[1] Here, then, high-titled nobles were seeking to take on farm revenue of a large area: no local entrepreneurship was even remotely involved. At the other end, again in Gujarat, we are introduced to 'the Prince of Revenue farmers, the chief of merchants, khwaja X' [Salahuddin Muhammad Shah village *sarkar* Surat] who was seeking the farm of a single village, the evidence coming from a collection of documents, compiled in c. 1650.[2] Here, then, we have the case of, perhaps, a true 'portfolio [proto-]capitalist'.

However varied the class of revenue-farmers, the general administrative doctrine was against the institution because of its inevitable oppressiveness. In 1634, praising a *jagirdar*, the author of *Mazhar-i Shahjahani* says that the *jagirdar* rejected the offer of local headmen (*arbab*) and others for taking the revenue-farm of a *pargana* at Rs one lakh, where the regular realisation was only Rs 20,000, because he knew that 'in the practice of *ijara* lies the ruin of the country'.[3] But then he did not have the acumen of some modern historians.

In his book Athar Ali had expressed some reserve towards Irfan Habib's then recent thesis of the 'agrarian crisis' in Aurangzeb's reign, the cause of which, following Bernier, was laid at the door of the *jagir* transfer system, and the consequent over-exploitation of the peasantry.[4] Athar Ali had thought that the imperial checks upon the *jagirdars*' exactions and internal

1. The new information collected for 1656-57 is analysed in *Apparatus*, p. xx.
2. *Medieval India – A Miscellany*, K.A. Nizami (ed.), I, Bombay, 1969, p. 80. See genealogical charts, pp. 82-5. The family had known marital alliances with seven Iranian families.
3. Abdul Aziz, *The Mansabdari System and the Mughal Army*, Lahore, 1945; W.H. Moreland, 'Rank (*mansab*) in the Mogul State Service', *Journal of Royal Asiatic Society* (JRAS), 1936, pp. 641-65.
4. Shireen Moosvi, 'Evolution of the Mansab System Under Akbar Until 1596-97', *JRAS*, 1981, pp. 173-85.

administration could not be regarded as entirely ineffective.[1] His doubts have been borne out by Shireen Moosvi's detailed study of the statistical evidence, which has strongly suggested that the 'crisis' of the 1660s was a passing phase, and conditions subsequently improved in Northern India.[2] Such an agricultural revival could hardly have been possible if there had been a continuously climbing curve of pauperisation due to excessive pressure from the Mughal nobility. One should rather ascribe the long-drawn-out scarcity of the 1660s more to abnormal failures of the monsoon than to the fault of any human agency.

Percentage (51.6 per cent) during the period 1658-78. Here too, except for a greater enhancement of the Iranis' share at the expense of the Turanis, the situation remained unchanged between the last years of Shah Jahan's and the first two decades of Aurangzeb's reign.[3]

If still more detailed research has not so far indicated the necessity of any significant revision in the view taken in the first edition of this book on the changes in the ethnic composition of the Mughal nobility under Aurangzeb, one item that was practically passed over in silence at that time does now need some comment as this was the social anthropology of the 'ethnic' groups that Athar Ali has established, largely following the classification and nomenclature of his Persian/English sources. He had assumed a complete lack of mobility among the groups. While it would be superfluous to say that, given the well-known caste and religious taboos, an integration of Irani and Rajput elements through intermarriages could simply not occur, there would still be room for the possibility that the Iranis and Turanis intermarried. For this it would be desirable to analyse marriages and reconstruct family trees. Irfan Habib, carrying out a comprehensive study of material on Nur Jahan's family, including that relating to 'marriages of members of Nur Jahan's family with those of other families', noted that 'with the single exception of the royal house, all these other families (with which marriages were contracted) are found to be of Persian origin'.[4] There is little reason to believe that Nur Jahan's family was exceptional among the Iranis. Yet, although the strong probability is that intermarriages among the main Muslim groups were rather rare, it would be fruitful to work out genealogies and patterns of marriage alliances of some of the higher noble

1. Irfan Habib, 'The Mansab System, 1595-1637', *Proceedings of the Indian History Congress*, 29th Session, 1967, I, pp. 221-42; and 'Mansab Salary Scales under Jahangir and Shah Jahan', *Islamic Culture*, vol., LIX, no. 2. 1985, pp. 203-27.
2. *Apparatus of Empire*, p. xx.
3. Frank Perlin, 'State Formation Reconsidered', *Modern Asian Studies*, 19.3 (1985), pp. 415-80.
4. Andre Wink, *Land and Sovereignty in India*, Cambridge, 1986.

families to determine the degree of mutual isolation of these groups during the seventeenth century. Too little work has been done on these lines so far.

When the first edition of this book came out, modern analytical work on the *mansab* system mainly consisted of a book by Abdul Aziz and an important article by W.H. Moreland.[1] Since the publication of the first edition of this book, Shireen Moosvi has gone very thoroughly into the evolution of the *mansab* system under Akbar;[2] and Irfan Habib has subjected the period between Akbar and Aurangzeb to two intensive surveys.[3]

These researches have not substantially modified the description of the *mansab* system Athar Ali had offered on the basis mainly of the evidence from the reigns of Shah Jahan and Aurangzeb. Rather, their attempt has been to show how the system developed into the kind he had portrayed from the time of its establishment under Akbar. Moosvi has demonstrated how the *sawar* rank originated out of the advance payments (*barawurdi*) for part of the maintenance of troops required by the *mansab*-number under Akbar. Irfan Habib has been mainly concerned with changes in the *mansab* pay and military obligations under Jahangir and Shah Jahan. What occasions surprise is that while new administrative measures and conventions heavily altered the profile of the *mansab* system within fifty years of the writing of the *A'in-i Akbari*, there was so little change in it after 1645. Aurangzeb during his entire reign of nearly fifty years made no significant change in the system, down to scales of pay, obligations according to *sawar* ranks and month-ratio, composition of military contingents, etc.

Such lack of concern for reform in the organisation of what was the 'steel frame' of the Mughal Empire during Aurangzeb's entire reign is hard to explain, even when full recognition is extended to Aurangzeb's anxiety to maintain a tried and tested system exactly as he had found it. Yet there were factors that made such rigid adherence to the inherited system difficult. One was the tendency to increase the number of *mansabdars* forced on the Mughal emperor by political exigencies. How these numbers increased during the seventeenth century was brought much in the first edition (pp. 7-11). Some new data given in the *Apparatus*, such as the number of *zat* rank holders of 500 *zat* and above at five different points forces the view that the increase was inexorable.

1595	1621	1637-38	1647-48	1656-57
123	242	419	443	518

1. Wink, *op. cit.*, p. 6.
2. Shireen Moosvi, *The Evolution of the "Mansab" System under Akbar Until 1596-7*, JRAS, London, 1981.
3. *Islam, Islamic Culture,* 1981

Of these, all the figures appear to be reliable except that for 1621, which could be an undercount.[1] Clearly, the tendency towards rank inflation is obvious. The question is whether it continued under Aurangzeb. As was admitted in the first edition of this work, no official lists of the kind are available for the period of Aurangzeb. The numerical data based on the lists of *mansab* holders of 1,000 *zat* and above which Athar Ali himself constructed, respectively for the periods 1658-78 (pp. 175-215) and 1679-1707 (pp. 216-71), must be regarded as incomplete; while relevant for examining relative shares of different ethnic groups, they are obviously deficient for the purposes of comparison with the earlier.

The whole question of the decline of the Mughal Empire has been recently clouded by the debate on the nature of that Empire. Taking cues from Burton Stein's *Peasant State and Society*, Frank Perlin[2] and Andre Wink[3] have tried to build up a picture of the pre-colonial state, which basically starts by discounting the information we have for the Empire from sources within it. Characteristically, they tend to dismiss much of the evidence from Mughal historians and documents (largely in Persian) as merely normative, or formalistic, given to 'semantic idiom'.[4] Such an attitude – it is so easy to put the words 'Empire' and its 'decline' within inverted commas and claim victory! – would, of course, make a study like the present one an illusory exercise. But there are hardly any recognised methods of historical research by which such a vast amount of record, largely mutually consistent in areas beyond the alleged 'semantic idiom', can be ignored for the purpose of any worthwhile consideration of the inner structure of the Empire and its role in society and economy. Part of the trouble, perhaps, is that much of the criticism of the Mughal material has come from those who are not at home with it. The argument they adopt would practically rule out the entire official and semi-official records of any government as admissible evidence for political or institutional history. It seems to Athar Ali that while Persian documentation of the Mughal Empire must be subjected, piece by piece, to such criticism as is to be applied to all historical evidence, it cannot be condemned as a class. The picture of the Mughal Empire that it offers, as of a centralised system, with due depiction also of factors and circumstances opposed to such centralisation, is a fairly credible one. In the author Ali's book too both sides of the picture are given emphasis, though Athar Ali's evidence comes overwhelmingly from the

1. *Mansab System*, Proc. Ind. Hist. Cong. 1967
2. Frank Perlin, 'State Formation Reconsidered', *Modern Asian Studies*, 19.3 (1985), pp. 415-80.
3. Andre Wink, *Land and Sovereignty in India*, Cambridge, 1986.
4. Wink, *op. cit.*, p. 6.

large store of Persian documentation. Whether this is a more reasonable way of reconstructing history than the one of proceeding from Perlin's theory of *watan* or Wink's of *fitna* as the cornerstone of Indian polity that Athar Ali leaves to the reader to judge.

SECTION [A]
[1659-1682]

I

The Deccan Viceroyalty in the Last Years of Shāh Jahān

As a prelude to the administration of the Deccan under Aurangzeb, we may consider it during the second Viceroyalty of the Deccan from 1652 to 1659 ending with his accession as Emperor.

This period is well illumined due to the availability of extensive documentation contained in the *Ādāb-i 'Ālāmgīrī* – a collection of letters mainly written on behalf of Aurangzeb before his accession by Munshi Qābil Khān[1]. This is supplemented by the documents preserved in A.P. State Archives, Hyderabad and the histories of the period [see map of Mughal India 1658 A.D.].

[I] Limits and Territorial Boundaries

By the end of Aurangzeb's first Viceroyalty, the Deccan comprised four provinces of Khāndesh, Berār, Aurangābād and Bidar[2], comparatively

1. Aurangzeb, *Ādāb-i 'Ālāmgīrī*, compiled by Muḥammad Ṣādiq [together with his letters written on behalf of Prince Akbar] in 1703-4, Br. Mus. Or. 177, ed 'Abdul Ghafur Chaudhurī, Lahore, Pakistan, 1971, 2 vols. I have made a selection of documents on the administration of Deccan during Aurangzeb's second tenure as Viceroy from *Ādāb-i 'Ālāmgīrī* for my M. Phil Dissertation entitled *Calendar, of Administrative Documents in Ādāb-i 'Ālāmgīrī*, submitted at A.M.U., Aligarh, 1991 [hereafter cited as *Calendar*]. Curiously in *Ādāb* Aurangzeb makes frequent references to his first Viceroyalty of the Deccan essentially for purpose of comparison with his second term as Viceroy.
2. A *farmān* of Shāh Jahān of 1636 to Hakīm Masīh-uz-Zamān proclaims that this *vilāyat* [i.e. Deccan] comprises five *ṣūbas* i.e *ṣūba* Daulatabad, *ṣūba* Aḥmadnagar, *ṣūba* Berar, *ṣūba* Khandesh and Telingana. *Bib. Nat. Paris, Blochet. Suppl. Pers.* 482, f. 67 [a]. However, a *parwāna* of Islām Khān of 1645 refers to four *ṣubas* of the Deccan *ibid*, f. 134 [b]. Anyhow there is a plausible explanation that Telingana did not have the status of the *ṣūba*. It was later merged with Bidar to form the *ṣūba* of Bidar. Although there is a possibility of apparently modifying the prevailing position yet J.F. Richards endeavour does not stand scrutiny in the light of the contemporary documentaly evidence which does naturally lead the writer to follow the correctly established facts without making any incorrect theorisation: The Mughal sovereignly and the institution of reproduction of sovereignly in the early modern period.

THE MUGHAL EMPIRE
UNDER SHĀH JAHĀN
1658
TIBET
KĀBUL
KASHMIR
LĀHORE
MULTĀN
DELHI
ĀGRĀ
AWADH
ALLAHABAD
BIHĀR
BENGĀL
ORISSA
AJMER
MĀLWA
TATTA
AHMADĀBĀD
KHANDESH
BERĀR
AURANGĀBĀD
BIDAR
BIJAPUR
GOLCONDA
SAFAVID EMPIRE
ARABIAN SEA
BAY OF BENGĀL

detached from the core of the Mughal Empire making them its periphery experiencing conquest and administrative consolidation relatively.

Ṣūba Khandesh, conquered by Akbar in 1601, with its capital at Burhanpur[1] which became the *sarkār* of Asir at a later stage was enlarged in 1634 by transferring the *sarkār* of Nandurbar, Bijagārh and portions of *sarkār* Handia in the south of the Narbada R. from *ṣūba* Malwa[2], as well as attaching forthwith *sarkār* Galna after its occupation in 1632. Baglana was added to it in 1658 twenty years after its annexation[3] to the Mughal Empire in 1638[4] [APPENDIX – A]. The boundaries of *ṣūba* Berar largely remained unchanged from Akbar's time except for inclusion in the north of the entire principality of Deograh as a *sarkār* transferred from *ṣūba* Malwa and the southern boundaries were affected due to the creation of *ṣūba* Telingana which was in subsequent period merged into *ṣūba* Bidar.

In 8th regnal year Shāh Jahān introduced grouping of the *sarkārs* of *ṣūba* Berar into two new administrative jurisdictions, by the creation of two new provinces, Pāinghāt and Bālāghāt[5], which between them comprised the whole of the Mughal Deccan. This arrangement was subsequently discarded except for the geographical nomenclature. Pāinghāt constituted five *sarkārs* of Narnala, Kherla, Gavil, Punar and Kalam whereas Bālāghāt comprised *sarkār* of Baitala, Mehkar, Basim and Mahur.

Ṣūba Aurangabad largely comprised the former kingdom of Aḥmadnagar annexed by Akbar in 1595-6 but its real annexation[6] with the seizure of

1. Burhanpur served as headquarters not only of Khandesh out of the entire Deccan until its replacement by Aurangabad in 1636. [*Cf.*, Irfan Habib, *An Atlas of the Mughal Empire*, [hereafter *Atlas*] O.U.P., Delhi, 1982, p. 36].
2. Lahori, *Pādshāhnāma*, II, pp. 62-3, [*Cf.*, *Atlas*, pp. 23, 34]. These were erroneously shown transferred to *ṣūba* Khandesh in 1636 instead of 1634 as shown by J.F. Richards [ed.] *Imperial Monetary System of Mughal India*, O.U.P., Delhi, 1987, p. 194 on the strength of R.A. Alvi's 'Mughal Geographical Accounts of Khandesh', *Medieval India - A Miscellany*, Vol. III, pp. 127-8.
3. Lahori, II, p. 105-7.
4. It was treated as a separate territory [*wilāyat*], but without the status of a *ṣūba* is also recorded as a separate unit in *Dastūru-l 'Amal-i 'Ālāmgīrī* c. 1659. MS, Br. Mus. Add. 6598 f. 120 [a], whose statistics belong to 1656. But it was later on joined to *ṣūba* Khandesh as one of its *sarkārs*. Its annexation to the Mughal Empire is attested by two *farmāns* of Shāh Jahān of 1638 and 1645 [*Blochet. Suppl. Pers.* 482, ff. 14 [a-b], 24 [a-b]]. But thenceforward it remained under the charge of the Viceroy of the Deccan. [*Cf.*, *ibid*, f. 150].
5. *Cf.*, *Bloch. Suppl. Pers.* 482, f. 23 [b], which contains a *farmān* of Shāh Jahān of 1647 in regard to their protection by directing Shāh Nawāz Khān to proceed from Malwa to Burhanpur to look after Pāinghāt and Rashid Khān to march from Nander to Aurangabad to control Bālāghāt.
6. Fateḥ Khān s/o Malik 'Ambar, who joined the Mughal service, killed Nizāmu-l Mulk, recited *Khutba* [Friday sermon], struck coins in Shāh Jahān's name, sent *peshkash*

Daulatabad was effected in 1633. In 1636, the *ṣūba* contained the *sarkārs* of Daulatabad, Aḥmadnagar, Paithān, Bīr, Jālnāpur[1], Junnār [Junair], Sangamner and Fatehābad [Dharur[2]] whereas the *sarkārs* of Junnar, Talkokan, Parenda and Sholapur which were in possession of Bijāpur Kingdom by the settlement of 1636 were subsequently ceded to it in 1657[3].

Shāh Jahān in his early years [i.e. 1635] created a separate region of Telingana by incorporating certain annexations from the Nizāmshahi Kingdom and portions of *sarkār* Pīthri[4]. However, this dispensation did not last long because consequent upon the annexation of Bīdar and Kalyan from Bījāpur Kingdom in 1657, the newly created *ṣūba* of Telingāna comprising the single *sarkār* of Nander was merged with the recent acquisitions so as to create the new *ṣūba* of Bidar. The *ṣūba* of Bidar comprised *sarkārs* of Nander, Kalyan, Bidār, Akalkot, Malkhaid, Yādgīr [Firuzgarh], whereas *sarkār* Ramgir ceded by Quṭbshah to the Mughal Empire in 1656 was subsequently made a *sarkār* of the *ṣuba*[5].

[II] Main Officials

When Aurangzeb was appointed as Viceroy of the Deccan for the second term in 1652 A.D., he again ratified that the Mughal Imperial administration acknowledged the distinctiveness of the four Deccan provinces by stationing a Viceroy of the Deccan at Aurangabad who exercised control over the provincial administration by appointing their governors because according to his own estimation he had high officials under him during his first Viceroyalty of the Deccan while none such except for the Deccanis were available to him during his second term. The problems were complicated further by the demand of the officials posted in the Deccan as *faujdārs* and *qila'dārs* etc for their promotions[6].

[tribute] consisting of elephants, horses, diamonds, studded weapons, through his son 'Abdur Rasūl, was favoured with the rank of 7,000/7,000 for strengthening the Mughal control [which does not incidentally find any mention in Athar Ali's *Apparatus, of Empire*, Delhi, 1985, hereafter *Apparatus*] and the *jama'* of fifty crore *dāms* yielding one crore rupees was assigned in *jāgīr* of the Imperial officials together with 21 strong forts of Qandahar [Kandahar] and Mahur and the areas along with fort equivalent to his *jāgīr* was given to him and the remaining portions of Nizāmu-l Mulk were annexed [*Blochet. Suppl. Pers.* 482, ff. 9 [a-b], 65 [a], 67 [b]].

1. Before the capture of Daulatabad in 1633 control of Jalnapur was important for the Mughals, which was regained only in 1616, [*Cf.,Atlas*, p. 55].
2. Lahori, I, ii, p. 62.
3. Muḥammad Ṣāliḥ, *'Amal-i Ṣāliḥ,* [ed.] Ghulam Yazdani, Bib. Ind. Calcutta, 1912-46, Vol. III, p. 262.
4. Lahori, I, ii, p. 62, p. 711.
5. Lachmi Narayan Shafīq, *Khulāṣatu-l Hind*, transcript, Department of History, A.M.U., Aligarh, p. 151.
6. *Calendar,* Doc. No. 1.17, *Ādāb,* Vol. I, p. 155.

From the very inception of the Sultanate period some administrative common terms have not been specially highlighted.

Aurangzeb as Viceroy appointed Mirzā Khān as the *nāzim* [governor] of *ṣūba* Berar in 1654 with the rank of 3,000/3,000[1], before which 'Abdullāh, s/o Rashīd Khān Anṣāri with the rank of 1,500/1,500 held the office[2]. Similarly Hādi Dād Khān, 1,000/300 was made the *nāzim* of Telingana in 1655, which position he enjoyed till his death in 1655[3]. Mīr Muḥammad Sai'd or Mīr Jumla with a rank of 6,000/6,000 was made the *ṣūbedār* [Governor] of Burhanpur [Khāndesh][4]. Aurangabad was the seat of Viceroy himself. These appointments presumably needed confirmation by the Emperor.

In addition, other important officials were there, Diyānat Khān[5] had remained the *Dīwān* of Bālāghāt till he was replaced by Murshid Quli Khān[6]. Multafat Khān held the *Dīwānī* of Painghat till 1656 when it was handed over to Murshid Quli Khān on the recommendations of Aurangzeb[7]. Practically this reform was largely carried out by Murshid Quli Khān, assisted for some time by Multafat Khān as it begain with the classic expedient of crop sharing and Aurangzeb's letters make it crystal clear that this applied to the entire territory, including the *jāgīrs.* Interestingly the particular form of sharing which was used is said to have been the innovation of Murshid Quli Khān himself. Actually the proportions to which the revenue was to be collected were based on a different scale. Practically speaking half of the produce was to be taken from crops raised on rainfall; and a third from crops irrigated from well, but in the case of sugarcane, fruits and spices, the share was to range from one-third to one-fourth, keeping in view the cost of irrigation and with respect of fruits the years the trees to bear fruits. Furthermore, different rates were also promulgated for crops irrigated from streams and canals. Ṣādiq Khān definitely says that the old system of assessing the revenue by the number of ploughs was still retained in certain areas, while the practice of measurement was introduced in others. Naturally for the purpose of the latter, Murshid Quli

1. Muḥammad Wāris, *Pādshāhnāma*, I.O., Ethe, 329, f. 22 [b].
2. *Calendar,* Doc. No. 1.10, *Ādāb,* Vol. I, p.146, Wāris, 184 [b], 198 [b].
3. *Calendar,* Doc. No. 1.29, *Ādāb,* Vol. I, p.181, Wāris, 222 [b], 248 [a], 261 [a].
4. *Ādāb,* Br. Mus. Or. 177, f. 116 [a] as cited in *Apparatus,* 6586.
5. *Calendar,* Doc. No. 1.4, *Ādāb,* Vol. I, p. 119, Lahori, II, 728.
6. *Calendar,* Doc. No. 1.5, *Ādāb,* Vol. I, p122. Khāfi Khān, I, 733, n, who otherwise follows Ṣādiq Khān in this passage here differently. He says that Murshid Quli Khān, appointed new *muqāddams* in villages which had no *muqāddams,* the heirs of the former *muqāddams* of these places having been disappeared through the adversity of fate.
7. *Calendar,* Doc. No. 1.15, 1.16, 1.17, 1.43, *Ādāb,* Vol. I, pp. 139, 142, 154, 206-8 and 237-8.

Khān is said to have determined the *rai'* for every crop and to have fixed the *dastūrs* per *bighā* after taking account of the prices. Though Aurangzeb did not say anything about the measurement yet since he declares that crop sharing had proved an expensive method he could hardly have anticipated its permanent fixture. Ṣādiq Khān actually says that Murshid Quli Khān measured the area of most of the *parganas*. Though the revenue records of *pargana* Papal [Berar], C. 1679, give detailed particulars concerning its measured area yet the decisive evidence is furnished by the village and area statistics of Aurangzeb's reign as these show that nearly nine-tenths of the villages of Berar and Aurangabad had been measured and nearly a half of those of Khandesh. It would naturally seem, therefore, that the major result of Murshid Quli Khān's reforms was the introduction of measurement, and that crop-sharing was only employed at the beginning to help in fixing workable *rai's* for the different crops[1]. Murshid Quli Khān is credited to have devoted so much attention to formulating the *rai's* that in order to prevent any inaccuracy he would himself pick up one end of the measuring rope [after Murshid Quli Khān's reforms] in Mughal Deccan. In Mughal Deccan, the payment of revenue in cash, based upon a very summary assessment, is described as an old practice, but after the brief interval of crop-sharing introduced by Murshid Quli Khān, payment in cash was re-established though it was founded on assessment by measurement. Interestingly enough the distribution of *taqāvi* for similar purposes of cultivation also formed an important part of Murshid Quli Khān's reforms in the Deccan for the purchase of bullocks, buffaloes and other necessaries. We are given to understand that his colleague Multafat Khān was the author of an ambitious proposal to advance Rs 40,000 to 50,000 "as *taqāvi*" from the Imperial treasury for financing the contruction of dams [*bānds*] in the provinces of Khandesh and Berar [Pāinghāt region], to be disbursed in the *jāgīrs* and also, presumably, in the Khāliṣā. Multafat Khān had promised that, if his scheme of financing bunds was accepted, the whole amount advanced could be realised within two years. However, collection in annual installments was also sanctioned. Murshid Quli Khān is said to have asked for repayment at the time of harvest, but in two installments.

Aurangzeb appointed Ziauddin Ḥusain as his *Dīwān* in 1653[2], who was promoted as the *Dīwān* of the Deccan in 1656 after the death of Murshid Quli Khān[3]. In 1652, Muḥammad Ṣafi was appointed *Bakhshi* and *Wāqi'a*

1. Ṣādiq Khān, Or.174, +f 185[b]-186[a], Or.1671, f. 91 [a]; Khāfi Khān, Vol. I, pp. 733-4.
2. *Calendar,* Doc. No. 1.10, *Ādāb,* Vol. I, p. 147.
3. *Selected Documents of Shahjahan's Reign,* [*SDSR*] ed. Yusuf Husain Khān, *Daftar-i Dīwānī,* Deccan, Hyderabad, 1950, p. 202, which does explain that Murshid Quli Khan of Bengal was a different person who was appointed as its governor.

Nawīs of the Deccan[1], which was held by Mīr Ja'far Astarabadi in 1655[2]. In 1656 it was transferred to Qazi Nizāmā Karharodi[3]. Aurangzeb secured the post of *Dārogha-i Top Khāna-i Deccan* [Superintendent of the Artillery of the Deccan] for Hoshdar Khān[4], which was previously held by Mīr Khalīlullāh[5] [1650-52]. From 1654 to 1656 it was held by Shamsuddīn[6].

Since the administration of the *sarkārs* of these four provinces was carried out through numerous important officials to whom we find frequent references in our sources *viz.,* Muḥammad Shāh Qadīmī[7] was appointed the *qila'dār* of Qandahar fort after the death of Amān Baig. *Ṣūba* Khandesh where Aurangzeb stayed in the first instance during his first Viceroyalty had several high Mughal officials. Saiyid 'Abdul Wahab, who was credited for the excellent administration of Baglana as its *faujdār* [military commandant] was succeeded by 'Umar Tarīn[8], who was censured by Shāh Jahān, and then by Asadullāh s/o Faizullah[9]. 'Usman Afghan, *faujdār* of Bijagārh in 1653 was replaced by Muḥammad Beg Khaishgī, an official of Aurangzeb and the former was pacified by grant of the *faujdāri* of Sulṭanpur and Nandurbar[10]. Manohar Das held the *qila'dāri* of Asir on the eve of Aurangzeb's second Viceroyalty[11]. Fathullāh s/o Zakariya was the *faujdār* of Chopda [*sarkār* Asir][12] while Mir Muḥammad 'Ali was the *qila'dār* of Galna[13]. Mīr Aḥmad[14] appointed as *faujdār* of Nasirabad [*sarkār* Asir] in 1652-3 was succeeded by Jalāl Khān Kākar in 1656[15]. Pratap Singh was appointed in 1652-3 as the *qila'dār* of Dhurb [*sarkār* Galna][16]. Muḥammad 'Inayat s/o Islām Khān was the *bakhshi* and *wāqia'Nawīs* of Burhanpur in

1. *Calendar,* Doc. No. 1.11, *Ādāb,* Vol. I, pp. 136-7, Wāriṣ, f. 229[b].
2. Wāriṣ, ff. 229[b], 249[b].
3. Wāriṣ, ff. 249[b].
4. *Calendar,* Doc. No. 1.11, 1.12, *Ādāb,* 136-7, 153, Wāriṣ, f. 164[a].
5. Wāriṣ, f. 169[a].
6. Wāriṣ, ff. 185[a], 205[b].
7. *Calendar,* Doc. No. 1.3, *Ādāb,* Vol. I, pp. 114-117.
8. Saiyid 'Abdul Wahāb s/o Saiyid 'Abdur Rahmān was appointed the *qila'dār* of Bāglānā in 1644, *SDSR,* p. 141. His appointment was also confirmed through a *farmān* of Shāh Jahān and *parwāna* of Islām Khān of 1645. *Blochet. Suppl. Pers.* 482, ff. 22[a], 134[b] and 140 [b].
9. Wāriṣ, 415[b] *Calendar,* Doc. No. 1.5, *Ādāb,* Vol. I, p. 121.
10. *Ibid.*
11. Wāriṣ, f. 145[b].
12. Wāriṣ, f. 205[b]; *Apparatus*, S-6178.
13. A.P. State Archives, Hyderabad [henceforth Hyd. 4037].
14. Wāriṣ, f. 157[a], *Apparatus,* S-5737.
15. Wāriṣ, f. 248[a] Shāh Nawāz Khān, *Maasiru-l Umara.*
16. Hyd. 3842, p. 473 of Jammun was *faujdār.*

1654[1]. Mir Ja'far was the *faujdār* of Chainpur [*sarkār* Handia][2]. Roshan Beg Khwāfi Khān was the *faujdār* of Sulṭanpur and Nandurbar[3].

Initially Aurangzeb was directed to stay at Burhanpur to administer Pāinghāt where after he was bound to proceed to Daulatabad to improve the administration of Bālāghāt as he was advised to consider both of them under him[4]. Names of some important officials of *ṣūba* Berar occur in contemporary accounts. Fatḥ Rohila [Afghan] was the *faujdār* of Nandapur Bālāghāt [*sarkār* Mahur] in 1653[5] whereas 'Ināyat Khān s/o Islām Khān was recommended for the *faujdārī* of [*sarkār*] Mahur[6] and Hoshdār for that of [*sarkār*] Kalam[7]. Bindraban was reported to be the *amīn* of *parganas* of Bālāghāt[8]. Imām Quli Turkomān was the *qila'dār* of Zafarnagar [*sarkār* Mehkar] in 1655[9] which post was subsequently retained by Mīr Aḥmad Khwāfi[10]. Aurangzeb also recommended the grant of *faujdāri* of Mahur to Murshid Quli Khān[11]. Shāh Jahān favoured Multafat Khān for Ellichpur for which subsequently Jalāl Khān's name was approved by the Emperor. But Jalāl Khān was made the *faujdār* of Punar due to his inexperience[12], vacating Ellichpur in 1653 in favour of 'Abdullah[13]. It was next year placed under the *faujdāri* of Mirza Khān[14].

Ṣūba Aurangabad had also several important officials as is known from our sources. Mirzā Khān, grandson of 'Abdur Raḥim Khān-i Khānān, who was appointed as the *qila'dār* of Aḥmadnagar in 1650, was replaced in 1653 by Shāh Beg Khān, who retained it till 1655[15].

1. Wāriṣ, f. 212[a], *Apparatus,* S-6202.
2. Ṣāliḥ, Vol. III, p. 245.
3. *Calendar,* Doc No. 6.5, *Ādāb,* Vol. I, p. 473. There are several other examples *viz.,* Raja Sangrām Singh, *Zamīndār* Jammun was the *faujdār* of Manjrud with the rank of 700/500 in 1653, [Wāriṣ 194 [a], who was succeeded by his g/son Sārang Dhar in the same year after his death [*Ādāb*, Vol. I, p. 151]. Similarly Pahārā Nauhanī was the *thānādār* of Bahādurpur in 1654 [Ṣāliḥ, Vol. III, p. 206] and Bakhtiyar Khān was the *thānādār* of Salher [*sarkār* Baglāna] [Hyd. 3705]. Imāmuddin Muḥammad and Nizāmuddin Muḥammad served as *Mīr-i 'Adl* and *Ṣadr* of Burhanpur respectively, [*SDSR*, p. 191] and Muḥammad Ṣāliḥ served as its *Wāqi'a'Nawīs* [*SDSR*, p. 185].
4. *Calendar,* Doc No. 1.44, *Ādāb,* Vol. I, p. 187.
5. *Calendar,* Doc No. 1.45, *Ādāb,* Vol. I, p. 180.
6. Wāriṣ, 148[b]. Nandapur has been recorded as Taundapur in the source, *Apparatus*, S-6609.
7. Wāriṣ f. 217 [b], *Apparatus*, S-6336.
8. Hyd. 4079.
9. Wāriṣ, f. 217 [b], *Apparatus,* S-6336.
10. Wāriṣ, f. 248 [a], *Apparatus*, S-6609.
11. *Calendar,* Doc. No. 1.20; *Ādāb,* Vol. I, p. 217.
12. *Calendar,* Doc. No. 1.9; *Ādāb,* Vol. I, p. 141-2.
13. *Calendar,* Doc. No. 1.10; *Ādāb,* Vol. I, p. 146.
14. *Calendar,* Doc. No. 1.16, or Wāriṣ, *f.* 198 [b], *Apparatus,* S-6133. Ināmullah was appointed as *thānādār* of *sarkār* Kalam.
15. *Calendar,* Doc. No. 1.8, 1.9, *Ādāb,* Vol. I, pp. 141, 145.

There after Multafat Khān was assigned the *qiladāri'* of Aḥmadnagar in 1656[1] where after Naṣīrī Khān[2] received its castellanship for whom Aurangzeb had endeavoured through Sa'dullah Khān.

Derwesh Beg Qāqshāl, *qila'dār* of Tirambak [*sarkār* Sangamner] was replaced by Shafqatullāh s/o Sazāwār Khān[3] in 1654 which was, however, subsequently held by Mirzā 'Alī s/o 'Arab Khān[4] Similarly, Izzat Khān held the *qila'dāri* of Fateḥabad and Dhārur in 1652[5]. Raja Debi Singh Bundela was made the *faujdār* of Bir[6]. In 1653, the castellanship of Junair was in-charge of Narsingh Das s/o Raja Dwārka Dās[7] and its *thānādāri* was in assignment of Nazar[8]. In 1655, it was in-charge of Muḥammad Ṭāhir Ṣaf Shikan Khān, who was succeeded by Nūrul Ḥasan Khān[9]. Mumrez Khān was appointed the *faujdār* of Junair[10], Abul Faẓal Ma'muri held the *faujdāri* of Onkapur[11].

In 1657 Hoshdār received the *faujdāri* of Chimargonda Kada and Bust [*sarkār* Aḥmad Nagar][12]. 'Abdul Nabī held the *faujdārī* of Rāherī [Raigarh] in 1656[13] and Rashīd Khān Anṣāri was entrusted with the military commandantship [*faujdāri*] of Dindori [*sarkār* Sangamner][14].

1. *Calendar,* Doc. No. 1.43; *Ādāb,* Vol. I, p. 274; Wāriṣ, f. 224 [a], *Apparatus,* S-6377.
2. *Calendar,* Doc. No. 15.1; *Ādāb,* Vol. II, pp. 727-8.
3. *Calendar,* Doc. No. 1.22, *Ādāb,* Vol. I, p. 151, Hyd. 4155; Wāriṣ, f. 194 [b], *Apparatus,* S-6043.
4. Wāriṣ 212 [b], *Apparatus,* S-6206.
5. *SDSR*, p. 180.
6. Wāriṣ, f. 198 [a].
7. Wāriṣ, f. 168 [a], *Apparatus,* S-5745.
8. Wāriṣ, f. 177 [b], *Apparatus,* S-5936.
9. Wāriṣ, f. 230 [a], *Apparatus,* S-6414, S-6415.
10. *Calendar,* Doc. No. 12.2; *Ādāb,* Vol. II, p. 744. These examples can be multiplied *viz.,* Dildost was the *thānādār* of Bījāpur, [*sarkār* Pattan or Paithān], [Wāriṣ, f. 195 [b], *Apparatus,* S-6045], Muḥammad Beg was appointed the *kotwāl* of Aurangabad [Hyd. 4277] and La'l Beg was the *darogha* [superintendent] of the stores of Daulatābād fort in 1658. [*SDSR*, p. 218].
11. *Calendar,* Doc. No. 11.6; *Ādāb,* Vol. I, p. 606. He was granted *thānādāri* of Lādsangwi [*sarkār* Jālnāpur] by removing Sai'd Khāndesi etc, *Calendar,* Doc. No. 11.5, *Ādāb,* Vol. I, p. 599.
12. *Calendar,* Doc. No. 15, *Ādāb,* Vol. II, p. 729.
13. Wāriṣ, 274 [b]; *Apparatus,* S-6603.
14. Wāriṣ 169 [b], *Apparatus,* S-5765. Aurangzeb's original *nishān* of 10 *Rajab* 17th regnal year [1644 A.D.] to Rashīd Khān Ansari, probably a relative of Sai'd Khān Chaghtā in response to his representation stating that his solicitation could not be acceded to recall him from the border due to Aurangzeb's summoning to the Imperial court, also assuring him of the princely favours with instructions to make his representations. [Photocopy of original is with me for which I am thankful to the owner Mr. Kabir of Bhopal [M.P.]].

The separate *sarkār* of Telingāna which was merged in *sarkār* Nānder later in *ṣūba* Bidar in 1657, had some high officials. Consequent upon the death of Amān Beg, the *qila'dār* of Qandahar fort, Muḥammad Shāh Qadīmī was appointed its castellan[1]; it was subsequently assigned to Muḥammad Beg[2]. In 1657, Ḥusāmuddin Khān was the *faujdār* of Telingana[3] before which he held the *qila'dāri* of Ūdgir [*sarkār* Nander[4]].

In 1653 Uzbek Khān was replaced by Khwāja Barkhurdar as *faujdār* of Ausa[5]. During the same period Ilhāmullāh s/o Rashīd Khān enjoyed the *thānādāri* of Nander[6].

Aurangzeb maintained cordial relations with his main officials including *Dīwāns* and *Bakhshīs*, *Nāzims* and *Ḥājibs*, as well as with other officials ranging from *Dārogha-i Top Khanā-i Deccan* to the *thānādārs* by not only remaining in regular contact observing their conduct through surveillance but also pleading their case either for promotion or for posting in view of the expediency of the situation with the Emperor. The *Ādāb-i 'Ālāmgīrī* is replete with numerous such instances [as shall be revealed from the next two sections]. Aurangzeb's frequent and loud protestation against undue dismissals and transfers of his officials reflect his deep attachment with his men whom he had gathered during the past two decades[7]. His spirited defence and bold and frequent pleading for the promotion and posting of his officials which were either turned down or modified or delayed or reluctantly accepted demonstrated Aurangzeb's sincerity in streamlining the Deccan administration.

[III] The *Jāgīr* Assignments – Problems of Low Monthly *Jāgīrs*

It was but natural that the *manṣabdars* were assigned *jāgīrs*, which were of varying categories, to meet the pay claim [*Ṭalab*] according to the *manṣab*. While the evolution of Mughal *manṣab* system ascribed to Akbar[8],

1. *Calendar,* Doc. No. 1.3, *Ādāb,* Vol. I, p. 117.
2. Wāriṣ 148 [b], *Apparatus,* S-5660.
3. Wāriṣ, f. 92 [b]; *Apparatus,* S-5222. He was appointed to this post after the death of Karamullāh with an increase of 500/400 enhancing his rank to 2,000/2,000 with the instructions to reach there immediately after the receipt of the Imperial *farmān*, protect the fort with utmost care, look after the welfare of the artillerymen as well as stores and other responsibilities of castellanship. *Bloch. Suppl. Pers*. 482, ff. 23 [b] - 24 [a].
4. Wāriṣ, f. 92[b], *Apparatus,* S-5222.
5. *Calendar,* Doc. No. 204, *Ādāb,* Vol. II, pp. 628-31.
6. Wāriṣ, f. 184[b], *Apparatus,* S-5991.
7. *Calendar,* Doc. No. 2.4, *Ādāb,* Vol. II, pp. 628-31.
8. For *manṣab* system see, W.H. Moreland, 'Rank [*Manṣab*] in the Mogul State Service', *JRAS,* London, 1936, pp. 641-65; A.J. Qaisar, 'Note on the Date of Institution of *Manṣab* under Akbar', *Proc. Ind. Hist. Cong.* [*PIHC*] 24th Session, Delhi, 1961,

its basic elements were retained by his successors with certain new features specially emerging under Shāh Jahān, *viz.*, new scales of pay, month ratio, conditional rank and new regulations fixing the strength of contingent under different *sawār* ranks[1], with which we are mainly concerned in regard to Deccan Viceroyalty during the last years of Shāh Jahān[2].

Jāgīrs were of different categories based on the ratio of their actual income [*ḥāṣil*] to their normal income [*jama'*, *jama'dāmi*] which was expressed in terms of month i.e. if its income was one-third of the *jama'* the *jāgīr* would be *chahārmāhā* or four monthly[3]. The month ratio of the *jāgīrdārs* changed from year to year and under Shāh Jahān the military obligations of a *manṣabdār* were fixed according to the month ratio of his *jāgīr*[4].

Although the conditions of *jāgīrs* in the Deccan were deteriorating yet these were to be assigned to the *jāgīrdārs* to meet their pay claims in view of the scarcity of *pāibāqi* and extra – Deccan *jāgīrs*. Towards the close of Shāh Jahān's reign the revenue realisation in the Deccan was only one-third or one-fourth of the *jama'* due to desolation of peasantry[5] and the practice of deduction of one-fourth or one-fifth or one-sixth portion of the Deccani *manṣabdārs'* pay claim had already become prevalent under Shāh Jahān[6], as the practice of reducing the pay claims of the Deccani nobles by a fourth was established in 1634.

Such a phenomenon had excessively disturbing effect on the income from the *jāgīrs* as there were no factors inhibiting expansion of fertile *jāgīrs* and the availability of full revenue-yielding *jāgīrs*, which naturally had an overwhelming impact on the working of *jāgīr* administration causing wide spread discontent. Diyānat Khān, who was assigned *pargana* Phulambari by the Imperial *Dīwāns* wanted to visit the court to plead his case due to

---

pp. 55-7, Irfan Habib, The *Manṣab* System, 1596-1637, *PIHC*, 29th Session, Patiala, 1967, 221-42, *idem* 'Salary and Pay Scales Under Jahangir and Shah J ahan, *Islamic Culture*, 1985; Shireen Moosvi. The Evolution of *Manṣab* System under Akbar until 1596-7, *JRAS*, London, No. 2, 1981, pp. 173-85.

1. M. Athar Ali, *The Mughal Nobility Under Aurangzeb*, Bombay, 1966, p. 40.
2. Even during Aurangzeb's first Viceroyalty Shāh Jahān issued a detailed *farmān* to Aurangzeb in 1641-42 for branding regulations in the Deccan, Zakir Husain, Aurangzeb's First Viceroyalty of the Deccan: A Reappraisal, *PIHC*, Delhi, 2010, pp. 310-17.
3. Irfan Habib, *The Agrarian System of Mughal India*; Bombay, 1963, p. 264.
4. Athar Ali, *Mughal Nobility*, pp. 26-30, 54-8. There is enough evidence in contemporary historical literature to prove this phenomenon. Even Shāh Jahān's previously referred to *farmān* of 14th R.Y. was issued on the report of Prince Muḥammad Dārā Shukoh as well as that of Islām Khān and Afzal Khān. *Bloch. Supp. Pers.* 482, ff. 46 [a] - 47 [a].
5. *Calendar,* Doc. No. 1.24; *Ādāb,* Vol. I, p. 166.
6. *Calendar,* Doc. No. 1.36, *Ādāb,* Vol. I, p. 149; *SDSR*, pp. 1-23, 88.

its low yield [*kam-ḥāṣili*]. However, Aurangzeb endeavoured to retain him due to his knowledge of the Deccan by exchange of his *jāgīr*[1].

Such a low income was reflected in month-ratio showing corresponding decline in the *jāgīrs* of most *manṣabdārs* in the Deccan which were not more than four-monthly' and often even less[2]. In the later years of Shāh Jahān transfer from Northern India to the Deccan entailed assignment of a low monthly *jāgīr*[3].

Aurangzeb correctly opined that grant of two offices of *Bakhshi* and *Dārogha-i Top Khana* to Ṣafi Khān was a burden on the *jāgīrs* of the Deccan in view of their desolation[4]. Murshid Quli Khān was assigned *pargana* Posad with abatement in *jama'* which was, however, low-revenue paying. Accordingly Aurangzeb ordered assignment of three lakh *dāms* from it and the rest to the equal to 5-6 was to be paid from elsewhere like that of Diyānat Khān[5]. It was brought to the Imperial notice that Murshid Quli Khān held '10-monthly' *jāgīrs* in Hindustan [North India] whereas notwithstanding increase in rank assignment of *Dīwānī* of Bālāghāt and expenses of *sih-bandīs* [auxiliary troops] his *jāgīr* in the Deccan was '5-monthly' whereas he required much to equal his income and expenditure which was further disbalanced by the introduction of branding regulations compelling him for maintaining 70% more contingent[6]. Curiously enough Aurangzeb also noticed that Murshid Quli Khān used to receive '12-monthly' *jāgīr* in Hindustan whereas his total *jāgīr* in the Deccan equaled to '6-monthly' which had caused inconvenience to the recipient. Since Aurangzeb expressed his inability either to assign any *jāgīr* or recommend enhancement in rank with Shāh Jahān's approbation, he pleaded his increase in his *manṣab* or grant of '8-monthly' *jāgīr*[7].

The above is an index of the sharp decline in month ratio which was reduced to 50% by transfer to Deccan from North India. Shamsuddīn, Superintendent of the Artillery of the Deccan who held '7-monthly' *jāgīr* in Bihar which was, however, compensated by assigning '7-monthly' *jāgīr*[8] in the Deccan to him. But the conditions had worsened to such an extent that Aurangzeb used to report them to the Emperor or the Central Ministers for taking corrective measures, for example, he asked Fāẓil Khān

1. *Calendar,* Doc. No. 1.4, *Ādāb,* Vol. I, p. 118, *SDSR*, pp. 1-2, 13 and passing.
2. *Calendar,* Doc. No. 1.35, *Ādāb,* Vol. I, p. 149.
3. Saiyid Najib Ashraf Nadvi [ed.] *Ruqa't-i 'Ālamgīr*, Azamgarh, 1930, p. 88.
4. *Calendar,* Doc. No. 1.11, *Ādāb,* Vol. I, p. 137.
5. *Calendar,* Doc. No. 1.5, *Ādāb,* Vol. I, p. 122.
6. *Calendar,* Doc. No. 6.4, 11.1, *Ādāb, p.* 466-7, 600-601.
7. *Calendar,* Doc. No. 1.20, *Ādāb,* Vol. I, p. 217.
8. *Calendar,* Doc. No. 1.21, *Ādāb,* Vol. I, p. 198.

to recommend the case of Rūḥullāh Khān due to deteriorating condition of the Deccan *jagīrs*.[1]

Aurangzeb conveyed to Shāh Jahān that 'Ināyat Khān, s/o Islām Khān held '8-monthly' *jāgīr* in Hindustan whereas his *jāgīr* in the Deccan was '5-monthly' he was granted the *faujdāri* of *sarkār* Mehkar with an increase in *manṣab* based on '5-monthly' ratio[2]. It was the natural corollary of the low yielding *jāgīrs*. In view of the declining revenues Aurangzeb strongly recommended assignment of Ankot etc to Shāh Beg Khān by fixing its *jama'* at one crore and sixty lakh *dāms* instead of two crore *dāms*, whereas, like Shāista Khān, he could be granted *jāgīr* worth forty lakh *dāms* from elsewhere.[3]

Though there is no need of multiplication of such examples, yet it is an irony of fate that Aurangzeb, as Viceroy of the Deccan encountered this problem of low income *jāgīrs* which one cannot overlook. Aurangzeb pleaded that the income from his *jāgīrs* in the Deccan was greatly low, and that the problem for him was further complicated by the transfer of his *jāgīrs* in Multan and Bhakkar and a reduction of Rs 17,00,000 where he needed better *jāgīrs* to keep his head high before the rulers of Bijapur and Golconda.[4]

Shāh Jahān however, laid emphasize upon proper administration of the Deccan especially that of his *jāgīrs* whereas Aurangzeb strove for securing better *jāgīr* assignments to himself and his officials outside the Deccan.[5] He even granted Baglana, which was originally in his *inā'm* grant without obtaining any alterative *jāgīr* in exchange. The Emperor asked him to send Shāh Beg Khān to the Imperial Court and suggested either to take his *jāgīr* or assign it to someone else. In consequence of Aurangzeb's failure in convincing Shāh Jahān in regard to this move he expressed his willingness to accept it in '10-monthly' *naqdi* without loss [*āfat*][6]. The Prince again faced censure on the ground that since he had sought Ellichpur without abatement he was now soliciting reduction in *jama'*, in response to which Aurangzeb's own commitment that whatever he would obtain from other *jāgīrdārs* its *jama'* would be fixed suitably which led him to his consent for Ellichpur. But in the event of refusal of reduction in *jama'* in this *jāgīr*, which he received in lieu of his *naqdi* he would suffer a loss of ten lakh

1. *Calendar,* Doc. No. 13.2, *Ādāb,* Vol. I, pp. 642-3.
2. *Calendar,* Doc. No. 1.44, *Ādāb,* Vol. I, p. 187.
3. *Calendar,* Doc. No. 1.16, *Ādāb,* Vol. I, p. 140.
4. *Calendar,* Doc. No. 1.1, *Ādāb,* Vol. I, p. 96.
5. *Calendar,* Doc. No. 1.6, *Ādāb,* Vol. I, pp. 116-7 and several other documents in *Ādāb-i 'Ālāmgīrī.*
6. *Calendar,* Doc. No. 1.9, *Ādāb,* Vol. I, p. 141.

rupees[1]. Aurangzeb's surrender of Ellichpur was interpreted as his failure in administering the Deccan which the Prince refuted on the ground that since the *pargana* had declined in revenue for the last twenty years how could it be brought to prosperity within one and two harvests[2].

Aurangzeb's remark proves that he used to minutely observe the position of each and every *pargana* of the Deccan on the basis of records of several decades ____ which is further proved by his detailed description of the state of revenues of various *parganas* under *jāgīr* or *khāliṣa* as shall be discussed in the next section in regard to Chananeri *Deshmukh* episode as he was the Chief of Indur in Telingana. Despite his being a keen observer one fails to reconcile his other statement that Ellichpur merely required *jāgīr* administration and improvement in agriculture[3], a task which could not be accomplished within two decades by his own admission as stated above.

Aurangzeb had never remained negligent in commending the endeavours of the improvers as is evident from his appreciation for Mīr Khalīlullāh and Murshid Quli Khān for enhancing income of *jāgīrs* of *parganas* of Daryapur and Bir respectively[4].

Shāh Jahān in disregard to ground realities offered some unrealistic option to the Prince *viz.* his allowing Aurangzeb for exchange of more revenue paying *jāgīrs* of other *jāgīrdārs* to which he showed his disinclination. Even when he resumed low revenue yielding *jāgīrs* worth, 1,27,00,000 *dāms* of some incompetent officials it did not meet Imperial approbation. When abatement in the *jama'* of some low revenue paying *parganas* was sanctioned Aurangzeb pleaded for '8 monthly' *naqdi* in lieu of his disputed '9-monthly' *jāgīr*[5].

Since Aurangzeb's such cryptic remarks, perhaps could not dispel the cobweb of suspicion he suggested for procuring Imperial orders regarding *jāgīr* affairs of other *jāgīrdārs* in context with Multafat Khān's request for loan, which during his first Viceroyalty he could advance on his surety[6].

In view of the deteriorating conditions of *jāgīr* in the Deccan Shāh Jahān ordered the resumption of Bir to *khāliṣa* and in lieu assignment of '10-monthly' *naqdi* to Aurangzeb[7]. In regard to a suggestion of the Emperor for resuming Rs 20,36,000 in his *jāgīr* from other *jāgīrdārs* Aurangzeb

1. *Calendar,* Doc. No. 1.8, *Ādāb,* Vol. I, pp. 144-5.
2. *Calendar,* Doc. No. 1.9, *Ādāb,* Vol. I, pp. 141-3.
3. *Calendar,* Doc. No. 1.9, *Ādāb,* Vol. I, pp. 141-3.
4. *Calendar,* Doc. No. 1.12, *Ādāb,* Vol. I, p. 153.
5. *Calendar,* Doc. No. 1.13, *Ādāb,* Vol. I, p. 126.
6. *Calendar,* Doc. No. 1.15, *Ādāb, pp.* 207-8.
7. *Calendar,* Doc. No. 1.16, *Ādāb,* Vol. I, p. 139.

unequivocally explained that in the event of its implementation all of them would become *jāgīrless* resulting in their dispatch to the Imperial court diminishing the strength of the army by one-third which was, however, needed owing to the military position of the Deccan. To resolve this *jāgīr* crisis he pleaded for assignment of extra-Deccan *jāgīrs* and cash [*naqdi*] from Malwa as was prevalent during his first Viceroyalty[1].

Shāh Jahān often used to criticize Aurangzeb and fixing upon him the responsibility of the mal-administration of the Deccan with the sarcasm that to avoid any loss to him all his *jāgīrs* were granted in the Deccan and he was granted ten crore *dāms* in '10 monthly' *naqdi* from Malwa with the authorisation to resume *jāgīrs* of his choice equal to two crore *dāms* from the *jāgīrdārs* including *pargana* Nandurbār. Āurangzeb politely declined the offer on the ground that such a policy would lead to the exodus of the *jāgīrdārs* to the Imperial Court due to non-availability of *jāgīrs* or if they were assigned *jāgīrs* elsewhere these were not enough, failing which *pāibāqi* lending to be low-income *maḥāls* would have to be assigned in lieu of their higher income *maḥāls*, demoralising them beyond redemption. Anyhow, Aurangzeb, in compliance with Imperial instructions, selected some areas from the *khāliṣa* and *jāgīrs* reports of which were sent to the Court with the hope that in exchange of his previous '10-monthly' *naqdi* and for expenses and calamities accompanying with *jāgīrdarī* he would be granted *jāgīr* worth two crore *dāms*, with rebate in income, making it '6-monthly'. Aurangzeb was however, honest enough to state that since income from Nandurbār did not suffer any loss he accepted the same for sixty lakh *dāms* like Prince Murād Bakhsh, who had previously held it[2].

In order to effect economy in government expenditure he suggested that in lieu of Rs 1,90,000 assigned to Jahān Āra Begum from *mandvi* [market] Jahānābād, Burhānpur, Shāista Khān should collect and dispatch to her the *naqdi* granted to Aurangzeb from Malwa to save the double transportation charges[3]. Aurangzeb was also rebuked on account of *pargana* Sulṭanpur held in *inā'm* grant of Prince Muḥammad Sulṭan and Nandurbār in *naqdi jāgīr* of Aurangzeb, subsequently excluded from their *dual-i jāgīr* and included in *khāliṣa*, which due to the carelessness of previous *jāgīrdārs* became desolate yielding 92,000 *dāms*. He pleaded that since the *Dīwāns* had ignored ten-yearly papers of the same they had designated the *parganas* as excellent and prosperous and Aurangzeb had

1. *Calendar,* Doc. No. 1.23, *Ādāb,* Vol. I, p. 157.
2. *Calendar,* Doc. No. 1.24, *Ādāb,* Vol. I, p. 165-8.
3. *Calendar,* Doc. No. 1.25; *Ādāb,* Vol. I, p. 201.

no choice, if Shāh Jahān assigned him '5-monthly' in lieu of his '10-monthly' *jagīr*[1].

Such persistent humiliations and adverse criticisms dejected Aurangzeb, who wrote to Jahān Āra Begum that if such a reduction was enforced then Baglāna, which was assigned in *inā'm-i altamgha*, during his first term as Viceroy, would suffice. However, Jahān Āra, pacified him by communicating news of the grant of Baglāna as his *inā'm*, two-third as *jāgīr* and one-third as *naqdi*. But ultimately the tyranny of the circumstances compelled him to remind his previous decision of retiring from administration, which he was not allowed to stick because under new dispensation his trusted officials, were being allowed, enticed and summoned to the Court like Malik Ḥusain by inducement of assignment of high rank during the last twenty years[2].

Aurangzeb favoured the *jāgīrdārs* to such an unprecedented degree that he even declined his *jāgīr* of Bir, yielding one crore *dāms*, whose revenues were increasing annually, instead preferred Mādhuji Bhonsla's '6-monthly' just for fulfilling his commitment of assigning Bir to Shah Beg Khān to accommodate his scattered *jāgīrs* worth, 3,50,00,000 *dāms* on the eve of the latter's summoning from Aḥmadnagar to Golcunda expedition[3]. In addition to presenting cases of individual *manṣabdārs* he also made representations to the court procuring orders for release of salaries of the petty *jāgīrdar* through his *wakil*[4].

Aurangzeb who held *naqdi jāgīr* worth '10 crore *dāms,* sought the intercession of Sa'dullah Khān to get the draft of his salary released, after getting deducted the Imperial claims against him[5]. In a similar fashion Aurangzeb approached Shāista Khān for securing his withheld payments from 'Umar Tārin[6] as well as his *naqdi jāgīrs*[7] because he stressed his dependence on *naqdi*[8].

Since Deccan was a deficit area an increase of 5,000 *sawār* [2x3h] could not move Aurangzeb to accept charge of ten forts otherwise his enhancement in rank would become nullified and he would even suffer further loss on account of extra-expenses on their maintenance[9]; he could

1. *Calendar,* Doc. No. 1.27, *Ādāb,* Vol. I, pp. 191-2.
2. *Calendar,* Doc. No. 9.2, 12.1; *Ādāb,* Vol. I, pp. 408-9; Vol. II, p. 746.
3. *Calendar,* Doc. No. 1.29, 1.30; *Ādāb,* Vol. I, pp. 161-2, 199-200.
4. *Calendar,* Doc. No. 11.2; *Ādāb,* Vol. I, pp. 579-8.
5. *Calendar,* Doc. No. 6.7; 1.30; *Ādāb,* Vol. I, 461.
6. *Calendar,* Doc. No. 8.3; *Ādāb,* Vol. I, p. 485.
7. *Calendar,* Doc. No. 8.4; *Ādāb,* Vol. I, p. 494.
8. *Calendar,* Doc. No. 8.8; *Ādāb,* Vol. I, p. 506.
9. *Calendar,* Doc. No. 8.5; *Ādāb,* Vol. I, p. 500.

only accept the fort of Asir entailing no expenditure and he also held the fort of Junnair[1].

His endeavour for recurring appointment of intelligent and honest *karorīs* and *'āmils* for his *jāgīr* till his arrival in the Deccan to realise not only the land revenue but also to see to it that the *jāgīrdārs* and *karorīs* could not harass the peasantry and his offer to administer the Deccan either with *naqdi* and *jāgīr* is illustrative of his devotion to duty[2].

One of the great problems of the *jāgīr* administration was posed by the promulgation as well as the implementation of new branding regulation of the 27th regnal year of Shāh Jahān which was directly related to the low revenue yield of *jagīrs*. The availability of a *farmān* of Shāh Jahān of the 14th regnal year to Aurangzeb during his first term of Viceroyalty also referred to by Aurangzeb during his second tenure unfolds background of this device in the Deccan, which was in tune with the situation.

Farmān to Aurangzeb [titles omitted]. "It was brought to the most sublime, most holy and most august notice of His Majesty from the *wāqia'* of the province of the Deccan that due to the low-yield of *jāgīr* [*kam ḥāṣili-i jāgīr*] of that province during this period the pay claim after branding [*Ṭalab-i dāgh*], from the time of his arrival he too got branded the contingent by free will and inclination and obtained one-fourth, as salary. When this fact was brought to the notice of that illustrious son through LuṬfullāh, *Bakhshī* and *Wāqia'Nawīs*[3], that fortunate son asked him to record the true fact in the *wāqia'* so as obtain the reply. Accordingly the said person brought it to the most holy and sublime notice of [His Majesty] that the Regulations of Branding and Verification [*ẓabita-i dāgh-o taṣḥiḥa*] are not prevalent in this province; if *dastūru-l 'amal* [administrative or fiscal regulations, administrative manual] is issued from the sky high [Imperial] Court then the Brand on horse for identification at inspection [*ṯalab-i dāgh-o taṣḥiḥa*] can be made according to it. The august Imperial order is issued that we send the Regulation of Branding and Verification with the exalted *farmān* [Imperial order]. From the officials whose entire *jāgīrs* are in Hindustan [North India], one is Rāi Satar Sāl, who most probably, has been himself maintaining a contingent larger than required under the Regulation and in this situation let that fortunate son assure that Rāi Satar Sāl and some others who maintain contingents according to Regulations

1. *Calendar,* Doc. No. 8.7; *Ādāb,* Vol. I, p. 505.
2. *Calendar,* Doc. No. 14.1, 14.2; *Ādāb,* Vol. I, II, pp. 675-7.
3. Luṭfullāh Khān s/o Lashkar Khān [Irani] holding the *manṣab* of 1,000/800 was the *Bakhshī* and *Wāqia' Nawīs* of Bālāghāt, [Lahori, II, p. 191 in 1049/1639-40] which was raised to 1,000/1,000 in 1052/1642-3, [Lahori, II, 290] in which year he died, [Lahori, II, 746].

to make claims [accordingly] and from rest of the persons who would not have cared for this whosoever has his entire *jāgīr* in Hindustan, an increase or decrease in his *jāgīr*, as per schedule, shall be effected in Hindustan and the rest shall be received in the Deccan. Let the *jāgīr* of Hindustan be governed according to the Regulation of Hindustan and the share of *jāgīr* in accordance with the income thereof be brought under stipulated Branding Regulation. Whosoever has his entire *jāgīr* there the current income [*ḥal-i ḥāṣil*] of his *jāgīr* be inspected and pay claim of branding [*t̲alab-i dāg̲h*] be made accordingly and consider this Regulation perpetual and verify it year to year and consider His Majesty's favours increasing day by day. Written on 2nd *Sha'bān* 14th regnal year. Written on the report of Prince Muḥammad Dara Shukoh, Islām K̲h̲ān and Afẓal K̲h̲ān [titles omitted][1]".

However, after 1641 another *farmān* of Shāh Jahān was issued in his 27th regnal year which had general applicability declaring that it has been represented to the Court that for the nobles and *manṣabdārs* that who receive cash instead of *jāgīrs* are paid for each horse branded [*asp dāg̲h̲i*] ... cash salaries are never to be fixed above 'eight-monthly' or 'four-monthly'[2].

He equally laid emphasize upon the amelioration of the conditions of the peasantry which was groaning under the oppression of the former Governors[3]. He was also vigilant that no loss could occur in revenue-collection without any oppression of the peasantry by the *jāgīrdārs* and *karorīs*[4]. Aurangzeb also took precautionary measures to save the peasantry from the enemy, punish the oppressors realising beyond assessed revenue notwithstanding Dara Shukoh's success in getting resumed Berar from Aurangzeb's *jāgīr* and unsuccessful bid for snatching the Deccan Viceroyalty from him[5].

Interestingly enough Tavernier depicts the country of Golcunda as being "fully" of tanks, which are said to have been made by building dams, which were "sometimes half a league long", so as to stock the water in natural depressions and use it after the rains for fields[6]. Similarly there was a great Kamthana tank of Bidar, made by dam built to its north, that was "verily" a "Tigris" and which freed the cultivators of the surrounding country from all dependence upon the rain[7]. Furthermore in the later years

1. *Bloch. Supp. Pers.* 482, ff. 46[a] - 47[a].
2. *Calendar,* Doc. No. 1.1; 14.1; *Ādāb,* Vol. I, pp. 96, Vol. II, 675-6.
3. *Calendar,* Doc. No. 14.1; *Ādāb,* Vol. II, pp. 675-6.
4. *Calendar,* Doc. No. 15.1, 15.4, *Ādāb* 737.
5. *Wāqi'āt-i 'Ālāmgīrī*, p. 39.
6. Tavernier I, 121-2.
7. *Ma'āsir-i 'Ālāmgīrī*, 308-9, *Epigraphis Indo-Moslemica,* 1937-8, 1-2.

of Shāh Jahān we also find the Mughal administration planning to advance nearly Rs 40,000 to 50,000 to cultivators in Khāndesh and the Painghat portion of Berar, for the purpose of erecting bunds or dams. In Banglore "They have brought into every town and village thousands of canals, cut from river for the benefit of cultivation[1] as these were most probably managed to the co-operative phad system, which still is continuing in the area[2].

In a nutshell, Aurangzeb succeeded in streamlining and improving revenue and financial administration, augmenting revenue resources and implementing revenue reforms of Murshid Quli Khān in the Deccan.

[IV] Revenue and Financial Administration

Consequent upon the annexations of 1636 during Aurangzeb's first Viceroyalty of the Deccan[3] it contributed over one-fifth of the total *jama'* [assessed revenue] of the Mughal Empire [1646-7], in contrast to its area which was even less than one-tenth of the total area. Surprisingly enough the *jama'* of the Mughal Deccan remained at par in 1650 as well. This level of *jama'* remained even less than 21% in 1656 during Aurangzeb's second term as Viceroy of the Deccan during which phase he made frequent complaints concerning the enormous difference between the estimated and actual income [*ḥāṣil*]. Aurangzeb stressed that the actual realisation of the Mughal Deccan was Rs 88,00,000 which was below even '3-monthly'

1. Ṣādiq Khān, Or 174, ff. 60[b]-61[a], Or 1671, f. 34[a].
2. *Royal Commission on AgricultureReport* 325.
3. *Cf.*, Zahoor Ali Khān 'The Mughal Campaign Against Bijapur, 1636, Geographical Interpretation, *Aligarh Papers on Indian History*, presented in *Ind. Hist. Cong.*, Dharwar, 1988, pp. 231-35. However, during the very period of nine months such imminent conquests [in 1635-6] became possible, Shāh Jahān succeeded in eliminating Jujhār Singh Bundela by a multi-pronged attack upon him, who had resorted to flight towards Deccan *via.* Sholāpur, under the command of 'Abdullah Khān Firoz Jung, Saiyid Khān Jahān Bārha , Khān-i Dauran, as Prince Aurangzeb was given the nominal charge of the command with Shāista Khān as his advisor. *Cf.*, Abha Singh, Jujhar Singh's Rebellion: A Reappraisal, *PIHC*, 1990, pp. 230-40. Shāh Jahān received both cash and kind a huge amount as tribute from the rulers of the Deccan [*Duniyādārān-i Deccan*], *Zamīndār* of Gondwana and the booty of Jujhar Singh usurped by him from Chaurāgarh amounting *in toto* to two crore rupees as that much amount would have hardly ever been accumulated by the monarchs of the world which was equal to the income of Tranxoiana. *Cf., Bloch. Supp. Pers.* 482, ff. 63[b] - 64[b], 65[b] - 67[a]. In 1632 Fateḥ Khān s/o Malik 'Amber who joined the Mughal service with the rank of 7,000/7,000 contingent upon the execution of Nizāmu-l Mulk also helped in conquering Nizāmu-l Mulk's territory in 1633 having a *jama'* of fifty crore *dams* yielding one crore rupees as well as some of his strong forts was allowed certain favours inspite of his misdeeds. *Cf.,Blochet. Supplement Persian*, ff. 9[a-b], The Shāh Jahān *Nama of* Inayat Khān, Delhi, 1990, pp. 67, 73, 77-78, 82-83, 97-99, 103, 107, 109, 112-116, 118-119.

[*sih-māhā*] or 24.3%. The civil and military expenditure of the Deccan, of course, excluding the salaries of the Officials from the *jāgīrs* arrived at Rs 31,76,000 of which Rs 25,43,000 were spent on the cash allowances of Aurangzeb and his sons whereas the expenses incurred on Artillery and other related expenditure required Rs 6,30,000 which could be provided by *k͟hāliṣa sharīfa*, tribute of Golcunda and Deogarh amounting to Rs 1,43,000 and the deficit of Rs 20,36,000 was made good with the reserve accumulated in the Deccan treasuries[1]. Aurangzeb also faced Shāh Jahān's strictures without any fault on his part[2].

We are well aware of the fact that *deshmukhs*, *despandeys*, *patels*, *muqaddams* all ensure the creation of the administrative arrangements of the erstwhile regime i.e. Deccan Sultanate as even the word *muqaddam* owes its origin to Delhi Sultanate period.

To Aurangzeb's utter dismay had occurred the shortfall in the revenues continued in 1652. The decline in agriculture prompted Shāh Jahān to appoint Aurangzeb as Viceroy of the Mughal Deccan with the specific instructions for improving cultivation and resettling villages. Aurangzeb himself blamed the prevalence of miscellaneous forms of revenue assessment and collection [*ẓawābiṭ-i gūnāgūn*]. Murshid Quli K͟hān's appointment as *Dīwān* for improving the agrarian conditions resulted into crop-sharing[3] as *taqāvi* [agricultural loans] were advanced to the peasants[4]. Even Shāh Jahān rebuked Aurangzeb for not sanctioning himself 40,000 to 50,000 rupees, as *taqāvi* for raising the irrigation bunds in the provinces of Khandesh and Berar[5].

Interestingly enough the financial obligations of Chananeri *Deshmukh,* whose descendent, all called Chananeri *Deshmukhs*, have been recorded in a letter from Aurangzeb during his second term of viceroyalty of the Deccan[6]. We are also informed that when the *jama'* imposed upon him was enhanced substantially, Chananeri *Deshmukh* sought permission to be allowed to pay the increase separately as tribute [*peshkash*] and not as part of the *jama'* to be paid annually to whomsoever it was earmarked in *jāgīr* or *k͟hāliṣa* as Aurangzeb naturally required Chananeri, to pay both, one amount as *jama'* [assessed revenue] as it was totally different from *peshkash* which was deposited into the Imperial treasury and an additional

1. *Calendar,* Doc. No. 1.23; *Ādāb,* Vol. I, pp. 156-8.
2. *Calendar,* Doc. No. 1.24; *Ādāb,* Vol. I, pp. 165-8.
3. *Calendar,* Doc. No. 1.18; *Ādāb,* Vol. I, pp. 134-5.
4. *Calendar,* Doc. No. 1.16; *Ādāb,* Vol. I, pp. 138-40.
5. *Calendar,* Doc. No. 1.15; *Ādāb,* Vol. I, pp. 206-8.
6. *Calendar,* Doc. No. 13.1; *Ādāb,* Vol. I, pp. 636-39, *Cf.,* Irfan Habib, *Agrarian System of Mughal India,* second revised edition, Delhi, 1999, pp. 223 and 225.

amount as *peshkash.* Thus, Aurangzeb endeavoured to reconcile realities of revenue administration with the formal law of *shari'at.*

In order to cope with the financial difficulties Aurangzeb used to augment the revenue resources[1] from all possible means of income including tribute from the *Zamīndār* of Deogarh[2], Jawar[3], conquest of Deogarh[4] and *peshkash* [tribute] from there as well as from Golcunda[5]. Aurangzeb was cautious enough in protesting over the new rates of the troopers which were too low to maintain a suitable horse, that ultimately led to its revocation. The problems of enforcement of Branding Regulations[6] also became the subject of Aurangzeb's objections as these were included not in the Realisation of *muṭāliba* [State dues] from Rāo Karan. The Branding Regulations again became a cause of consternation in the Deccan[7] which was against the interest of the *manṣabdārs*[8].

We come to know about measures for realising the tribute from Quṭbu-l Mulk, side by side the threat to attack on Golcunda[9]. Notwithstanding Aurangzeb's endavours for realising tributes he had strived to recommend release of Inderman, *Zamīndār* of Dhandhera[10]. Aurangzeb also evinced much interest in improving the conditions of the Deccan[11]. He however simultaneously, settled the exchange rate of *hūn* of Quṭbu-l Mulk's *peshkash,*[12] which helped in realisation of the settled amount of his tribute[13].

The Ā'īn does not provide us with any relevant information about the Mughal Deccan beyond saying that Berar was under *nasaq*[14].

Ṣādiq Khān, however, does tell us that in the Deccan province neither measurement nor crop-sharing had been followed "since ancient times". "On the contrary the established practice was that each of the villagers and a pair of oxen, grew what crop he liked, whether food grain or port-herbs and paid to the authorities [*sarkār*] a little money on each plough varying with the territory and the *parganas;* and there was no [further] enquiry about, or

1. *Calendar,* Doc. No. 1.26; *Ādāb,* Vol. I, pp. 163-4.
2. *Calendar,* Doc. No. 1.28; *Ādāb,* Vol. I, pp. 211-3.
3. *Calendar,* Doc. No. 1.29; *Ādāb,* Vol. I, pp. 161-2.
4. *Calendar,* Doc. No. 1.31; *Ādāb,* Vol. I, pp. 214-15.
5. *Calendar,* Doc. No. 1.32; *Ādāb,* Vol. I, pp. 218-19.
6. *Calendar,* Doc. No. 1.35; *Ādāb,* Vol. I, pp. 178-9.
7. *Calendar,* Doc. No. 1.36; *Ādāb,* Vol. I, pp. 148-50.
8. *Calendar,* Doc. No. 1.38, 1.40; *Ādāb,* Vol. I, pp. 158-9, 230-2.
9. *Calendar,* Doc. No. 1.42; *Ādāb,* Vol. I, p. 219.
10. *Calendar,* Doc. No. 1.44; *Ādāb,* Vol. I, pp. 186-7.
11. *Calendar,* Doc. No. 12.4; *Ādāb,* Vol. I, pp. 828-31.
12. *Calendar,* Doc. No. 4.4; *Ādāb,* Vol. I, pp. 276-8.
13. *Calendar,* Doc. No. 4.5, 4.6; *Ādāb,* Vol. I, pp. 305-308.
14. Ā'īn I, 478.

regard paid to the quality of crops"[1]. It seems that this might have been the general practice, but from a document prepared in 1642-43 it appears that in some *parganas* at least a kind of *nasaq* based upon measurement was applied. Moreover writing from the Deccan in 1653 Aurangzeb concurred with Shāh Jahān's view that the "different methods" [*ẓawābit-i gūnāngūn*] followed by the revenue authorities were a cause of the ruin of the country[2]. This might have been the general practice but from a document prepared in 1642-43 under Aurangzeb's first Viceroyalty of the Deccan it appears that in some *parganas* at least a kind of *nasaq* based upon measurement was being applied. However, 1679 Papel document does show that nearly nine-tenth of the villages of Berar and Aurangabad had been measured and nearly a half of those of Khāndesh.

Though Murshid Quli Khān introduced crop sharing, yet it was an expensive method as Aurangzeb himself declared that when it was introduced in the Deccan the cost of revenue collection doubled simply from the necessity of organising a watch and ward on the crops[3].

We come to know about measures for realising the tribute from Quṭbu-l Mulk, side by side the threat for attack on Golcunda[4]. Notwithstanding Aurangzeb's endavours for realising the tributes he was strived to recommend release of Inderman, *Zamīndār* of Dhandhera[5]. Aurangzeb also evinced much interest in improving the conditions of the Deccan[6]. Aurangzeb however simultaneously, settled the exchange rate of *hūn* of Quṭbu-l Mulk's *peshkash*,[7] which helped in realisation of the settled amount of Quṭbul Mulk's tribute[8].

We are well aware of the fact of the problem of difference between paper *jama'* and actual realisation persisted as neither Murshid Quli Khān's reform nor Aurangzeb's claims of doubling the revenues in certain fiscal units nor Shāh Jahān's manipulations of salary rates for cavalry could be of much significance.

---

1. Ṣādiq Khān, Or 174. F. 185 [a-b] 1671, f. 90[b]- Khāfi Khān, 1732n.
2. *Ādāb-i 'Ālāmgīrī*, f. 36[a] ed. I, 139.
3. *Ādāb-i 'Ālāmgīrī*, Or 170, f. 118[a], this letter is missing in the printed ed.
4. *Calendar*, Doc. No. 1.42; *Ādāb*, Vol. I, p. 219.
5. *Calendar*, Doc. No. 1.44; *Ādāb*, Vol. I, pp. 186-7.
6. *Calendar*, Doc. No. 12.4; *Ādāb*, Vol. I, pp. 828-31.
7. *Calendar*, Doc. No. 4.4; *Ādāb*, Vol. I, pp. 276-8.
8. *Calendar*, Doc. No. 4.5, 4.6; *Ādāb*, Vol. I, pp. 305-308.

II

The Deccan Provinces [1659-1682]

1. Viceroys

There is no denying the fact that the office of the Governor of a province was an extremely important one in the Mughal Empire which was divided into numerous provinces each of which was under the administration of the Governor who was designated as *nāzim, ṣāhib-i ṣūba, ṣubedār* or *faujdār-i ṣūba*. The provincial Governors, like the principal minister at the centre were normally appointed from amongst the officers holding highest *manṣab* [rank], forming the hard core of the ruling class[1].

Since the Deccan provinces enjoyed a special status because these were four in number, they had a Viceroy, which policy could not be abandoned even by Aurangzeb as Emperor. Furthermore the four older Deccan provinces Aurangabad, Berar, Bedar and K͟hāndesh which experienced conquest and administrative consolidation relatively late as the Imperial administration recognised the uniqueness of the Deccan provinces by stationing a Viceroy of the four Deccan provinces at Aurangabad who exercised authority over the provincial administrations. Aurangzeb, like other provincial Governors, appointed Governors to the four Deccan provinces, together with a Viceroy. Whenever we find occasional blanks in respect of some Deccan provinces it may be presumed that no Governor was appointed, the province was assumed as part of the superior Viceroyalty of the Deccan, which was generally held either by a prince or a high noble. The following table is illustrative of the position of the Governors of the Deccan who along with the Viceroy served the four provinces at different times and who were sometimes also transferred from one province to another province of the Deccan or altogether shifted to elsewhere. Initially most of Governors were those who had loyally served Aurangzeb during his second Viceroyalty.

1. For details see P. Saran, *Provincial Government of the Mughals*.

Table 1: Governors Of Deccan Provinces [1659-1682]

R.Y.	Deccan	Bedar	Khāndesh	Berar	Aurangabad
1st	Prince Mu'azzam	Khān-i Zamān Mīr Khalil [I]	Wazir Khān [T] Mir Jumla [I]	Saiyid Ṣalābat Khān Ikhtiṣaṣ Khān [Ind.]	
2nd	Prince Mu'azzam			Saiyid Salabat Khān Ikhtiṣaṣ Khān [Ind.]	Wazīr Khān [I]
3rd	Shāista Khān			Shāh Beg Khān [I]	
4th	Shāista Khān	Khān-i Zamān Mīr Khalil [I]		Shāh Beg Khān [I]	
5th	Shāista Khān	Khān-i Zamān Mīr Khalil [I]			
6th	Prince Mu'azzam	Khān-i Zamān Mīr Khalīl [I]			
7th	Prince Mu'azzam	Khān-i Zamān Mīr Khalīl [I]	Wazīr Khān [I] Daūd Khān Qureshi [Ind.]		
8th	Mirzā Raja Jai Singh [R]		Wazīr Khān [I] Daūd KhānQureshi [Ind.]		
9th	Mirza Raja Jai Singh [R]		Khān-i Zamān Mīr Khalil [I]	Iraj Khān [I]	Khān-i Zamān Mīr Khalil [I]
10th	Diler Khān [Af]		Khān-i Zamān Mīr Khalil [I]	Mir Khalil [I]	
11th	Prince Mu'azzam		Mukhtār Khān [I]	Daūd Khān Qureshi [Ind.]	
12th	Prince Mu'azzam		Mir Shamsud-din [I]		
13th	Prince Mu'azzam		Daūd Khān Qureshi [Ind.]		
14th	Prince Mu'azzam		Daūd Khān Qureshi [Ind.]		
15th	Bahādur Khān Koka [I]	Mukhtār Khān	Daūd Khān Qureshi [Ind.] Hoshdār Khān [I]		
16th	Bahādur Khān Koka [I]	Mukhtār Khān Mir Shamsuddin [I]	Hoshdār Khān [I]		
17th	Bahādur Khān Koka [I]	Qalandar Khān [I]	Mukhtār Khān Mir Sham-suddin [I]		

(Contd...)

18th	Bahādur Khān Koka [I]		Mukhtar Khān Mir Shamsuddin [I]		
19th	Bahādur Khān Koka [I]		Mukhtar Khān Mir Shamsuddin [I]		
20th	Bahādur Khān Koka [I]		Mukhtar Khān Mir Shamsuddin [I]	Khān-i Zamān Mīr Khalīl [I]	
21th	Diler Khān [AF]	Khān-i Zamān Mīr Khalīl [I]	Mukhtar Khān Mir Shamsuddin [I]		
	Asad Khān [I]				
22th	Prince Shah ʻĀlam				
23th	Prince Shah ʻĀlam		Bahādur Khān Koka [I]		
	Prince Shah ʻĀlam				
24th	Bahādur Khān Koka [I]				
	Bahādur Khān Koka [I]		Iraj Khān [I] Mir Zamān Mīr Khalīl [I]		

Sources: Muḥammad Kāzim, *ʻAlamgīrnāma,* ed. Khadim Ḥusain and ʻAbdul Hai, Bib. Ind. Calcutta, 1865-73, pp. 129, 191, 198, 219, 233, 338, 416, 426, 439-40, 462, 476, 485, 564, 578, 592, 624, 627, 634, 741, 761, 818, 854, 869, 874, 903, 904, 907, 913, 919, 924, 970-72, 988, 1000, 1022, 1029-30, 1032, 1036 and 1037; Saqi Mustaiʻd Khān, *Maasir-i ʻĀlamgīrī,* Bib. Ind. Calcutta, 1871, pp. 45, 49, 60, 110, 114, 124, 144, 158 ,161, 189, 205 and 206; *Akhbarat-i Darbar-i Muʻallā*, 14RY, 15RY, 18RY and 20RY, *Ādāb-i ʻĀlamgīrī,* compiler, Abul Fateh Qābil Khān, ed. Abdul Ghafur Chaudhuri, Lahore, 1971, Vol. II, pp. 997, 1043, 1054 and 1105-8, Bhim Sen, *Nuskha-i Dilkusha,* Br. Mus. Or 23, ff. 67[b]-68[a], Shahnawaz Khān, *Maasirul Umara,* ed. Maulvi Abdur Rahim, Bib. Ind. Calcutta, Vol. I, 188, 768, Vol. III, 620-23.

The nature and tenure of appointments and the kind of officials appointed as Viceroys and Governors in the Deccan provinces are reflected in the above table which shows one Prince, four Iranis, one Afghan and one Rajput each as Viceroys of the Deccan and yields an average tenure of two years and one month. Similarly the Iranis enjoyed predominant position as provincial Governors because 16 are Iranis, 2 are Turanis and 2 are Indian Muslims during Aurangzeb's first phase as the Emperor.

A further analysis of the table indicated that the Imperial court discouraged long tenures for Governors and generally transferred or recalled them within 2-3 years which practice was also followed by Aurangzeb especially in view of maintaining their efficiency in administering the Deccan.

When Aurangzeb marched from the Deccan in January 1658, he appointed his son Prince Muḥammad Mu'azzam, as Viceroy, to manage the Deccan affairs due to his vast experience of its administration. Beginning from January 1658 till Aurangzeb's final return in March 1682, a period of 24 years intervened during which duration six Viceroys were appointed to the Mughal Deccan, among whom Prince Mu'azzam [later Prince Shah 'Ālam], held the office for 11 years, Bahādur Khān for 6 years, Shāista Khān for 3 years, Jai Singh for 2 years, Diler Khān for one year and Asad Khān for a few months.

Although these Viceroys often remained busy in meeting the Maratha menace who were devastating the Imperial dominions, yet they carefully managed the Mughal administration of the Deccan. Aurangzeb due to his sagacity and political dexterity saw to it that maximum help and cooperation was extended to the Viceroys. Accordingly even on the eve of the fratricidal wars of succession he directed Aṣālat Khān, to proceed to the Deccan with Prince Muḥammad Akbar during the Prince's sojourn from Daulatabad to Aurangabad[1]. Aurangzeb issued orders to Muḥammad Ṭahir Khurāsāni, entitled Wazir Khān, to administer the affairs of Daulatabad and serve Prince Mu'azzam staying at Burhanpur[2].

Keeping in view of the problems of administering Deccan, encountered by Prince Muḥammad Mu'azzam, Aurangzeb through his *Mīr Bakhshi* Muḥammad Amīn Khān issued orders on 5 January, 1659 to Sarfaraz Khān [5,000/4,000], Randola Khān [4,000/4,000], Jadu Rai [4,000/2,500], Rustam Rai [2,500/1,200] and Dattaji, the Imperial officers, who were deputed for the Deccan by the Emperor, that whosoever would not have marched from Buhanpur to Bālāghāt would remain there without proceeding ahead. Similarly those who would come subsequently would also act accordingly. If, however, all of them considered dispatch of contingent necessary to their *jagīrs* they were allowed to do so whereas they were asked to stay there accompanied with another corps without yearning for further injunction in the matter[3].

Aurangzeb in order to have an eye over the Viceroys and to monitor their activities used to summon them to the Imperial court, *viz.,* he asked Prince Mu'azzam to hand over the administration of *ṣūba* Khāndesh to one of his trusted associates to procced to the Mughal Court[4].

1. *Ādāb,* Vol. II, p. 1032.
2. *Ādāb,* Vol. II, p. 1052.
3. *SDAR*, AR no. 4956.
4. *Ādāb*, Vol. II, p. 1058.

It was the well established practice that all the instructions regarding the affairs of the *ṣūba* were sent by Aurangzeb to the Viceroy/ Governor, who subsequently conveyed them according to the orders[1]. It was incumbent upon him to maintain peace and tranquility as the executive head in addition to protecting the *ṣūba* and deciding the criminal cases[2]. The Viceroy used to play an important role in recommending promotions and demotions in *manṣab*, as the Viceroy of the Deccan was bound to protect the four *ṣūbas* of the Deccan as well as was held responsible[3] for its management and mal-administration. The Imperial officials serving in that *ṣūba* [i.e. four Mughal provinces of the Deccan] were asked not only to accept the Viceroy as their leader but also to obey him and act in accordance with his instructions and he was supposed to exert his utmost in discharging the Imperial assignments[4].

It was but natural that side by side the appointment of Viceroy and the Governors other provincial officials were posted by Aurangzeb in the Deccan following his accession to the Mughal throne.

2. *Dīwān*

The *Dīwān* or the chief provincial fiscal officer entertained same predominant position or level of authority as the Viceroy used to enjoy. He was the principal executive in the revenue administration as he was primarily responsible for ensuring proper assessment and collection of the land revenue. He was not only responsible for encouraging the extension of cultivation by advancing agricultural loans [*taqāvi*] but tax concessions to persons bringing virgin lands under plough[5].

The *Dīwān* of the province had control over treasury through *darogha* [superintendent] *sazāwal* [transmittal officer], and *qabz nawis-i manṣabdārān* [receipt writer of the *manṣabdārs*], administered mint through *darogha-o-amīn* [superintendent and head], *ṣāḥib-i 'iyār* [assay-master],

1. *Cf., Akhbārāt-i Darbar-i Mu'alla*, Sitamau transcript, p. 339.
2. Abul Fazl, *Ain-i Akbari,* tr; Jarrett, Calcutta, 1949, Vol. II, pp. 37-41.
3. *SDAR,* pp. 49, 52-4, 60, 111-12. These promotions and demotions in rank were effected on the recommendations of Mirza Raja Jai Singh and Bahadur Khān.
4. *Cf., Blochet Supplement Persian,* Bib. Nat. Paris, Ms no. 482, ff. 21[a]-22[a] concerning appointment order of Mirza Raja Jai Singh as the Viceroy of the Deccan instructing them not to deviate from his advice and remain submissive as well as obedient to him.
5. Parmatama Saran, 'Provincial Government of the Mughals', Allahabad, 1941, p. 189; J.F. Richards, Document Forms of Official Orders of Appointments in the Mughal Empire, Cambridge, 1986, pp. 18, 32-5. Irfan Habib, *Agrarian System,* p. 222 and Shireen Moosvi, Aurangzeb's *Farmān* to Rasikdar on Problems of Revenue Administration, 1665, in *Medieval India,* [ed.] Irfan Habib, Delhi 1994, pp. 197-208.

and *chauksi-o-wazan kash* [assayer and weigh master], controlled finance by *baramad nawīs* [auditor of accounts] and *istifa* [claims, settlements] and checked army through *Dīwān-i fauj* [finance officer of the army] and *peshkār* [secretary to the finance officer], to smoothly run the financial administration. It also shows the Imperial administration's care to control expenditure and transfer of funds. Consequent upon Aurangzeb's victory over Jaswant Singh and Qasim Khān's combined forces, he confirmed Multafat Khān[1] as *Dīwān* of the Deccan bestowed the title of 'Azam Khān with the rank of 4,000/2,500, which office was held by Amanat Khān[2] in 1662, and Makramat Khān[3] in 1667, and 'Askar Khān[4] in 1678-80. Not only each province in the Deccan had its own *Dīwān* but even each *sarkār* had a separate post of *Dīwān*, *viz.* Mir Zainul 'Abidin was the *Dīwān* of *ṣūba* Khāndesh[5], whereas Khwaja Muḥammad'Usmān held the *Dīwānī* and *Bakhshigari* of *ṣūba* Bidar[6]. Muḥammad Shafi was the *Dīwān* of *ṣūba* Berar[7], Lal Chand was the *Dīwān* of *sarkār* Ramgir which was once held by Nasrullah[8] and the *Dīwānī* of *sarkār* Baglāna was assigned to Tirkam Das[9] whereas Sanjar Beg was appointed as the *Dīwān* of *sarkār* Parenda[10].

Thus, in pre-1682 Mughal Deccan there was one *Dīwān* of the Deccan, four provincial *Dīwāns* and 37 *sarkār* level *Dīwāns*. The memorandum of actual revenue realisation of *jagīr* and numerous other papers used to bear the seal of the *Dīwān* and in cases of detailed revenue statistical data the seal of the *Dīwān* was affixed[11]. The most able and successful technical-cum-professional officers serving as *Dīwāns* of provinces might hold ranks as low as 300 to 500 *zāt* and *sawār*. Sometimes the office of the *Dīwān* was coupled with other offices. Khwaja Todar Mal was *Dīwān-i Buyūtāt*[12]

1. Abul Fazl Ma'muri, *Tarikh-i Aurangzeb*, Ms, Br. M. Or 1671, f. 98[b]; Bhimsen, *Nuskha-i Dilkushā*, Ms, Br. M., Add. 23 884, f. 14[b]; *"Ālamgīr Nāma*, pp. 51, 75, 92; *Ādāb*, II, p. 1006.
2. *SDAR*, p. 6.
3. *Selected Waqai' of the Deccan* [1660-71] [*SWD*] [ed.], Yusuf Husain Khān, Hyderabad, 1953, pp. 94-5, *SWD*, pp. 94-5.
4. *SDAR*, 62.
5. *SWD*, pp. 23, 126-7, 132-4.
6. *SDAR*, pp. 60-61.
7. *SDAR*, pp. 89-90.
8. *SWD*, pp. 73-4, 78.
9. *SWD*, pp. 68-9, 133-4.
10. *SDAR*, p. 32.
11. M.A. Nayeem, *Mughal Documents*: *Catalogue of Aurangzeb's Reign*, Andhra Pradesh State Archives, A.P. 1981, Vol. I, part II facsimiles of Doc. Nos. H/I/I, H/I/2, H/I/82, H/I/99, H/I/114, H/I/131 etc *Cf.*, J.F. Richards 'Official Revenues and Money Flows in a Mughal Province', in [ed.] J.F. Richards, *The Imperial Monetary System of Mughal India*, OUP, 1987, p. 229.
12. *SWD*, pp. 94-95, 137-8.

of Deccan. There were separate *Dīwāns* in the army[1] as well as in the provincial flotilla[2].

3. *Bakhshī*

On the executive side, the provincial *Bakhshī* or chief military inspection officer in-charge of certifying *manṣabdārs* for receipt of *naqdi* or *jagīr* assignments occupied a significant position. He made arrangement for military and provincial news-collection. As military in-charge he made inspection of horses, review of soldiers of the *manṣabdār* and issue of orders for their payments. 'Askar Khān was the *Bakhshī* of the Deccan[3] who was also assigned additional charge of *wāqia' nawisi*[4] in view of his responsibilities. It was the duty of the *Bakhshī* to confirm the antecedents of a claimant for the *manṣab*. We are informed that when Bahādur Khān Koka recommended the name of one Imāmuddin Ḥusaini from amongst the great Saiyids renowned in Gujarat and Khāndesh, in 1676 great Aurangzeb got verified his credentials by the *Dīwān* of the Deccan including the applicant's capacity for *manṣab*[5]. Kamyab Khān was also made *Bakhshī* of the Deccan[6].

Likewise there were four provincial *bakhshīs* in the Deccan provinces of pre-1682 era, *viz.,* Mir 'Abdul Hadi was the *Bakhshī* and *Wāqia'Nāwis* of Burhanpur / Khāndesh[7]. Ghiyasuddin, son of Islam Khān was made the *Bakhshī* of *ṣūba* Aurangabad by transferring Mir Abul Ḥasan[8].

4. *Faujdār*

The *faujdār* and *thānadār* were among the important posts in the provinces. The *faujdārs* in the Deccan provinces played a prominent role in streamlining the administration of military and civil affairs where territorial jurisdiction was designated as *faujdāri* which had no uniform size, as such a form of intermediate administration of cutting across the *sarkār* boundaries [but never across *ṣūba* or *pargana* lines] because it might consist of a *pargana*, or a group of *parganas* or of a *sarkār*, or more than a *sarkār*. The *faujdāri* jurisdiction not necessarily coincided

1. *SDAR,* pp. 60-61.
2. *SDAR*, pp. 10-12.
3. *SDAR*, p. 120.
4. *SDAR*, pp. 125-7.
5. *SDAR*, pp. 109-110.
6. *SWD*, p. 170; we are also informed that Muḥammad Hadi was *Bakhshī* of *ṣūba* Khāndesh in 1662; *SWD*, pp. 140-141; *SDAR*, pp. 135-6.
7. *SDAR*, pp. 148-150.
8. *Ādāb,* Vol. II, p. 1115.

with the territorial boundaries of the *parganas* or *sarkārs* which, however, invariably reflected Imperial need for intensive control, and surveillance, and the various levels of cooperation or antagonism among the local *zamīndārs* or variation in terrain helped to determine the extent of territory assigned to a *faujdār* which was the *faujdāri* or territorial jurisdiction in administrative domain of a *faujdār*. The *faujdārs* used to supervise the *thānadārs*, commandants of military checkpoints, and numerous commanders of road petrol [*rāhdārs*]. Due to his commanding several hundred armed heavy cavalry the *faujdār* was a visible, and formidable reminder of Imperial authority in the countries[1]. Insofar as the appointment of the *faujdār* was concerned, generally *manṣabdārs* ranging from 500 to 5000 were appointed because the charges of *faujdār* varied considerably in importance. In Deccan there was the *faujdāri* of Karnatak[2], and Baglana[3] to which nobles of very high rank were appointed. The approximation of duties of the *faujdār* can be gauged from following actual appointment order of 7 February 1663 "Presently, the position of the *faujdāri* of Karnatak *ṣūba* Daruz Zafar Bijapur, upon the transfer of Dargāh Quli Khān, as per the back endorsements is conferred upon Ṭahir Muḥammad Khān. Let him fulfill diligently the duties and customary obligations with rectitude and propriety. He must not permit the slightest matter to escape his vigilance and care. He must exert to punish the malfactors and rebels, to demolish the strongholds of such a group, to protect and succor the subjects and revenue payers and to prevent iron-smiths from manufacturing matchlock. He must order all those who in all the *thānas* of the *faujdāri maḥāl* are appointed to keep order, not to exact any of the forbidden taxes and none should become unruly and seditious. He must guard the highways so that travellers and wayfarers may move back and forth with composed minds and nowhere theft and highway robbery should occur. If the property of any person is stolen or plundered he must recover it from the thieves and highwaymen, and return such goods to the rightful owner, and punish that ill-fated group. Let the *deshmukhs, deshpandiyas, muqaddams*, peasants, and cultivators recognize him as the permanent *faujdār* and consider the office belonging to the said Khān. They should know full injunction in the matter, and act accordingly[4]".

Saiyid Manṣur was assigned the *faujdāri* of Baglana which was previously held by Saiyid Ḥasan whereas Sharza Khān was granted the

1. Noman Ahmad Siddiqi, 'The *Faujdār* and *Faujdari* Under the Mughals'; *Medieval India Quarterly*, 4, [1961] pp. 22-35.
2. Abu'Ālam Ḥaidarabadi, *faujdar* of Carnatic held the rank of 2000/500. *Cf., SWD*, p. 5, *Akh* 8 Zilqada 39 R.Y.
3. Saiyid Mausur Barha, *faujdar* of Baglana held the rank of 3000/1500 'Ālamgir Nāma, pp. 140, 337; Masirul *Umara*, II pp. 449-52; *SWD*, pp. 126-7, 137-8, 172.
4. *SDAR*; p. 41.

faujdāri of Sulṭanpur and Nandurbār[1]. Shah Beg Khān was entrusted with the *faujdāri* of the environs of Aurangabad[2]. Suhrab Khān, held the *faujdāri* of Balapur[3]. Likewise Ḥusamuddin Khān was made the *faujdār* of *sarkār* Bijagarh[4]. Isma'il Khān received the *faujdāri* of Jalnapur[5].

Although the *faujdār* as an active interventionist occupant was a formidable reminder of the Imperial authority throughout the countryside, yet he was also bound to ask the other officials to follow the dictates. We are told that Diyanand Ray, wrote to Khwaja Beg, *faujdār* of *sarkār* Ramgir intimating him, that Lal Chand, *Dīwān* of *sarkār* Ramgir was performing duties whimsically, with the instructions that if Lal Chand was acting in collaboration with Khwaja Beg that was commendable failing which he would be dismissed and replaced by someone else[6].

Faujdāri was so important an office that notwithstanding representation it could be denied to the heirs of the deceased as was the case of the *faujdāri* of Erandol. Despite all exhibitions of improvement of the heirs of the deceased *faujdār* Aurangzeb declined the assignment of *faujdāri* paving way to their submission for posting at Burhanpur so as to save them from starvation[7].

Due to their extraordinary importance the *faujdārs* never hesitated in misusing their authority or misappropriating money through fraudulent means whenever they got an opportunity. The *deshunkh* and other local officials made a representation against the high handedness of Nuṣrat s/o Fateḥ Jang, the *faujdār* of *Sarkār* Basim, *Ṣūba* Berar Bālāghāt, who plundered with impurity the household items, horses, five thousand rupees and extracted money from the daughters and widows of the *maqaddam*, which resulted into the appointment of another *faujdār*[8]. It was but natural that the Emperor censured the *faujdārs* in1681 for their failure to check river crossing and highways of the Deccan which led to supply of provisions and war equipments to the Marathas, Bijapur and Hyderabad[9].

5. *Qil'adār and Thānadār*

The post of the *qil'adār* was quite important because several strategic forts commanded by independently commissioned officers known as

1. *Ādāb*, II, 1100.
2. *Ādāb*, II, pp. 1156-71.
3. *Ādāb*, II, p. 885.
4. *Alamgir Nāma*, p. 199.
5. *Alamgir Nāma,* p. 454.
6. *SWD*, p. 74.
7. *SDAR*, p. 67.
8. *SDAR*, pp. 89-90.
9. *SDAR*, pp. 131-2.

qila'dārs were substantially garrisoned by the Imperial troops. Even appointment orders for the *qila'dārs* of major forts were assigned under a direct and independent authorisation from the Emperor. Since there were numerous important ones in the Deccan the articulation of royal authority can be seen from the following table because the Emperor himself directly appointed most reliable *manṣabdārs* as *qil'adārs* or fort commanders some of whom to hold petty ranks.

TABLE - 2

Sl. No.	*Name of the qil'adār*	*Name of the fort*	*Rank*	*Unconditional*	*Conditional*
1.	Bakhtiyar Khān[1]	Zafarabad	3000/2500	3000/1500	1000 *sawār*
2.	Iraj Khān[2]	Sholapur	2500/2300	2500/1800 [300, 2-3h]	500 sawār [300, 2-3h]
3.	Barkhurdar Khān[3]	Usa	2000/2000		
4.	Saiyid Muḥammad Khān[4]	Parenda	1500/1000	1500/1000	500 *sawār*
5.	Qalandar Khān[5]	Aḥmadnagar	1500/1000 [200, 2-3h]	1000/700	500/300 [200, 2-3h]
6.	Abdul Aziz[6]	Sunnair	1500/700	1000/500	500/200
7.	Suhrab Khān[7]	Udgir	1500/900	1500/800	100 *sawār*
8.	Mas'ud Khān[8]	Chandor	1500/700		
9.	Rustam Khān[9]	Bhaipur	1500/900	700/500	400/400
10.	Mirza 'Ali[10]	Fatehabad Dharur	1500/600	1000/400	200 *sawār*
11.	Ihtimam Khān[11]	Udgir	1500/		
12.	Mu'nim Khān[12]	Aḥmadnagar	2500/1000		
13.	Saiyid Ḥusain[13]	Ramgir			
14.	Jansipar Khān[14]	Zafarabad	1000/500		
15.	Iraj Khān[15]	Sholapur	2500/2000		
16.	Qalandar Khān[16]	Nandgaon	1500/1000		
17.	M'utaqid Khān[17]		2000/2000	2000/2000	

The above table, though not an exhaustive inventory clearly, shows the status of the *qila'dārs* by indicating the names of the castellans and the forts, and their ranks including unconditional and conditional. The *qila'dārs* were responsible for the maintenance of forts, and procurement of war equipments, and provisions. They were also liable to be promoted, demoted or transferred.

Since the *jagīrdars* were not merely satisfied with their *qila'dari* they also used to solicit the *faujdāri* of their *qila'dari* jurisdiction *viz.,* Rehman Quli Beg, *qila'dār* of Garha was also granted its *faujdāri* with an increase of 50 *sawār*[1]. Saiyid Muṣtafa, *qila'dār* of Hathgarh solicited the *faujdāri* of 2-3 *parganas* from security point of communication as also to check Murathy[2].

Ūdājī Ram who held the *qila'dāri* and *faujdāri* of Mahur for three generations solicited the restoration of *faujdāri* which was transferred to 'Abdullah Khān Shirazi[3].

Although next to *faujdār* and *qila'dār* was the post of *thānedār* yet the precise nature and the duties of the *thānedārs*, and the degree of control exercised over them by local *faujdārs* is not quite clear. 'Abdur Rasul 800/300 was appointed to the *thānedāri* of *pargana* Jamkheda[4]. Qādir Dād Khān 1000/800 [600x2-3h], who previously was assigned the *thānedāri* of *pargana* Bir, which was given in the *jagīr* of Bahādur due to which the former's conditional rank was resumed and he was posted in the army of Prince Muḥammad'Azam Shāh in 1682 by the Emperor[5] with the rank of 1000/500[6].

Interestingly some of the *thānedāris* were so much important that nobles of high rank were appointed to them *viz.,* the *thānedāri* of Gulshanabad which was granted to Jadaun Rai Deccani.

Hence it is difficult to imagine that control over these *thānedārs* was ever exercised by local *faujdārs* in the Deccan. Contrary to it there were numerous small *thānedārs* to which only petty *manṣabdār* were appointed. In a nutshell it seems that *manṣabdārs* from the rank of 200 upwards were generally appointed *thānedārs*. The *thānedārs* and *qila'dārs* were bound not to allow the flow of provisions to the enemy as specifically mentioned in a *dehsāla* of 1689 to 14 *thānedārs* and 5 *qila'dārs* to block the passage of provisions to Bijapur and a bond to this effect was also obtained from them as well[7].

6. *Qāzi, Ṣadr, Muḥtasib*

Under the Mughals the judiciary was a separate but not an independent institution which, however, required specialiaed academic training due to which *qāzis* and *ṣadrs* could expect careers in one branch only. The *qāzis* were rarely assigned executive and financial duties, probably for avoiding their administrative interest. They could partially put a check on the tyranny

1. *SWD*, p. 169.
2. *SDAR*, pp. 82-3.
3. *SDAR*, pp. 80-81.
4. *SDAR*, p. 136.
5. *SDAR*, p. 135-6.
6. *SDAR*, pp. 114-5.
7. *SDAR*, pp. 127-8.

of the executive. Even the high Mughal officials and administrators could prefer the interference by the judiciary in the administration. Even Mahabat Khān protested to Aurangzeb against the increase in the power of the *qāzis* of the Empire. He wrote in his letter that the Empire depends now on the *qāzis*; and a *qāzi* is only satisfied with bribes[1].

The Mughals employed provincial *qāzis* drawn from the ranks of the *ulema'* for every *sarkār*, city and *qaṣba* as they used to decide the civil cases, settle disputes, restrain people from indulging in evil deeds, enforce the laws of Islam, and arrange for marriage. The *qāzis* were also appointed when the need arose due to conversion of the chief of a territory. The *qāzis* of the *sarkār* even used to appoint the deputy *qāzis*. We are told by Jalal Khān Kakar that since *parganas* of Seoni and Timurani *sarkār* Handia were in the *zamīndār's* charge who had embraced Islam which had made the presence of a *qāzi* extremely necessary so as induce the Muslims to follow the Islamic laws and settle the matters according to Islamic *shari'at*. Accordingly the *qāzi* of the *sarkār* i.e. Qazi Shihābuddin, was directed to appoint his deputy as *qāzi* thereat with conditional *madad- ma'āsh*[2].

It is an established fact that in 1659 Aurangzeb revived the office of *muḥtasib* and placed these officers under the control of the *qāzis* throughout the Empire to enforce prohibition against wine drinking, apostasy and blasphemy and to help in the regulation of markets and commerce[3]. However, there are instances of assigning this office to the *qāzi*, as in case of above Qāzi Shihabuddin, who was also granted the office of *iḥtisab* and even *khitābat* of two *Eids* in 1661 A.D.

There are instances of the appointment of new *qāzis* following the transfer of the previous *qāzis* through the Imperial order as was the case of Mulla Aḥmad Sherwani, who was appointed in February 1662 A.D. upon the transfer of Qāzi 'Abdul Wāsi' for which he also received conditional and unconditional allowances, treasuries of the cities from Aḥmadabad, Aurangabad and Burhanpur[4], which shows their appointment and transfer by the Emperor.

The provincial *ṣādr* was responsible for regulating state grants to worthy, generally religious recipients. The Imperial *ṣādar* and the chief *qāzi* assigned men well-versed in the Islamic law to vacancies for judges and *muḥtasibs* etc.

1. *Cf., Mughal Nobility*, p. 146.
2. *SDAR*, pp. 15-16.
3. *Cf.,* M.Z. Siddiqi 'The Muhtasib Under Aurangzeb', *Medieval India Quarterly*, 5; 1963, pp. 113-9.
4. *SDAR*, pp. 15-16.

[II] Other Provincial Officials

Although there used to serve several other provincial officials in Mughal provinces of the Deccan in addition to the above yet only some other important officials can be mentioned here fleetingly. As far as the higher officers are concerned the act of their authorisation and approval emanated directly from the central administration in the offices of the *wazir* or head *Dīwān* of the Empire, whereas appointing authority issuing the orders was probably, the provincial *Dīwāns* in respect of subordinate offices. The Imperial inspector general, or *Ba<u>kh</u>shīu-l Mamalik*, sent his own subordinates to the provincial military contingent known as *Ba<u>kh</u>shī-i fauj*[1] or *Dīwān-i fauj*.

The Mughal administration assigned the gathering and reporting of public events and secret intelligence both to the news writer posted in the *pargana* at the *pargana* headquarters and to the superintendents of the posts. The *wāqia' nāwis* was supposed to be official in every matter including administration and protection of his *jagīr*. Throughout each expedition, this specially appointed fiscal officer and his staff maintained minute details of all transfers including extraordinary expenditure incurred by the commander or any of his subordinates. However, all these accounts were adjusted by the treasury after the return of the army.[2]

However, it could be transferred and his rank reduced as happened in case of the *wāqia' nāwis* of Chandor[3]. It was the duty of the *wāqia' nāwis* to make utmost endeavours in discharging his responsibilities as well to send *roznāmcha-i wāqia'* every week to the Imperial record office as is evident from the appointment order to Mir 'Azizuddin, the *wāqia' nāwis* of Islamgarh[4]. At provincial level it was so important an office that even it could be assigned to provincial *Ba<u>kh</u>shī*. Furthermore, 'Askar <u>Kh</u>ān, *Ba<u>kh</u>shī* of the Deccan was also burdened with this responsibility. The Mughal espionage system was so strong that when the *wāqia' nāwis* came to know of the arrival of the ship of Shāista <u>Kh</u>ān from Rakhang [Arakan] port to Ishaq Pattan port near Cicacol he sent a communication on 17 August, 1661 so as to confirm the news of the death of Shuja' [na-Shuja'] from the captain of the ship to get it entered in the news report[5]. Even another news report from Hyderabad city on 30 August 1661 as per the written statement of Mir Qasim, an employee of *sarkār <u>kh</u>aṣṣa*

1. *SDAR*, pp. 113-4.
2. J.R. Richards, 'Mughal State Finance and the World Economy', *Comparative Studies in Society and History*, 1981, p. 294.
3. *SDAR*, p. 11.
4. *SDAR*, p. 100.
5. *SWD*, p. 3. *SDAR*, pp. 125-7.

sharifa at Muchhli Pattan port confirmed that the ship of Chauliya, who was previously a servant of Shāista Khān, had come from Rakhang port and reported that Shuja' was killed, and the sons together with their sisters were imprisoned by the *zamīndār* of Rakhang, and the sons had their sons and previously Muḥammad Amin Khān, *Bakhshiul Mamalik* was also apprised[1].

Postal communication in the Mughal Empire served an extremely crucial purpose through which network the news could he conveyed. Its administration was entrusted to a *manṣabdār* when Saiyid Tajuddin was given the charge of *dāk chauki* or postal communication of the army, Bahādur Khān Koka by the Imperial order, was directed to instruct the Meoras and other staff of the *dāk chauki* to secure bond from them for not interfering with the peasants and inhabitants of towns and villages and wayfares situated therein, not bringing anyone's paper / letter along with the *nalwas* [post containers] and delivering the *farmāns* and letters issued from the Imperial court to the officials [*mutaṣaddis*yāni] thereat and sending the petitions and news reports [*'arāiz-o-waqāi'*] to the officials posted in the said army under his imitation as per rule. He has also to ask the Meoras [i.e. messengers who belonged to the Muslim Meo community] to send the *nalvas* every month otherwise any delay by them would be penalised [by deductions] from their payments by the clerks of the Imperial record offices. He was bound to write true facts without any partisanship and jealousy[2].

[III] Local Administration

Side by side provincial administration of the four provinces of the Deccan, the imperial court laid an equal emphasize on the local administration. Since the *Dīwān* seems to have made the great majority of appointments it is but natural that he also recruited, appointed and monitored the occupants of the semi-official or intermediary posts found in the four Deccan provinces.

1. *Chaudhurī*

It is but natural that the Imperial *Dīwān* and the *Dīwān-i Khāliṣa* also confirmed the appointment of a *chaudhurī*, who was firmly identified with the Imperial regime and he was obviously supposed to assist all Imperial officers sent to his locality for collecting revenues, and sometimes, he could, however, find himself under tremendous pressure to make up any

1. *SWD*, p. 7.
2. *SDAR*, pp. 47-48; For details see Irfan Habib, Postal Communication in Medieval India, *Proceedings of Indian History Congress*, 1985.

accumulated arrears. In return for these services a part of land revenue through remissions, concessions and commissions annually up to 5% of the revenues was collected. The *chaudhurī* was designated differently in the Mughal Deccan, as *deshmukhs* who was basically a *zamīndār*.

2. *Majmua'dār*

In every *sarkār* there used to be a *majmua'dār*, who used to play an important role in revenue collection. However, sometimes, he appeared to have indulged in misappropriation or suppression of facts of embezzlement together with other officials. We are told about such an episode in three news reports of 3 May, 10 May and 9 June 1661 in which the *majmua'dār* suppressed the facts of misappropriation of land revenue by the *Dīwān* of *sarkār* Ramgir, for whom they severely punished him financially[1].

3. *Kotwāl*

The central figure for general urban administration was the *kotwāl* or the city magistrate, who acted with the *qāzi* and the *qila'dār* of the city in assuring the entire responsibility for maintenance of peace, order and security of the city, *qaṣba* and its immediate neighbourhood. Significantly, the duties of the *kotwāl* and his stature were somewhat reduced at the provincial capitals serving as the seats of the provincial governors. However, elsewhere, in every important town, he was the most prominent figure, whose city guards and watchmen and various other bodies of armed footmen, were the urban police. Compared to any other officer, he was more responsible for controlling the urban crowd and for mitigating and controlling the sectarian violence, which could break out in any of the Deccan provinces as is convincingly proved by a report from Aurangabad of March 1663. It was reported that Manṣur, a beggar, resident of Begumpur, Aurangabad represented that Rajab had killed his son by dagger. Furthermore, Man, Dadu and Sahu had brought embroided cloth etc to the market for sale. Peemji, a butcher brought three of them to the *kotwāl* complaining that they had stolen these goods. Accordingly a thorough investigation revealed that they along with others had plundered a *carvan* of Gujarat at village Parchi, situated in *pargana* Nandurbar, and whatever share they had obtained, which they had brought for sale. Therefore, the *kotwāl* imprisoned three of them[2].

4. *Shiqdār*

The Imperial administration strictly checked the activities of the

1. *SWD*, pp. 65-8, 71-2.
2. *SWD*, p. 51.

shiqdār and *kotwāl* as a lady reported the matter of kidnapping her grandson by Sikandar and 'Alāul, *shiqdār* and *kotwāl* of *pargana* Dangiri. Accordingly the Prince's order was communicated to Ghiyasuddin Khān on 6 November 1674 asking him to depute ten *ahdis* [gentlemen troopers] so as to escort them along with the grandson. When Saiyid Muḥammad, *shiqdār* and *thānedār* brought the information under *qāzi*'s seal to the effect that due to Maratha invasion 'Alāul and Sikandar who were dismissed had gone from there, it is strictly ordered to produce three of them otherwise a harsh sequence could follow[1].

The *shiqdār* played same role of maintenance of law in rural areas. A *shiqdār* was ordered to hang over a thief, who had killed a peasant, in *pargana* Ūdgir[2].

The *Dīwān* of the Mughal Empire also recognised the local power and resources of numerous local magnates by formally designating them as *zamīndārs*. It is an established fact that those *zamīndārs* whose domains were situated within the zone of direct Imperial administration maintained a relationship with the Imperial administration quite similar to that of *chaudhurīs*, in coordinating between the state, and rural and town society. Since the post of *chaudhurī* was very significant in the local administration loyal, and influential *zamīndārs* were appointed as *chaudhurīs*.

5. *Qānūngo*

In every *pargana* there was a local record keeper and accountant or *qānūngo* who used to work in tandem with the *chaudhurī*. The office of the *qānūngo* was hereditary because on his death, his legal successor was appointed to the post and he was confirmed in his office by an Imperial *sanad*[3]. Generally, holders of these offices were recruited from the literate secretariat castes like Khatris or Brahmins. The *qānūngos* by controlling the data on the revenue administration, and by accumulating wealth overtime, became quite important local figures under Aurangzeb[4]. Their terms of service and tenure were similar to those of *chaudhurīs*; they received tax free grants on the revenue proceeds and other perquisites.

It was the part of the duty of the *qānūngo* to dispatch, year by year, the record of revenue and area taxed for the last ten years [*mawāzino-i dah sāla*], the records of the cash revenue rates for each crop [*dasturu-l 'amal*] and other papers from the accounts for the collection and assessment of

1. *SDAR*, p. 105.
2. *SWD*, pp. 45-6.
3. *Ahkam-i Ālamgiri*, f. 216[b].
4. For details see. S.Z.H. Jafri, *Sarkār* Qanungos: 16th-17th Century Documents, *PIHC*, 1985.

the current year for the perusal of the provincial *Dīwān*. The *qānūngo* was also informed about the appointment of the *Dīwān* of his *sarkār*[1] as well as other officials.

6. *Muqaddam*

The village headman or *muqaddam* played a crucial role in streamlining the local administration. He was not only informed about the important appointments of officials concerning the revenue and other matters but was also bound to recognize them, as such his condemnation and appreciation was given weightage. We come across a representation submitted by the notables and peasantry of Tajalka Chahār Thāna, *sarkār* Basim, *ṣūba* Berar, Bālāghāt to the Viceroy of the Deccan on 21 January 1671 complaining against the high handedness, and plunder of a *faujdār*, who had even imprisoned the daughters and widows of a *muqaddam*. This was taken seriously because of the truthfullness of the matter as a result of the inquiry, and another *faujdār* was appointed[2] thereafter.

7. *Chaudharī-I Sāi'r*

The headman of the *sai'r* revenues or the *chaudhurī-i sāi'r* assumed responsibility for proper administration and taxation of town and urban markets. He had to pay a fixed fee. Majority of these *sāi'r* headmen were either bankers [*mahājans*] money changers [*ṣarrafs*] or leading merchants of the town or the city of the area. They provided an important link between the local and central administrations and a medium of controlling urban commerce for the Empire.

There are some other officials dealing with the local administration like *patwārī* or village accountant etc whose role can never be underestimated.

The above discussion not only clearly establishes the increasingly effective, efficient and internally differentiated bureaucracy but also the integration of the administration of the four provinces of the Mughal Deccan with the rest of the country because like centre, primary administrative appointments were made within the four provinces as well in view of the fact that the Deccan was always relatively detached from the core area of the Empire in North India.

1. *SWD*, pp. 133-4.
2. *SDAR*, pp. 89-90.

III

Army Organisation and Deployment in the Deccan

1. Manṣab and *Jāgīr* Assignments

Manṣab [rank] indicated the position of its holder [*manṣabdār*] in the official hierarchy under the Mughals because they owed direct subordination to the Emperor irrespective of their *manṣab*. The *manṣab*-holders of the Mughal Empire were assigned dual numerical ranks; the first number representing his *ẓāt* ['personal'] and the second *sawār* [cavalry]. According to the sanctioned schedule, the *ẓāt* rank determined the personal pay of the *manṣabdār* and the *sawār* rank, the size of cavalry contingent maintained by him for the Emperor's service as well as the pay he was to receive to meet his expenses for maintaining it. His pay claim [*ṭalab*] consisted of the total amount sanctioned for both *ẓāt* and *sawār*, and this could be met either by payment in cash from the imperial treasury or by assigning to him territories in his *jāgīr* as official estimated [*jama', jama'dami*] of course had exactly to equal the pay due to him[1]. The conditional rank assigned in view of the services required of a particular officer at a particular post was normally cancelled and the additional *jāgīr* resumed in the event of the *manṣabdār's* transfer from the post. This fact is amply proved by a *dastak* of the Prince. Muḥammad A'zam Shah on 28 July 1682 issued to Kamyab Khān, *Bakhshi* of the Deccan provinces that consequent upon the transfer of Qādir Dād Khān from the *thānadārī* of *pargana* Bir, which was assigned in the *jāgīr* of Bahādur Khān, the Emperor ordered for cancellation of his conditional *manṣab* as per the following specifications:

1. For details see, W.H. Moreland, "Rank [*Manṣab*] in the Mogul State Service", *JRAS*, London 1936, pp. 641-65, A.J. Qaisar, 'Note on the Date of Institution of *Manṣab* under Akbar', *PIHC*, Delhi, 1961, Irfan Habib, 'The *Manṣab* System, 1596-1637', '*PIHC*, Patiala, 1967, *idem*, *Manṣab* and Pay-Scales under Jahangir and Shahjahan, *Islamic Culture*. Hyderabad 1985, Shireen Moosvi, 'The Evolution of *Manṣab* System under Akbar until 1596-97', *JRAS*, London, No. 2, 1981.

1000 [*ẓāt*]
800 *sawār*
do-aspa barāwurdi
200[*sawār*] 600[*sawār*]
According to *barāwurdi*
1000 [*ẓāt*]
1000 *sawār*
500 [*sawār*] conditional was reduced
1000 [*ẓāt*]
500 *sawār*[1]

Conditional ranks were normally added to the previous *ẓāt* and *sawār* ranks, *viz.,* Muḥammad Aiyyub who was assigned 250/20 and *sawārs* conditional to his posting in the Deccan as he was granted the duties of *bakhshigari*, *wāqia'-nigāri* and *amīnī-i dāgh-o-taṣḥiḥa* of the army of Shaikh Minhaj posted to administer Gulbarga and other *parganas* of Bijapur in December 1676 A.D. He was recommended an increase of 50 *ẓāt* by Bahādur Zafar Jung Kokatash[2].

From the statistical information in respect of 1000/800 [200x2-3h] it can be deduced that it can be stated 1000/800+200 which means that 200 were *duaspa sih aspa,* whereas the rest of the rank was termed as *barāwurdi.* From the point of view of pay and military obligation, the rank of 800, of whom 200 were *du-aspa sih aspa*, really meant 1000 *sawārs*.

In making out the pay certificates, against pay claim [*ṭalab*] for dual ranks the pay on *ẓāt* [maintenance of self, family and personal establishment] account was termed *kasab* [personal] and the *sawār*, *tabinān* [contingent][3]. It is an established fact that the pay for both *ẓāt* and *sawār* gradually divided from Akbar to Shāh Jahān and the scales fixed by Shāh Jahān were continued by Aurangzeb without any modification as is amply demonstrated by the *Dastūru-l 'Amals* of Aurangzeb's reign.

Theoretically speaking all *manṣabdārs* were directly appointed by the Emperor. Another method of recruitment was based on the recommendations of the prominent nobles, specially governors and commanders which

1. *SDAR,* pp. 135-6. It further orders for his posting in the army accompanying the Prince and excluding his name from the list of appointees thereat.
2. *SDAR,* pp. 113-4. This is clearly stated here that 50 *ẓāt* and 20 *sawār* were conditional.
3. See *Mughal Documents, 'Catalogue of Aurangzeb's Reign*'; A.P. State Archives, Hyderabad, 1981, Vol. I, part ii, facsimiles XV-XIX, Doc Nos H/I/, H/I/1; H/I/2, H/I/6, H/I/82; H/I/99; H/I/114; H/I/131.

were normally accepted[1]. Recommendations by the Princes were generally accepted. Even increase in rank was recommended by high officials[2].

There are instances of demotions in rank on the recommendations of the high nobles *viz.,* Mirza Raja Jai Singh due to the failure of Sarafraz K͟hān 5000/4000 [1000x2-3h] in accompainment with him had reduced 1000/1000 from his rank which was accepted by Aurangzeb on 1 May 1665 demoting him to 4000/3000 [1000x2-3h][3]. Yaswant Rao's 200 *sawār* rank was reduced due to his killing of a Brahmin[4]. K͟hān-i Zamān who originally held 5000/2000 [300x2-3h] was reinstated to 4000/2000 unconditional while 1000/300 [2x3-h] as conditional[5].

Similarly A'bdur Reḥmān Bijāpurī previously entitled Sharza K͟hān held the rank of 3500/2000 out of which 1000/1000 were reduced. However, he was reinstated to 2500/1500 by curtailing 1000/500 in March 1670[6].

Interestingly enough we come across incidences of the dismissal from *manṣab* and reinstatement of the same *manṣab* on a fresh *tajwīznāma* [recommendation] *viz.,* Vaisaji s/o Madhiy Ghorapara's [holding 300/60[7]] and his removal and reinstatement. Proceeding to anywhere without permission could even result into dismissal from service as Seru Beg s/o Ilahwardi K͟hān b/o 'Abdur Rasul faced removal from service due to visit to Shah Aurangabad without consent[8]. The intervening period between dismissal and reinstatement was excluded from payment[9]. Efforts were made to get entered promotions and demotions in rank in the *wāqia'*[10].

The month scales probably arose due to variation between the official assessment of revenue [*jama'*] of *jāgīr* and the actual revenue collections [*ḥāṣils*] due to which the *jāgīrs* were declared 1 monthly to 3 monthly. In the reign of Aurangzeb a transfer from Northern India to the Deccan meant a *jāgīr* on a lower month scale[11]. Although Aurangzeb as Viceroy of

---

1. On the recommendation of Mirza Raja Jai Singh Mulla Aḥmad Naitha the leading noble of Bijapur was given the rank of 6000/6000 *'Ālamgir Nāma*, 919-920; *Futuhāt-i 'Ālamgīrī*, ff. 103 [b], 116 [c], 117 [c], 165 [b]; *Akhbarat* 8th RY; *SDAR*, pp. 116-7.
2. *SDAR*, pp. 52-4, 107, 124-5, 140, 148-150.
3. *SDAR*, p. 49.
4. *SDAR*, pp. 63-4.
5. *SDAR*, p. 111-2.
6. *SDAR*, p.70.
7. *SDAR*, p. 71-2.
8. *SWD*, p. 103.
9. *SDAR*, pp. 108-109.
10. *SDAR*, pp. 76-8.
11. *SDAR*, p. 84.

the Deccan sought relief for two to three monthly *manṣabdārs* which as Emperor, he seems to have forgotten because he continued Shāh Jahān's scales even in the Deccan[1].

The Rajputs received 8 to 6 monthly *jāgīrs* even in the Deccan a curtailment which led to representations[2].

There used to be a number of deductions against sanctioned claim [*muqarrara ṭalab*] largest number of which was made in case of the Deccanis comprising Bījapurī, Haidarabadi and Maratha *manṣabdārs* who served under the Mughals[3]. This deduction of one-fourth known as *waza'-i dām-i-chunthāī*, that was continued under Aurangzeb from the total *dāms* of both the ranks.

However, Aurangzeb ordered that if, one had come direct from Iran and it was proved that he had served none of these governments then 1/4th deduction was not allowed[4].

Khaurāk-i dawwāb [fodder for beasts] or *rasad-i khurāk* was deducted from the *ṭalab* [pay claim], which was not, however obligatory on all the *manṣabdārs*[5]. *Irmas* was another deduction for demand for supplies. *Du-dāmī* or 5% was another deduction. *Jurmana* or fine for deficiencies was another deduction. We are informed that in 1677 the Deccanis had been exempted from paying the expenses of *khurāk-i filan-i ḥalqa* [feeding of elephants of the Imperial stables] due to 'their distressed circumstances and the low income of their *jāgīr*[6]. The *muṭalib-i* was a type of recovery of government claims against the *manṣabdār*[7].

A general order was issued in 1662 A.D. for the dismissal of *sawārs* in respect of those holding the rank upto 250 *ẓāt* as we find in case of Muḥammad Taqi [who was made the superintendent of the *Dīwān's* court] with the rank of 100/10 and Muḥammad Iḥsan holding 100/15 as his rank[8]. However, in less of his *sawār* rank 50 *ẓāt* were enhanced as per the request of Amānat Khān in September 1662. This is further proved by the following

1. For details see, *Mughal Nobilty*, pp. 46-9.
2. *SDAR*, p. 84 which contains petition of Maharaja Jaswant Singh's father-in-law.
3. *SDAR*, pp. 63-4 contains an Imperial order of 11 Rabi, 10 RY for the deduction of 1/4th from the Deccan if they served under Bijapur and Haiderabad states, even if they had originally come from Iran. In case of some it was exempted as well *Cf.,SDAR*, pp. 71-2, 80-81] [*Cf.*, Mamuri, *Tarikh-i Aurangzeb*, f. 156 [b]].
4. *SDAR*, pp. 63-4.
5. *SDAR*, pp. 32-3 recording exemption of *khurāk-i dawwāb* to Maulko Bilal.
6. *SDAR*, pp. 114.
7. *SWD*, pp. 84-5, 80-81, 233.
8. *SDAR*, p. 47.

table of *manṣabdārs* posted to administer Talkokan[1]. However this seems to have been cancelled subsequently in 1672[2].

Table – 1

Sl.No.	*Name of Manṣabdār*	*Rank*
1.	Lodi Khān	2500/1500
2.	Mahmud Khān	300/80
3.	Lal s/o Jalal	250/
4.	Ḥusain s/o Jalal	200/
5.	Shahbaz s/o Jalal	250/
6.	Qaim s/o Nizam Lodi	150/
7.	Daulat s/o Salim	100/
8.	'Alāul	100/
9.	'Alāul s/o 'Abdur Razzāq	80/
10.	Maternal grandson of Jalāl Ḥusain	150/
11.	Bahar s/o Ni'mat	150/
12.	'Abdullah s/o Fida	100/
13.	Shaikh Faizullah s/o Saiyid Muḥammad	80/
14.	Shaikh 'Abdur Rahim	80/
15.	Sarwar s/o Darya	80/

The Mughal *manṣabdārs* were assigned *naqdi* or *jāgīr*, the payment of *naqdi manṣabdārs* was made from the *khāliṣa* where *jāgīrdārs* were assigned *jāgīrs*. *Jāgīrs* assigned in lieu of salary due to *manṣabdārs* were known as *jāgīr-i tankhwāh* or *tankhwāh-i jāgīr*[3]. Furthermore a *jāgīr* assigned to a *manṣabdār* contingent upon his appointment to a particular post was known as *mashruṭ* or conditional. *Jāgīrs*, independent of rank, involving no obligation of service, were known as *inā'm*. The *jāgīr* assignments were calculated in *dāms* on the basis of *jama'dāmī* of the areas of the assignments, which was worked out by the revenue statements of ten years [*mawāzana-i dah sala*] of the provinces of the Empire. During Aurangzeb's second Viceroyalty of the Deccan the actual *ḥāṣil* came to an average of these monthly or one-fourth of the *jama'*. Accordingly adjustment was allowed which was designated as *takhfif-i dāmi* so as to keep the *jama'dāmī* equal to *jāgīrdar's* pay and the balance was adjusted by the payment in cash or assignment of additional *jāgīr*. If however, the actual collection exceeded the *jama'dāmī* or 'month ratio'

1. *SDAR*, pp. 4-9.
2. *SDAR*, p. 102.
3. *SDAR*, 27-8; *Dilkushā*, f. 139 [a].

the difference was either recovered or the *sawār* rank was increased. Asad Khān, conveyed to Aurangzeb that Mukarram Khān had informed him that the actual income of his *jāgīr* in the Deccan exceeded the 'month ratio' sanctioned to him. The Emperor ordered for an increase of 100 *sawārs* in the rank of Mukarram Khān to adjust the excess of his income[1].

Transfer of *jāgīrs* was a permanent feature of the Mughal administration which is well documented by the contemporary chronicles, collection of letters and documents. Ādab-i '*Ālāmgīrī* is replete with such details.

Only *waṭan jāgīrs* were exempted from transfer. In a representation to Aurangzeb it was stated by Raja Inder Singh that it was the established practice that after the death of the holder of *waṭan, manṣabs* were granted to their heirs as per the assessed revenues of their *waṭans*[2].

2. Control Over *Manṣabdārs'* Contingents

Since *manṣab* was dual in nature which included both *ẓāt* and *sawār*, the *manṣabdārs* were assigned either *jāgīrs* or paid in cash to meet out expenses on both accounts. Insofar as the Imperial control over *manṣabdārs* is concerned it began from the time of assignment of *sawār* rank from the second half of Akbar's reign to force every *manṣabdār* to actually maintain the exact number of horses and cavalrymen expected of him for the Imperial service. However, due to inherent dishonesty among most of the nobles it was not possible to eradicate it through an Imperial command. In order to check all evasions of military obligation, the introduction of *dāgh* [branding] for the horses and *chehra* [descriptive roll] for the men was an important innovation of Akbar[3].

During Akbar's reign each *manṣabdār* was bound to bring to muster the number of men indicated by his *sawār* rank, penalty was imposed for any default. Probably a *manṣabdār* of 100 *sawār* had to bring at the maximum 50 horsemen under Akbar[4]. During Jahangir's reign slackness was shown in checking the contingents maintained by the *manṣabdārs*[5] which was apparently reorganized by Shāh Jahān. Shāh Jahān gave formal status to the actual position in respect of contingents maintained by the

1. *Akhbārāt*, Sitamu Transcript [12th R.Y. of Aurangzeb, p. 233].
2. *SDAR*, p. 121. Since the *jama'dāmī* of Raja Inder Singh's *waṭan jāgīr* exceeded the pay due to his rank he solicited that either his rank be increased to equal the *jama'dāmī* or *jamā'dāmī* be decreased to equal the pay for his existing rank because in either case none would be assigned a share in his *waṭan-jagir*. Accordingly his *manṣab* was increased. *Ruqaat-i 'Ālāmgir*, p. 167, Lahori, I, p. 161.
3. *Ain-i Akbari*, Vol. I, pp. 135, 266-7.
4. *Ain-i Akbari*, Vol. I, pp. 123-4.
5. Moreland, *JRAS*, 1936, pp. 641-65.

manṣabdārs and his modifications with regard to *dāgh* are known from a passage in the *Pādshāhnāma* of 'Abdul Ḥamid Lahori. It is stated there that it was the law of the Empire that these *manṣabdārs*, who had *jāgīrs* in any of the *ṣūbas* of Hindustan [North India] and were posted in the same province in which their *jāgīrs* were situated, were to bring to the muster horsemen equal in number to one-third of their *sawār* rank. But if posted outside the *ṣūbas* of their *jāgīrs*, they were only obliged to one-fourth and if in Balkh and Badakhshān, one-fifth. This one-fifth rule was applied to all those posted in *ṣūba* Kābul[1]. The *manṣabdārs*, holding *naqdi jāgīrs* who were paid in cash were required to muster their contingents according to one-fifth rule which is clearly mentioned in a *dasturu-l 'amal* of Shāh Jahān of 27th R.Y.[2], which are confirmed from *Khulaṣatus Siyaq*, written during late Aurangzeb period[3].

Since the rule of one-fourth was applied in the Deccan, the *dāgh* of *taṣḥiḥa* was made accordingly under Shāh Jahān and Aurangzeb as is evident from a *farmān* of Shāh Jahān of 2 *Shaban* 14th R.Y. [1641-2 A.D.] to Prince Aurangzeb, during his first Viceroyalty of the Deccan as already mentioned in Chapter I is quite significant as it does contain details regarding the maintenance of *mansab* by Rai Satar Sal[4] etc as given in a unique manuscript in Bib. Nat. Paris[5].

The significance of this *farmān* can become more clear if we refer to the schedule issued in 14th R.Y. of Shāh Jahān, by Islam Khān because the present *farmān* refers to that schedule[6].

Yet another method of control over *manṣabdārs'* contingent was the fixation of month rates under the heading *tabinān* [contingent] specially in regard to 2-3 months which according to Aurangzeb's letter of 29th R.Y. of Shāh Jahān quoting an Imperial order to convey that the pay for '3-months' for which Rs 17/8 and Rs 15 have been respectively sanctioned [elsewhere] has been fixed [in the case of the Deccan] from the beginning of the month of Mihr Kharif Yunt Il, at Rs 20 per head per month or at the same rate as for 4 months[7].

The pay calculated from rates previous to Shāh Jahān's 27th R.Y. in respect of the Deccan which was better for the lower categories than those continued in the Deccan subsequently [3-2 months]. That is why Aurangzeb

1. Lahori, II, pp. 505-7.
2. Ali Muḥammad Khān, *Mirāt-i Aḥmadi*, Baroda 1928, Vol. I, p. 228.
3. *Khulaṣatus Siyaq* MS; S.S. Coll 410/143 MAL AMU, Aligarh, f. 54 [c].
4. Rai Satar Sal s/o Rao Ratan [R] held the rank of 3000/3000 during 14 RY of Shahjahan, [corr. 1641-8], Lahori I [b], 297.
5. Bib. Nat. Paris, Ms No. 482 Persian, ff. 46[a]-47[a].
6. *SDSR*, pp. 79-84 and *Dasturu-l 'Amal 'Ālamgīrī*, MS, Br. M. Add. 65, 99, ff. 121-3.
7. *'Adab-i 'Ālamgīrī*, Lahori, 1971, Vol. I, p. 178, *Cf.,Calendar*.

as Viceroy of the Deccan had so strongly solicited modification of this order which was a harsh one and become so grateful when Shāh Jahān made an exemption in the case of the Deccan for those placed in the 2 and 3 months-scales[1].

Although many of the detailed regulations prescribed for branding and checking the contingents of the *manṣabdārs* have come down to us specially in the *Zawābit-i'Ālamgīrī* and *Khulaṣatus Siyaq*[2] yet original documents help us in understanding the ground realities of this regulation. A *dastak* of 21 July 1660 issued to Shaikh Muḥammad, *Bakhshi* of the ships in favour of Yaqūt Khān *faujdār* of ships holding the rank of 2000/700 [100x2-3h] instructs for branding through verification and replacement, which indicates the number of men and horses each 149 out of which 132 men and horses each were alive whereas 2 each had died. In regard to remaining each 15 men and horses a list of deceased abscondees is given there along with the horses[3].

Shāh Jahān's *farmān* of 1652 stress for completing or ignoring fraction of horses required under branding *viz.,* one horseman was to be considered adequate for branding purposes under the one-fourth rule because the extra fraction of one-fourth 'horseman' was disregarded. *Tāzi'* horses were also branded in the Deccan[4].

Aurangzeb in his 25th R.Y. issued an order that all the *manṣabdārs* serving in the Deccan up to the *ẓāt* rank of 5000 should bring their horses [required against the same rank] for branding[5]. That is why Jadun Rai Deccani like 'Abdul Aziz Khān and his tribe solicited exemption from branding[6].

3. Forts

The forts in the Deccan played a very significant role not only in defending the surrounding areas but also acted as a catalyst in running the administration, serving as ordinance depots and granaries, stationing the armies and their training centres, housing treasuries and accommodating other important provincial officials. As the nucleaus of defence Aurangzeb saw to it that besides appointing high officials as the *qila'dārs* of strategic forts none of the forts was to be left defenceless or without a castellan for a moment.

---

1. *Ibid.*
2. *Zawabit-i 'Ālamgīrī*, ff. 38[a] – 40[6].
3. *SDAR*, pp.10-12.
4. *Mirat-i Ahmadi*, Vol. I, pp. 228-9.
5. *Akhbārāt*, 21st *Shawwal* 25th R.Y.
6. *SDAR*, pp. 114-5.

There were numerous forts of military importance in addition to a cluster of countless small forts as these safeguards of fortified strongholds were distributed throughout the Mughal Deccan. The position of some forts of crucial significance, the status of the *qila'dārs* and the number of the contingents maintained by them in 1670 A.D. can be gauged from the following table:

Table- 2[1]

Sl. No	*Name of the qila'dār and the fort*	*Manṣab*	*Un-conditional*	*Contingent*	*No. of Contingent*
1.	Bakhtiyar Khān, *qila'dār* of Zafarabad	3000/2500	3000/1500	1000 *sawār*	-
2.	Irij Khān, *qila'dār* of Sholapur	2500/2000	2500/1800 [300x2-3h]	500 *sawār* [300x2-3h]	969
3.	Barkhurdār Khān, *qila'dār* of Ausa	2000/2000			668
4.	Saiyid Muḥammad Khān *qila'dār* of Parenda	1500/1500	1500/1000	500 *sawār*	500
5.	Qalandar Khān, *qila'dār* of Aḥmad Nagar	1500/1000 [200x2-3h]	1000/700	300 [200x2-3h]	-
6.	'Abdul Aziz Khān, *qila'dār* of Sunnair	1500/700	1000/500	500/200	-
7.	Suhrab Khān, *qila'dār* of Udgir	1500/900	1500/800	100	300
8.	Masu'd Khān, *qila'dār* of Chandor	1500/700			234
9.	Rustam Khān, *qila'dār* of Bhalipur [Nagpur]	1000/900	700/500	200/400	-
10.	Miraz Khān, *qila'dār* of Fateḥabad Dharur	1000/600	1000/400	200 *sawār*	166

The above table does indicate the *manṣabs* both conditional and unconditional, except in two instances and the number of contingents maintained by them except for '4 [four] *qila'dārs* which were lost due to wear and tear. The conditional *manṣabs* were contingent upon their holding the *qila'dāri* of the forts in question.

The forts indicated above were held by the *umara* whose ranks ranged from 3000 to 1000. It was compulsory for every *qila'dār* to remain inside the fort, failing which any punishment like reduction in rank or transfer could be imposed. When it was conveyed to Aurangzeb in April 1676 that Lashkari Beg, *qila'dar* of Gālna fort leaving behind his son had emerged

1. *SDAR*, pp. 73-5.

from the fort to welcome, Mir Nūrullah, the *faujdār* of Thaner and Ner, not only he earned the imperial wrath by suffering reduction of 20 *sawārs* in his rank but also censorious remarks of the Emperor that in future he would not come out of the fort, otherwise he would stand transferred[1]. Similar penalty for coming out of the fort for hunting was imposed on Jan Sipar Khān, *qila'dār* of Zafarabad fort[2].

Since the *qila'dārs* maintained law and order as well as trained the army in archery and cannonding we find detailed description of such practices. For example, Saiyid Ḥusian, castellan of the Ramgir fort in consultation with the *Dīwān* and Saiyid Jamāl *sawār*, who was appointed *amīn* of archery of the army posted atop the fort by Naṣrullah, [*Dīwān* of *sarkār* Ramgir] observed the archery of Sadi Sadiwal, and he in accordance with the regulation of the Deccan forts marked first, second and third as per the following details and some were week in archery and he specially noted the absence of Ghiyasuddin, *Dārogha* [superintendent] of the said fort:

[Total]	=	97 persons
First	=	54 persons
Second	=	35 persons
Third	=	7 persons
Week [zabūn]	=	1 person
[Total	=	97]
Sadi Somri	=	47 persons
First	=	26 persons
Second	=	18 persons
Third	=	3 persons
[Total	=	47]
Sadi Ghanshiyam	=	49 persons
First	=	27 persons
Second	=	17 persons
Third	=	4 persons
Week	=	1 person
[Total	=	49]
Sadi Bhikari	=	Dismissed
First	=	1 person

Furthermore Saiyid Jamāl also inspected the 500 Baksariyas posted thereat, who were categorised first, second and third except for a few who were found week. But out of them 91 persons, who were dismissed from the archery of Bhikhari Hazari, were bent upon fomenting trouble because

1. *SWD,* p. 83.
2. *SDAR,* pp. 29-30.

they did not possess their *taṣḥīḥa* [verification] and archery [certificates] with their *sadiwals*[1].

Under such rigorous training and strict vigilance it was but natural to take strict disciplinary action against the malefactors for streamlining the administration and maintaining high standard of military discipline. Accordingly an Imperial order issued through Ṣafi Khān, the *Bakhshiu-l Mamalik* [chief pay master general] was received by Saiyid Ḥusain, the *qila'dār* to the effect that let Mir 'Abdul Ma'bud, be appointed as *Hazari* in place of [Mir] Bhikhari and those mischief mongers who were accompanying him were to be expelled and replaced, which was handed over to Ghiyasuddin to be conveyed expeditiously to Mir [Bhikhari] for compliance.

In regard to the previous and present strength of the matchlockmen and the extraordinary size of the fort, Aurangzeb remarked that forts bigger than the fort under discussion did not possess so huge an army as large army shall be fixed for that fort due to which the contingents shall have to be stationed for its protection[2].

The above does reflect the measures introduced for training the armies as well as endeavours for maintaining peace and tranquility in the forts. It was also obligatory on the part of the *qila'dār* to procure the provisions as lack of provisions was intolerable and it was essential to arrange for six months all types of provisions taking into consideration the strength of army and other dwellers of the fort. The *Dīwān* or *naib Dīwān-i buyūtat* was kept well informed about the actual position of the provisions. The *qila'dār* was duty bound to make arrangements for procurement of provisions inside the fort[3].

There used to be abundant provisions in the forts as is known from the report of the Parenda fort where there was no space left in the grainary for stocking additional provisions, which were adjusted in the salary of contingents posted thereat[4].

As established by the *dastak* of Todar Mal, *Dīwān-i Buyūtat* of *ṣūbas* of the Deccan to Khwājā Badri Das, *Naib Dīwān-i Buyūtat* of *sarkār-i Khaṣṣa Sharīfa* to look after the purchase and sale of grains from graineries, undertake the repairing work of the buildings of the forts and *sarais* [inns][5]. The highandedness of the *qila'dārs* used to become the

1. *SWD*, pp. 63-4.
2. *SWD*, pp. 68-9.
3. *SWD*, pp. 137-8, *SDAR*, pp. 82-3.
4. *SWD*, pp. 94-5.
5. *SWD*, pp. 139-140.

subject of representation. A *maḥẓar* under the seal/signature of Saiyid Manṣur, *faujdār* of Baglana, Mani Ram *hazāri*, Gurdās and Man Singh, *sadiwal* on 21st December 1662 posted at Aurang Garh fort complained that SulṬan Quli Beg, the *qila'dār* was demanding Rs 1900 as three month's salary of the entire contingent for himself, failing which was threatening the complaints' for the transfer, as he had not received 15 months' salaries[1].

Even carelessness in arranging the war equipment was treated a cognizable offence which was punished. A complaint in respect of Jan Sipar K͟hān, *alias* Mir Bahādur Dil was, from the *waqi'a* of *ṣūba* Zafarabad [Bidar] was brought to the Emperor's notice in February 1662 in regard to his negligence in procuring iron rockets and his coming out of the fort for deer hunting led to a reduction in his conditional 200 *sawār* out of 1000/600 from his rank and his dismissal from the *qila'dāri* of small-citadel of Zafarabad as the deputy of K͟hān-i Zamān except for his appointment under him[2].

The position of the forts used to be ascertained. It was reported on 18 April 1662 that Malik Ḥusain Muḥammad had come to note down the position of the provisions, contingents and the length and width of the cannons of the forts of Baglana as per the *dastak* of Muḥammad Hadi, *Bak͟hshī* of *ṣūba* K͟hāndesh.

The *dastak* of the abovementioned *Bak͟hshi* clearly stipulated that in accordance with the imperial order written by Ṣafi K͟hān, *Bak͟hshiul Mamallik*, the details of the length and width of the cannons, weight of the cannon-balls, lead, gun-powder and iron rockets available in the entire forts of *ṣūba* Khandesh was sought in addition to position of contingents, matchlockmen, cannondiers and staff of the forts[3].

This type of information definitely shows the extraordinary interest which Aurangzeb evinced in strengthening the defense potentialities of the forts of the Deccan which is further proved by the memorandum of the Imperial orders concerning postings and campaigns in the Deccan *viz.,* Irij K͟hān, castellan of Sholapur sent documents describing the conditions of the said fort stating that 13 cannons of three types as well as soliciting 20 more cannons and 500 additional matchlockmen as 1000 matchlockmen were insufficient[4].

In January 1671 Bark͟hurdār K͟hān, the *qila'dār* of Ausa, requisitioned provisions for the fort including the iron cannon-balls and the services of

1. *SDAR,* pp. 39-40.
2. *SDAR,* pp. 29-30.
3. *SWD,* pp. 140-141, *SWD,* p. 170 contains similar instructions concerning Galna and Baitala forts.
4. *SDAR,* p. 65.

sadiwals etc which was partially fulfilled[1]. Interestingly enough details of cannondiers both European and Mughal posted in the forts of Sholapur and Kalyan, their monthly salaries and other related matters: in 1682 A.D. are found[2].

Special attention was paid to European cannodiers as we come to know from a news report that five European cannondiers were posted at the fort of Parenda from the imperial court, out of whom two of the Europeans had run away one of which was traced and brought to the fort. The presence of the European cannondiers was ensured as is clear from the attendance record of Duke Ferdin and other cannondies at Sunnair fort[3], which became possible in an age when European gunners were a common sight in many parts of Mughal India. The *qila'dārs* used to test the potentiality of the cannons[4].

The forts used to serve as treasure troves because we come to know that the Baridi coins of the Deccanis used to be weighed according to the copper[5] by the *taḥvildar* [treasurer]. Even during the course of transportation of the Imperial treasury the treasure was deposited in the forts as was conveyed by Khān-i Zamān that the treasury was kept inside the Zafarabad fort till the end of the rainy season whereafter it would be transferred to the treasury of Shah Aurangabad[6].

The forts became the centres of Mughal resistance against the Marathas. Sometimes the *qila'dārs* also lost their lives due to assassin's dagger or any other reasons as we know about the assassination of Iḥtishām, *qila'dār* of Ūdgir which was done in October, 1662[7].

4. *Bargīs*

Malik 'Amber is credited for having trained the Marathas as the *bargīs* in the gurrilla warfare [*jung-i qazzāqi*]. If Marathas were a nation then Malik 'Amber was the father of the nation. Consequent upon Malik 'Amber's utilisation of the Maratha chiefs and their followers known as the *bargīs* [hit and run] in popular parlance the Mughals had begun to realise the importance of the Marathas in the Deccan campaigns because, Maratha turn-coat played a pivotal role in inflicting a crushing defeat on Malik 'Amber in 1616 by Shāhnawāz Khān. Beginning from Shāh Jahān down to

1. *SDAR,* pp. 138-40.
2. *SWD,* p. 92.
3. *SDAR,* pp.134-5.
4. *SWD,* p. 70
5. *SWD,* p. 155.
6. *SWD,* p. 10.
7. *SWD,* pp. 153, 157.

Aurangzeb the rise of Maratha power manifested in the establishment of an independent Maratha kingdom in the Deccan by Shivajī[1].

The difference in Maratha armies with those of the armies of the Mughal Empire or the Deccan Sulṭanate lay in the *bargīs*, the ill-clad, ill-armed, marauding Maratha soldier, having his advantage solely in numbers and the ability for dispersed warfare[2]. This fact is clearly recorded in 1675-6 by Fryer who described troops of Shivajī, 'all Naked Starved Rascals, 'but fitter for any Martial Exploit having been accustomed to Fare Hard, Journey Fast and take little Pleasure[3]. Manucci recalled that the early Maratha troops had only lances and long swords two inches wide[4]. Obviously such equipment did not require large resources. It is evident that the *bargīs* were essentially lance-wielding peasants riding on country ponies, which receives further corroboration from a contemporary account:

> "It came to be represented [to the Emperor Aurangzeb] that Marathas obtained collaboration from the peasants [*muzari'ān*] of the Imperial dominions. It was thereupon ordered that the horses and weapons found in every village should be confiscated. When this happened in many villages, the peasants, providing themselves with horses and arms, joined the Marathas[5]".

Since Shāh Jahān's time Mughals came in further contact with the Marathas as is evident from *Ādāb-i 'Ālamgīrī* and other sources, *viz.,* we came to know about the crushing defeats inflicted on Shivajī and other Maratha chiefs during last years of Shāh Jahān by Multafat Khān[6]. Aurangzeb's involvement in the fratricidal wars of succession at a time when he was required to turn on Shivajī so as to crush him forever, paved the way for his initial successes[7]. We came to know that before he set out to win his throne in 1658, Aurangzeb urged his officials to make out capital punishment to "peasents, *deshmukhs,* and *patels* of the *parganās* of the Imperial territories; who have gone over to the side of the enemy [Shivajī] and his associates and have exerted themselves in guiding or abetting those ill-destined ones"[8].

1. *Cf., Mughal Nobility*, p. 29.
2. Irfan Habib, '*Essays in Indian History – Towards a Marxist Perception*', Delhi, 1995, p. 250.
3. John Fryer, *A New Account of East India and Persia being Nine Years' Travels*, 1672-81, II, edited by William Crooke, London, 1912, pp. 66-8.
4. Manucci, *Storia do Mogor*, III, p. 505.
5. *Nuskha-i Dilkushā*, f. 139[a-b], translation done by Irfan Habib in *Essays in Indian History*, p. 253.
6. *Ādāb*, II, p. 680.
7. *Cf.,* M.N. Pearson, Shivaji and the Decline of the Mughal Empire; *Journal of Asian Studies*, No. XXXV, Vol. 2, Feb. 1976, 226.
8. *Ādāb*-i *'Ālamgīrī*, f. 175 [a-b]. It will be a mistake to consider Shivaji and the

Aurangzeb made utmost endevours in annexing the Maratha territories especially of Shivajī and he even assigned *jāgīrs* in the country of Shivajī [*mulk-Siva*] *viz.*, Antaji Khandakata, 3000/2000; and five other *manṣabdārs* were recommended *jāgīrs* in Shivajī's territory which were approved as well[1]. Similarly numerous *manṣabdārs* including previous officials of Shivajī were assigned *jāgīrs* for administering the Talkokan country [*mulk-i* Talkokan] which was a narrow coastal tract, in May 1660 [which Mughals had claimed in 1657][2] and again in 1660, when Aurangzeb instructed Shāista Khān to enter it and suppress the activities of Shivajī[3]. Even some of them were granted conditional *sawār* rank during the second campaign[4]. The lists of the Imperial officers serving in Talkokan for the second time unambiguously designate Talkokan as country of Shivajī[5]. Although it is interesting to note that the Mughal news-reporters were so much vigilant that they used to report even the movement of Maratha armies.

Yet it is equally curious that while one hundred *sawārs* from the contingent of Jadu Rao proceeded from the town [*Qaṣba*] of Junnair towards the Imperial army it was reported that 2000 infantry of Shivajī [Siva-i *maqhūr*] entered *tappa* Parah of *pargana* Junnair on 30 November 1661[6]. Previously on 19 November 1661, 1000 infantry of Shivajī had indulged in revenue realisation from the said place etc[7]. Such plunders with impunity evoked spontaneous but harsh Mughal reactions as is evident from the following:

> "In 1661 Aurangzeb ordered multi-pronged attack on the country of Shivajī. He ordered Namdar Khān to march against Shivajī with 4000 *sawārs* under his command while Rao Bahādur, shall be the vanguard of that army whereas another 4000 *sawārs* will be dispatched under

---

Maratha Chiefs as the leaders of a peasent uprising as the fiscal and political practices of the Marathas bore the deepest imprints of the *zamīndārī* origins. However, it is interesting to read in the English records of "a very great report of peace settled between the Mogul and Sevageo" in 1665, under which Shivaji was "to deliver up all the castles and country which he has taken from the Mogul" and in return "to the Kirge Besy [*Deshmukh, Desaī*] of all the country of the Deccan. *English Records on Shivajī,* 11, 575.

1. *SDAR*, p. 13. The other *manṣabdārs*, naming Sanbhaji, Jānuji and Muḥammad Sharif, were granted *jāgīrs* in July 1662 in the country of Shivaji or Talkokan, *SDAR,* pp. 34-5.
2. *'Amal-i Ṣāliḥ*, III, 1262; *SDAR*, p. 107, gives names of former officers of Shivaji who were favoured thus: Raghuji, 1000/500, Ambaji with 4-monthly *jāgīrs* and one-fourth deductions.
3. *'Ālamgīr Nama*, pp. 574-8.
4. *SDAR*, pp. 4-9.
5. *SDAR*, pp. 16-7.
6. *SWD*, p. 161.
7. *Ibid.*

whomsoever Maharaja Jaswant Singh will recommend. Aurangzeb ordered Sarbuland Khān to attack Shivajī's country from another direction over the head of 4000 *sawārs* appointing Rao Amar Singh Chandrawat as vanguard of the army whereas another 4000 *sawār* shall be deputed under the commander of Maharaja Jaswant Singh. Lodi Khān was bound to remain in *thana* Talkokan where ever Maharaja will depute him in accompaniment with 3000 *sawārs* and another 3000 *sawārs* shall be deployed under Maharaja's recommended commander. Furthermore Mukhtār Khān shall command 2000 *sawārs* as per Maharaja's recommendations[1]".

Thus, an army of 24,000 was sent against Shivajī. If the rest like Nāmdar Khān could have been sincere then Shivajī would have been crushed. But the conditions were so unfavourable that when Nāmdar Khān urged Shāista Khān to make a direct attack on Shivajī, the shrewd noble retorted that if the Deccan campaign was so quickly concluded, an invasion on Qandahar would be ordered; and if that too succeeded, the contingents would be disbanded[2].

Marathas were so much dready that they sometimes used to take away the wounded Mughal *manṣabdārs*[3]. Even sometimes merchants had the same fate in store. One Ḥāji Ibrāhīm[4] who was interned by Shivajī was released in March 1663.

Aurangzeb due to the advisability of the situation had to open the gates wide to admit the Marathas in his service with succeeding years[5] notwithstanding their marauding activities.

There were instances and suspicion of collusion between the Mughal commanders and the Marathas. Jaswant Singh was even suspected of having a hand in Shivajī's night attack on Shāista Khān's camp in 1663[6]. During the same year Aurangzeb charged Prince Shāh 'Alām with culpable negligence in crushing the Marathas and he was replaced by Jai Singh as Viceroy of the Deccan. After the discomfiture of Shāista Khān, Jai Singh first concentrated his fire against Shivajī, compelling him to seek terms at

---

1. *SDAR*, p. 19. In accordance with an English report of 1675, the hardships suffered by the peasants were so severe there that all people pray that the Moors may regain the country, *English Fadories* in *India*, N.S. I, 332. Moreover, they had to live by plunder only, for Shivaji's reputed maxim was, "No Plunder No Pay" ed. Fryer, p. 341.
2. *Nuskha-i Dilkushā*, f. 123[a].
3. *SWD,* p. 47 which narrates the case of one Muḥammadi.
4. *SWD,* pp. 53-4.
5. Even non- Marathas previously serving under the Marathas were admitted to Mughal service *SDAR,* p. 35; M.A. Nayeem, *Mughal Documents*, Vol. I, II, III, IV/100, IV/126, V/832.
6. *Nuskha-i Dilkushā*, f. 24 [a-b], Mamuri, f. 131 [a], Khāfi Khān, II, p. 175.

Purandhar, so as to take the Marathas into a subordinate partnership so as to crush Bijapur, with their help[1].

It may be specifically emphasized that since the time of Aurangzeb's first Viceroyalty of the Deccan in [1636], Shivajī's father Shahji was being patronized by 'Ādilshāh against the Mughals. Mahabat Khān accompanied with the Mughal army defeated the Marathas. Multafat Khān, Aurangzeb's castellan of Aḥmad Nagar expelled Minaji from the Mughal dominions while 3000 Mughal troopers were posted against them. Aurangzeb's bid to conquer the twin Saltanates of Golcunda and Bijapur in 1656 created further dissensions with Shivajī who began to indulge in nefarious activities since 1657 onwards against the Mughal Empire. We also come to know, as stated above, that from the beginning of Aurangzeb's reign, even Marathas occasionally used to join the Mughal service. Notwithstanding Aurangzeb's policy of alertness concerning Shivajī and the Marathas towards the end of the second term of his Viceroyalty of the Deccan in 1659 we encounter with several letters of Aurangzeb to Shāista Khān on the disturbances created by Shivajī, Minaji and other Maratha leaders and their pleaders and supporters[2]. However, Aurangzeb's monumental *farmān* of 4th August 1665[3], issued to Mirza Raja Jai Singh, who was then at Purandhar fort, of course, after the submission of Shivajī, which proved a turning point in the Mughal-Maratha relations, almost for a quarter century which thoroughly highlights his policies about Purandhar and Bijapur campaigns simultaneously involving annexation of Shivajī's 23 forts, issuance of a *farmān* to him with Aurangzeb's palm impression, approval of the terms of the treaty of Purandhar, made by Jai Singh with Shivajī and numerous other matters of utmost historical significance *viz.,* military administration,

1. 'Ālāmgir Nāma, p. 913; *Nuskha-i Dilkushā*, f. 31 [b], Khafi Khān, II, p. 184.
2. Aurangzeb, '*Ādāb-i* 'Ālāmgiri, collection of letters written on behalf of Prince and or Emperor Aurangzeb by his *Munshi*, Abul Fateḥ Qābil Khān, [ed.] Abdul Ghafur Chaudhuri, Lahore 1971, Vol. I, pp. 512-21, Andhra Pradesh State Archives, Doc. No. V/2003[6] which tells us that Gobind Rao, s/o Chandra Rao, came from the country of Shivaji to join the Mughal service. He was recommended *jagīrdārī* of his territory [*mulk*] with 1/6th portion in the old country [*mulk-i-qadim*] with the *Manṣab* of 500/50.
3. *Cf.,* G.T. Kulkarni, A Note on Mirza Raja Jai Singh's Purandar and Bijapur Campaigns An Unpublished *Farmān* of Aurangzeb [1665 A.D.], *PIHC*, Kolkata, 2011, pp. 274-83. I have obtained a copy of this *farmān* through the kindness of Dr. G.T. Kulkarni who has critically examined its historical significance. Since the translation of the *farman* is not exhaustive it needs a fresh rendering because it is not crowded with Arabic diction as these are the titles of Prince and some nobles whose credentials have been identified in the footnotes [see Appendix - B]. *Cf.,* Mirza Raja Jai Singh's correspondence entitled *Haft Anjuman,* Ms of Munshi Udairaj and Jagdish Narayan Sarkar's English translation, *The Military Dispatches of a Seventeenth Century General.*

diplomacy, arrears of *peshkash,* cession of Sholapur etc, etc. A *farmān* was also issued to Shivajī's son on the solicitation of Mirza Raja Jai Singh about the approval of the treaty of Purandhar in 1665 A.D. as mentioned in Jai Singh's military dispatches published in *Haft Anjuman* in 1969 by Jagdish Narayan Sarkar. The *farmān* does prove that ending Shivajī in his submission Aurangzeb sincerely endeavoured to get him engaged actively against the Bijapuri forces of 'Ali 'Ādil Shah II in accompaniment with Jai Singh in the Mughal administration's war efforts by positively utilising Shivajī in ultimately annexing Bijapur and the events of May-August 1665 as it was received and acknowledged on 22nd September 1665. We are also well-informed about the Mughal military organisation *viz.,* numerical strength of infantry, mounted musketeers, gunners, arms and equipments, military administration, espionage, logistics and discipline. Military administration in reducing Shivajī to submission which Aurangzeb was also desirous of using against Bijapur in the event of the failure of diplomacy. Along with the positioning of guns, supplies of *rahakalas*, cannon balls, lead, gun powder and other war equipments like short spears were procured in adequate quantity to various army contingents and forts. Deficiency in the stipulated number of 1000, men was made good through fresh recruitments from other tribes. Recruitments through *manṣab* policy regarding three grades of *manṣab* have been highlighted. Aurangzeb's policy of encouraging competent Rajputs and the experienced men to carry out demolition work is superb. Aurangzeb got maintained continuously adequate supply of 1000 mounds of grains on every fort and area.

In regard to diplomacy concerning 'Ali 'Ādil Shah II Aurangzeb sought Mulla Aḥmad's visit to settle issue of *peshkash*, cession of the fort of Sholapur and other *maḥals* of Nizamul Mulk through negotiation as Aurangzeb preferred policy to force and expediency to might as he even covered Shivajī through diplomacy as well owing to which he allowed territories both in Konkan and Bijapuri Bālāghat yielding nine lakh *hūns* to Shivajī. Aurangzeb wanted settlement of Bijāpuri problem failing which there would be clash of armies. The *farmān* contains well thought out arrangements - the strategy tactics, preparations of war with Bijapur and Shivajī as Aurangzeb was not only an Emperor but a great military strategist.

We are informed that on the recommendations of Prince Shāh 'Ālam and Jaswant Singh, Shivajī was pardoned, following his flight from Agra, and his son Shambhaji was given the rank of 5000/5000. Furthermore Shivajī was also allowed to annex as much of the Bijapur territory, as his resources permitted, or else he was to confine himself to his territory in accordance with the advice of the Viceroy of the Deccan[1] as the rise of the Maratha power manifested in the establishment of a Maratha state in the Deccan which could become possible due to ultimate failure of Mirza Raja Jai Singh's successful campaign of 1665 resulting into the conclusion of the treaty of Purandhar yet the fruits of his military victory were snatched away to a great extent by Shivajī's flight from Agra in 1666.

Interestingly enough Mirza Raja Jai Singh was one of the leading exponents of a forward policy in the Deccan as he was dispatched as Viceroy to retrieve the situation in the Deccan after the failure of Shāista Khān who was also ordered by Aurangzeb to enter into Konkan in 1660 to suppress the activities of Shivajī as it was ceded to Bijapur during Aurangzeb's first Viceroyalty of the Deccan under 1636 settlement and reclaimed only in 1657 during Aurangzeb's second term as the Viceroy of the Deccan. Jai Singh naturally concentrated his ire against Shivajī, compelling him to seek terms of treaty of Purandhar. Fundamentally his scheme was aimed at bringing the position of the Marathas into a subordinate ally for making an attempt with their help upon the kingdom of Bijapur. It seems that Aurangzeb was not willing to commit such a large force to the Deccan as Jai Singh requisitioned nor did Aurangzeb approve of the recruitment and promotion of the Deccanis which Jai Singh proposed for sowing dissension among the Adilshāhis as is also proved from the contents of Aurangzeb's *farmān* of 1665 A.D. Dispatch of this *farmān* was the victory of Jai Singh's aggressive policy. Ultimately, neither Jai Singh's policy nor that of his critics succeeded. But owing to compulsion of circumstances the Emperor gradually began to indulge in the last two decades of the seventeenth century against all the three Deccan powers, the 'Ādilshāhis, the Quṭbshāhis and the Marathas. But notwithstanding opposition to Jai Singh's forward policy or its support Aurangzeb remained undecided to such an extent that Shivajī could neither be crushed nor reconciled as he began to send messages demanding *chauth* from the Mughal officers as in the event of any default he used to threaten to lay waste the country[2].

As mentioned elsewhere that at the 71st session of the Indian History Congress, Dr. G.T. Kulkarni, presented a paper on a unique *farmān* of Aurangzeb to Mirza Raja Jai Singh, then the Viceroy of the Deccan, dated 4 August 1665. Since this long *farmān* contains a large amount of

---

1. Bhismen, *nuskha-i-Dilkushā,* Br. M. Or 23, f 35 [a-b]. A document is found in Yusuf Hussain Khān [ed.], *Selected Documents of Aurangzeb's Reign* issuing warrant for search and arrest of Shivaji immediately following his flight from Agra.
2. *Cf., Selected Documents of Aurangzeb's Reign* [ed.], Yusuf Hussain Khān, Daftar-i-Diwan-o-Mali-o-Mulki, Hyderabad 1959, AR No. 30 19th Ramazan 14th RY [20th June 1671].

details regarding military and administrative matters yet there is need for its full translation. This has been carefully done in my book, *Medieval India: Studies in Polity, Economy and Society, 14th-19th centuries, Delhi, Primus 2019.* But despite all trials and turbulations this *farmān* of Aurangzeb remained the arch-stone or guiding principle of the Mughal-Maratha relations for almost a quarter century. We are aware of various developments between 1656 to 1665 A.D.[1] about the successive Viceroys of the Deccan like Prince Mua'zzam, Shāista Khān and again Prince Mua'zzam and the changes that occurred from 1665 to 1689 that gradually began to change the entire scenario. Diler Khān also served actively as Viceroy of the Deccan whereafter Shah 'Alam who succeeded him in 1668 [till 1672] showed slackness in pushing the Marathas along with Raja Jaswant Singh[2]. Bahādur Khān, who was the Viceroy of the Deccan from 1672 to 1676, was repeatedly suspected of being friendly with the three Deccan powers of Golcunda, Bijapur and the Marathas. Diler Khān again became Viceroy of the Deccan and he was again replaced by Prince Shāh 'Ālam as Viceroy of the Deccan and he was alleged for secret alliance with the ruler of Bijapur in 1682-83. The crisis became so much deep that in 1685 Shāh 'Ālam was imprisoned on the charge of being in secret alliance with Quṭb Shah and being friendly to Shambhaji.

Manṣabs began to be granted to the Marathas from Jahangir's time but to seek Shivajī's cooperation who had his own political centre and ambitions was a totally different matter. Shāista Khān, was so hostile to the Marathas that he never recruited them even as cavalrymen or foot-troopers[3]. The Maratha policy of Jai Singh came to be tested when Shivajī appeared at Agra for the grant of a suitable *manṣab*. Numerous nobles led by Jaswant Singh, who dismissed Shivajī as a "petty *bumia*", Ja'far Khān and Ra'd Andaz Khān deadly opposed to any concessions to Shivajī, whereas Jai Singh's cause was espoused by Amin Khān, Saiyid Murtaza Khān and 'Āqil Khān, Aurangzeb, however, remained undecided and he had failed to win over Shivajī with a grant of 5000/5000, with the result that he was neither crushed nor conciliated, instead the Maratha leader had fled from his court which resulted merely into the issuance of a *dastak* to Mir Muḥammad Shafi *thanedār* of Baitala to this effect:

> 'Since the wretched and miserable Siva along with his son, fled away from His Majesty's presence and the most sublime and the holy order was promulgated from the imperial court in regard to his arrest together

1. *Cf.*, Zakir Hussain, An Opening To Rajaram? A *Farmān* ofAurangzeb of 1689, *PIHC*, Delhi, 2011, pp. 319-23.
2. Mamuri, f. 130 [a].
3. *Mughal Nobility*; p. 106.

with his son, *aḥadis* [gentlemen troopers] have been deputed from here accordingly. Consequent upon the receipt of the *dastak* [order] he should also direct his agents that they in collaboration with each other, must remain alert and consider injunction in the matter'[1].

The result of the entire exercise was this that in 1667 [as mentioned elsewhere] on the recommendations of Shāh 'Ālam and Maharaja Jaswant Singh, Shivajī was pardoned and his son Shambhaji was given the rank of 5000/5000; Shivajī was also allowed to annex as much territory of Bijapur as his sources permitted, or else, he was to confine himself to his own territory and bound to act in accordance with the advice of the Mughal Viceroy of the Deccan[2]. Due to slackness in punishing the Marathas in 1668 by Prince Shāh 'Ālam and Jaswant Singh, Diler Khān expressed his displeasure and difference.

The situation had reached to such an extent that according to a memorandum [*yāddāsht*] dated 9th September 1668 to Partap Rao, chief of the contingent army of Sambhaji, son of Shivaja [Raja Shivajī][3] that *nisar* [gift of a noble] of Rs 500 was offered. It further stated that the *manṣab* of Sambhaji was 5000/5000 [2x3h] '6 monthly' one-fourth deduction [*chauthāi*] was exempted.

However, such favour did not yield expected dividends, instead Shivajī's men unabatedly remain engaged in realising the revenues of the *jāgīrs* of Mughal *jāgīrdārs*. Even the Marathas used to plunder the Mughal *jāgīrs* to such an extent that not a single *dam* was left to be realised by the *jāgīrdār*[4], which, sometimes, left the *qila'dār* in the fort high and dry[5] even compelled him to seek financial assistance.

The Marathas had basically *zamīndār* leaders and peasant armies. However, under the Marathas peasant resistance was completely submerged because the potential peasant rebel become a *bargi* trooper of the Marathas where there was no pay, only the risk of death and the chances of plunder[6]. Though Shivajī also maintained conventionally paid, better equipped cavalry and artillery, yet the combined endeavours of the *bargīs* and Marathas were aimed at loot and plunder.

---

1. *SDAR*, pp. 54-5.
2. *Nsukha-i Dilkushā,* ff. 35 [a] 36 [b].
   Nauskha-i Dilkushā, ff. 34-35 [o]; *Futūhāt-i 'Ālamgīrī*, f. 59 [o].
3. Aurangzeb recognized Shivaji's title of Raja early in 1668 as well as *manṣab* for Shambhaji and the peace which had lasted for two years only. Sarkar, *Short History*, p. 206.
4. *SDAR*, pp. 71, 90-91.
5. *SDAR*, p. 177.
6. Frayer, A new Account, I, p. 310.

In order to save the Mughal territories from Maratha devastation or their unwelcome presence or any corresponding obligation to guard it Shivajī demanded *chauth* [or *chauthaī*] without rendering any yeoman service, which befittingly suited to the founder of a brigandage state where no plunder no payment was the cardinal principle. In 1671 Ūdājī Ram's plenipotentiary represented that the army of Shivajī had reached *sarkār* Mahur and plundered *pargana* Amarkher, *jāgīr* of Ūdājī Ram. Furthermore the enemy was encamped in the surrounding areas and was demanding *chauth* from every *pargana*, due to which the entire *jāgīr* of Ūdājī Ram was ruined. Accordingly he solicited Imperial orders for 'Abdullāh Shirāzi for exerting a bond to the effect that in the event of collecting a single dām by the Marathas on account of *chauth* he would be held responsible otherwise Ūdājī Ram was ready to give thing in writing to face the ire, if a single *dam* was collected from the *parganas* by the army of Shivajī, contingent upon his reinstatement to its *faujdārī* as well[1].

Surprisingly enough the Mughal officials did not hesitate in attributing the devastation of Mughal territories by the Mughal armies as well as is evident from the written communication of Suhrab Khān, [the castellan of Ūdgīr] who alleged the desolation of *pargana* Ūdgīr by the Imperial armies and the accursed Marathas owing to which the entire peasantry had run away to such an extent that for the last two years neither any revenue was accuring nor any loan was forthcoming, which was, however, vehemently refuted by Prince Mua'zzam, the Viceroy. When Suhrab Khān reported that the accursed [i.e. Shivajī] had sent the message to remit 1/4th of the revenue [i.e. *chauth*] otherwise they would run over it, and merchandise of those merchants who due to fear had stayed at Tilanga[na] was lifted away by the Marathas.

Accordingly he was assured of the arrival of the army. The *qila'dār* further reported arrival of 60-70,000 cavalryman and a few thousand foot-troopers towards the close of night, near the fort, which was encountered through the cannon balls and muskets due to which they turned towards Tilanga[na], and the spy brought the news that the accursed Shivajī [Siva *maqhūr*] was verily at these places. He was, assured of rewards. The said *qila'dār* complained against the desolation of his *jāgīrs*, which had made the maintenance of his contingent of 200 *sawārs* and 400 gunners difficult whereas he had also sought additional 400 gunners by way of assistance till the disturbance of Shivajī was over[2]. Shivajī plundered 51 villages of Aḥmadnager, Junair and Parenda in 1670.

1. *SDAR*, pp. 80-81.
2. *SDAR*, pp. 86-8.

Since the relations with Shivajī had strained to such an extent that on 19 March 1671, Partap Rao s/o Gannuji was summoned from Baglana by Prince Mua'zzam, Viceroy of the Deccan on the charge of writing a letter to Shivajī. When the matter was referred to Neknām Khān, the *faujdār* of Baglana he recommended internment in the event of his committing such a crime, side by side showing his ignorance of the entire episode. Ultimately Partap Rao was dismissed[1].

Shivajī was himself not a liberator of the peasants[2], as is evident from numerous events *viz.*, Muḥammad Taj s/o Fateḥ Jang Khān, on 18 March, 1671 accompanied with a contingent of 500 *sawārs* attacked 30 *kurohs* away from Nander and fought with the army of Shivajī. Consequently he brought heads of 40 Marathas and 20 horses as well as got liberated 50 *muqaddams* of the villages of the country of Telingana[3].

The Marathas used to take full advantage of the absence of the *jāgīrdārs* from their *jāgīr parganas* as is confirmed from an anonymous complaint of June 1671 of seizing all his *jāgīr parganas* seeking permission to proceed there which was, however, denied[4]. However, the Mughal *manṣabdārs* who successfully fought against the Marathas were rewarded. It was reported to Prince Mu'azzam on 10 January, 1672, that the Marathas, numbering about 10,000 cavalrymen and 3-4,000 foot-troopers had surrounded *qaṣba* Nander from all sides for 3 days and nights. But Yashwant Rao with Shaikh Aiyyub, agent of Diler Khān by strengthening the entrenchment killed most of the enemies, wounded several of them and inflicted a crushing defeat on them to such an unprecedented degree that when as soon as one of their *sardārs* [chiefs] was killed they fled away with utter shame towards Telingana and *sarkār* Mahur. Thenceforward he was rewarded an increase of 50 *ẓāt* raising his *manṣab* to 300/140[5].

The conditions of peasants became equally intolerable in the Mughal held territories because, as stated above the Marathas imposed their own tribute in addition to Mughal land revenue demand. Bhim Sen noted that 'the troops of the Marathas who come in for the sack of plundering the country, extort money from every *pargana*, in accordance with their desire

1. *SDAR*, pp. 92-3.
2. Satish Chandra, 'Social Background to the Rise of the Maratha Movement during the Seventeenth Century', [*ESHR*, 3, 1973, pp. 207-17; *idem,* Shivaji and Maratha Landed Elements, in Medieval India, Society, the *Jagirdari* Crisis and the Village, Delhi 1983, pp. 128-38, P.V. Ranade, 'Feudal Content of Maharashtra Dharma, *IHR*, I, 1974, Delhi, 44-50; *Agrarian System*, pp. 349-50.
3. *SDAR*, pp. 93-4.
4. *SDAR*, pp. 97-8.
5. *SDAR*, p. 102.

and let [their horses] graze on and trample upon the cultivated fields[1].

As soon as war began between the Marathas and the Mughals, the conditions of the peasantry could only worsen beyond redemption. The conduct of the Mughal army in the Maratha territories is thus described in a news report of Aurangabad of 26 January, 1662:

> "When the news was received that towards Lohgarh fort etc which would be about 20 *kurohs* from *qaṣba* Pune majority of villages of the accursed enemy [i.e. Marathas] are inhabited. Thereupon Shāista Khān, deputed Nāmdar Khān and other *manṣabdārs* on 23 January, 1662. The said Khān went there and set ablaze about 70-80 villages on the way on the very day and plundered the grain etc and stayed near the fort of Tarkan adjacent to the aforesaid fort. Since the inhabitants of the said villages had taken away the animals and goods on the mountains the said Khān encamped there for the second day accompanying him for searching out the livestock and undertaking enslavement on the mountains, and they reached there, seized over 1,000 animals, and enslaved 300 men and women approximately. On the third day marched ahead, set fire and plundered the villages near the forts of Tarkan, Lohgarh, Awsapur and Longi and returned"[2].

The position remained unchanged even in 1675 as recorded by a contemporary observer:

> 'Laying waste all in their road, both villages, fodder, and corn; for their castle they drive them along with them, and take them, their wives and children for slaves; so none escape except those can fly fastest, or hide themselves in the woods, which they also set on fire, to leave them destitute of those recesses[3]'.

Even Shivajī's own administration was equally repressive because he 'left the Tiller hardly as much as will keep Life and Soul together, in the core of his own kingdom[4]. Notwithstanding such unbearable conditions a large number of peasants were compelled to turn to him, by force of circumstances, to serve him as *bargīs*. Such a vicious circle of oppression and depredations on both sides resulted into swelling number of *bargīs* on the Maratha side and the Mughal Empire splintering irretrievably.

---

1. *Nuskha-i Dilkushā*, f. 139 [b]; *SDAR*, pp. 108.
2. *SDAR*, pp. 27-8.
3. Frayer, *A New Account*, p. 310.
4. *Ibid*, pp. 311-12.

IV

Revenue and Financial Administration

[I] Khāliṣa and Pāibāqī

[A] *Khāliṣa*

Lands not assigned in *jāgīr* whose revenues were reserved for the Imperial treasury were known as *Khāliṣa* Sharīfa or *Khāliṣa*. *Khāliṣa* seems to have been fluctuated from 5 to 25 per cent of the total *jama'* [estimated revenue] incurred of the Mughal Empire. However, it appears to have been consisted of shifting territories scattered throughout the Empire. The total extent of the *Khāliṣa* varied considerably under *Karori* Experiment of [1575-6, 1579-8], *jāgīrs* of the nobles having been resumed by Akbar [1556-1605], practically placing the whole of the Empire in the *Khāliṣa*, large amounts of cash payments had to be made to them by the Imperial treasury[1]. Later in his reign, of course, after the dismantling of the *Karorī* Experiment in 1580, *Khāliṣa* appears to have been accorded for one-fourth of the total *jama'*. Under Jahangir [1605-27] *Khāliṣa*'s jama' fell less than 5% of the total *jama'* of the Empire which shrank to 28 crores of *dāms*[2]. The *jama' of Khāliṣa* was gradually expanded under Shāh Jahān so that it rose to one-seventh or 120 crore of the total *jama'* of 880 crores in 1647[3] which accounted for 13.6% approximately. In Aurangzeb's 10th R.Y. the *jama'* of the *Khāliṣa* reached to nearly one-fifth of the total of the Empire[4]. The proceeds [*haṣil*] of the *Khāliṣa* prior to the Deccan annexations were approximately 26.1 million rupees[5].

The Emperor's share mainly consisting of the cash income out of the revenues of *Khāliṣa* and tribute from the feudatories, out of which he paid a large number of *naqdī manṣabdārs* and other high officials and

1. *Agrarian System*, p. 271 and *n*.
2. Qazwini, *Pādshāh Nāma*, transcript of Riza Library in Deptt. of History, p. 423; Muḥammad Sharif Najafi, *Majalis-us-Salatin*, Ms. Br. M, or, 1903, ff. 115 [a-b].
3. Lahori, II, pp. 710-13, *Agrarian System*, 271-3.
4. *Miratul 'Ālam*, f. 214 [b].
5. *Agranian System*. p. 273 *n*.

maintained his own personal troops [*aḥadis*], artillery and the whole palace establishment besides meeting expenditure in the provinces.

It is an established fact that since the Imperial treasury had to disburse salaries to the *naqdī manṣabdārs* and others in cash, the tendency in the *Khāliṣa* too [like *jāgīrs*] must have been overwhelmingly towards collection in cash. A large chunk of the income assigned to Emperor's own establishment from the *Khāliṣa*, less salaries paid out to *manṣabdārs,* was expanded on the royal establishment which under Akbar amounted to 6 percent of the total estimated revenue[1], which position was perhaps equally true under Aurangzeb.

The above data show that the *Khāliṣa* covered a very large portion of the Empire, but the Emperor was also in command of a considerable income collected directly by his treasury.

As stated above that the *Khāliṣa* also tended to collect revenues in cash. However, in actual incidences, we find commutation of kind into cash as is established from four documents entitled āwārja-i muṭalibāt-i *Khāliṣa* Sharīfa mutafarriqat [miscellaneous balance of the claims of the crown lands] of 1081 AH/ 1671 AD[2] in *pargana* 'Ādilābād *sarkār* Asīr, *ṣūba* Khandesh.

The replenishment of *Khāliṣa* Sharīfa was always taken care of. In view of its special significance the second Imperial *Dīwān,* the *Dīwān-i Khāliṣa* Sharīfa was appointed, who was in-charge of the reserved or the centrally administered lands of the Empire and of all the revenues coming directly to the current treasury. When Aurangzeb, as Viceroy of the Deccan, for the second time encountered difficulties in obtaining sufficient *jāgīrs* against his *manṣab* pay claim in the Deccan he was suggested by Shāh Jahān to resume requisite *jāgīrs* of the *manṣabdārs* into the *Khāliṣa*, which suggestion was, however, politely declined by Aurangzeb, due to some administrative reasons[3].

Aurangzeb also claimed for the *Khāliṣa* the land revenue from varying proportions of villages and *parganas* of the four provinces of the Deccan. Agents of the *Khāliṣa* transferred these collections directly to provincial treasuries immediately after receipts. Funds thus gathered could be stored or transported elsewhere for Imperial purposes. However, unfortunately we do not possess synoptic statement of the *Khāliṣa* for the older Deccan provinces in the first half of Aurangzeb's reign. Imperial *Khāliṣa* officers

1. Āīn, I, edited by Blochmann, p. 9.
2. Inayat Jang Collection, National Archives, New Delhi [hereafter IJC] IJCI/ 13/ 0-14, IJCI/ 13/ 0-32, IJC/ 13/ 0-43, IJCI/ 13/ 0-63.
3. *Ādāb*, p. 157; *Calender,* p. 44.

in the Deccan used to receive perhaps 42 percent of the total established collections of revenue.

More significant were the sums received by the *Khāliṣa* accounts of the Deccan treasury because all *sāīr* revenues, custom duties, and other miscellaneous collections went to provincial treasuries under this heading [as the headings found on all related documents] of four Deccan provinces testify.

Furthermore all tribute [*peshkash*] payments made by local officers went to the *sāliyāna* because surviving documents, after ample evidence prove, that the Mughal Imperial fiscal officials in the Deccan recorded the collections of these *peshkash* payments from the local aristocracy of the Deccan provinces, as these were not mere formalities, but represented a source of considerable funds for the Imperial administration.

There is no denying the fact that the Deccan treasury endeavoured to locate agreements and to enforce collections in all the *sarkārs* of the Deccan provinces. Special messangers used to carry sums of the *peshkash* owed to the *Khāliṣa* Sharīfa to the Deccan treasury at Aurangabad. Although *Khāliṣa* consisted of shifting territories scattered all over the Empire yet the Imperial administration in the Deccan maintained details of the same as is evident from a memorandum of the villages of the *Khāliṣa* from *tappa* Raheri, *pargana* Islamabad [mod. Bhivandi] *sarkār* Talkokan-i Nizamu-l Mulki, *ṣūba* Aurangabad of 34 RY/ 1690 A.D. which contains data for the year 1657. It gives the number of villages as five which had a *jama'* of 2,10,931 *dāms* yielding Rs 1,111/ 14½ out of which 1,40,847 *dāms* were earmarked for *Khāliṣa* Sharīfa. Thereafter village-wise break up of *Khāliṣa* Sharīfa together with *madad-i ma'āsh* assignment is given[1].

Interestingly enough even the *jizya* was included in the *Khāliṣa* Sharīfa stipulating that Shaikh Najmuddin, *Qaẓi* of *pargana* 'Ādilabād [*sarkār* Aīsr, *ṣūba* Khandesh] had to pay Rs 283½ *in toto* according to the *nuskha* of Muḥammad Mehdi, *Dīwān* of *ṣūba* Khandesh as per the following: Rs 150 for the *jizya* of *pargana* 'Ādilabād and Rs 133½ as per the *nuskha* of Khwaja Muḥammad 'Usmān, *Dīwān* of *ṣūba* Khandesh from the *jizya* till 1090A/ 1680 AD, which, he could not pay till 1681 AD[2]. However, we have no information about the total *Khāliṣa* Sharīfa position during Aurangzeb's first phase of the Deccan.

In 1636, Shāh Jahān under the active leadership of Aurangzeb, then Viceroy in the Deccan, achieved his strategic goals in the Deccan because Bijapur and Golcunda were made tributary states in a new formal settlement.

1. IJCI/ 34/ 0-17 and IJCI/ 34/ 0-18.
2. IJCI/ 23/ 11-28 and IJCI/ 23/ 11-30.

Although it, however, brought some stability to the Deccan frontier for the first time, yet it was a temporary phase in the nature of a cease-fire. Shāh Jahān was content to have Bijapur and Golcunda as tributary states, but the court faction was obviously in favour of annexation, attracted by their great wealth, which inevitably prevailed[1]. Formal invasions against Bijapur and Golcunda were sanctioned in 1656-7, which again proved abortive because another peace treaties were made with the two states which lasted for next 30 years contingent upon the payment of *peshkash* by them, which invariably formed part of the *Khāliṣa* Sharīfa.

On 23 August, 1661 Fateḥ Jung Khān, *faujdār* of Nander sent messages through his *harkāra* to Muliya, Quṭbul Mulk's *harkāra* for Saiyid Muzaffar, Mulla 'Abdus Ṣamad and I'tmād Rao and verbally summoned the *harkāra* through his *bakhshi* telling him to remit to him whatever was paid per annum to the late Rashīd Khān failing which threatened attack on frontier villages. Accordingly Ḥakīm Nizāmuddin Aḥmad asked whether he should strive for collecting the amount of stipulated *peshkash* or endeavour for *faujdār's* goodwill[2]. Till 25 August 1661, Rs 50,000 and 1,20,000 hūns were released on account of *peshkash.* Previously Rs 1,00,000 were received from the total *hūns* and deposited in the central treasury at Aurangabad, whereas 10,000 *hūns* and Rs 50,000 were given to Khān Muḥammad, an official of Shāista Khān to be remitted as it is in the imperial treasury of Aurangabad, while both Quṭbul Mulk and 'Ādil Shāh promised to pay the freshly stipulated *peshkash* regularly. However, due to the outbreak of the wars of succession the arrears of *peshkash* and other related claims could not be fully materialised to the satisfaction of Aurangzeb. But since 1661 we find numerous instances of the payments or promises or problems of payments especially by Quṭbul Mulk, who had to remit ten lakh rupees annually as *peshkash*, which may be summarised chronologically to give an idea of the magnitude of the demand:

On 17 August, 1661 one diamond belonging to Mohan Das was sent by Quṭbul Mulk to Khān-i Zamān to Zafarabad to be delivered to Amānat Khān for onward transmission to the imperial court where it would be assessed and adjusted against *peshkash*, if it would meet Aurangzeb's approbation otherwise it would be returned back[3]. Remainder of *hūns* would be sent to the Imperial treasury of Aurangabad after 26th August, 1661. As far the amount of tribute is concerned it was imposed on the *ḥavaldārs* on the current year's revenue that would be collected from Quṭbul Mulk's men accordingly[4].

1. For details of tribute see, Introduction to *Calendar,* pp. XXXV-XXXX.
2. *SWD,* p. 5.
3. *SWD,* p. 3.
4. *SWD,* p. 6.

It was reported on 31st August, 1661 that 75011½ *hūns* on account of *peshkash* from Quṭbul Mulk was deposited in the central treasury at Aurangabad through Khān-i Zamān[1].

Mullah 'Abdus Ṣamad made an agreement with Muḥammad Naṣir, the Mughal *ḥājib* on 16th September, 1661 to remit 2,00,000 *hūns* [as *peshkash*] from October, 1661 to July 1662 in the following five installments:

[i] From 1 *Rabi'* I to end *Rabi'* II : 44444½ *hūns.*

[ii] From 1 *Jumada* I to end *Jumada* II : 44444½ *hūns.*

[iii] From 1 *Rajab* to end *Shahaban* : 44444½ *hūns.*

[iv] From 1 *Ramazan* to end *Shawwal* : 44444½ *hūns.*

[v] From 1 *Ziqada* to end *Ziqada* : 22222 *hūns*[2].

It was communicated on 30th September, 1661 A.D. that Mir Qasim 'Ali, of the Imperial treasury, received and remitted 5000 *hūns* out of the total *peshkash* from the *ḥavaladār* of Machhlipattan port[3].

It was known on 19 January 1662 that Rs 5000 as *nisār* to the Imperial *farmān* were offered in front of Muaḥammad Ḥusain, *mutaṣaddi* at Machhlipattan by Muḥammad Nabi, an official of Ḥakeem Niẓāmuddin Aḥmad.

It was complained that they were responsible for remitting Rs 10,00,000 as the fixed tribute, for payment of which Mulla 'Abduṣ Ṣamad had stood surety as per the installment and agreement, as they were offering lame excuses. Accordingly the matter was discussed with Quṭbul Mulk on 19th February 1662 and the *ḥājib* / [envoy] demanded amount from Mulla 'Abduṣ Ṣamad according to installment and agreement. It was pleaded that the amount was not received from the *ḥavaldārs* which proved unconvincing; hence 4000 new *hūns* were exchanged through *ṣarrafs* [money-changers] into [Mughal] rupees and the remainder were paid in '*Ālamgīrī* coins for which money receipts of Rs 1,00,000 were given. Mulla' 'Abduṣ Ṣamad executed a bond to remit the amount in accordance with the installment and agreement[4].

It was ordered on 9 April 1662 that a sum of Rs 1,25,987 ½ ['*Ālamgīrī* coins] out of the stipulated *peshkash* of Rs 10,00,000 per annum be sent through *hundwi*[bill of exchange] of the *ṣarrafs* to the central treasury of Aurangabad and dispatch the paper of *hundwi* to Amānat Khān, enabling him to obtain money from the money changers and remit it in the imperial treasury[5].

---

1. *SWD*, pp. 7-8.
2. *SWD*, p. 11.
3. *SWD*, p. 12; *SWD*, p. 14.
4. *SWD*, p. 16.
5. *SWD*, p. 17.

On 13th May 1662 Rs 69,811¾ out of the fixed *peshkash* of Rs 10,00,000 for which 'Abduṣ Ṣamad stood surety was paid.

It was conveyed on 16 May 1662 that a sum of 2444 *hūns* and 6½ *annas* from the amount of *peshkash* and Rs 3,259 as *'ulufa* [salary] of Mir Muḥammad Ḥusain ṬabaṬaba was obtained from *peshkash* as per Aurangzeb's *farmān*. It was ordered that 2044 *hūns* and 6½ *annas* and Rs 3,259 be given to Muḥammad Ḥusain, *mataṣaddis* of Machhlipattan Port and the remaining 400 *hūns* be allowed to Mīr Muḥamamd Ḥusain ṬabaṬaba and Rs 34,000 as amount for procuring imperial requirements was given to Muḥammad Ḥusain, *mustaṣaddi* of the port[1].

The above mentioned details give us a peep into the real state of tribute affairs of Quṭbul Mulk, who was, however, with some lapses was punctiliously busy in making matters easy in regard to *peshkash* as compared to 'Adil Shāh whose valuation of *peshkash* is known only from a *siyaha* document of 24th December 1661, which were merely 10 rings as per following specifications of quality and price tabulated hereunder[2].

Table – 1: List of the valuation of the tribute of 'Ādil Khān

Sl. No.	*Kind of ring*	*Quantity*	*Quality*	*Weight*	*Price/without deduction*
1.	Ordinary gold ring with diamond bezel	one	diamond	10 *surkh* [10 masha ? gold]	Rs. 810 Rs. 648
2.	Ordinary silver ring with lotus …	one	diamond	7¼ *surkh*	Rs. 3500 Rs 2800
3.	Silver ring en-grossed with ruby bezel	one	ruby	3 *surkh*	Rs. 250 Rs. 200 As per Jahan Ara's order Rs. 280
4.	Gold enamel ring with ruby bezel	one	ruby	8 *surkh*	Rs. 250 Rs. 200
5.	Ordinary gold ring with ruby bezel	one	ruby	5 *surkh*	Rs. 900 Rs. 800
6.	Gold enamel ring with ruby bezel	one	ruby	3½ *surkh*	Rs. 200 Rs. 160

1. *SWD*, p. 22.
2. *SDAR*, pp. 23-4. The imperial administration also appointed Mīr 'Abdul M'abud as *ḥājib* at Bijapur in January 1671 by Muḥammad Niṣir to look after his duties as envoy, who was found to send weekly news report of Bijapur to the Imperial court probably to command obedience, [*SDAR*, p. 83].

7.	Ordinary gold ring with ruby bezel	one	ruby	3 *surkh*	Rs. 50 Rs. 40
8.	Gold enamel ring with ruby bezel	one	ruby	5 *surkh*	Rs. 102 Rs. 80
9.	Ordinary gold ring with ruby bezel	one	ruby	?	Rs. 102 Rs. 80
10.	Jewel studded gold ring with ruby bezel	one	ruby	3½ *surkh*	Rs. 80 Rs. 64

The above table shows the real worth of the *peshkash* received from 'Ādil Khān price of which has been calculated Rs 6,244 or Rs 6,274, if we take into consideration the increase of Rs 30 in respect of item No 3 by Princess Jahan Ara and it arrives at Rs 5,072 without deduction. It also brings home the point that the *peshkash* drawn from Bijapur was a token one merely recognizing Mughal overlordship whereas tribute to a tune of ten lakh rupees per annum was imposed and extracted from Golcunda in the real sense of the difference. The annual tribute in the settlements of 1636 and 1656-7 remained the same i.e. 2 lakh hūns annually from Quṭbul Mulk and the only difference remained in the exchange value of *hūns* which rose from Rs 4 to Rs 4½ and finally Rs 5 in 1654 and the arrears accuring on account of variations in exchange rates of *hūn* becāme a matter of dispute. However, tribute from Golcunda remained an enormous source of income of the *Khāliṣa* Sharīfa in the Deccan in Aurangzeb's first phase of the Deccan.

[B] Pāibāqī

Lands which were those *parganas* temporarily in charge of the Imperial officials pending reassignment of pay salaries of *manṣabdār / jagirdārs* were known as *pāibāqī*[1] ... These unassigned and unclaimed revenues [*pāibāqi*] that were temporarily collected by the agents of the imperial administration were placed in the provincial treasury. Under ordinary circumstances these *pāibāqi* lands would have comprised but a small proportion, certainly under five percent of the total provincial revenues of the Deccan.

It is a well-established fact that the Deccan had always been a deficit area specially from the closing years of Shāh Jahān's reign as its actual *ḥaṣil* was hardly 25% of the *jama*' or *jama'dami* [estimated revenue] by which *jāgīrs* were assigned in lieu of pay which was due to the desolation of the Deccan peasantry as revenue collection in the Deccan had declined

1. *Khulaṣatus Siyāq*, f. 24 [b]; *Waqāi 'Ajmer*, pp. 74, 375-6; Ma'muri, ff. 156 [b]-157[a]; *Cf.*, M. Athar Ali's Review on J.F. Richard's *Mughal Administration in Golcunda*, OUP, 1975, in *Journal of Asian Studies*, 1976, p. 159; *Agarian System*, pp. 259- .

enormously. Even during his second Viceroyalty of the Deccan, Aurangzeb was advised to resume *jāgīrs* of nobles yielding Rs 20,36,000 to *Khāliṣa* so as to make good of his *jāgīr* income, which Aurangzeb, however, suitably refused to accept as such dispossessed *manṣabdārs* whose *jāgīrs* thus resumed would become *jāgīr*-less and they would have to be sent to the Imperial court[1]. This implies the scarcity of *paibāqī* towards the end of Shāh Jahān's reign, a phenomenon which Richards even could not discern during the last phase of Aurangzeb's reign.

We have, however, no evidence to suggest that the situation had improved tremendously only in Aurangzeb's reign.

In view of the extraordinary importance of *pāibāqī* the *amīn* of *pāibāqī* was appointed, who together with his staff and the *amīn* of other lands set the current assessment for the villages and *parganas* in the provinces based upon the rolling ten year average yield and market figures for production of annual yield per crop and per unit of area [*mawāzana-i deh sāla*]. It was his duty to administer the *pābāqī maḥāls* properly.

Due to scarcity of *jāgīr* there used to be a mad rush for assignment of *jāgīr* from *pāibāqi*. When due to the transfer of Muḥammad Momin, son of Shāh Beg Khān the amount of *khurak-i dawwāb* [animal fodder] in *pargana* Thaner, *ṣūba* Khandesh, which was resumed to *pāibāqī* in 1663 was subsequently assigned to Muḥammad Amān, son of Muḥammad Amīn, maternal grandson of Shāh Beg Khān[2]. A *parwāna* [order] of Shāista Khān of 13th December 1661 entrusted, 1,37,90,000 *dāms* accuring from the *pāibāqi maḥāl* of Jadu Rai and 3 others in *pargana* Poona, *sarkār* Junnar, *ṣūba* Aurangabad to Raziuddin Muḥammad[3].

During the first phase of Aurangzeb's Deccan policy we rarely find any mention of the *pāibāqī* which *inter alia* establishes its extreme scarcity. It is no more astonishing that even *pāibāqī* worth one lakh *dāms* was recommended by Shāista Khān in January 1662 for a Maratha official with the instructions to recognize him as holder of that much *dāms*[4], which shows the immense significance which the *pāibāqī* had acquired in Aurangzeb's early reign.

In view of the scattered evidence which does suggest that claims

1. *Ādāb*, I, p. 157; Richards, *Mughal Administration*, pp. 199-200. For an opposite view see Zakir Husain, 'The Working of the *jagir* System in the Deccan during the Later Years of Aurangzeb', *Journal of Objective Studies*, Delhi, 1990, Vol. II, No. 1.
2. M.A. Nayeem, *Mughal Documents*, Vol. I, part II, A.R. No. V/2/09.
3. *Ibid*, p. 72-3 Another document [*ibid*, p. 1014] entrusted Randola Khān, 95,40,000 *dams* due to shortage of *pāibāqi*.
4. *SDAR*, pp. 25-6.

made by the <u>*Kh*</u>*āliṣa* in Aurangzeb's reign were relatively high. We can also add the unmarked and unclaimed revenues whose revenues were temporarily collected by the agents of the central administration to this as yet undetermined amount. Thus, both types of revenues probably formed one fourth of the total revenues of the Deccan amounts to 2,96,70,00,000 *dāms*[1].

[II] Land Revenue Assessment and Realisation

Since the Deccan was always relatively detached from the core area of the empire in Hindustan or North India, the four Mughal Deccan provinces of Aurangabad, Berar, Bidar and Khandesh definitely experienced conquest and administrative consolidation comparatively late in the centralised imperial administration of the seventeenth century. The people of the Deccan had suffered considerably between predatory armies and frequent draughts leading to famine. With the settlement of 1636, the imperial administration began making endeavours to reform and systematise the revenue assessment and realisation of the Deccan.

Interestingly enough, the Deccan administration reached a definitive stage of consolidation as late as 1652. The renowned *Dīwān* of the Deccan, Murshid Quli <u>Kh</u>ān, through an imperial order, carried out the sweeping series of reforms in the agrarian administration. His aim was to bring the four Deccan provinces fully into the classical *ẓabt* or regulation revenue system of the North India. It need no recital as major extension of the *ẓabt* system occurred in the Deccan by Murshid Quli <u>Kh</u>ān who made a three pronged effort by recruiting new, reliable revenue assessors and collectors, providing incentives for the extension of cultivation, and reorganising assessment, and collection of land tax by the *ẓabt* system of Hindustan because the greater part of the Mughal Empire was administered directly under the *ẓabt* system. One can argue that the essence of his measure lay in, first, establishing crop-sharing or more specifically *kankūt*, for some time, in order to establish the *rai's* [harvest yield crop-rate] for various crops in different districts, such as food grains, vegetables, high-grade crops, varying the government share according to crop and natural or artificial factors, by taking into consideration the prices, fixing the value of the out-turn of cultivation, enabling to collect the revenue rates according to the crop after measuring the land. Thereafter he worked out the cash rates or *dastūru-l 'amals*. The chief characteristic of his system was an ongoing systematic cadastral survey of agricultural lands for establishing field-by-field tenures and cropping patterns within each village and *pargana*. It was but natural that armed with this detailed statistical data, Murshid Quli <u>Kh</u>ān could fix

1. *Miratul 'Alam*, ff 214[b]-215[b]; *Ẓawābit-i 'Ālamgīrī*, ff. 3 [a], 5 [b].

the land revenue on a field by field basis of a maximal level of cultivated area for each village and the kinds of crops / groups, with reduced rates for cash crops like sugarcane and records of previous market rates over the previous ten years. The state claim was for cash payment of revenue while the *Dīwān* also improved the system of *taqāvi* [i.e. advances or loans] made to peasants to encourage expansion of arable land. Obviously over a large part of the Deccan the older system of imposing land revenue based on the number of ploughs was now replaced by a system of measurement[1].

Under the *ẓabt* system, the allowance for crop failure was made by excluding from revenue assessment, the areas denoted *nābūd* [crop-less] which could not exceed 12½ percent of the sown area. The loans designated *taqāvi* 'strength giving' were sanctioned under the *ẓabt* regulations which were normally to be repaid at harvest. Furthermore grant of tax concessions or whenever revenue rates were allowed to encourage land cleaning and colonisation, which were, however, gradually enhanced every year until the full rates were fixed in the fifth year[2]. The revenue demand was stated primarily in cash in the *ẓabt* system and this system of assessment, could be replaced by another, such as assessment in kind or crop-sharing, and vice-versa. Generally it appears that the share of produce taken as revenue ranged from one-third to half in most parts of northern India and Deccan[3].

Consequent upon these changes measurement of villages *viz.,* 2,832 villages in *ṣūba* Khandesh constituting 45 percent of the total were assessed and surveyed under the zabt system[4], whereas the remaining 3,507 villages were brought under less exacting assessment, involving crop sharing in fixed proportion at the time of harvest. Another system of revenue assessment was the old Khandeshi plough tax lump sum per plough [*sarbasta tashkhīs*] which was imposed in the case of the more remote areas. It was the customary calculation that a peasant with a pair of oxen could cultivate an area of one *aut* or 80 *bighas* and would be taxed accordingly. It can be safely assumed that the *ẓabt* system was more intrusive into the fabric of local society as compared to other methods of assessment.

The total area of the four older provinces of Deccan was approximately 1,23,221 miles [i.e. Aurangabad=38518 Bidar 17552, Berar 44147 and

1. *Agrarian System*, pp. 227-8; R.A. Alvi, 'Murshid Quli Khān in Deccan', *PIHC*, 33rd Session, 1972, p. 207.
2. *Agrarian System*, pp. 212 & n., 249-256
3. *Ibid*, pp. 190-230.
4. *Agrarian System*, p. 4.

Khandesh 23004] which equaled 3,17,660 sq. km[1]. Murshid Quli Khān's meticulous reorganisation of the agrarian administration of the Deccan provinces determined the mode and level of Imperial revenue collection for the next century[2]. We presume that later adjustments were made in the total revenue demand. However, the actual collections varied. Ultimately the resources of the provinces were undoubtedly established in the Imperial records and the official mind. The same system became so deeply entrenched in the Mughal revenue administration that any deviation from it could not be tolerated as is evident from the following statement probably made in late 1670's or early 1680's:

> "Ruḥullah Khān convened the imperial order that in the records office of the Deccan *Hundwi* is not written on the *chitthi-i deh ba dehi* [village to village accounts]. The fact remains that since the very inception of the conquest of the country [i.e. Deccan] the *chitthi* is obligatory because there are *Hindwi* knowing *deshmukhs* and *deshpāndiyas* in the *parganas* and it is essential that the *sarrishtas* [records] of the central and provincial *qānūngos* [*qānūngoyān-i ḥuzūr o ṣubajāt*] should be in conformity and no difference should be allowed. If order is issued then the *chitthi* in *Hindwi* script of the *qānūngos* or without seal and signature of the *Dīwān* with the symbol [*nishān*] may be sent regularly to Hindustan [North India] according to the *dastūr-i 'amal* [practice/ revenue schedule] of Murshid Quli Khān[3]". Even Aurangzeb in the late Seventeenth Century stressed on the system of revenue administration in the Deccan[4].

As stated earlier that Murshid Quli Khān, the *Dīwān* commissioned by Aurangzeb during his second term as the Viceroy of the Deccan in 1652 and the *Dīwān* was given a royal mandate to introduce large scale revenue reforms. He proved so able an improver and revenue administrator[5] that he enhanced the revenues by 25% in a large area as compared to Diyānat Khān, who was the *Dīwān* of Bālāghāt before Murshid Quli Khān.

Shāh Jahān considered the implementation of miscellaneous regulations [*ẓawābit-i gūnāgon*] as the chief cause of the ruin of the Deccan, which

1. The approximate area for the seventeenth century is taken from area tables for Khandesh and Malwa, Aurangabad, Berar and Bidar. It is not certain that the total includes Baglana because it has not been specifically mentioned. *An Atlas*, pp. VII-VIII.
2. *Cf.*, an āwāraja of *Kh*ālisa Sharifa of 1722 of *ṣūba* Berar Bālāghāt stating that the revenue administration or '*amal*-i Murshid Quli Khān was still valid, IJC VIII/89/607.
3. IJCI/ 0/ 0-580.
4. IJCI/411.
5. For details see Ṣādiq Khān, *Shahjahan Nāma,* Or 174; ff. 90; Khāfi Khān, II, 735; *Ādāb*, pp.134-5, 138-140, 148; *Calendar,* pp. XXXI-XXXV, 33-5, 37-8, 62.

according to Aurangzeb was further deteriorated by the mismanagement of the former Viceroys appointed between the interregnum of his first and second Viceroyalty i.e. from 1644 to 1652 because he claimed that he had streamlined the revenue administration during his first term as Viceroy of the Deccan from 1635 to 1644. This was true to some extent because in the interviewing over 8 years the agriculture had ruined and the peasantry had fled away due to the oppression of Viceroys and *jāgirdārs*[1].

Side by side the *ẓabt* system, the *'amal-i batāi* was considered equally helpful in improving the revenue affairs of the Deccan, which represented a claim on behalf of the state to a share of the actual crop. Khafi Khān has drawn our attention to a third method of assessment which was the *batāi* system or sharing of the crop between the government and the cultivator. Murshid Quli Khān introduced three kinds of sharing: [i] the producer of land only depended on rain and the crop was to be shared equally between the peasants and the government. [ii] the crops of rabi' and kharif obtained from well-water were to be divided between the producer and the government so that one-third of it was taken by the government and two-thirds were to be received by the peasants. [iii] However, for the crops like grapes, sugarcane, plantain, opium, poppy, sandal wood, turmeric, mango, cumin seed, etc one-ninth to one-fourth was to go to the government and the rest was to be left to the peasant[2]. This is generally opined that it was a temporary measure adopted for evolving a reliable crop rate [*rai'*] as both the *Dīwāns* of the Deccan i.e. Murshid Quli Khān and Multafat Khān were engaged in introducing *ghalla bakhshī* or *batāī* in Pāīnghāt and Bālāghāt. It, however, seems to have been a permanent measure of the revenue assessment where a simple sharing of the harvested grain took place, one share being left to the revenue payer whereas the other set apart for the state or its assignee because in regard to the officials posted in the Deccan we find an Imperial order of 7th August 1664 taking strict action for failure in proper implementation of crop sharing which reads:

> In regard to Riā'yat Khān it was represented to His Majesty that he did not make proper effort in realising the revenue of Surat Port and it also occurred in some other *parganas* where he had enforced crop-sharing [*'amal-i batāi*]. The world commanding and world obeying order was issued that 100/50 be reduced from his unconditional *manṣab*. Accordingly

1. For details see, *Ādāb*, I, pp. 100-138-40, *Calendar*, pp. 2, 33-35, J.N. Sarkar, *History of Aurangzeb*, Vol. I, Delhi, [reprint] pp. 99-100, S. Moinul Haq, *Prince Arangzeb: A Study*, Karachi 1962, pp. 38-39, Najib Ashraf Nadwi, *Muqaddama-i Ruqa'at-i Alamgir*, Azamgarh, 1981, [reprint], pp. 195-6.
2. A.J. Syed, *Aurangzeb in Muntakhabul-Lubab*, Asia Publishing House, Bombay, 1977, p. 59.

his unconditional 800/100 was reduced to 700/50 leaving 700/250 in which 200 *sawār* rank was contingent upon serving as castellan of Zafar Nagar[1].

According to a contemporary estimate, the *jama'dāmi* of [estimated revenue figures by which *jāgirs* were assigned in lieu of pay] of the provinces of the Deccan of 1667 was 2,96,70,00,000 *dāms*[2] which was 32.1 percent of the total *jama'* of the Empire. From 1667 to 1691 the share of the Deccan in the *jama'dami* of the Empire was 35.5 percent[3], which was 9,24,17,16082 *dāms* that was not a substantial rise. We can conclude that the *jama'dāmi* of the Deccan was one-third of the total *jama'* of the Empire.

When any *manṣabdār* was assigned the *jāgir* he got it assessed. We find that Saiyid Ḥaji and Shihabuddin, sons of Muḥammad Sai'd, *qila'dār* of SulṬangarh had gone towards Bhargaon for fixation of *jama'* [*tashkhis-i jama'bandi*] of their father[4]. Similarly Nūr Khān Lodi, *manṣabdar* from *pargana* Laling came to Khwāja Burhāni, *amīn* for revenue assessment [*jama'bandi*] and returned back after fixation[5]. This fact is also confirmed from innumerable *jāgīr* assignments [*daul-i jāgīr*] and āwāraja documents. Even it was obligatory upon the *Dīwān* to know the assessment of *jama'* of the *parganas* etc as is known from an appointment order of the *Dīwān* of *sarkār* Baglana *ṣūba* Khandesh of 1st December 1661 which *ipso facto* reads thus:

> The incumbent [i.e. Khwaja Trikam Das] should know the true facts of the assessment of *jama'* of the *parganas* like Khwaja La'l Chand, the ex-*Dīwān*. He should obtain the *sarrishta-i kāghaz* [register of papers] properly under signatures of the *desāis* and *qānūngos* so as to send it to the Imperial record office. He should not allow that any one of the *jāgirdārs* could oppress the peasantry. Let the peasantry make endeavour in cultivating cultivable and irrigated lands [*bardāshtan-i zamīn o bāghāt*][6].

We find that in early 1650's the Mughal administration on the solicitation of Multafat Khān, proposed to advance [*taqāvi*] of Rs 40,000 to 50,000 to cultivators in Khandesh and a portion of Berar for the purpose of erecting *bands* [dams] for impounding water for providing irrigation[7]. Surprisingly

1. *SDAR*, p. 44.
2. *Miratu-l 'Alam*, ff. 214 [b]-215.
3. *Zawabit-i 'Alamgiri*, ff. 3 [a] – 5 [b].
4. *SWD*, p. 128.
5. *SWD*, p. 168.
6. *SWD*, pp. 133-4.
7. *Ādāb*, I, pp. 207-8.

we find several series of connected documents specially during the second phase of Aurangzeb's Deccan administration as the Emperor, indicating the source of irrigation, if any, which mainly relate to *parganas* of 'Ādilābād, Laling and other areas of *ṣūba* Khandesh[1] as the officials were duty bound to look after the irrigation facilities as we come to know that Saiyid Manṣur, *faujadār* of Baglāna had been appointed to see the irrigation canal[2]. Although it is impossible to estimate the total area irrigated by the lakes and tanks, small or magnification of ordinary reservoirs yet it may be safely assumed that it was quite considerable because tanks or reservoirs played an important role as a source of irrigation in the Deccan.

The *jama'* of the Deccan in 1654 was estimated by as 1,44,90,00,000 *dāms* which rose to[3], 2,96,70,00,000 *dāms* in 1667 after 13 years. It became more than double in a span of 13 years, which further increased to 9,24,17,16082 *dāms* between 1667 to 1691, of course, within the next 24 years.

However, the question does arise that whether this increase in *jama'* ever commensurate with the actual *ḥaṣil*? What was the actual yield? What was the nature of the problems faced in revenue collection? What were the effects of the Maratha fiscal demands upon the Deccan in a number of forms? And so on and so forth.

The actual revenue realisation in 1654 was one crore rupees excluding 12 lakh rupees on account of natural calamities such a low *ḥasil* had a deep connexion with the deteriorating agrarian conditions in the Deccan.

Furthermore *jama'* was a long way from *ḥaṣil*. Aurangzeb during his second term as Viceroy of the Deccan represented to Shāh Jahān that "the *jama'dāmi* of these provinces after the reduction is 1,44,90,00,000 *dāms*. The actual *maḥṣul* [revenue] thereof, including the deduction of Rs 12,00,000 which the *Dīwāns* had not written off but shown as due to *āfat* [natural calamity], arrives at one crore rupees, which does not cause to average to 3-monthly of the *jama'dāmi*[4].

Although low revenue yield, accompanied with war plunder, tribute and massive agrarian tax collections combined to generate resources for the Mughal Deccan yet due to revenue embezzlements from the liquid reserved stored in the provincial treasuries the picture became astoundingly

1. IJC 1/11/432, 1/11/492, I/11/569; I/11/571.
2. *SWD*, p. 128.
3. *Ādāb*, Vol. I, pp. 156-8, *Calendar*, pp. 43-5.
4. *Ibid*; This position was equally true during Auranzgeb's reign as is clearly stated in a document of February 1660 that all the Deccan was getting 3 monthly *ḥaṣils*. MA Nayeem, *Mughal Documents*, I, ii, pp. 96-7.

grimy even before the crisis of the Deccan wars[1]. Even, *dīwān*, *faujdār* and *amīn* etc were charged for embezzlement of 26, 839½ *hūns* in June 1661[2].

However, leaving aside such occasional aberrations, endevours were always made to the extension of cultivation for the maximisation of land revenue. Thus, for instance on 24 June 1661, Saiyid Manṣur, *faujdār* of Baglāna, appointed Ankus Rao, son of Jankha Behal, to bring 25 *ghair'amali* [uncultivated] and 2 *'amali* villages under plough by giving him presents[3].

The extraction of *chauth* by Shivajī from 1670 onwards, was, however, a great factor in draining the land revenue resources of the Deccan because it was based upon a claimed 25% share of the Imperial tax assessment and established collections. The *chauth*, when fully collected equal to 8 million rupees which was exacted from Mughal or so called foreign territories[4]. In a nutshell the problems of the revenue administration and diminishing returns were the chief characteristics of the Mughal Deccan in pre-1681 era.

[III] The *Deshmukhs / Desaīs, Deshpāndes* and other *Zamīndārs*

The Imperial authority for realizing the revenues rested on the services of the *zamīndārs* of the country side in the Deccan provinces, without whom any order was impossible within this group of *zamīndārs*, the leading figures were the *deshmukhs*, who were semi-hereditary officially recognised intermediary officers[5], who acquired dominant power and high status in each *pargana*.

We are given to understand that during 1690 AD Khwas Khān was fixed the amount of two lakh rupees as *peshkash* as he was *deshmukh* of Bijapur. Generally in the old country one-fourth of the *peshkash* is realised

1. M.A. Nayeem, *Mughal Documents*, I, ii, pp. 8, 61.
2. *Ibid*, p. 24.
3. *SWD*, p. 125.
4. A.R. Kulkarni, '*Maharastra in the Age of Shivaji*', Poona 1969.
5. If we go by the classification imposed by Nurul Ḥasan, Land Control and Social Structure in Indian History making an important and necessary distinction between the intermediary, more powerful *zamīndārs* and primary or smaller village level ones it was followed by Muzaffar Alam; "The *Zamīndārs* and the Mughal Power in the Deccan", *Indian Economic and Social History Review* [IESHR], X1. [March 1974], pp. 74-91. However, most Mughal documents from the Deccan provinces do not distinguish between the two levels of *zamīndārs* whereas primary *zamīndārs* were nothing more than peasants [*ri'āya*]. *Land Control and Social Structure in History*, [R.E. Frykenberg, ed., in S. Nurul Ḥasan, Aspects of *Zamīndāri* System in the Deccan, 1695-1707, pp. 17-21, *PHIC*, 1969].

in advance while in the remaining half of the *rusum* which are taken every year by the government yet in Bijapur it is totally different where previously Rs 10,000 were realised while Rs 1,00,000 remained unrealised after the grant of the *faramin*[1].

Although *deshmukhs* [and *zamīndārs*] were autochothonous lords of the land, most of the *deshmukhs*, as a result of generations of transmitted experience became collaborators of the imperial administration in the Deccan under Aurangzeb as well. The Mughal provincial *dīwāns* used to make contracts, and negotiate continued terms of service with these intermediaries for creating a formal link between the state and the *deshmukhs* where after the *deshmukhs* received a patent of office or *sanad*, couched in Persian, providing up to 5% allowance on tax-collected, retention of tax-free lands, and protection for *deshmukhs* of the local position and status. They also used to execute bonds promising to pay in installment, stipulated appointment fee, to collect taxes in collaboration with the agents of the *jāgīrdārs* or *karorīs*[of the *khāliṣa*], to submit required periodic reports, and to encourage extension of cultivation[2].

The *deshmukhs* or *desāis* were hereditary chiefs or *zamīndārs* of a *pargana*. Furthermore in the Deccan provinces *zamīndārs* usually meant regional [*pargana*] aristocrats, *nāyāks*, *muniwārs*, *deshmukhs*, *desāis*, *deshpāndes* and so on. Any how the so called primary *zamīndārī* system of north India type was generally absent in the Deccan[3]. They were usually peasant by caste. The importance of such local magnates in the local administration of the Mughal Deccan was well established as they had to be maintained and created throughout due to political and social necessities. *Deshpande*, the hereditary accountant was a Brahmin, because of his literacy.

The myth of the invincibility of the Mughal might was so important a factor that it had made the *zamīndārs* submissive and subservient in the Mughal Deccan. When Marathas under Shivajī appeared to have challenged the Mughal might the *zamīndārs* in the Deccan became recalcitrant and tumultuous. A contemporary observer criticized the Maratha-Mughal conflict even at the very beginning as recorded here under:

> "Most of the villages, in the *ṣūbas* of the Deccan are in control of the *deshmukhs* and the *deshpāndes* of the *parganas*. In the country which is under the possession of our men, a number of *deshmukhs*

1. IJCI/32/8-1.
2. *Cf.*, J.F. Richards, 'The Imperial Crisis in the Deccan'. *Journal of Asian Studies*, XXXV, No. 2, Feb, 1976, pp. 252-3.
3. *Cf.*, *CEHI*, I, p. 254.

and without [acquiring] the *sanad* they are misappropriating the *rusum* and *inā'm*"[1].

Bhimsen opined that the *zamīndārs'* support to Shivajī emboldened him to challenge the Mughal power in the Deccan; however, after Shivajī's death they became the active collaborators of the Mughals in oppressing the peasantry[2].

The *deshmukhs*, sometimes, connived with the mischievous elements; a daily news report of October 1661 brings to light such connivance of the *deshmukh* of *pargana* Lohnair, who used to keep Bhils for committing theft according to the statement of the *muqaddams* of the area[3]. Even, Chait Singh, the *zamīndār* of village Mansul, of the said *pargana*, was alleged to be a villain as he used to indulge in highway robbery, probably on the invitation of the *deshmukh*[4]. The *deshmukhs* of the Mughal Deccan, occasionally remained in collusion with the *deshmukhs* of the Deccan kingdoms, *viz*. Dawal, *deshmukh* of *pargana* Varval, in *sarkār* Nander who was in league with Subhāni, *deshmukh* of *pargana* Kaulas with Quṭbul Mulk's territory was ordered to be arrested by Shāista Khān, in May 1662[5].

However, such stray incidents never posed a threat to the Mughal endeavours of systemisation of Imperial administration in the Mughal Deccan, which was also aimed at restoring internal peace and security.

Since *deshmukhs* and *deshpāndes* were generally hereditary, they invariably held their appointments on the basis of a *sanad* or Imperial order and they could also be removed from their posts by the Emperor. That is why we find a daily news report of the city of Ellichpur in *ṣūba* Berar conveying that Kishna, *deshpāndia*, dismissed from the office had filed a suit with the *mutaṣaddi* of the city of Aurangabad claiming his hereditary rights.

But the appointment of *deshmukhs* and *deshpāndes* was, as a rule, for life and so while *jāgirdārs* came and went, they stayed on permanently.

The *gumāshta* [agent] of every *jāgīrdār*, had to rely utmost on the help of these two officials in assessing and realising the revenue. They were bound to assist him, but they were equally responsible to check the accounts of collections and to see that no irregular exactions were made from the peasantry[6].

The *Desāis* played a crucial role in financial administration of the Deccan provinces, as they used to be clubbed with *qānūngos* and *muqaddams*[7].

1. IJC, Nos. 259-260 as stated in M. Alam, The *zamīndārs* p. 75.
2. *Dilkushā*, ff 130, [a] 140 [a].
3. M.A. Nayeem, *Mughal Documents*, I, ii, p. 527; SWD, p. 193.
4. *Ibid*, pp. 89-90.
5. *Ibid*, p. 128; *SWD*, p. 127; *Ibid*, p. 19.
6. *Cf., Mughal Nobility*, p. 87; *SDAR*, pp. 21-22; 25-6;
7. *SWD*, pp. 133-47.

In addition to intermediary *zamīndārs*, there were also other *zamīndārs* who used to pay the stipulated *peshkash*, which was, totally distinct from *mal*[1], that is again confirmed from a document of June 1659 of the Deccan that [a rolling of ten year average on crop returns and market prices and *peshkash* of the *zamīndārs* from all the *parganas* of the Deccan was collected[2].

The above-mentioned categories of intermediaries [*zamīndārs*] held prescriptive rights of controlling the peasantry over a specified area were allowed to retain a minor share of the formal revenue-demand, revenue-free lands, and enjoy their local positions of power in lieu of enforcement of the revenue realisation and order in the countryside.

Although reference to the principality of Ramnagar occurs in the Ā'īn yet its chief is said to have submitted to Akbar [*Mirat*, I, 134]. However, a fresh imposition of tribute [*peshkash*] was negotiated in 1638 [Lahori, II, 109]. But *Mirat Suppl.*, 228, shows it as a separate capital *sarkār*. Though its modern capital, Dharampur is not mentioned and in our sources yet it required this name only in 1766, [Bombay, Gazetteer, Vol. VI, 25n].

We have find a representation of Bindraban under the seal of Yar Ali that "*Pargana* Ramgir comprising four *chaklas* and 27 *tappas* whose length from East to West is 100 *kurohs* and the width from South to North is 35 *kurohs* as majority of the central portion [*qalb*] sand the gregoreous jungle in view of the fact that a portion of the said *pargana* comprises the *khaliṣa sharifa* where the maximum is in assignment of the different *jāgirdārs*. The miscreants have become obtained power and majority where the mountains and jungles of the aforesaid *pargana* have become the abode and resort of the refractory and other mischief-mongers and miscreants. Meanwhile the plenipotentiary of the ancestoral slave has written that due to the grace of the [Almighty Lord] the *faujdār* of Ramgir is with the increase of 750 *swars* conditional upon the devotee of the sublime court was ordered that the grace and benediction of this week this *pargana* is included in the *khaliṣa* and the requirements worthy of work are assigned so that the duties of such service in length and width and the custody of the *reza-riaya* [peasents] is (i) God the Almighty willing is granted so that increase in prosperity and its administration and control is done otherwise its *faujdari* is alloted to such a person over the head of a contingent comprising the 300 *swars* from the contingent of the late Khan-i-Zaman and above one thousand matchlockmen should remain with the destiny of

1. *Cf.*, *Nuskha-i Dilkushā*, f. 140 [a].
2. *The Mughal Documents* [I, ii, fasimile. role of Doc. No. V/210 *mawāzana*. Ac. No. 4958 of AP State Archives.

the aforesaid person so as to cope with the miscreants. It was most difficult to be communicable.

The *peshkash* was also collected from the big *zamīndārs* as well, who occasionally pleaded for its exemption *viz.,* the *zamīndār* of Rāmnagar, sought the same, by offering some gift, through Saiyid Manṣur, *faujdār* of Baglāna[1], in view of the fact that a fresh imposition of tribute on this principality was negotiated in 1638[2].

The brother of 'Abdul Hadi, *zamīndār* of Yalgharp held the rank of 150/100, who was granted *jāgīr* from the said *pargana*, *sarkār* Nander, *ṣūba* Ẓafarabad *alias* Telingāna in 1659[3]. The *zamīndār*, in his capacity helped the imperial administration. We have learnt from a daily news report of *sarkār* Ramgir about the visit of the above said 'Abdul Bari, *zamīndār* for his meeting with the *faujdār* thereat as they were so much hand in glow that they jointly used to go for hunting.

But notwithstanding this mutual understanding the *jāgīrdārs* were many a time compelled to subdue the rebellious *zamīndārs*. Jalāl Khān Kākar, in a similar incident of crushing a defiant *zamīndār* marched towards Hoshangabad, [in *sarkār* Handia].

Sometimes the officials of big *zamīndārs* indulged in burning the villages as we come to know from a daily news report of Ellichpur city that the *deshpāndia* of *pargana* Karamandgaon represented about the burning and devastation of three villages of the said *pargana* by the men of the *zamīndār* of Chanda, which illicited serious action by the Mughal administration by seeking the *zamīndār's* explanation in the first instance. Strict action was also initiated against Durga, son of Bābū, *ḥawaladār* of *pargana* Sarpur, belonging to Chanda [principality], for lifting away the goods and cattle from the *parganas* of *sarkār* Ramgir[4].

The *zamīndārs*, sometimes, possessed *manṣab*, *viz*., 'Abdul Bari, *alias* Allu, neo-Muslim, had besieged Udairāj, *zamīndār* of *pargana* Sibalgaon, holding the rank of 100 *ẓat*. A battle was fought between them leading to causalities on both sides. Ultimately the said *zamīndār* concluded a peace, gave Rs 1,000 in cash and one horse and Jalal Khān reciprocated it by gifting a horse and returning from there in May 1662[5].

1. *SWD*, p. 134.
2. Lahori, II, p. 109. The *zamīndār* of Ramnagar solicited the permission to visit the imperial court which was granted and a *farmān* was promised to be issued. *Blochet Suppl. Persian*, No. 482, f. 97 [a].
3. M.A. Nayeen *Mughal Documents*, I, ii, facsimile Doc No. H/I/2. Telingāna was no more a *ṣūba* after 1657 and its reference is curious *Cf., Atlas*, Sheet 15/Notes; *ibid*, pp. 90, 120-121; M.A. Nayeem, *Mughal Documents*, I, ii, p. 21.
4. SWD, p. 297.
5. SWD, p. 86.

Similar incident was reported on 16th May 1662 about the chastisement of Donger, *zamīndār* of Mahagaon, [*sarkār* Mahur, *ṣūba* Berar] by Sarfarāz Khān [Deccani], *jāgīrdār*. The *zamīndār* who became recalcitrant was chased from the mountain where he had taken shelter to another mountain[1]. Jalāl Khān also planned to admonish the same *zamīndār* by his own troops without any help from Sarfarāz Khān, Deccani [otherwise the country would have been destroyed by excessive marching of armies][2].

The local collaborators of the Marathas including the *deshmukhs,* if we take into consideration the statement of Bhimsen, who accuses that, the *zamīndārs* and the *deshmukhs* supported Shivajī[3]. But the evidence adduced by us, during the first phase of Aurangzeb's Deccan policy does not fully corraborate this assumption, because Shivajī himself suppressed many a *deshmukhs* to hide his *swaraja* and he ruthlessely exterminated some of the *deshmukh-zamīndārs*[4] which was their home country or due to which many of them joined service either under 'Ādil Shāhi or Mughal governments. Shivajī even tried to convert *peshkashi zamīndārs* into *khiraji* ones. Furthermore, the importance of the Deccan and the Maratha revolts increased only when Aurangzeb himself moved south in 1681[5].

Haqiqat [true facts] of the *peshkash* of Udaiji Ram *alias* Babu Rai *deshmukh* of the *parganas* of *sarkār* Mahur etc that Rs 2,50,000 in the name of Udaiji Ram *alias* Jagjivan, father of the aforesaid person in accordance with the *Tamassuk* of 25th of the month of Khurdad 8th regnal year of His Magesty [*Ala Hazrat*] the title of Emperor Shahjahan in the *awarja* of the *mukhtar* of the *mansabdars* in accordance with the calculation [*tashkhkhus*] of the former *diwans nuskha* according to the specification [*nuskha*] of Nawab Jamlatul Mulki Madarul Mahani Allami *Fahani* Jumalatul Mulk Asad Khan.

It is no more than an intractable problem to assess the strength of Imperial authority in the Deccan countryside because the imperial administration successfully assimilated, armed, militant local chiefs and notables into the imperial state as *zamīndārs*. It is therefore, more appropriate to call the *zamīndārs* of all hues as Mughal collaborators in the Deccan till 1681.

1. SWD, p. 88.
2. M.A. Nayeem, *Mughal Documents*, I, ii, p. 19.
3. *Nuskha-iDilkushā*, f 140 [a].
4. *CEHI*, I, p. 197.
5. Satish Chandra, 'The Maratha Policy and its Agrarian Consequences', in B. Parsad [ed.] *Ideas in History*, Delhi.

SECTION [B]
[1682-1707]

V

Expansion of Mughal Power in the Deccan

[I] Territorial Expansion and Creation of New *Ṣūbās*

From the imperial viewpoint, the revolt of Prince Akbar, during the war in Rajputana in 1681 finally brought a crisis situation in the Deccan, where he sought refuge at Sambhaji's court[1], which was, to the utter disliking of Aurangzeb. Consequent upon the conclusion of the Rajput campaign Aurangzeb moved south, with his entire court and a large Imperial army, to Aurangabad, which served as the headquarters for the Mughal Viceroy.

There is no denying the fact that in Aurangzeb's move south, the usual motive for expansion was very much present in order to obtain more and more resources to maintain the alligence of the nobility. Furthermore, failure of Bijapur to control the Maratha menace and the support of Golcunda to the Marathas compelled Aurangzeb to dispense fully of the Marathas and stabilise the southern frontiers of the Mughal Empire permanently by annexing Bijapur and Golcunda. Thus, Aurangzeb ultimately decided on the solution which he on the scene had argued for thirty years before: complete elimination of the last troublesome tributary states of Bijapur and Golcunda by their outright annexation[2].

Thus, consequent upon the march of Aurangzeb to the Deccan in 1681-2 accompanied with his household, court and grand army began an era of continuous conquests which began to change geographical contours of South India. It may be convincingly argued that recurring wars and incessant diplomatic pressure had a sense of inevitability on an irreversible sequence of events, which ended with the final victories over Bijapur and Golcunda in 1686-87. Aurangzeb had conquered and annexed the Sulṭanats of Bijapur, Golcunda and the Maratha Kingdom by 1689, whereafter his

1. *History of Aurangzeb,* IV, B. 35, ff.
2. Richards, *Mughal Administration*, pp. 45-46; M.N. Pearson, 'Shivāji and the Decline of the Mughal Empire, Symposium: Decline of the Mughal Empire', *Journal of Asian Studies*, Vol. XXXV, [February 1976] p. 231.

armies launched a protracted seige of the Maratha stronghold of Jinji, the far southern refuge of Raja Ram, the new Maratha leader and conquered it in 1698. Thus, the Mughal Empire expanded confidently in the Deccan during the late 17th century [see map of six Mughal Deccan Provinces in late senventeenth century].

It is in this backdrop that one should see the expansion of the Mughal Empire in the Deccan, which in penultimate analysis resulted into the territorial expansion and creation of new *ṣūbās.*

In 1685, the Mughal army moved into Bijapur, and staying outside the capital began investment and massive siege and in September 1686 after a costly military engagement, Sikandar 'Ādil Shāh was capitulated and Bijapur became a Mughal province. Thus, the *ṣūba* of Bijapur was finally created upon the annexation of the 'Ādilshāhi Kingdom of Bijapur, which constituted the entire former Kingdom with its boundaries existed on the eve of annexation, of course, with the exception of Naldrug and Gulburga, which, however, had been annexed some years earlier[1]. The Mughal *ṣūba* of Bijapur comprised the following *sarkārs* and 2 principalities:

> *sarkār* Dabhol, *sarkār* Parenda, *sarkār* Raybagh, *sarkār* Miraj, *sarkār* Akluj, *sarkār* Bijapur, *sarkār* Naldrug, *sarkār* Gulbarga, *sarkār* Nuṣratabad-Sagar, *sarkār* Belguam, *sarkār* Torgul, *sarkār* Mudgal, *sarkār* Adoni, *sarkār* Raichur, *sarkār* Nadyal, *sarkār* Bankapur, *sarkār* Hanigeri and two tributary principalities of Bednur or Kanara and Mysore[2].

During the siege of Bijapur the Mughals intercepted a message of sending reinforcement comprising an army of 40,000 by Abul Ḥasan, King of Golcunda attacking from the east on the Mughal army while Marathas attacking from the west that led to temporary conquest of Hyderabad in 1685 by the Mughals, which they vacated after a truce. In fact, Aurangzeb waited till the completion of the siege of Bijapur before directing his energies to the final conquest of Golcunda. On 14 January 1687, Aurangzeb began his final assault on Golcunda because he considered Golcunda and Maratha nexus a challenge to the Mughal authority in the Deccan.

Besides leveling charges of favouring Hinduism and Shi'ism over orthodox Islam and financing Sambhaji's attacks on the Mughal dominions while keeping Golcunda free form the Maratha entourage Abul Ḥasan was found guilty of withholding Rs 1,62,22,278 as arrears in tribute in 1687[3].

---

1. *Nuskha-i Dilkushā,* ff. 68[a], 69[b].
2. *Atlas,* Sheets 14[A] and 16[A]. Notes pp. 56-7, 63-4.
3. IJCI/2/1 as cited in Richards, *Mughal Administration,* p. 48.

After protracted siege of Golcunda fort by treachery and night escalade Aurangzeb simultaneously issued a proclamation formally annexing the entire Kingdom of Golcunda which became the Mughal province of Hyderabad as Golcunda was renamed as Hyderabad with official epithet *Darul-i Jihad* [land of war] which comprised 20 *sarkār* of Golcunda proper, located north of the Krishna R. that, however, remained literally true during the early phase.

The Mughal province of Hyderabad also contained the territory of Golcunda upon its annexation in 1687 with the exception of Ramgir which in 1656 was ceded by the QuṬb Shāh, being made later a *sarkār* of *ṣūba* Bedar[1]. The *ṣūba* of Hyderabad comprised the following *sarkārs*:

> *sarkār* Kolas, *sarkār* Elgandal, *sarkār* Koilconda, *sarkār Golcunda*, *sarkār* Bhūngir, *sarkār* Nalgonda, *sarkār* Khammam-mett, *sarkār* Elluru, *sarkār* Rajamundry, *sarkār* Sikakol, *sarkār* Pangal, *sarkār* Ghanpur, *sarkār* Devarkonda, *sarkār* Guntur, *sarkār* Kondapalle, *sarkār* Machhlipattan and *sarkār* Niẓampattan.

Aurangzeb made few drastic modifications in the boundaries of the former Kingdom of Golcunda. A far-reaching decision was made in this initial stage, that radically disputed from the previous practice, which was concerned with Aurangzeb's detachment of the Karnatak, previously administered as a single *ṣūba* under Golcunda, from administrative jurisdiction of Muḥammad Ibrāhīm, a former Golcunda general, who had suddenly defected to the Mughals, the Mughal governor of Hyderabad province. We also come to know that in 1688, the 12 *sarkārs* south of Gundlekamma and Krishna river were designated the Hyderabad Karnatak by the Mughals so as to distinguish them from the *sarkārs* conquered by Bijapur further south. The Karnatak *sarkārs* of Hyderabad were divided into Bālāghāt [uplands] and Pāinghāt [lowlands]. The Bālāghāt included *sarkār* Siddharat, *sarkār* Ganjikota, *sarkār* Gooty, *sarkār* Cumbum and *sarkār* Kanchi [seat of administration of Karnatak Pāinghāt], *sarkār* Chandragiri, *sarkār* Survepalli, *sarkār* Ūdgīr, *sarkār* Tiruvottiyur and *sarkār* Chingleput. The above *sarkārs* of Karnatak of Hyderabad were acquired by the Golcunda Kingdom in 1655.

In addition, the following *sarkārs* were also the part of Hyderabad: *sarkār* Wandiwash, *sarkār* Jinji, *sarkār* Palaiyamkottai, *sarkār* Vellore, *sarkār* Jagdev, *sarkār* Valikandapur and *sarkār* Varadavur. The Mughal province of Hyderabad was further augmented by the annexation of two principalities of Tanjavur and Trichnapalli [the Kingdom of Madura] which were submitted to the Mughals in 1694.

1. Shafiq, p. 153; Thākur La'l, f. 89[a].

The three distinct largest administrative divisions of Hyderabad i.e. Hyderabad, Golcunda and Karnatak resembled the Mughal provinces because Aurangzeb himself remained in Hyderabad for approximately four month so as to make *in situ* supervision of the assimilation of the newly conquered territories into the Mughal Empire.

It is quite interesting to note that the Karnatak of Hyderabad, only totally conquered by Golcunda by 1650s was, as a matter of fact, formed a sub-consolidation, was not as much advanced as was in Golcunda.

Keeping in view of the typical conditions prevailing in the Karnatak, the Emperor brought this entire vast region under a single administrator, with his seat at Kanchi [Conjeevaram]. Separation of the Karnatak from Golcunda or Hyderabad and its recognition as a distinct administrative and political unit has two important consequence, *viz.,* maintenance of the administrative boundary and the requirements of the Mughal administration formed a new political entity in the Deccan. The *faujdār* of Karnatak, who was at par with the Governor of Hyderabad, was directly answerable to the Emperor which decorated the status of Hyderabad as a political and economic centre because he sent his tax and tribute collections to Aurangzeb.

Thus, the gradual culmination of the long drawn imperial endeavour to conquer the Muslim Kingdoms of the Deccan resulted in the territorial expansion and the creation of two new *ṣūbās* of Bijapur and Golcunda under the centralised Imperial administration. However, administrative and political consolidation in Bijapur and Golcunda was incomplete after 1686-87. The Mughal commitment of the best military and administrative resources of the Empire to continued expansion led to further territorial expansion by the unceasing draining of wars against the Marathas in the Deccan in an eagerness for further expansion up to the sea-shores.

[II] Administative Problems of the Newly Conquered Areas

The newly conquered areas posed a many administrative problems for Aurangzeb. When Aurangzeb first considered the problems of administration in the newly annexed areas he detached the Karnatak from Hyderabad province, which was previously administered as a single province, under Golcunda, from the administrative jurisdiction of the Mughal governor of *ṣūba* Ḥaiderabad, which by any standard had far reaching administrative significance. To distinguish it from Karnatak-i Bijapur it was designated as Karnatak-i Hyderabad, which was annexed by Golcunda in late 1650s wherein political and administrative consolidation was less advanced.

In view of its peculiar prevailing conditions the Mughal emperor appointed a single administrator to this region with his seat at Kanchi[1]. It was factually a sub-kingdom whose administration was in reality a provincial headquarters at Hyderabad. The *faujdār;* if he did not combine his office with the *Dīwān;* had a *Dīwān* and other provincial officials. The central administration of Golcunda/ Hyderabad no longer controlled the tax revenues from Karnatak.

The former Golcunda Kingdom had enlisted the support of same *zamīndārs* by appointing them as commanders [*sardārs*] of locally raised horsemen or *sihbandīs*. Aurangzeb also induced *sardārs* to shift their allegiance to him. Accordingly, he ordered to 'Ali 'Askar K͟hān, the Golcunda officer, who was appointed as governor of the Karnatak in early 1688 to remove those of his subordinates sent by Abul Ḥasan Quṭb Shāh along with resumption of their *jāgīrs,* except for making an exemption in regard to the *jāgīrs* of Ismāi'l K͟hān and Yacham Nair [or Achpat Nayar] etc who were *zamīndārs* [i.e. *sardārs*] as well[2]. Thus, conciliatory endeavour was temporarily successful because Aurangzeb's orders had a soothing effect as they contained plundering attacks on the Governor of Karnatak for two years up to January 1690 because Ismāi'l K͟hān Mak͟ha, Yacham Nair and other Golcunda *sardārs* joined the Mughal service[3]. Both of them probably did not become *manṣabdārs*[4]. However, the Marathas at Jinji in December 1687 attacked and occupied Kanchi, the capital of the Hyderabad Karnatak, which began a ten-year war in the Karnatak. The above mentioned one together with two *sardārs* helped the Mughal Imperial administration in expulsing the Marathas out of Kanchi, the seat of administration, up to Wandiwash.

But the Imperial administration had always a problem of shifting loyalties of the *sardārs,* who occasionally used to engage in collaboration with the Marathas especially in 1689 when Raja Ram, brother of Sambhaji became the Maratha King. Upon the execution of Sambhaji Aurangzeb divulged his future plans to his third son Muḥammad A'zam Shāh in a *farmān,* dated 27-8 March 1689.

1. See for details: see J.F. Richards, *Mughal Administration in Golconda*, London, 1975, 62, 64 as Kancipuram.
2. Bhimsen, *Nusk͟ha-i Dikush*ā, f. 95 [a], *Cf., History of Aurangzeb*, Vol. II, pp. 567, J.F. Richards, The Hyderabad Karnatak: 1687-1707, *Modern Asian Studies*, IX, 1975, pp. 243-4.
3. *ibid.*
4. Ismai'l K͟hān Makha or Makka is frequently mentioned as *manṣabdār* in 'Inayat Jang Collection *viz.*, I/ 41/ 8-102; I/ 42/ 1-32; I/ 42/ 6-120; I/ 42/ 7-30; I/ 42/ 8-18. But he received *manṣab* in 1691-2, *Cf.*, IJC, I/ 34/ 4-20, whereas Yacham Nair or Achpat Nayar held the rank of 6000, *Nusk͟ha-i Dilkushā,* f. 112 [b].

"… there are two alternatives namely, that either Raja Rām must make his submission to the Emperor through the mediation of this Prince or that his fort [Raigarh] must be strictly besieged. The first clause concerns with the surrender of the fort, which after the capture of faithless Sambha, belongs to the Mughals and was seized by him [Raja Rām] at the instigation of some fools. He should be brought to the second clause i.e. sieze should be made vigorously and discontinue this useless talk, establish *thānas* [military check posts] and administer the territory and forts … before the commencement of the rainy season… He should proceed to Ghat [Range] on the pretext of a hunting excursion so as to acquaint with the position of Kamahi pass… Yāqut Khān due to the fooly of Nāhir Khān sent the representation of Raja Ram to the Imperial Court through his son, who did not turn up[1] …".

However, all these plans proved futile because Raja Ram moved towards Jinji from Maharashtra. The new Maratha king conceived of retaking Golcunda and Bijapur Kingdoms so as to put the Mughals on the defensive in the Deccan. Aurangzeb's alleged religious policy of destruction contemplating the temples of Karnatak alienated Yacham Nair[2], who joined Raja Rām and marched towards Karnatak. Hyderabad, joined by Ismāi'l Khān Makka along with former Golcunda officers and local *zamīndārs* outnumbering and isolating the Mughal detachment resulting into the flight of the *faujdār* of Karnatak-i Hyderabad[3].

However, the Imperial administration had overcome this problem because by October 1690 the Mughals under Zulfiqar Khān, once more fully controlled all the key points in the Hyderabad Karnatak. Ismāi'l, sensing his chance for recovery from this debacle rejoined the Mughal service. We find that not only Ismāi'l Khān Makka but his son Parwarish Khān also joined the Imperial service. Ismāi'l Khān held the rank of 5,000/ 4,000, six-monthly, in 1698-9 for which he was assigned a sum of 4,17,00,000 *dāms* whereas his son enjoyed the *manṣab* of 1,500/ 500, four-monthly. When he complained to Aurangzeb that 'I am unable to work, if contingent is provided from the government and something is granted for the livelihood than I can proceed to my posting' the emperor ordered for total payment of his *jāgīr-i zāt* and that of his son as per rule while after obtaining the bond for the contingent [*tabinān*] the remaining half be granted wherefrom he like[4]. Later Aurangzeb transferred him to Maharashtra as *faujdār* of Raheri

1. National Archives of India, Acquired Documents NAI – 1697.
2. This has become a subject of unnecessary contention *Cf.*, J.F. Richards, *op. cit.*, pp. 62-64 and *idem* The Hyderabad Karnatik pp. 244-47.
3. *History of Aurangzeb,* Vol. V, p. 68.
4. IJC, I/ 41/ 12-39.

with the rank of 6,000/ 5,000 in place of 'Abdur Razzāq Lari. Thus, the former rebel, detached from his holdings in the Hyderabad Karnatak was profitably re-employed outside Golcunda by the imperial administration to avoid any problem[1].

Contrary to Ismāi'l Khān Makka, Yacham Nair began a series of raids from his home territories against the neighbouring Mughal *sarkārs,* while Zulfiqār Khān lured him back into Mughal fold by a high rank of 6,000 *ẓat* and an enormous *jāgīr* yielding revenues worth 9,00,000 rupees and subsequently on Aurangzeb's orders executed him in 1694 for treason[2], whereafter his eldest son KumaruYachama Naidu was allowed to succeed with a rank of 6,000/ 6,000 with all titles and honours of his father. Thus, the Mughal administration succeeded in controlling the evidently troublesome area[3].

Similarly Mughal administration successfully dealt with another important Telgu, Sāyapanair Kumār Venkatadari [or Sauyapanid], a *muniwār* and the Kumma chief of the northern districts of Karnatak as 'Ali Mardān Khān, *faujdār* of Hyderabad Karnatak confirmed his local position with all privileges and perquisites enjoyed under Quṭb Shāhs[4]. The Mughals followed the Quṭb Shāhi tradition of allowing local peace keeping operations to *muniwārs* or *kāwalis* for policing the major roads and markets over large trade of Hyderabad Karnatak to resolve such administrative problems[5].

There remained instability and political uncertainty during the last decade of 17th century in the Hyderabad Karnatak region as compared to other *ṣūbās* of the Deccan because war with the Marathas became the main concern for the Mughal administration. Therefore, no real effort, like that of Golcunda, was made for assimilating the Hyderabad Karnatak to the *ẓabt* or standard administration; instead the *faujdār* thereat and his *qila'dārs* and *thānadārs* scattered throughout the region merely endeavoured to hold on in difficult times. That is why that during intervals between Maratha depredations, these isolated officials collected whatever revenues could be gathered, but did little else, due to unfavourable circumstances.

Aurangzeb had established a semblance of a provincial administration by placing the establishment of Karnatak under 'Ali Mardān Khān, who,

1. *Ma'āsirul Umara,* Vol. I, p. 291; *Ma'asir-i 'Ālamgīrī,* pp. 357, 369, 387, 550.
2. *Nuskha-i Dilkushā,* fol. 116[a]; Manucci, *Storia do Mogor III,* 271, 2; *History of Aurangzeb*, V, pp. 95-6.
3. T. Rama Row, *Biographical Sk* etc.*hes of the Rajas of Venkatagiri, Madras,* 1875, pp. 44-7.
4. J.F. Richards, *op. cit.,* pp. 249-50.
5. *Ibid.,* p. 250.

from 1690 to 1692, acted as both *faujdār* and *Dīwān*. The Karnatak *faujdār* succeeded in establishing and maintaining his authority because he was even able to assert his right to complete control over all revenue agents in the Karnatak including salaried agents of the *Dīwān* and those serving under Babu Pandit, head *qānūngo* of *ṣūba* Hyderabad, because Aurangzeb ordered that they report to 'Ali Mardān K͟hān, not to his adversary Zulfiqār K͟hān. Even he did not show his willingness to accept Rs 13,70,000 of all the *maḥāls* of *sihbandī* which was granted to former *faujdārs* of Karnatak due to which it was resumed to *pāibāqī*, instead he insisted that after assigning the *maḥāl* recommended by Zulfiqār K͟hān, the balance of pay claim paid from the [Imperial] *K͟hāliṣa* and got it sanctioned as well and that too in *hūn* amounting to 7,70,000 *hūns* [Rs 25,02,500] without getting deducted the difference in exchange rate[1].

Due to capture of 'Ali Mardān K͟hān by the Marathas from 1692 to 1694 the entire Karnatak came purely under military administration as Aurangzeb gave full administrative powers to Zulfiqār K͟hān, who suffered severe setbacks and the region was so steadily battered by the Mughal-Maratha movements that a contemporary participants of these campaigns observed that "under previous regimes [i.e. Golcunda and Bijapur], the Karnatak had been extensively cultivated, now a many places had been converted into wastes due to the passage of armies who oppressed the people"[2].

Consequent upon the final capitulation of Jinji in 1698 the position had changed considerably because of the appointment of Dāūd K͟hān Pannī, as deputy *faujdār* of Hyderabad Karnatak and subsequently of the seven *sarkārs* of recently conquered Bijapur Karnatak. Dāūd K͟hān Panni streamlined the administration of the Karnatak. But he had to concede to Maratha extortions which, however, could not ultimately restore order to the confused administration of the region as per the expectations of the central Imperial administration.

But the immediate problem in 1690s was the financing of a large, locally raised, military force in the Karnatak Hyderabad and the Karnatak *Dīwān* had to finance over a dozen big fortresses seized from the Quṭb Shāh. Furthermore, the *Dīwān* was also bound to find funds so as to make payments to 37,000 *sihbandīs*. Finally the central treasury assumed complete responsibility for pay and supplies of the fortresses from the *K͟hāliṣa* parganas of the Karnatak including payment of the 37,000

1. IJC, I/ 34/ 4-20 to I/ 34/ 4-28 containing complete details of 'Ali Mardān K͟hān's assignments etc
2. *Nusk͟ha-i Dilkushā*, fol. 114[a].

sihbandīs under the command of 'Ali Mardān Khān[1]. Almost the entire formal revenues amounting to Rs 82,00,223 of Karnataka went to internal administration and military defence and the Emperor could draw profit, if any, only from the production of the diamond mines in the Karnatak because Aurangzeb used whatever revenues could be extracted from the Karnataka to finance 8 years long struggle against the Marathas at Jinji. Upon the capture of Jinji by the Mughals in 1698 they assumed control of the additional seven districts designated as the Bijapur Karnataka yielding Rs 65,00,000. However, Aurangzeb's military engagements and the tremendously deteriorating condition in the Deccan precluded any concerted endeavour at administrative consolidation. In the last decade of his reign Aurangzeb was content to have a military occupation of the Karnatak, to such an extent that even the entire income was expanded in meeting out the pay claims of the *sihbandīs* and the contingents of the forts. In order to reduce expenditure of the Hyderabad Karnatak in 1703 an excellent *faujdār* was recommended by removing numerous *thānadārs* and *faujdārs* because one fort commandant was sufficient in each fort and Rs 15,00,000 of *sihbandi* paid to him and the contingent of each fort was to remain in the *morchal* [the watch at the door of a fortress] of every fortress paying way for saving Rs 30,00,000 to be included in the *khāliṣa*. Aurangzeb approved saving but declined appointment of a new *faujdār* or any deputy of Nuṣrat Jung as it would become counter-productive while appreciating savings in *sihbandi* the same was ordered to be handed over to Dāūd Khān. Since even half of the revenues were not accruing to the government which position could be averted by removing *thānadārs* and assigning *pāibāqī* in the salary of *sihbandi* transferring some excellent *maḥāls* in entirety to *Khāliṣa* in lieu of savings in *sihbandi* so as to achieve visible economy [in government expenditure]. The implementation of this scheme was possible in consultation with Khān Nuṣrat Jung which was also corroborated by the said Khān's letter. When the Emperor's orders were solicited for submitting a self-contained note in response to his letter for His Majesty's perusal, then Aurangzeb replied that 'since it was the work of the *dīwān* let it be submitted to Asad Khān[2]'.

The savings, affected in this way were utilised for defraying the salaries of the troops engaged in wasteful siezes of Maratha fortresses in the western Deccan due to Aurangzeb's policy of *qilāgīrī* [conquering the forts] versus *mulkgīrī* [conquering the country]. By 1703 the economic profile of the entire Deccan was as tabulated hereunder[3]:

1. IJC, I/ 34/ 4-20 to I/ 34/ 4-28.
2. IJC, I/ 45/ 5-86.
3. IJC, I/ 45/ 5-85.

Table - 1

Sl.No.	Classification of Revenue	Annual Receipts in Rupees and Annas	Percent of Total
1.	*Khāliṣa*	2,03,893.1	1.30
2.	*Jāgīrs* [Assigned to other *manṣabdārs*]	35,06,959.3½	22.30
3.	*Jāgīrs* [Assigned to Fort Commanders and others i.e. troops]	11,21,037.11	7.13
4.	*Sih-bandī* [under Nuṣrat Jang *Qiladārs* and *Thānadārs* in Karnataka]	70,30,641.4	44.71
5.	*Maḥal-i* Kaveripattan etc under the control of the *Zamīndārs*	13,72,402.8	8.73
6.	*Pāibāqī* [including under control of Pāligārs, *peshkash* at Rs 3,79,530]	7,09,542.5	4.51
7.	*Pāibāqī* [including under control of Pāligars, *peshkash* at Rs 8,30,650]	17,79,966.13½	11.32
	Total	**1,57,24,443**	**100**

The above table demonstrates some financial advantages to the Mughal administration as a sequel of the Maratha capitulation. The central revenue administration attempted to alleviate the *jāgīr* crisis by allocating lands worth 3.5 million rupees to *manṣabdārs* who were not holding official positions in the *ṣūba*. We also find similar details about the economic position of the entire Karnataka in 1706 where the value of the *Khāliṣa* lands jumped fivefold to nearly one million rupees per annum as compared to 1703 position. Tribute from Pāligārs added over 0.7 million rupees as compared to 1.2 million rupees of 1703 under this head. As far as allocation under *sih-bandis* is concerned it declined to 5.25 million rupees in 1706 in comparison to over 7 million rupees, which suggests that some improvements were made in this respect in the light of the above mentioned suggestions[4]. But the central question which remains to be answered as yet relates is the extent to which the actual collections approached above figures. If may be presumed that Dāūd Khān's vigorous efforts brought the collections reasonably close to the actual demand and agricultural position also began to improve considerably. The Mughal occupation of the Karnatak failed to achieve administrative unity and consolidation and even it could not be brought under the *ẓabt* system; instead the Mughals used whatever administrative machinery was left by the Quṭb Shāhs due to wars with Marathas. Notwithstanding the administrative failure the Mughal officers defended this enormous region against the determined internal and external

4. *SDAR*, pp. 233-5.

opposition. It is equally important from administrative and political point of view that the Mughals eventually expelled the Marathas completely out of the Bijapur Karnatak below Madras.

The administrative problems in newly conquered areas had its various manifestations because the Mughal control failed to carry with it increased political and administrative consolidation. For example, extension of the Imperial boundaries led to a perceptible decline in Mughal state power as exercised from Hyderabad, whereas the Telegu warriors, who in previous regime, served as troop commanders [*sardārs*] and local administrative intermediaries emerged self-sufficient *rajas* especially in Godavari region of coastal Andhra or the district of Srikakulam [Persian: Sikakul], Rajamundry, and Elluru as a result of Mughal conquest of the area. We find the QuṬb Shāh could not introduce the system of *parganas* systematically. The more productive narrow coastal plains were subject to direct military control of Mughal Imperial administrators. Furthermore, both Rajamundry and Elluru districts had more systematic administrative arrangement where *deshmukhs* of Razu caste helped in tax-collection because they were also collaborators and intermediaries under the Mughals as the Imperial administration at Hyderabad negotiated terms with these intermediaries and auxiliaries comprising *deshmukhs, muniwārs* and *sardārs*.

In order to avoid further administrative problems Aurangzeb left untouched the administrative arrangements and old personnel in more remote parts of the newly conquered *ṣūbās* including Godavari region side by side attempting to establish a formal administrative structure in uniformity with other Mughal provinces.

True to his reputation, Aurangzeb diplomatically continued the old officials temporarily, because Saiyid 'Abdullāh *sar-i lashkar* of Quṭb Shāh served under the administrative control of 'Ali Mardān Khān, Governor of Rajamundry and later *faujdār* of Hyderabad Karnataka and helped the Imperial administration till his death in post 1694. Thereafter Muṣtafā Quli Khān was appointed *faujdār* of Srikakulam, Elluru, Kondapalli and Kondavidu districts and the parts of Machhilipattam and Niẓāmpattan. By doubling his administrative responsibilities Aurangzeb did not increase the *faujdār*'s military and administrative establishments[1].

During his tenure of administration he strived hard to collect maximum revenues most ruthlessly even from his Razu and Valama *sardārs*, putting in disarray the equilibrium of political and administrative system.

1. *Cf.,* J.F. Richards, 'Mughal Retreat from Costal Andhra', *Journal of Royal Asiatic Society*, 1978, p. 54.

Even his rapacious avarice disgusted Sitarama Pasupati, a Razu *sardār* [commander] who for the first few years of Mughal administration remained a faithful auxiliary. Such administrative problems were further accentuated by the continuous expropriation of the Telgu chief culminating into the rebellion of Sitarama Pasupati in September 1694 and the *faujdār*'s efforts at pacification and settlement miserably failed. The prevailing draught and partial failure encouraged dissidence by smaller chiefs as well. In 1695, the rebels dictated terms to the *faujdār*, who delegated all administrative authority to his nephew accordingly.

Taking advantage of this humiliating agreement Jan Sipār Khān, sought his son's appointment as *faujdār* to restore Mughal prestige which was lost due to his total disregard for the proper conduct of administration. However, Aurangzeb directed each *faujdār* in Hyderabad to send the reinforcements to Muṣtafā Quli Khān[1], which saved the situation. But during temporary halt in 1696 the *faujdār* was unable to give any meaningful consolidation to his area of control, instead in 1697 the rebellion was again broke out making rebel coalition overwhelmingly victorious leading to the defeat of Imperialists and the death of Muṣtafā Quli Khān. Jān Sipār Khān's desire was temporarily fulfilled due to the appointment of his son as *faujdār*, which he had to vacate subsequently in favour of Faqīrullāh Khān, son of the deceased *faujdār*. But he also lost the coveted post which was assigned to Mehdi Khān Bek, who in 1700 faced rebellion of nearly all Razu *sardārs*, again paying why for the succession of Faqīrullāh Khān as *faujdār* of Srikakulam in 1702. But the failure of local administration was detrimental to the Mughal interests. The lock luster of Mughal administration of coastal Andhra gave much autonomy to this region as state within state began to emerge there.

Riza Khān, former Mughal officer turned bandit chief came right on the gates of Machilipatnam with a force of 9,000 to 10,000 men in February, 1703 whose plundering and daring ritually closed the Machilipatnam – Hyderabad trade routes from his capital at Wakinkira, he captured and held Kondavidu Guntur districts for several months during which period as out parties to ravage the country side thus met with little or no resistance either from the Mughal *faujdar* or from the local Telgu aristrocracy. Simultaneously the Bedar leader Pidiyah Nayak who executed a long distance said from his force. Unfortunately marching from his capital at Wakinkira he captured and held fort in the Guntur district for several months. This could become possible due to the engagement of Faqirullah Khan in a conflict with Koldinder Ranga Razu *deshmukh* and *maniwar* of Elluru district as in February 1703 he made a firm demand of Ranga Razu

1. *Akhbārāt*, Sitamau transcript, 39 [6 Zilhijja], p. 45.

for his arrears of revenue from Elluru district. Runga Razu immediately took his family and followers north across the Godavari and return what troops he could muster with the help of Raju Chiefs in that area where Faqirullah Khan started chasing him which however remained unfulfilled due to change of Rustam Dil Khān, who started tax collection with utmost brutality in this region, that was harmful to the Mughal administration which provided a Mughal retreat from direct administration over Srikakulam, Rajamundry and Elluru districts and thereby making Mughal officials in effectual figureheads, which gradually diminished Mughal administrative and political control there.

Since the Mughal administration encountered troubles in conquering Bijapur due to the buffer kingdom of Pam Nayak, the Bedar ruler, strategically located between Bijapur and Golcunda as Sakar, the heavily fortified capital, was his seat of administration, where from he sent all available contingents and provisions during the siege of Bijapur and subsequently of Golcunda. Aurangzeb reattributed him by occupying Sakar through negotiations and renaming it Nuṣratabad and Pam Nayak and his family etc were brought to Aurangzeb, who granted him the *manṣab* of 5,000/ 4,000[1]. His sons Jagna[2] and Nand[3] became *amirs* like members of Pam Nayak's entourage *viz.*, Pidiya Nayak[4], all of whom are designated as Deccani *zamīndārs* in our sources. Aurangzeb utilised their services[5] side by side completing Mughal conquest of Bedar territories by also ceding Raichūr controlled by another Bedar chief. But the Bedars still continued raising problems for the local administration especially by Pidiya Nayak, [a Mughal *manṣabdār*] nephew and adopted son of Pām Nāyak]. He slipped from the Mughal camp on the pretext of getting new recruits and fresh supplies and equipments and silently moved to Wakinkira with his family and followers where he fortified the town, emplaced the guns and collected more troops. Therefore he created administrative problems by collecting the taxes from villages near Wakinkira and blocking the major roads. Furthermore the Bedar troops detained and plundered all caravans passing through the region, and raising his strength to 14-15,000 Bedar archers and musketeers and 4-5,000 cavalry. Pidiya Nayak delayed serious Mughal attention from 1688 to 1691 notwithstanding the fact that the revenue realisation in Nuṣratabad [Sakar] came to a standstill in 1691 due to the commotion of Bedars[6].

1. *Nuskha-i Dilkushā*, f. 95[b], I.A. Arshi [ed.] Tārikh-i Muḥammadi, 1099 AH.
2. Jagna Nayak held the rank of 5,000 / 5,000, *SDAR*, p. 205, Manuir, f. 205[b].
3. Nand Nayak held the *manṣab* of 1,500 / 700, *SDAR*, p. 205.
4. Paraya Nayak or Pidiya Nayak was granted the *manṣab* of 5,000/ 5,000.
5. *Muntakhabul Lubāb*, II, p. 370. *Cf., History of Aurangzeb*, V, pp. 214-5.
6. IJC, I/ 33/ 7-46, I/ 34/ 3-9.

Pidiya Nayak, the leader of the Bedars claimed a legitimate right to rule, which predated the Mughal invasion of Pam Nayak's Kingdom. Aurangzeb was right in ignoring his claim by recognizing Jugna Nayak holding *manṣab* of 2,500/ 1,500 one of Pam Nayak's natural sons as "legitimate heir to that country[1]". He also became *deshmukh*[2] of Nuṣratabad *Sakār*.

The Mughal expedition against Wakinkira in 1691 proved abortive as Pidiya Nayak paid 9,00,000 rupees for undisturbed possession of Wakinkira; however till 1696 his raids into the newly conquered Mughal territories grew more and more damaging to the east in *ṣūba* Hyderabad and to the west of Gulbarga *sarkār* of *ṣūbā* Bijapur to the extent that Aurangzeb himself took notice of it that the men of Pidiya Nayak were realising revenues of *parganas* near Bijpur and ordered Khwāṣ Khān to enquire from Rudra and report to him[3].

It appears that temporary reconciliation between Pidiya Nayak and the Mughal administration took place because we are informed that in 1698-99 he had made a representation for grant of *jāgīr,* which automatically entailed *manṣab.* However, due to some unforeseen eventuality he could not visit the Emperor thereby depriving himself of any *jāgīr* assignment[4].

In 1700, Khān Firuz Jung pleaded *sardeshmukhī* etc of *pargana.* Kankūrtī Koki and Talikota etc *maḥāl* of *ṣūba* Bijapur and the *rusūm* [perquists], *in'ām* lands and villages of Nuṣratabad [Sakar] etc for Pidiya Naik, which was acceded to by the Emperor, who remarked that "whatever Pam Nayak enjoyed during the reign of Sulṭan Muḥammad 'Ādil Khān as per the authentic *sanad* was approved and a portion from 'Ali 'Ādil Khān's government would also be granted he should demand the *sanads* and inspect". Firuz Jung tried to obtain *sanads* but failed to procure them, which perhaps closed this chapter forever[5].

Firuz Jung, who also organised an expedition to eliminate the troublesome Bedar leader who dissuaded from doing so through his diplomatic maneouvering and promise to pay 9,00,000 rupees, which was never fulfilled as Aurangzeb himself personally led last campaign against Wakinkira. But the Mughal administration failed to contain his scope of activities west into Bijapur and east deep into Hyderabad province. The Bedars used to plunder newly annexed provinces with utmost impunity either independently or in association with Maratha bands, which was difficult to stop.

1. Khafi Khān, II, pp. 526-528.
2. Jugna *deshmukh* received enhancement in rank. *Mā'asir-i 'Ālamgīrī,* p. 305.
3. IJC, I/ 38/ 2-10; I/ 38/ 3-10.
4. IJC, I/ 41/ 10 - 84.
5. IJC, I/ 43/ 1-51.

To suggest that Aurangzeb failed to assimilate the most capable and important Bedar leader into the Imperial administration, as tributary chief, *deshmukh* or *manṣabdār*[1] is half truth because the Emperor made a sincere effort not only to grant him *jāgīr* but also to offer *sardeshmukhī* of his former Kingdom. Actually it was the failure on the part of Pidiyah Nayak himself to report to the Emperor and to produce proper documentation in favour of his claim for *sardeshmukhī.*

Such elements always created administrative problems of unmanageable magnitude in the newly conquered territories in 1680s and 1690s when marauding rebellious *zamīndārs* and the local chieftains, Bedars, Gonds and Telgu warriors raided deep into the imperial provinces, which also caused precipitous decline in revenue collections. One such extremely notorious bandit of Hyderabad was Pap Rai, who in late 1690s indulged in organised highway robbery in one of the interior districts of Hyderabad[2]. When the local *faujdārs* and *zamīndārs* threatened him he became a military retainer of Venkat Rao, the Telgu *zamīndār* of Kaulas wherefrom he drank up the blood of his new master by extorting money from his subjects, which posed an explicit challenge to the Imperial authority.

Incomplete political and administrative consolidation in Bijapur and Golcunda after 1686-87 and Aurangzeb's purpose behind his fiscal policies in Bijapur and Hyderabad for further aggressive expansion and his general approach in these newly annexed provinces resulted into under administration and over-exploitation which created serious administrative problems of far reaching consequences. Such a situation further confounded the confusion in tackling the administrative problems to an unprecedented degree by dispassionate administration of the empire which was, however, not completely free from ignoble desire for aggrandizement and plunder.

It can be summed up in a nutshell that for mitigating administrative problems Aurangzeb made Hyderabad proper as the object of sustained administrative reorganisation during the years 1687-1700 while endeavours at a similar administrative consolidation in the Hyderabad Karnatak were frustrated by the 1689 rebellion of the Telgu *nāyaks* and the sudden flight of Raja Rām, the Maratha king to Jinji in 1690, which compelled Aurangzeb to devote to a prolonged war with the Marathas. These protracted, arduous and bitter campaigns gave respite to other mischief mongers to foment troubles as they turned to predatory raids in the newly annexed territories to give vent to their pent up feelings for the fulfilment of their ambitions,

1. J.F. Richard,'The Imperial Crisis in the Deccan, *Journal of Asian Studies*, XXXV, [Feb], 1976, p. 248.
2. J.F. Richards and Velcheru Narayana Rao, 'Banditry in Mughal India: Historical and Folklore Perceptions', *IESHR*, XVII, 1980.

thereby offsetting Mughal designs of forceful expansion and administrative assimilation.

III. Assignments in the Newly Conquered Areas

The conquest of Golcunda, Bijapur and the Maratha Kingdom from 1686 to 1689 led to the specific policy decision in respect of the assignments in the newly conquered areas. Initially assignments in extremely rare cases were made from Bijapur and Golcunda. However, theoretically speaking, the annexation of these two former kingdoms could have generated additional revenue resources sufficient to offset the influx of Deccani nobles coming from Bijapur, Golcunda and the Maratha kingdom. It may also be argued that if Aurangzeb had successfully secured and stabilised his new southern frontiers, he could well have utilised the resources of Bijapur and Golcunda to meet his additional costs as well. It may be opined that the most obvious choice would have been for Aurangzeb to assign all the productive lands in the newly conquered provinces to meet the increased annual demand for the *jāgīrs*[1] because a contemporary revenue manual stated that land tax collection should have enhanced annual Imperial revenue by 23% or 53 million rupees over the previous Empire wide collections of 252 million rupees[2].

These new provinces and their resources could have been used to provide *jāgīr* [salary assignment] to any *manṣabdārs*, new or old, who required them. But Aurangzeb, as a deliberate policy decision; instead retained the bulk of revenues from the greater part of most productive and fertile lands in Hyderabad and Golcunda to meet strategic objectives in the south. Instead in the often complex pattern of revenue payment detailed in the *āwārja* or balance documents, we find detailed *pargana* wise āwārjas[3] of numerous *sarkārs* of the *ṣūbās* of Aurangabad, Khandesh, Berar and Bedar, which furnish statistical information about the assignment of *jāgīrs* to a number of officials, serving in Hyderabad or Bijapur, whose *jāgīrs* were assigned in the above said four provinces. Furthermore, countless officials, holding *jāgīr* assignments in old Deccan provinces have been shown posted with the armies of the high nobles, serving in the newly conquered former kingdoms of Bijapur and Golcunda. Furthermore, this

1. *Cf.*, J.F. Richards: 'The Imperial Crisis in the Deccan', *loc cit*, pp. 238-9.
2. *Ẓawābit-i 'Ālamgīrī,* as cited in I. Habib, *Agrarian System,* p. 409.
3. These list individual *jāgīr* assignments within each *pargana* for a particular point in time as we find several *āwārjas* of different years of a single *pargana* as well. These documents were usually drawn up in order to ascertain the available revenues open for reassignment to *manṣabdārs*. *Cf.,* J.F. Richards, 'Official Revenues and Money Flows in a Mughal Province', *Loc. cit.* p. 2.

policy is further depicted from the document of 29th month of Rabi II 38 - 1695-96 AD sent to Muhammad Jåfar in regard to the [details of] *sair hāṣil.* "Refuge of chieftancy and nobility, of excellent and sublime status, worthy of cooperation Mir Muhammad Jåfar who should be in the protection and safety of the sublime Almighty Lord in full satisfaction that previously was communicated that the Imperial order was issued that the full revenue paying *painths* which belong to the *jagirdars* should be considered in the Imperial *khaliṣa.* That refuge of ministry should despatch that time facts of the full revenue yielding *painths* of the *parganas* of *ṣūba* Daru-l Jihad Hyderabad concerning has *diwan* with the register of [the last] five years under his own verification be sent in writing so as to present it before His Majesty so that the concerned register is received. Accordingly it is hereby written that no more delay should be done in the matter so that the register of the aforesaid *painths* be arranged in accordance with the previously written one so as to be despatched as expenditionsly as possible so that the position of the income of *tankhwah* and the present revenue statistics is brought to notice"[1].

Thus the concentration of reserving revenues for *khaliṣa* was specifically without any hitch or hesitation. Except for a few *āwārjas* from Hyderabad and Bijapur, the rest relates to four old Deccani *ṣūbās,* which again confirms Aurangzeb's policy of placing the choicest areas as *khāliṣa* and *Pāibāqī* in the newly conquered provinces as is especially evident from the tabular information furnished about Hyderabad[2]:

Table – 2

Sl.No.	*% of Classification of Land*	*Revenues Collected in Rupees*
	44% *Khāliṣa*	Rs. 67,00,000 Annual Collections
	56% *Pāibāqī*	Rs. 88,00,000 Annual Collections
	100% Total	Rs. 1,55,00,000 Annual Collections

Contrary to above we do not come across references in a few *āwārja* papers of Hyderabad and Bijapur showing a reciprocal tendency of corresponding assignments from these two newly annexed provinces serving in older Deccani *ṣūbās.* The following table clearly depicts this phenomenon in late 17th century:

1. IJC I/38/6-5.
2. IJC, I/ 32/ 0-95 to I/ 32/ 0-128.

Table – 3

Sl. No.	Name of manṣabdār/ jāgīrdār	Place of Posting	Jama'dāmi in Dāms	Ḥāṣil in Rupees	Place of Assignment	Reference
	Peet Singh s/o Jagat Singh	*qila'dār* of Karnatak	3,18,500	3234	*sarkār* Sangamner *ṣūba* Aurangabad	IJC I/41/4-17
	Mehdi Quli s/o Ḥāji Muḥammad	*Amīn-i Pāibāqī* of Nuṣratabad, Bijapur	1,99,000	1660	*sarkār* Sangamner *ṣūba* Aurangabad	IJC I/41/4-17
	Khwāja Suhail s/o Mīr 'Abdul Jabbar	*Dārogha-i* Jawahiri Bazar, Bijapur	80,000	833/6	*sarkār* Daulatabad	I/46/12-46
	Mīr Muḥammad Qāsim s/o Mīr 'Abdul Mu'āli	Buyūtāt-i Ḥyderabad	26,25,000	3263	*pargana* Kanher *sarkār* Daulatabad [Aurangabad]	I/45/1-160
	Saiyid Nuṣrat s/o Saiyid Koka 'Ali 'Ādil Khān	Posted at Bijapur	6,50,755	4203	*sarkār* Aḥmadnagar *ṣūba* Aurangabad	I/45/5-4
	Ghulām 'Ali Khān	Posted at Karnatak-i Hyderabad	4,49,370	4069/7	*sarkār* Aḥmadnagar *ṣūba* Aurangabad	I/0/0-645
	Dāūd Khān deputy of Khān Nuṣrat Jung	*Faujdār* of Bālā & Pāīnghāt Karnatak-i Hyderabad	2,00,21,479	2,29,297	*pargana* & *sarkār* Bir, Aurangabad	I/45/82-21
	Muḥammad Ja'far s/o Iftikhār Khān	*Bakhshi* & *Waqianigār* of Hyderabad	11,89,688	14,866	*pargana* & *sarkār* Bir, Aurangabad	I/45/8-50
	Ḥāji Jamāl s/o Iraj	Posted at Hyderabad	1,54,000	1,954	*sarkār* Pathri *ṣūba* Berar	I/44/10-124
	Ya'qub Beg s/o Chirāgh Beg	Posted at Bijapur	75,000	948	Partappur, Kalyan *ṣūba* Berar	I/0/0-540
	Muḥammad Murād s/o Jamāl	Posted at Bijapur	65,500	916	Partappur, Kalyan *ṣūba* Berar	I/0/0-540
	Amānullāh Beg s/o Muḥammad Beg Khān	*qila'dār* of Elgundal	2,10,000	2,496	Partapur, Kalyan *ṣūba* Berar	I/46/7-16, I/0/0-764
	Gopal Chand s/o Bindraban	*Mushrif* of stores of the forts of Hyderabad	1,06,000	1,202	*pargana* Parangaon *sarkār* & *ṣūba* Khandesh	I/0/0-2008
	Muḥammad Sai'd s/o Muḥammad 'Ali	*Dīwān* of Karnatak	1,15,000	903	*pargana* 'Ādilābād *sarkār* & *ṣūba* Khandesh	I/0/0-2008

	Saiyid Tājuddin s/o Fatḥuddin	Posted at *Chabūra-i Kotwāli,* Khandesh	1,25,000	837	*pargana* 'Ādilābād *sarkār&ṣūba* Khandesh	I/0/0-2008

The above table which does not aim at cataloguing the stipulated data is illustrative of the fact that assignments were made from older *ṣūbās* for those officials posted in the two erstwhile kingdoms. However, we do not come across details of *jāgīr* assignments from Bijapur and Golcunda during the early phase of their annexation. Even the *pāibāqī* lands especially in Hyderabad remained as it is without re-assignment for extended periods of time.

But there were certain exceptions to this rule. It was reported that *pargana* Medak included in *khāliṣa* in *ṣūba* Hyderabad having *jama'dāmi* of 1,28,51,000 yielded Rs 3,10,365 was partially assigned in *jāgīr* in 1698 notwithstanding the fact that the *maḥāl* of *khāliṣa* could not be assigned in *jāgīr* without the imperial order on the plea that it could be assigned in need[1].

Interestingly enough the revenue figures of the 20 *sarkārs* of *ṣūba* Hyderabad support the assertion of practical exclusion of *ṣūba* Hyderabad from *jāgīr* assignments. It is related that within two years after the annexation of Hyderabad i.e. in 1689, the chief fiscal officer of the province designated as *dīwān,* had in fact completed a reassessment of the provincial revenues. In his revised revenue assessment he imposed as selective enhancement by *pargana* of 13% which raised the Mughal demand to 15.5 million rupees per year. During the course of this revenue settlement, the *dīwān* under direct imperial instructions classified each *pargana* as either *khāliṣa* or as *pāibāqī* lands[2], suitable for *jāgīr* assignments, which, however remained under imperial control without reassignment for longer periods of time.

We are aware of the fact that Aurangzeb set aside nearly half of Hyderabad revenues for the central treasury in 1689. But Rs 88,00,000 in *pāibāqī* lands also remained unallocated out of which only Rs 20,00,000 were selected by *dīwān* of the Deccan to meet the needs of the provincial governor, the *dīwān, faujdār* and fort commanders and their garrison and for the ongoing expenses of Hyderabad. Similar arrangements, of course, took effect in Bijapur.

Since the contingent posted thereat is in the eyes of His Majesty by keeping in view the tumultuousness and the vastness of this *suba* [Bijapur] the requisite strength of the accursed Beds in collaboration with the Marathas [Ashqiyas] and the *zamindars* have firmaly determined that consequent

1. IJC, I/ 41/ 8-38.
2. IJC, I/ 32/ 0-95 to I/ 32/ 0-128.

upon the return of His Majesty to vehemently attack once forever. Since the total amount in the aforesaid country and cumcum Salut [?], Konil, Righ and Saundur which are in control of the Marathas have been assigned in salary out of which not a single *dam* is obtained. About 12,80,000 is the balance of demand and the contingent when he maintains excessive demand which is increasing day by day as keeping of the contingent is also must. Hopes that *pargana* Chit, Karanchki, Molowar and Narkunda which are in assignment of the Nawal Khan and the Deccans be granted by the grace of the Almighty Lord which the *khaliṣa* of Imtiyazgarh and Firoznagar is assigned to the applicant so that the Almighty God willing the Imperial territory is kept in control so that the port be kept properly and all contingent and the army is paid and the miscreants be engaged in continued prayers.

Notwithstanding these deductions, areas having revenues of six million rupees annually should have been open for general assignment in 1689 while another unknown amount would also have been available in Bijapur. In view of the tremendous clamour for *jāgīrs* these lands would have been expeditiously allocated to the *manṣabdārs*. In contrast, Aurangzeb imposed significant restrictions on the assignment of these tracks[1]. Even in 1702 Aurangzeb himself conceded that, "presently there is approximately eight million rupees of *pāibāqī* under the administration of the *dīwān* in Bijapur and Hyderabad excluding the Karnatak little of which has proved beneficial to the state".

When as per the selection [*intikhāb*] Saiyid Lutf Muḥammad represented to His Majesty that Ram Gonda, *desai* of *pargana* Khanapur became the expense holder of the fort of Bhimgarh owing to which he does yearn for a *farmān* for *deskat* of the said *pargana* as per the *asnads* (certificates) certificate of Deccanis. Hopes for the *Parwana-i-Diwani* whereupon after the capture of the fort the *farmāns* may kindly be issued which was approved and *sanad* was given accordingly in Bijapur. When Zulfiqar Khan wrote that Muḥammad Ḥasan *zamindar* of Dabhol *sarkar* was present in the conquest of *qila'* Islamgarh with 5,000 infantry in the army, in *suba* Bijapur, as the forts of the Marathas had come under the control of the Imperial army and majority of the excellent *mansabdars* were seized and brought to the army. Accordingly in view of excellent services and for the habitation of the *deshmukhs* the *zamindari* thereof was recommended for which *sanad* may kindly be given which was assigned as well.

Before proceeding further one should be tempted to know the real state of assignments of *jāgīrs vis-a-vis* the *khāliṣa* in the newly annexed

1. *Cf.*, Richards, *Mughal Administration,* pp. 105-107; IJC, I/ 46/ 12-167, I/ 46/ 12-178.

provinces. Wizārat Khān's detailed report[1] of 1699 brings to light the hopeless state of *Khāliṣa* in Bijapur:

> "The expenses of pay claim [*ṭalab*] and salary of the garrison of the forts, *manṣabdars, aḥadis* [gentlemen trooper] and *barqandāz* posted in Darūẓẓafar [i.e. Bijapur] and the procurement of the provisions of the forts etc stipulated expenses, use of *bān* and *barūt* [gun-powder] and the equipments of artillery etc which are required for the forts and the army and the repairs of the forts the entire revenues of the *khāliṣa* do not suffice and the claimants always complain, and sometimes, the arrangement of the *kārkhāna* is kept suspended. If *pargana* Okhli etc 12 *parganas* are reverted to the *khāliṣa* than the maintenance of prospective increase in revenue and supply of [provisions of] *kārkhānas* is possible, otherwise expanses of this province is difficult"[2].

Such an alarming situation had already alerted the Emperor, whose cryptical remarks on the income and expenditure of this *ṣūba* previously submitted by Kār Ṭalab Khān during his tenure of *dīwani* shows the imperial contention for improving the economy of the *ṣūba*: "The income and expenditure should be equal and every possible effort should be made that *khāliṣa* and *peshkash* be maintained according to the term of administration of 'Ali 'Ādil Khān and expenditure should be minimized[3]".

The situation on the economic front was found so disturbing that when the income and expenditure of *ṣūba* Bijapur were perused by His Majesty that "Rs 25,000 were in assignment of Kār Ṭalab Khān as *sih-bandī* [auxilliary troopers] of *pargana* Almala, [the Emperor observed] that *sih-bandī* was excessive, which should be given in the *jāgīr* of the Governor[4]".

In order to remove anomalies in income and expenditure of *ṣūba* Bijapur, Aurangzeb after his initial reaction observed that: "Much difference is shown [in income and expenditure] from the writing of the Governor and the *Dīwān*, what is wrong if they [i.e. *jāgīrdārs*] are given in lieu of this *maḥāl* [i.e. 12 *maḥāls* recommended for inclusion into the *khāliṣa* in Bijapur] except for *aimma,* otherwise since all are posted and united then how the *maḥāls* be resumed: Order that, "income and expenditure should be equalled and they [i.e. *jāgīrdārs*] should be given from *pāibāqī* with abatement in lieu thereof[5]".

1. IJC, I/ 41/ 10-19 to I/ 41/ 10-59.
   IJC I/36/10-1.
2. IJC, I/ 41/ 10-49.
3. IJC, I/ 40/ 10-49.
   IJC I/36/9-9.
4. IJC, I/ 40/ 9-13.
5. IJC, I/ 41/ 10-49.

However, in a subsequent order the Emperor adopted a different posture that: "As of now any transfer and change cannot be affected; so long as the royal standard is in this vicinity, only whatever is possible can be given. As soon as His Majesty returns, the Almighty God willing, the *sanad* of transfer and change shall be issued[6]".

Since there were some restrictions on the allotment of even *naqdī jāgīrs* in the newly annexed kingdoms it was but natural that Aurangzeb, after one year discontinued *naqdī* to Rustam Dil Khān, Governor of Hyderabad in 1694 for maintaining 4,000 infantry, notwithstanding the Governor's engagement in warfare incapacitating any one to accept *jāgīr* [except for *naqdī jāgīr*]. Accordingly he was ordered to consider the said infantrymen as disbanded[7]. In contrast, special favour was shown to those officials posted in Bijapur and Hyderabad who were generally immune from payment of *muṭālība* [state demand] except for *musāi'da* [financial assistance] and *taṣarruf*[8].

Aurangzeb obviously had no intention of placating the *manṣabdārs* demanding pay at the expense of the imperial treasury because nearly Rs 70,00,000 in annual revenues from Hyderabad provided a substantial increase to the extent of 26% to the *khāliṣa* of the entire Mughal empire. Furthermore any land similarly allocated in Bijapur would have raised the figure. Demonstratively such collections from Hyderabad obviously helped easier administration and transmission for military operations in the Deccan than those revenues collected in the Northern provinces.

The total number of the *mahals / parganas* of the newly conquered *suba* of Bijapur exceeds 3.80 out of which 20 *mahals* given hereunder have been included in the *khāliṣa sharifa* hereunder on the suggestion of Wizarat Khan, which is hardly 5% of the total area of *suba* Bijapur. On the other hand only 4% of the area was allocated in *jagirs* on the suggestion of Wizarat Khan. However in yet another case we again find one more suggestion of including 12 *mahāls*.

As the expenses of the *ṭalab* and *tankhwah* of the contingent of the forts *mansabdars*, gentleman troopers, *barqandazs* posted in *suba* Daruzzafar of administration of the stocks of the forts etc, the stipulated expenses and the use of *bān* and lead and the requirements of artillery which they bring with the forts and the armies, and the repairs and of the forts as the income from the [limited] *khaliṣa* do not suffice while the *arbab-i ṭalab* always complain and even the running of the *karkhanas* sometimes becomes

6. IJC, I/ 42/ 12-51.
7. IJC, I/ 36/ 1-4.
8. IJC, I/ 36/ 4-1, I/ 36/ 4-2.
IJC I/41/8-215-220.

insufficient. Accordingly if Okhali etc 12 *mahāls* are totally included into the *khaliṣa* then the growth of prosperity and the increase in the revenue and the administration of the factories are possible otherwise expenses of this *sūba* become difficult for which orders may be given.

Thereafter Aurangzeb ordered thus "Let the income and expenditure be equalled and from the *paibaqi* in lieu thereof be given with abatement".

Rs 19,40,739/11¼ as the revenue realisation of 1080 while Rs 9,76,577 as the *mahsūl-i paibāāqi* of 1103 in accordance with the term of administration of Ali Adil Khan has been shown.

Aurangzeb recorded that "Much difference is shown from the written statement of the Governor and the *Diwan*, if in lieu of this *mahal* except for the *aimma*, grants be given then there shall be no difficulty otherwise since all are busy in the service and campaign then why it should be taken from them"[1].

[Since very limited *mahals* were assigned in *jagirs* hardly 4% it was but natural that the *khāliṣa* and even *pāibāqī* was kept unalloted for several extended years. These 13 *mahals* had a *jama* in 1080 A.H. / 1669-70 A.D. of 13 crore and 2901 *dāms* while its *hasil* in different years yielded Rs 6,83,188 / 11½. However, Aurangzeb also stressed that "Income and expenditure should be equated and in exchange of it, it should be given from *pāibāqī* with abetments".

Table - 4

Actual income and expenditure [*madakhil-o-makharij* of *sūba*] Daruzzafar Bijapur

INCOME

12,06,455
Previous 6,06,097
Mahal in entirely 40,00,278
Pargana Haveli Daruzzafar Nausair *Balda pargana* Hindi = *Muqarrara hasil* = Rs 101000½
Pargana Eklaud *mahal muqarrara hasil* = Rs 75,000
Pargana = Nanah *mahal* = *Muqarrara hasil* = Rs 3,89,409
Pargana Ankalkot *mahal* = *Muqarrara hasil* = Rs 11,606
Pargana Babar dil *mahal* = *Muqarrara hasil* 1105 A.H. = Rs 30,000
Pargana Jalka *mahal* = *Muqarrara hasil* 1106 = Rs 80,000
Pargana Jamkhand *mahal* = *Muqarrara hasil* of 1106 A.H. = 5,504
Pargana Kaukabpur Jaroda = *mahal*
Pargana Kadam *mahal* = *muqarrara hasil* = Rs 9,065/-
Pargana Haisli *mahal* = *muqarrara hasil* 1106 A.H. = Rs 44,935/-
Dehat = Rs 1,80,912
Different villages which have been fixed in the following *mahals* for the administration etc. = Rs 1,55,821/5
Pargana Imtiyazgarh = Rs 24 villages
Stipulated *hasil* of 1103 A.H. = Rs 35,625

1. IJC I/41/10-49, I/41/0-55, I/39/10-52, I/39/10-53, I/39/10-54, I/39/10-56, I/39/10-58, I/39/10-59.

Pargana Haveli Ghazipur = 15 villages = stipulated *hasil* 1103 A.H. = Rs 16,158/-
Pargana Haveli Firoznagar = 13 villages, stipulated *hasil* of 1103 A.H. = Rs 25,002/8
Pargana Qamarnagar 75 villages, stipulated *hasil* of 1105 A.H. = Rs 34,050/12
Pargana Masli Badu 15 villages, stipulated *hasil* of 1104 A.H., Rs 21,868/12
Pargana Moga – 7 villages, stipulated *hasil* of 1103 A.H., Rs 18,710
Pargana Nirangal, villages = 3 villages, stipulated income = Rs 6,118/12
Pargana Nusratabad *alias* Sakar 63 villages, stipulated *hasil* = Rs 505
Pargana Nasirabad, 35 villages, stipulated *hasil* = 1103[1]
Dehat-i-Kanat-i-Almas [villages of diamond mines]
Stipulated realisation = 25,091
Paibaqi, sair, painth and *chaukis* etc which as per current register was received in the office according to 1103 which was recorded that shall be utilized in proportion for preparing the *nuskha* = Rs 1,06,905/11
Meanwhile = 5,19,359
Mahals which were fixed in the crown land
Rs. 13 *Mahal* for different years = Rs 3,62,359/-
Previous *k͟hāliṣa* = Rs 6,667; Current *k͟hāliṣa* = Rs 3,56,691/12
Pargana Islampur *alias* Barhampuri = Rs 10,528
in accordance with the *ta'ahud* of *karori* in the month of *kharif* till the end of *Rabi*
Previous *k͟hāliṣa* = 2 villages, stipulated Rs 1,000, meanwhile 9,527
Pargana Okli etc 39,899
Stipulated *hasil* 1105 A.H. 3,52,431
Previous *k͟hāliṣa* Rs 5,666/4, Current *k͟hāliṣa* Rs 47,164
Pargana Okli, *pargana* Nagauri = Rs 37,966
Pargana Kota 35,452, *pargana* Hibarka 24,707
Previous *k͟hāliṣa* = villges Rs 1,116, remainder 36,670
Previous *k͟hāliṣa* = 1250, meanwhile 34,202/12 Current *k͟hāliṣa*
Previous *k͟hāliṣa* = one village 6,000, meanwhile Rs 21,707
Pargana Bodri 11,965, *pargana* Bardaw 39,073, *pargana* Kaukabpur Bakinga 41,276/12
Pargana Sindgi 3,680/13, *pargana* Mangal Baidiya 63,369
Pargana Honowar 26300, *pargana* Hawani 22,612/15
Pargana Hosor 7,635/-
On account of the designation of Jagdeo Raj, *zamindar* of Srirangapattan *pargana* Banavar during the term of administration of Mir Abdul Wahab was deposited in the treasury of the province of Daruzzafar [Bijapur] which was ordered to be deposited from 1104 A.H. in the treasury of Sira Fort. Meanwhile in accordance with the copy of the application which in accordance with the representation of the supplicant of His Majesty's Court was represented that was as heretofore was approved and ordered in the treasury of the province 48,000 *hūns* per *hūns* = Rs 3/¾ stipulated amount = Rs 1,56,000
Till date the *sanad* of the *diwani* of the province has not been received.

EXPENDITURE

Rs 18,59,919/13
Wizarat Khan

In accordance with the Sheet of the application	Posted in the army of the Governor [administrator] of the province	Alamgir Shahi 1108 A.H./1169AD
Rs 1,52,992/15½	Rs 3,57,525/13½	

Rs 5,58,029/9½
It was reduced as Except for *ibtiya-k͟hana* [sale house] *kiraya* [rent] of labour as per the following details: *topkhana-i jinsi* [artillery] etc which is suspended on demand, *sih bandi*, right of collection, perks of *fotadars* and the caretaker which shall be implemented after the preparation of the matter [*nuskha*] shall be put to implementation.
On account of stock = Rs 7,55,870/15½

Rs 2,40,957 was implemented	*Talab-i Ahsham* till *Jumada* II 41 R.Y.
Rs 5,14,913/15½ = Rs 14,115/10	Rs 11,09,521

1. IJC I/41/8-115.

GOVERNMENT SANCTIONS: ACTUALS

INCOME

Rs 12,06,455

Nuskha-i ṭalab [demand] 9,04,435

Peshkash of the *zamindār* of Sondha, *Ta'alluqa ṣūba* Daruzzafar is entered in front of His Majesty as it was ordered to be deposited in the treasury of the province = Rs 90,000

[A] On account of previous *peshkash* = Rs 25,000

On account *suba* etc = 16 *mahals* of *ta'alluqa* = Rs 15,000

Altama = Rs 5,435

EXPENDITURE

Situation in Daruzzafar Bijapur

Rs 5,59,903/4¼

Rs 1,32,544/4½ reduced from the total stocks, provision of grain, *ahsham* [contingent]

Asār-i Mubarak, mosque of congregational prayer with Balghūr *Khāna*		Masoleum of late Aurangzabadi Mahal Rs 3,473/10	
Khurak gawan [animal fodder]	*Khurak-i mahabusan* [food for the prisoners]	*Rozina Daran* Rs 3,504/12	*Ghuraba* 13230/-
Ahdiyan Tir Andazi [Arrow shooters] and *qautar* 49951/4		Shagrid *paisha* 93878/4	

Naqqar *Khāna* [Drum house] & *Gharyal Khāna* [watch house]	*Darush Shifa* [Hospital] wa Luluai Rs 10,230	Qaular *Barqandazan* = 24191/4
Qaularkhana Cannondiers [*Top* and azān] Rs 4,409/8	Awards Rs 801	
Contingent = Rs 1,32,729	Stock [*zakhira*] Rs 1,49,921/11	
23631 which is given on account of the *rasam* of grain = 138807	Rs 1,09,922/12 Rs 40,000	

Qita'jinsi = Rs 10,61,004/15¾

Reduced 4,21,485/5½

= Rs 6,36,517/10¼

[Amount] from they get the salary = Rs 9,56,449/6½

Reduced from it 4,24,485/5½

[Balance] = 5,32,914/1

Stock in addition to lead and *sarab*	Contingents
46 forts	46 *qilas* [forts]
6,05,948/3½	*ṭaujih* of 10 forts not received
= 4,04,091/3	stipulated which after the contingent that
Balance = 2,00,957	after one year two month as salary is paid in
	Grain = 36 *qilas* [forts]
	Stipulated = Rs 3,51,500
	19494/2 on account of *qitajat*
	Rs 3,32,007

Different villages are fixed for the contingents

Pargana Imtiyazgarh = 35,625	*pargana haveli* Ghazipur = 16,158	*pargana haveli* Firoznagar = 25,000	*pargana* Nirangal = 6,168/12
Pargana Dhar *alias* Dhawar = 1' Makki Madu Rs 10,322/8	Rs 21,468		

[Expenditure]

Waqia' of the contingent in accompaniment of the Governor of the Province 2,04,341/1-

On account of the Calf and Camel shed in accordance with the sheet of the application = 21,590/1	In addition to the *mansabdars* and monthly cash payment holders whose *parwana* [order] of salary has been received 1,82,759/-
Mansabdārs etc = 35,659 In accordance with the sheet of application = 23,461	In addition to the name of the *qila'dars* of Arak, Daruzzafar Bijapur in accordance with the Regiment of His Majesty

Similarly when a *parwangi* of Sibghalullah was received that Almas Amber chained to have *Sahar* of *Deshmukh* by Adil Khani concerning 12 *parganas* of Ikhlaspur, *sarkar* Conjipuram, *sūba* Bijapur then Aurangzeb asked to 'keep an eye on the well being of the empire, habitation and the happiness of the peasantry which should be given to any one by having any eye on the *rusūm* and income so as to fix the *peshkash*[1].

Similarly an escalation in demand for *jāgīr* assignment in the last decade of the 17th century would have reflected in a reduction of the Hyderabad *k͟hāliṣa* while the reverse occurred. Aurangzeb granted no *jāgīr* in *k͟hāliṣa* territories [barring exceptions], instead, he enlarged Hyderabad *k͟hāliṣa* considerably in 1695 and 1697 by transferring two *sarkārs* from *pāibāqī* status to *k͟hāliṣa*, which automatically removed from possible assignment as *jāgīr* lands with potential revenues of 1.7 million rupees.

However, a considerable reduction in the Hyderabad *k͟hāliṣa* lands took place in 1700, when Aurangzeb shifted 24 *parganas* – worth revenues of 1.2 million rupees to his youngest son Prince Muḥammad Kām Bak͟hsh, who received these *parganas* and some in Bijapur[2] as well in order to enable him to strengthen his power base in the Deccan enabling the Prince to use Bijapur and Hyderabad as a refuge in ensuing war of succession after Aurangzeb's death.

When the Prince showed his inability to collect the revenues worth Rs 30,000 out of Rs 1,33,420 the Emperor immediately retorted that "When the Governor and Prince do not realise the revenue than what others shall procure and administer". The Emperor further observed that "Loss [in revenue] is due to poor revenue administration[3]".

Aurangzeb, true to his reputation of gathering sources of funds to meet the wage bills for his field armies operating in the Deccan against the Marathas set aside the choicest areas as *K͟hāliṣa*; viz., he ordered for resumption of full revenue yielding *peinths* of Hyderabad belonging

1. IJC I/36/6-....
2. IJC, I/ 44/ 5-56.
3. IJC, I/ 45/ 7-41.

to *jāgīrdārs*[1], in 1696. Even the *jāgīrdārs*, interfering with the *bāg͟hāt* [irrigated lands] of Hyderabad, suffered the resumption of their *jāgīrs* into the *k͟hāliṣa*[2]. Similarly majority of the *faujdārs* and *thānadārs* who seized the revenues without getting the verification faced the resumption of their *jāgīrs* by the *dīwān* in collaboration with the Governor[3] in 1704.

Due to the perpetual increase in *k͟hāliṣa*, *sarkār* Elluru was included in the *k͟hāliṣa* in 1700, the *jāgīrdārs* from their lucrative assignments, who had to remain content with scattered *pāibāqī*[4] because the Emperor observed that "There is plenty of *pāibāqī* in Karnatak, whether Karnatak-i Bijapur or Karnatak-i Hyderabad. Assignment can even be made from the *pāibāqī* of Golcunda[5]". Contrary to the above the Imperial injunction disallowed assignment to anyone from the *k͟hāliṣa*[6] while transfer of *jāgīr* was naturally tantamount to dismissal from service[7]. A *pargana* in As'adnagar [Akluj] *ṣūba* Bijapur held by the Maratha *jāgīrdārs* alleged to have yielded 12 monthly income was recommended for inclusion in the *k͟hāliṣa*[8].

Such recommendations generally flowed from the pen of the revenue officials, *viz.*, some *parganas* of *sarkār* Medak, *ṣūba* Ḥyderabad, which were destined to be full revenue – paying became the part of *k͟hāliṣa*, in lieu *jāgīrs* were recommended from the *pāibāqī*[9] on the strength of such representations that "sufficient *pāibāqī* was lying unassigned in *ṣūba* Bijapur; neither it was assigned nor it was useful for the state, while the Deccani pay claimants were becoming numerous, unruly and useless[10]".

Surprisingly *jāgīrs* could be assigned from low yielding *k͟hāliṣa*[11] of Ḥyderabad and Bijapur. When Sher K͟hān Jamand, *faujdār* of Gadag represented that *pargana* of his newly assigned *jāgīrs* across the Krishna [river] was for his advanced *taqāvi* [agricultural loan] to the peasants and he made it populated which was recently included in *k͟hāliṣa*, in lieu of which he was offered *jāgīr* from Gadag which was desolate as it was infested with the Marathas. Consequently he was assigned from *pāibāqī* to mitigate his problem, notwithstanding clear order for non-transfer of *jāgīrs* of serving officials[12].

1. IJC, I/ 38/ 6-5.
2. IJC, I/38/9-10.
3. IJC, I/ 46/ 12-180.
4. IJC, I/ 42/ 6-120.
5. IJC, I/ 42/ 6-30.
6. IJC, I/ 39/ 11-70.
7. IJC, I/ 41/ 6-122.
8. IJC, I/ 41/ 8-122.
9. IJC, I/ 41/ 1-102; IJC, I/ 41/ 8-209.
10. IJC, I/ 42/ 1-69.
11. IJC, I/ 41/ 10-178, I/ 42/ 12-18.
12. IJC, I/ 43/ 1-29; I/ 43/ 1-30; I/ 43/ 1-31.

In view of the paucity of funds the Imperial *Dīwāns* clearly stated that there was ban on the *naqdī* [*jāgīr*][1] which, however, was not unchangeable because when in lieu of the salary of 2,000 cavalry and 3,000 infantry the ground realities were not in consonance with Khān Firoz Jung, cash [*naqdī*] was ordered that it was got commuted into *jāgīr,* which was a temporary Imperial dispensation[2].

Ostensibly Aurangzeb formulated the rule that whether from Bijapur Karnatak or [Hyderabad Karnatak] ... *khāliṣa* and the salary of the *jāgīrdārs* was to be fixed according to rules and regulations[3]. However, the above formulations were evolved because when Mīr 'Abdullāh etc one thousand *sawārs* were granted *manṣab* ranging from 20 to 250 and they were sanctioned pay claim from the *pāibāqī* of *pargana* Bhaknur etc *ta'alluqa* Islamgarh, Hyderabad they were conferred the orders for the assignment of the *maḥāls* in their salaries on the production of branding certificates subject to verification and memorandum. However, from the very date of grant, no cultivation took place and over two years no cultivation was done in the *maḥāls* of Hyderabad[4]. Such was the state of *jāgīrs* in Hyderabad and Bijapur because in piquant situations even *maḥāl-i ghair 'amli* [uncultivated *maḥāls*] from Bijapur were recommended[5]. Furthermore keeping in view of the unfavourable position of income and expenditure of the *maḥāl* of Bijapur Karnatak it was ordained that income and expenditure should be equal notwithstanding the temporary arrangement for the cash payment of the garrison and stores[6].

The problems of *jāgīrs* in newly annexed regions were enormous. Even Diler Khān 7,000 / 7,000 complained against the resumption of his three *jāgīr maḥāls* including *pargana* Rattihalli, *ṣūba* Bijapur, allocated in salary of the contingent, which led to their mutiny[7]. When Chin Qilīch was granted *faudārī* of Bijapur Karnatak following Ma'mur Khān's transfer then Aurangzeb remarked about the position of *pāibāqī* meant for the *jāgīr* of new incumbent "the income of *pāibāqī* is neither useful for the state not for the peasantry, as it is not received. Unlimited *pāibāqī* shall not be available in *maḥāl-i ghair 'amli* [uncultivated tract][8]".

The problems, sometimes, cropped up due to the administrative technicalities *viz.,* the *Dīwān* of Bijapur Karnatak reported about the

1. IJC, I/ 43/ 1-78.
2. IJC, I/ 43/ 5-37.
3. IJC, I/ 45/ 5-86.
4. IJC, I/ 46/ 0-101.
5. IJC, I/ 44/ 12-51.
6. IJC, I/ 44/ 11-112.
7. IJC, I/ 45/ 7-65.
8. IJC, I/ 45/ 9-38.

complaint of the garrison who solicited the *jāgīrs* of *jāgīrdārs* adjacent to the fort. Similarly when 2545 men of Wani s/o Gautam, posted at Nuṣratgarh fort who received in cash and *jāgīr* since the very beginning suffered resumption of *jāgīr* by the *Dīwān* of Bijapur Karnatak, the Imperial order maintained the *status quo ante*[1] in 1705.

When Sarfrāz Khān's *jāgīr* affairs were brought to the Emperor's notice then he observed:

> "Although the said Khān has contingent yet, perhaps it does not correspond with his *jāgīr* until the receipt of written communication of the Prince, *Bakhshī* and the *Dārogha-i dāgh-o-taṣḥīḥa* [superintendent of branding and verification] about the availability of the contingent commensurating the *tankhwāh* it [remainder pay-claim] cannot be given from the Old Country. If he want, then it can be granted from Bijapur and Hyderabad, from the uncultivated country[2]".

The above shatters the myth built up so cautiously by Richards about the extraordinary revenue resources of the new provinces. Even abatement in New Country was purely discretionary as it was refused to Dāūd Khān[3].

In the event of resumption of *jāgīr* to *khāliṣa*, alternatives were there, either it could be granted from *pāibāqī* or by transferring someone elsewhere. However, a new device was pressed into service, when *pargana* Satara [*ṣūba* Bijapur], *jāgīr* of Muḥammad Akram, which was reverted to *khāliṣa*, was ordered to be delivered in cash, whatever was accruing to Muḥammad Akram, through the *Dīwān* in 1704.

Remedial measures were taken for the proper administration of *jāgīrs* especially in the newly conquered territories *viz.,* to remedy the overvalued *jāgīrs* where collections did not come close to the nominal revenue assessment. Aurangzeb granted a standard one-third reduction on the nominal valuation of all *jāgīrs* assigned in Hyderabad[4]. It was also ordered that as far as the Deccanis were concerned they were granted three-fourth from the *Mulk-i Qadīm* [Old country] and one-fourth from the *Mulk-i Jadīd* [Newly conquered country][5]. In so far as the old Deccanis were concerned they covered the Deccani *manṣabdārs* of Shāh Jahān's reign upto his 31st R.Y. [1657 AD][6]. In regard to the *takhfīf* [reduction] it was clearly stipulated that no abatement was allowed in the event of conforming the *ḥāl-i ḥāṣil*

1. IJC, I/ 50/ 11-5.
2. IJC, I/ 45/ 7-10.
3. IJC, I/ 45/ 7-78.
4. Richards, 'The Imperial Crisis in the Deccan', *loc. cit.*, p. 241.
5. IJC, I/ 41/ 10-127.
6. IJC, I/ 46/ 12-167.

[actual realisation] with the month ratio as happened in *pargana* Mangal Badiya [*ṣūba* Bijapur][1].

Richard's contention that many *manṣabdārs* refused unproductive *jāgīrs* does not stand scrutiny, instead they endeavoured for *jāgīrs*[2]. Furthermore contrary to above, numerous absentee *manṣabdārs* in Hyderabad and Bijapur suffered due to lack of adequate help from the provincial administration except for influential and powerful nobles who had direct access to their *jāgīrs* while the petty salary claimants lacking sufficient resources to protect their *jāgīrs* suffered accordingly.

The *jāgīr* assignment in the newly conquered areas was not so much beneficial as it appears to be, because the annexation could not mitigate the problems of *jāgīr* assignees, who were normally assigned *jāgīrs* outside their serving *ṣūbās* or less productive ones.

The above does provide a peep into the position of *jāgīr* assignments the two newly annexed Kingdoms towards the close of 17th and the beginning of the 18th centuries as shortage of *jāgīrs* in 1690s was not an artificial one, which fact has been ultimately admitted by J.F. Richards himself[3].

1. IJC, I/ 46/ 5-73. For details of *jāgīr* administration see my paper 'The Working of the *Jāgir* System in the Deccan during the Last Years of Aurangzeb', *Journal of Objective Studies,* Vol. 2, no. 2, July 1990, pp. 72-80.
2. Richards, *Mughal Administration*, p. 202, Athar Ali, Review on Richards, *Mughal Administration*, *Journal of Asian Studies,* XXXV, February, 1976, p. 162.
3. *idem*, The Seventeenth Century Crises in South Asia, reproduced in his Power Administration and Finance in Mughal India, 1995, 637.

VI

Provincial Administration

[I] Emperor As Viceroy?

The great biographer of Aurangzeb, Sir Jadunath Sarkar, attributed his ultimate failure to his Deccan adventure; according to Sarkar, the decline of Aurangzeb's administration began when he let himself get bogged down in the Deccan from 1682 to his death in February 1707[1]. Satish Chandra, Irfan Habib and M. Athar Ali have linked the 'crisis in *jāgīrs*' to the stress of military campaigns in the Deccan during the emperor's last years[2]. It is, therefore, all the more surprising that there has been no large scale study yet of the Mughal administration, of the Deccan, except for J.F. Richards' pioneering work, *Mughal Administration in Golconda,* Oxford, 1975. Richards tended, as pioneers often do, to cast doubt on the "Deccan-ulcer" theories of his predecessors, by citing documents from both the A.P. State Archives and the Inayat Jang Collection, which they had sparingly used, if, indeed, at all[3]. Those scholars had essentially relied on the contemporary chronicles, Aurangzeb's own letters and the *Akhbārāt-i darbār-i mu'alla.* Their generalisations thus tended to rest largely on contemporary generalisations rather than on precise or primary evidence from archival documentation.

What is offered here is a selection of precisely such documents drawn from the Inayat Jang Collection relating to the last ten years of Aurangzeb's

1. Jadunath Sarkar, *A Short History of Aurangzeb,* 2nd ed. [revised], Calcutta, 1954, pp. 424 ff.
2. Satish Chandra, *Parties and Politics at the Mughal Court,* Aligarh, 1959, pp. v/vi-x/xii; Irfan Habib, *Agrariarn System of Mughal India,* revised ed., Delhi, 1999, pp. 312, 316; M. Athar Ali, *The Mughal Nobility under Aurangzeb,* revised ed., Delhi, 1997, pp. xx-xxii, 92-94.
3. To take one example, Irfan Habib notes that he has not been able to explore the "rich material" in the Inayat Jung Collection [*Agrarian System*], revised ed., pp. 478-9, and his use of A.P. State Archives material is obviously restricted to the published volumes of documents. Of course, much of this material is tangential to his main concerns.

reign. This collection was first described at length by A.I. Tirmizi,[1] and there is a brief description by J.F. Richards[2]. These divest me of the obligation to describe again this massive collection of Mughal archives in the Deccan, covering the period 1658-1774 and comprising some 135,000 documents.

I should rather explain the nature of documents that are here studied. I have picked out a number of such documents as contain Aurangzeb's own personal orders [preceded by words such as *naql-i khaṭṭ-i anwar,* 'copy of the luminous hand-written note [of the Emperor]', etc, on the assumption that such a selection would tell us what kinds of matters went up to the Emperor for decision, and what kinds of decisions were thereupon taken. What one gets here, then, are the threads leading to the top of the pyramid and then downwards. It is not the whole story: the peasants are largely out of the picture, though the Inayat Jang Collection has numerous other documents where they are very much 'in'. But the selection nevertheless meets my narrow object of inquiry: What was the nature of the problems Aurangzeb was facing in the Deccan, as viewed by himself and his administration, and how did he and his officials tackle them.

I begin below with no prior assumptions, but simply present the picture as we have it from these documents that number about fifty-five in all. The National Archives numbers which they carry are invariably given, and so too the dates wherever we have them. The archives numbers also include the regnal year of Aurangzeb, which began with 1 Ramazan; the first regnal year was deemed to have begun with Ramazan 1068 [2 June 1658]. All Hijri dates have here been furnished with their Christian-era equivalents.

Some other matters need also to be borne in mind. When the kingdoms of Bijapur and Golkunda [Golcunda] were annexed in 1686 and 1687, the Deccan had the following provinces: [1] Khandesh; [2] Daulatabād with its capital at Aurangabad; [3] Berar; [4] Bidar; [5] Bijapur; and [6] Haidarabad. The whole of South India excluding Kerala was called Karnataka, and this was divided into two sets of *Sarkārs,* one belonging to the *ṣūba* of Bijapur, the *'Karnatak-i Bijapuri',* and the other to Haidarabad, the *'Karnatak-i Haidarabadi'.* Before 1682, there used to be a *Nāzim* or Governor in each province, but the *Nāzim* of the *ṣūba* of Daulatabad, with headquarters at Aurangabad used to exercise some amount of control over them, and is, therefore, aptly called Viceroy of the Deccan in modern texts. When Aurangzeb himself arrived in the Deccan, it ceased to be a viceroyalty and Aurangzeb himself supervised the individual *Nāzims.*

1. *Studies in Islam,* Delhi, 1[3], 1964, pp. 174-84.
2. *Mughal Administration in Golconda,* pp. 317-19.

The Deccan territories were also divided into two categories. The 'Old Territory' [*mulk-i-qadīm*], which had come into Mughal possession by the end of Shāh Jahān's reign and the 'New Territory' [*mulk-i-jadīd*], which had come into Mughal possession in Aurangzeb's reign. The latter comprised the whole of Bijapur and Haidarabad provinces and parts of Daulatabad and Bidar provinces.

We can now proceed to what our documents tell us.

[A] Financial Difficulties

The financial drain on the Empire that the Deccan presented is shown by [the statement of the annual] income and expenditure of the *Khāliṣa* in the province of Daulatabad, submitted on 7 Ziqa'd 45 Regnal Year [16 April, 1701]:

INCOME	*EXPENDITURE*	*EXCESS OF EXPENDITURE*
Rs 8,71,542	Rs 19,03,596	Rs 10,32,054

The document draws attention to this excess of expenditure. It is stated that despite receipt of "bill [*hundīs*] from Hindustan, which took place previously", the hue and cry of unpaid claimants always used to take place. Now, apparently, such transfers from North Indian treasuries had ceased. The Emperor had ordered "Let *Khāliṣa* be expanded to meet the expenditure, but not the expense of [*jāgīrs* assigned for meeting] pay-claims of the army which are considerable." The caveat left the matter unresolved. The final orders as now given were equally weak:

At this time, people cannot be transferred [to yield *jāgīrs* for *Khāliṣa*].

Perhaps, after death [or transfer], land can be given to *pāibāqī*.[1]

A similar situation is indicated by Inayat Jang Collection document[2] in the case of the province of Bijapur in 1080 [?1108 AH = A.D. 1696-97], the *Khāliṣa* had a *jama'* of Rs 13,04,910, as 6, and *ḥāṣil* of Rs 6,83,187, as 11, 1/2. The total annual income 'in various years', meaning perhaps the average annual income, including that of *pāibāqī,* was put at Rs 9,78,577 and the annual expenditure at Rs 15,04,396 as 15, 1/4. The deficit thus exceeded Rs 5,25,000. The report pointed out that the expenditure was incurred because of pressure of military needs, salaries of *manṣabdārs,* horsemen, musketeers, stores of forts, rockets, gunpowder, repairs of forts; etc. The deficit had caused delays in salary payments, generating protests

1. See IJC, I/46/12-167 &178; The *Pāibāqī,* one should perhaps explain, comprised lands that were available for assignment in *jāgīr* and were in Imperial officials' hands [often on paper only in the Deccan] pending such, assignment. See Irfan Habib, *Agrarian System of Mughal India,* revised ed., pp. 308n. 312-13, 324, 325 & n.
2. [IJC, I/41/10-48].

from claimants. Aurangzeb characteristically contented himself with an impossible piece of advice, namely, economy.

The income and expenditure should be kept equal. They [pay-claimants] should be paid out of *pāibāqī* by way of *jāgīrs*] with reductions [in *jama'* presumably].

The income from *Khāliṣa* was, however, often sought to be increased. Thus, on 29 Rabi II, Regnal Year 38, it was ordered that all profitable market places [*paintha-ha-i sair-ḥāṣil*] in the province of Ḥaidarabad were to be taken into the *Khāliṣa*.[1]

[B] Pressure on Resources: Situation of the *Pāibāqī*

In 1975, J.F. Richards raised doubts over the alleged phenomenon of 'crisis of *jāgīrs*' in the later years of Aurangzeb, which figures in the writings of Satish Chandra, Irfan Habib and M. Athar Ali. Richards' doubts rested mainly on a document giving a high amount of *pāibāqī* [land available for assignment in *jāgīr*] in *ṣūba* Ḥaiderabad upon its annexation.[2] Athar Ali responded by setting out a statement of distribution of assignable lands in *Karanata-i Ḥaidarabadi,* 1706, which broadly brought out the small size of *Khāliṣa* and *pāibāqī* in that area.[3]

Much of the dispute can be settled [perhaps, against J.F. Richards!] by IJC-I/0/0-486 [Old No. I/14/129], which unfortunately lacks date but obviously belongs to Aurangzeb's late years. It contains the following statement submitted to the Emperor:

> The Emperor observed that it is repeatedly said that there is no *pāibāqī* left, and that I should take a *muchalka* [bond] from the Chief *Bakhshī*, Mukhliṣ Khān, that there should be no more [demands on] *pāibāqī* except on necessity[4]. The situation is that in the Old Country [*mulk-i qadīm*], the *pāibāqī* is being assigned away in [*jāgīr* in lieu of] pay, upon orders of the Emperor and the pleas of the representatives of pay-claimants, except for Pune and Tilkokan, etc, which is really of the character of new country. In the New Country [*mulk-i jadīd*], *viz.*, Bijapur and Haidarabad, the *pāibāqī* is considerable [almost eighty lakh rupees], since, owing to its low income, the [claimants'] representatives do not accept [*jāgīrs* from it] in accordance with the *jama'* and plead for reduction [in *jama'*], keeping in view the low receipts, on the ground that according to the prescribed *jama'* for

1. [IJC, I/38/6-5].
2. J.F. Richards, *Mughal Administration in Golconda,* Oxford, 1975, pp. 158, 308-9.
3. M. Athar Ali, *Mughal Nobility under Aurangzeb,* revised ed., Delhi, 1997, pp. xx-xxii.
4. Text not clearly decipherable.

> pay-assignment [*jama'-i tankhwāhi*] they would have to bring to brand contingents according to rule, and this obligation they would not be able to meet owing to low receipts, whereupon with the brand-report [*daghnāma*] not reaching the office, the *jāgīr'* would be transferred. Should concession be granted in the branding of contingents, they can bring the brand-reports in time. [It is] submitted for orders.

The statement goes on to give the *pāibāqī,* in terms of estimated income [*jama'*] and the actual [*hāṣil*]: the former was 1, 62, 58, 93, 576 *dāms* and the latter Rs 1, 85, 58,618, as. 14, 3/4, but the significance of the figures is weakened by the fact that they appear to apply to the whole Empire, still even for the Empire as a whole, the receipts are on the low side, some "five-and-a-half monthly" in official Mughal parlance. The ratio would have been much lower in the newly conquered territories of the Deccan.

Aurangzeb's response to all this is brief:

> First, the *jāgīrs* should be assigned out of the *pāibāqī* in the well-ordered Old Territories, along with those assignable against *manṣab* promotions. The disorderly, useless Deccanis should be confined to the New Territory, and to the Old [only] with reduction [of *manṣab*-claim]; and only thereafter, other places.

This was in line with the general distrust shown towards Deccani elements in the nobility and with the desire to retain the plums of Empire for the older nobility. But the decision did not resolve the real problem, *viz.,* the contraction of *pāibāqī* in the settled territories.

Aurangzeb continued to be irritated by *manṣabdārs'* refusal to accept *jāgīrs* out of *pāibāqī* in disturbed territory. On one document dealing with assignment in *ghair-'amalī* [unsubjugated territory], Aurangzeb wrote:

> Pune and Chakna and *pāibāqī* of Junair and Bara Maval, etc, *maḥāls* that no one accepts and wishes for, are many. They can be given to all.

Another document[1], shows that the pressure for *jāgīrs* upon the 'Old Territory' [in the Deccan] was intense. Dated 14 Zi'qad, Regnal Year 42, it contains a statement of the claims of 'Abdu'r Raḥmān Khān, 1500 *zāt,* 900 *sawār,* and Farjām Khān, *900l, 3005, for jāgīrs* in *pargana* Raipur, Baglana, Aurangzeb rejected the proposed arrangement, saying:

> [that it] cannot be given, since both claimants are not permanently posted to the Deccan. There are so many claimants from the Deccan. At present Ṣafshikan Khān is without *jāgīr* it is better it is given to him.

---

1. There is much *Pāibāqī* in [*ṣūba*] Haiderabad. Let them assign [*Jāgīrs*] from those *maḥāls* after usual reduction. IJC I/45/11-12.

This shows that *jāgīrs* in the Deccan were primarily reserved for those regularly serving them, in order to ease the pressure upon them.

On the other hand, there were hardly any takers for *pāibāqī* in the 'new territory' where little revenue could be collected. The Mughal chancery seems to have invented the term *gosht o istikhwān* ['flesh and bone'] to indicate that the pay-claimant should be satisfied with getting both meaty and unattractive *jāgīrs,* the latter being given from the *pāibāqī* in *ghair-'amalī* areas. This is the burden of IJC, *I/42/1-32*. It relates to the *jāgīr*-claims of Ismā'il Khān Makka whose *vakīl* did not agree to the transfer of his *jāgīr* in 1101 AH [? 1110 AH = AD 1698-99] to *pargana* Kalpkor with a reduction of the *jama'* to two-thirds. Aurangzeb rejected Ismā'il Khān's protest and ordered:

> IJC, *I/42/1-32* Even Princes wished to relinquish *jāgīrs* which did not yield enough income. Upon his transfer, Jānsipar Khān's *jāgīrs* in *pargana* Kaulas, *ṣūba* Haidarabad, with revenue receipts of Rs 1, 34,000 was assigned to Prince Kām Bakhsh. The Prince argued that he would have to empty troops [500 horse and 1000 infantry] costing him over Rs one lakh a year, so that in three years he would not be able to recover a single year's salary for himself. He thus pleaded for *jāgīr* somewhere else. Aurangzeb reacted to the plea [9 *Jumada*-1 Regnal Year 45=12 October, 1701] with the following caustic comment:
>
> If the Governor and Prince cannot administer it, how can anyone else do so? If reduction [of *jama'*] is desired, let it be given.

In IJC, *I/42/1-78*, dated 15 Ziqa'd 42 Regnal Year, [24 June 1698] it is stipulated by the Emperor that newly recruited Deccanis are to be given *jāgīrs* out of the *pāibāqī* of Imtiyazash [Adoni, Karnatak-i-Bijapuri], "which has not till now been given in pay-assignment or made over to the *Khāliṣa*", i.e. revenue had simply not been collected there. In territories where order had been established and so were *'amali,* they were not entitled to hold *jāgīrs;* these were to be resumed and converted into *Khāliṣa.* We can, again, see here that the large *pāibāqī* shown on paper, immediately after the conquest, had no reality since it yielded no revenue, being still *ghair-'amalī.*

[C] Pressure on *Jāgīrs*

Aurangzeb was troubled by the extensive exactions of illegal cesses called *sibtī* [lit. 'written, recorded'], [*vide* IJC, *I/47/1-17*], he recorded not only his anxiety on the score, but also indicated why these were occurring [IJC, *I/46/6-26*]:

> It has been reported that the *sibtī* has become very extensive in the Deccan provinces because of the transfers of *jāgīrs* and reductions of *manṣabs.* The news-recorders [*wāqi'a-nigārān*] and intelligence reporters [*sawānih-navīsān*] should report who is responsible. In our period what has not happened that will not now happen - forbidden things, illegal innovations are causes of devastation of the country!...

Similarly, most of the *faujdars* and *thanadars* etc till the issuance of the *parwana-i sibti* in accordance with His Majesty's orders, representation and *parwangi* obtain the order [*parwana-i uhda*] without the imposition of crop as per the *muchalka*, obtain the *parwana-i sibti.* Since a long time has passed that they have not get the *asnad-i sibti* who are in control of the revenue while without assessment *nustkha-i sibti* is not valid. Previously the *diwans* of the *subas* was written that all those who have not obtained the *parwanajat-i sibti* there *jagir* should be confiscated. It was written that whosoever has control do not abstain should be treated as ordered. Aurangzeb strictly ordered that "Let the *diwan* in cooperation of the *nazim* [Governor] resume it, there is no delay in it then it should not give the *parwana-i sibti*; there is no regulation in North India [Hindustan] that the *parwana-i 'uhda* be given"[1].

Clearly, Aurangzeb was aware that the *jāgīr* transfers pressed the *jāgīrdārs* to be oppressive during the short periods they held *jāgīrs;* they would act similarly when their *manṣabs,* and, therefore, salaries were reduced. This was written 4 *Rabi'll*, R.Y. 46 [28 August, 1702].

The pressure upon *jāgīrdārs* is indicated also by IJC, *I/45/5-207.* Mu'izzuddin 'Umar, deputy of *Qila'dār* of Salher [Sulṭāngarh] in Baglana pleaded that his brother and cousin posted with him had 'not received their *jāgīrs.* In the meantime his own *jāgīr* had been reduced by the reduction in his *mashrūṭ* rank. Could this reduction be adjusted against the *jāgīrs* due against his brother's and cousin's claim? The answer was No, Aurangzeb noted:

> Transfer and exchange cannot be sanctioned. Let the due claims be met out of the *pāibāqī.* There is no end to such pleas.

A report on the situation in Karnatak-i Bijapuri dated 10 *Rabi'* I, 45 Regnal Year [31 August 1700], in IJC, *I/45/5-86* brings out very well why the *mashrūṭ* ranks [from which local levies or *sihbandīs* were usually maintained] had to be reduced:

> The situation is that the entire conquered territory has been assigned to meet expense on *sihbandīs,* etc, and even half of it is not secured to the government. If the *thānadārs* are not so numerous, there is reduction

1. IJC I/46/12-180.

in the *sihbandīs,* and the *sihbandīs* can be paid out of the *pāibāqī;* and so as a result of economy in the expenditure on *sihbandīs,* some entire good *maḥāls* can be reserved for the Imperial *Khāliṣa,* whereby a visible improvement in the financial situation can take place.

In this particular case, Aurangzeb apparently declined to take the recommended measures, merely demanding that everything should be done "according to rules and regulations" [*ẓabita-wa-dastūr*]. Although there was pressure on *jagirs* yet attempt was made to pay 8 monthly *jagir* instead of 10 monthly to Khan Firozjung as it was observed by Aurangzeb that:

> "It was not properly understood by granting one-third reduction so as to reach the *hasil* suitably"[1].

[D] Low Income from *Jāgīrs*

How much the actual income [*ḥāṣil*] of *jāgīrs* as against the estimated [*jama'*] had fallen in the Deccan becomes clear from Aurangzeb's response to information about *pargana* Kanti, contained in Inayat Jang Collection[2]. He had inquired if the whole of this *pargana* could be given in *jāgīr* to officers of his great noble Khān Bahādur. When the details of revenues and current assignments in the *pargana* were collected, it transpired that at 5002,411 *dāms* of *jama'* and Rs 71,000/- *annas* 12, in *ḥāṣil,* it was "7-monthly". This made Aurangzeb change his mind and think highly of its *deshmukh.* He wrote:

> The *ḥāṣil* is highly in excess. Let a good revenue collector [*'āmil*] [of the *Khāliṣa*] be appointed. The *deshmukh* should be enrolled in service and the *faujdārī* jurisdiction be assigned to him. Let the *jāgīrdārs* be given in exchange their pay-assignments in the Deccan or Hindustan.
>
> The document is dated 23 Jumada I, R.Y. 41 [27 November 1697].

IJC, I/40/10-27, [dated 25 Sha'ban 40 R.Y. 19 March 1697] is concerned with *pargana* Narsi[?], whose *ḥāṣil* at Rs 40,000 is said previously to have been 2 monthly. Then it was granted against a pay claim of 1, 42, 00,000 *dāms,* to accord with which the *jama'* had been increased [*taufīr*] by a fourth [*sawāī*]. In other words the *ḥāṣil* of the *jāgīr* was now less than 'one-and-a-half monthly'! Aurangzeb thereupon seems to have rather unwillingly agreed to a reduction in the *jama'* of *jāgīrs* which yielded low *ḥāṣil,* presumably even below 2-monthly.

1. IJC I/46/3-50.
2. ICJ/41/8-19.

But this was for ordinary assignees. For princes the *jama'* was kept exceptionally low. Thus, it was transpired that *pargana* Muṣtufābād had been assigned to Prince [A'zam] in 1102 A.H. [A.D. 1690-91] on the basis of the *ḥāṣil* of 1098 A.H. [A.D. 1686-87]. The revenue receipts in 1105 A.H. [? 1110 A.H. = 1698-99] despite natural calamities amounted to '15-monthly', i.e. they are in excess of the *jama'* by 25 percent. The rule was that the *jama'* in such cases should be raised to equal the *ḥāṣil,* so as to make the *jāgīr* 12-monthly. This was naturally opposed by the Prince who wanted that the increase in *jama'* should be waived. IJC, I/43/10-7 records Aurangzeb's orders hereon thus:

> In future the *jama'* should be so increased as to make it 12-monthly. The past is exempt.

The Prince thus got away with the excess collections of the previous years.

Although we find that in 36th R.Y. of Aurangzeb it was a prevalent practice that who so ever does increase his *jagir* by endeavour and effort which, if transferred then he shall be compensated accordingly according to which the horses of the contingent shall be brought for inspection. During the term of Makramat Khan the former *diwan* was issued the order that whomsoever's *jagir* is transferred as per the Imperial order he should be compensated accordingly and whosoever pleads for the transfer then after a gap of 2½ years he should be granted excess in *mahsul*. However, it was ordered during the term of late Amanat Khan to subsequently grant him such in a case just for ten months which was however continued by Aurangzeb[1].

[E] *Jāgīr* Assignment

It was held to be a rule that as far as possible *jāgīrs* should not be assigned in fragments. Aurangzeb noted in one document[2] dated 12 Zilhij Regnal Year 41, = 2 July, 1697] that he had repeatedly observed that Baglana should not be held in partnership [*shiraka na-darad*] [APPENDIX - A].

Elsewhere when of *pargana* Parner, *sarkār* Junnair, it was reported that after Ismāi'l Khān Makka had been assigned *jāgīr* out of the *Khāliṣa* there, there were still small claims of *manṣabdārs* accompanying him to be met, which it was proposed should be given out of the same *pargana* by

1. IJC I/36/0-3.
2. [IJC, I/41/2-3] He further recorded that it [Baglana] used to be assigned to one individual. It has been conquered during the term of our [first] Viceroyalty. As far as possible it should not be assigned in fragments and seeking it under *Khālisa* and posting a *karori* and place it in charge of the *Dīwān* of Khandesh.

carving them out of the *Khāliṣa,* Aurangzeb concurred. He was recording his observations as follows:

> Why does Ḥamīduddīn Khān [*Dīwān*], once he has abandoned [part of *Khāliṣa*] in exchange [for *jāgīr*], not give up the whole? To have scattered territories [in *Khāliṣa*] is bad, and so is such *jāgīr* bad.[1]

Since for most of the matters of the *Diwāni* the representations are presented by the Governors of Aurangabad for which another order has been issued to present the important … through Prince Kam Bakhsh then Aurangzeb ordered that:

> Let the important affair which are must be communicated in writing which should be personably while so as to represent therein[2].

Aurangzeb seems to have kept in mind the families of those who died fighting for him. When Qādirdād Khān died in action, he had a large estate demand [*muṭālaba*] against him. His son 'Ināyatullah protested that it should not be deducted from his *manṣab*-pay, but from that of his brothers who were in actual possession of the *jāgīr.* When this report, dated 8 Ziqa'd Regnal Year 45 [16 April, 1701] was placed before Aurangzeb, he wrote:

> The demand [*muṭālaba*] against Qādirdād Khān, who died in action, is waived, except for whatever has been so far realised. It should not be taken from the heirs.[3]

On Muftakhar Khān's death in battle, his son 'Azizullah sought a *jāgīr* in the Deccan, but was unable to obtain it. A *jāgīr* was proposed for him in *pargana* Ner, Khandesh. Aurangzeb wrote on the proposal:

> *Jāgīr* should be given. Why is it not given? Why is it not given in Hindustan among those posted with Yar Muḥammad Khān? His father too had died in action. He does not have the capacity to bear the hardship of the campaign.

As for Ner, Nūr Khān's *jāgīr* these had been resumed upon his dismissal for some cause. His brother Jalaluddin Khān had been called to the court. Aurangzeb was now inclined to favour the brothers since their father [unnamed] too had died in the battle. So Aurangzeb added to the above note:

> The *maḥāl of waṭan* [home-*jāgīr*] is to be treated as loan [not property]. Jalāluddīn Khān has prior claim on it [*pargana* Ner?]. If not, then Nūr Khān by restoring him to an annual pay of two lakh [*dāms*], for his father has died in action.[4]

1. IJC, I/42/10-114.
2. IJC, I/46/9-41.
3. IJC, I/45/11-52.
4. IJC, I/47/12-30.

We may suppose that the Emperor was here thinking of *waṭan* in giving the same *jāgīr* to Jalāluddin Kh̲ān or Nūr Kh̲ān as his father had held. But he had then ruled out any parity with his inherited *jāgīr* [*waṭan*], by saying that the grant of *waṭan* too was a loan not a property transfer, and so it would be always subject to recall.

The wheels of Mughal administration normally moved very slowly and its bureaucratic structure could thwart Imperial orders. Two Maratha *thānadārs* of Shikarpur, Santa and Hanho petitioned that the Emperor had granted two villages out of *pāibāqī,* which they had not received, although *pāibāqī* in the *pargana* was available. Aurangzeb wrote in irritation:[1]

> In these petty matters, which belong to the *Dīwanī's* jurisdiction, why keep delaying [till the Emperor's approval]. When *pāibāqī* is available, and pay-assignment out of it has been ordered, such insistence [on fresh Imperial sanction] is improper.

The report on the case was submitted to the Emperor on 18 Muharram 47 Regnal Year [3 June, 1703].

A similar sense of irritation as shown when a plea of Ma'mur Kh̲ān for a *jāgīr* in *ṣūba* Bijapur was submitted with the report that the expense on *sihbandīs* in Bijapur province had already been judged excessive by the Emperor. Aurangzeb observed:

> The matter need not be given such length and width. Ma'mūr Kh̲ān does not want a *jāgīr* in Bir, but in Bijapur. He may be given [*jāgīr*] in Bijapur and those who are transferred as a result be given [*jāgīr*] in Bir.

When a report showed that after Ya'qut Kh̲ān's transfer, *pargana* Patur was not given over either to *kh̲āliṣa* or in *jāgīr,* awaiting perhaps its assignment on reduced *jama'* to Prince Kām Bakh̲sh, Aurangzeb wrote:

> Let them issue the *sanad* [for the Prince]. Hereafter let not such negligence occur, for it will not have good consequences. Why so much delay? It was transferred from Ya'qut Kh̲ān; but not given to *kh̲āliṣa* nor in pay-assignment.[2]

The date of the document is 2-Muharram 42 Regnal Year [11 July, 1698].

Aurangzeb's anger at the territory remaining un-assigned and so in *pāibāqī* during the intervening period is explained by his comments in another case, where he said of a balance remaining unassigned that-

> It be given to whoever wants it. The income on *pāibāqī* belongs neither to government nor to peasants; it is just being lost.[3]

1. IJC, I/47/11-113.
2. IJC, I/42/3-46.
3. IJC, I/46/11-103 and 104.

Obviously temporary lapses of *jāgīr* into *pāibāqī* brought no or little revenue to the government.

When the *jagir* of Sazawar Khān, from the *pāibāqī* of *pargana* Chitguppa etc, who was the dismissed *qila'dār* and *faujdār* of Muhammadabad [Bidar] Aurangzeb ordered that:

> "The rule is again stated and fixed that by transferring the dismissal, the newly replaced be given as owing to the transfer of Sazawar Khān who previously held the *mansab* it should be given to Jalaluddin Khān as well as owing to the transfer of Ghairat Khān it should be given to Sazawar Khān and thereof it exceeds the dismissed be restored"[1].

Similarly when the *intikhab* [selection] of the *faujdar* of Dhurp demands [*matalib*] of Iradat Khan the *qila'dar* and were brought before His Majesty then he asked for its submission which were presented that consequent upon the death of Samundar Khan, *qasba* Firozabad etc were assigned to him whereafter he ordered that:

[Since] It is the mistake of Kirpa Ram, head *peshdasht* it is again ordered that it should be granted to the newly assigned person first and if it is in excess then to other as he is well aware of all rules [and regulations] as from the time of his father till date 50 years have elapsed that is why it has happened. First all the demand be given to the *mansab* as perhaps the *mansab* of Iradat Khān is less than the deceased and if the demand is still pending then the *awarja* be intenationally sent" [2].

[F] *Faujdārī* Rights and Jurisdictions

The office of *faujdārī* could be a very lucrative office if its holder used force to get what he wanted. It was reported in the *Waqā'i* of Prince Bedar Bakht, 10 Sha'ban Regnal Year 46 [30 December, 1702] that Ranchhor, *mahajan,* and inhabitants of the township [*qaṣba*] of Patan, then in the *khāliṣa,* had complained that *faujdār*, Imām Bakhsh, had seized Rs 20,000 from them, and added-then with an eye, perhaps, to the Emperor's religious zeal-that Imām Bakhsh did not conform to the *shari'at,* carefully attaching a statement of the *Qāzī* and *wāqia'-nigār* to this effect. The Emperor thereupon recorded his orders, 4 *Ramazan* 46 [2 February, 1702] as follows:

> Patan is assigned [in *jāgīr*] to that son [Bedar Bakht]. A soldierly man, of good behaviour, helpful for prosperity, should be sent. The township and fort are given to him. Wizārat Khān be told to send the record

1. IJC, I/46/10-31.
2. IJC, I/46/10-17.

> [*fard*]. The *manṣab* of the dismissed man [Imām Bakhsh, *faujdār*] should be reported to us by the *Bakhshī*.[1]

Imām Bakhsh's *manṣab* was in fact reduced by 50 *zāt*, 20 *sawār*.

It seems that the *faujdārs* and *thānadārs* had to obtain *parwāna-i sibtī* or official licenses to permit them to collect tolls and dues. These were apparently given for particular seasons and presumably against some payments to the treasury, which thus could have a share in their collections. But these officials used to give undertakings to produce the *sibti* certificates within forty days, and then would go on season after season collecting the dues without obtaining the certificates. If they were warned against it, they did not listen. Aurangzeb confirmed the previous order that such officials' *jāgīrs* were to be resumed:

> The *Dīwān* with the help of the Governor is to resume [the *jāgīr*], willy nilly. Here, if there is delay [in the officials' applying for it], the *parwāna-i sibtī* is not to be issued.[2]

In Mughal administration, *jāgīr* and *faujdārī* were different jurisdictions, but big *jāgīrdārs* were often granted *faujdārī* jurisdictions over their *jāgīrs*.[3] When this did not happen, there could be conflict between a *jāgīrdār* and the *faujdār*. The case came before Aurangzeb of *pargana* Sopa, *sarkār* Junnair, where the *jāgīrdār* Yāsīn Khān held *faujdārī* over part of his *jāgīr*, but not in that part which lay in *patta* Barahti, of which Badal Singh was the *faujdār;* and 'Abdu'r Raūf then made allegations of illegal exactions against Badal Singh, and armed clash between his men and those of Badal Singh occurred. Aurangzeb wrote thereon:

> Why is someone else *faujdār* within the *jāgīr* of Yāsīn Khān? The *thāna* of Sopa is in his charge. So also [this] *thāna* should be in the charge of Yāsīn Khān. The Second *Bakhshī* should understand [the facts] and report.[4]

Thāna here means obviously a police post of *faujdārī* jurisdiction. This was written apparently in Ziqa'd 47 Regnal Year [March-April, 1703].

[G] Local Administration

W.H. Moreland had studied the position of *pargana* Headman [*Chaudhurī*] of the Mughal Empire' largely on the basis of certain

1. IJC-I/47/11-34.
2. IJC, I/46/12-180, dated 27 Shawwal, Regnal Year 46, 27 March, 1702].
3. IJC I/47/1-71.
4. Irfan Habib, *Agrarian system of Mughal India,* rev. ed., p. 339 n, where that is said to have been "the general practice" under Aurangzeb.

documents relating to the Deccan.[1] The term *chaudhurī* of Northern India corresponded to *desāi* or *deshmukh* in the Deccan, and *qānūngo* to *deshpāndiyas*[2]. Moreland had seen no particular differences in the nature of the duties of the two offices of *chaudhurī* and *qānūngo,* while Irfan Habib has tended to stress the differences fairly heavily.[3] From document of Inayat Jang[4] Collection it transpires that under the Niẓāmshāi regime the office established in the *pargana* of Daulatabad was of *deshmukh* only. It is, reported that a claimant to the office of *deshpāndia* possessed a *farmān* of Shāh Jahān confirming Bahādurji in the office of *deshmukh,* as originally given through a *sanad* of Malik 'Ambar ["Siddi 'Ambar"]; "The office of *deshpāndia* was not included therein." Subsequently, another *farmān* gave both offices to Dataji, son of Bahādurji. In Aurangzeb's 31 Regnal Year both offices were confirmed jointly to Dataji's sons, Raghoji and Jadon. This was contested by Kaneri, son of Meghrani, who claimed to hold *sanads* of the Niẓāmshāh ["Be-nizām"] and Malik 'Ambar in favour of his ancestors for the office of *Deshpāndia* of the same *pargana.* His claim was, however rejected: 2 Sha'ban Regnal Year 41 [13 February 1698].

From this case it is obvious that the two offices were not really well differentiated in the Deccan and could be held by the same person. Obviously, Kaneri's claim that the office of *Deshpāndia* was originally separate in the *pargana* and belonged to his family did not carry conviction.

One more factor appears from this document. Although family inheritance was respected, conditions could be added with each confirmation. When the brothers Raghoji and Jadon obtained the office in Aurangzeb's Regnal Year 31 [A.D. 1687-88], they were obliged to pay Rs 3,00,800 as *peshkash* and get 7,00,000 *bīghas* of waste cultivated [in order to pay revenue]. These were thus offices that carried a large income.

Such income probably attracted professional bankers and financiers as well. An incumbent of the office of *Deshpāndia* of *pargana* Murtazabad complained that Mahda, a *sahūkar* of the Imperial camp, was aspiring to get the office transferred to himself and was getting support in this from the *faujdār* and *qila'dār,* Muḥammad Ashraf.[5]

[H] Maintenance of Military Contingents

It was a long-standing complaint in the Mughal Empire that commanders were not maintaining their contingents according to their

1. *JRAS*, 1938, pp. 511-21.
2. Habib, *Agrarian System of Mughal India*, rev. ed., pp. 331-335.
3. *Ibib.*, pp. 331-38.
4. IJC, I/41/10-142.
5. IJC, I/38/0-14.

manṣabs. Interestingly enough one IJC document contains the complaint of Sazāwār Khān that he and his kinsmen were the principal *jāgīrdārs* in *pargana* Nasik [Gulshanabad]. A balance of pay [*ṭalab*] was still due against which *jāgīrs* needed to be assigned. He pointed out that the adjoining *parganas* of Wan and Dindauri "are assigned in pay to different Maratha people who do not at all possess contingents", and pleaded that he be given *jāgīrs* at their expense. Aurangzeb first called for a report on the *jāgīrs* held by Sarfarāz Khān and his kinsmen which were spread over seven *parganas* in the Deccan, the pay-claim being 7,30,37,000 *dāms*, while the *jāgīrs* assigned had the *jama',* of 5,82,39,55, *dāms* only. Despite this shortfall, Aurangzeb turned down the plea, recording the following observation:

> Though the said Khān does maintain a contingent, it is not perhaps as much as he can maintain from the *jāgīrs* he has. Unless there is a certificate from the Prince, the *Bakhshī*, and the Superintendent of Brand and Muster-roll about the presence of his contingent in accordance with his [*manṣab*] - salary, a *jāgīr* cannot be given in the Old Territories. If he wishes, the *jāgīrs* can be given in Bijapur and Ḥaidarabad from unsubdued territory [*ghair-'amal*].[1]

IJC, *I/45/11-12*, which bears Mun'im Khān's seal, enlarges upon the Maratha *manṣabdārs* as especially failing to maintain troops:

> Most Marathas, despite their not maintaining their contingents are in possession of their *jāgīrs* on the basis of brand-reports [*dāgh-nāma-hā*] submitted many years ago to the office of the *Dīwān*, and they would receive their pay-assignments in future as well. They do not bring their contingents for inspection-certificate [*taṣḥīḥa*]...
>
> Aurangzeb recorded on this the following orders:

They should give *taṣḥīḥas.* Whoever does not have any contingents or has less [than the standard], his *jāgīr* should be resumed.

Another device used was to deny good *jāgīrs* to those suspected of being without contingents. It was noticed in a statement of 27 Shawwal Regnal Year 46 [27 March 1702] that Takoji, etc, had been assigned "good *jāgīrs*" in *pargana* Shivgaon, within 'Old Territory', and received *jāgīrs* in Raibagh in 'New Territory' with 50 percent reductions of *jama'* whereas it had been laid down that "newly enrolled Deccanis, without contingents, should receive most of their *zāt* pay-claim in the New Territory without any, [*jama'*] – reduction". Aurangzeb reaffirmed this position, noting that -

1. IJC, I/45/7-10.

'Old' means [territory acquired] up till 31st Regnal Year of His Majesty [Shāh Jahān]; and from [our] accession to-date, all [acquisitions] are 'New'. Seeing the [state of] contingents from the reports of the Superintendent of the [Brand] Certificate [*Taṣḥīḥa*], and the imperial Brand [*Dagh-i-Huzūr*] and Mun'im Khān, all [of these] are without contingents. Their *zāt* is however] retained. If they have anything in the 'Old Territory' it should be resumed[1].

Aurangzeb, however ordered that:

Difference between the old and new Deccanis be made on account of maintenance of the *tabinān* [contingent][2].

A different case was that of Khwāja Muḥammad Naqshbandi. This religious divine had been deprived of his *manṣab* of 600 *zāt,* 100 *sawār,* and later restored to 500 *zāt,* 50 *sawār.* But he maintained no contingent and so lost 30 *sawār* in rank. But a report of Rabi' I Regnal Year 45 [10 August 1701] stated that he had produced no brand-certificate [*dāghnāma*] and so got no *jāgīr* against his *sawār* rank. He, on his part, had made this the reason to demand that the resumed 30-*sawār* rank be restored. Aurangzeb now judged this man right and wrote:

For the Khwāja it will be better that he joins the Army of Prayer and get an annual pension without calamity or suffering, since he does not have the capacity to bear hardship of the journey here.[3]

The Khwāja in his representation thereafter also quoted this observation approvingly, pointing to his own great age [a mere 46 years]. He noted that Aurangzeb had fixed his pension at Rs 3000 a year, large amount those days. But the Khwāja still wanted more, for he had a family and was in debt. Obviously, he was not to be lightly shaken off.

Aurangzeb also used to encounter numerous embarrassing situations. We are requited with a statement of Muḥammad Saifullāh, *Naib Dīwān* of Aurangabad referring to the communication of Muḥammad Ja'far, *Wāqi'a nigār* [news reporter] to appoint someone recommended by him to the office of *Karorī* by transferring Muḥammad Sharīf, *Karorī* of Bir which he refused to entertain without any fault of him. Similarly, when he also refused to act according to *Wāqi'a Nigār's* advice to appoint his candidate to a vacant post which he denied as well. Consequently he threatened him of misleading entry in the diary of event to which Aurangzeb reacted then:

"It is not acceptable without any investigation. Since *Bakhshī* and *Wāqi'a Nigār* have been transferred no representation has been

1. IJC, I/46/12-167 & copy, I/46.12-178.
2. IJC, I/46/10-13.
3. I/45/5-44.

received. Behavioural pattern of the *Khānazads* [sons of nobles] etc is devoid of devotion, honestly, and compassionate attachment with this Government, and the interested ones whose intensions are not accomplished, indulge in enmity to the extent of suspicion and in just imputation throwing him [His Majesty] in perturbation and consternation due to which persistence of imperial assignments is lost, hence consider it obligations to represent minutely."[1]

Conclusion

These documents make it clear that by Aurangzeb's last years the pressures of financial crisis in the Deccan were manifest. By its own resources it could not support the Mughal effort against the Marathas and the Imperial budgets in the Daulatabad and Bijapur provinces. This meant that the deficits had to be met by treasure transfers from North India and by assignments of *jāgīrs* in North India to *manṣabdārs* posted in Deccan. In other words, there would have to be a constant drain on North Indian resources. This must be remembered as a possible justification of the policy of detachment from the Deccan which Aurangzeb's successors pursued.

As a component of this financial drain, one can find that the 'crisis of *jāgīrs*'in the Deccan is well illustrated by a number of documents. The apparent *pāibāqī* reserve in Ḥaidarabad and Bijapur provinces is deceptive since it largely comprised territory claimed on paper and not actually subjugated. These were hardly territories that any *manṣabdār* would care to hold to obtain his pay. *Jāgīrs* in the 'Old Territory', on the other hand, were hard to obtain, and the documents show how many *manṣabdārs* were just left without *jāgīrs*.

At the same time, while creaky and slow, we see the Mughal administration nevertheless functioning. The bureaucratic structure was intact; records were compiled and maintained; reports and accounts were sought and given. Finally, like modern files, the papers come before the Emperor for his orders. Generally, we find that Aurangzeb read the papers and gave, in most cases, alert and sensible responses. He becomes vague and general, only when matters like financial deficits could not be resolved by a few precise instructions. Still, we can see some kind of strategy being pursued to curtail malexpenditure and secure better military efficiency. The strategy was not adequate, as events were duly to disclose. But one cannot say that none was tried.

[II] *Nāẓims and Faujdārs*

It is but natural that the post of the governor [*nāẓim*] in the Mughal

1. IJC, I/45/4-70 & I/45/4-7.

Imperial administration was a very significant one. The Mughal Empire was divided into a number of provinces [*ṣūbās*], each of which had been variously known as *nāẓim, ṣāḥib-i ṣūba, ṣūbedār, faujdār-i ṣūba* etc. On the pattern of two principal ministers at the centre, the *Dīwān* and the *mīr ba<u>kh</u>shī*, the provincial governors were normally appointed from among officers holding the highest ranks or *manṣabs*. One can assume that they always formed the hardcore of the provincial bureaucracy. The administrative hierarchy in the Mughal administration in the Deccan like *Nazims*, *faujdārs* and *suba* official has been explained for better understanding of the working of the administrative apparatus of the Mughals.

It is an established fact that the jurisdiction and powers of the governors have been analysed often enough.[1] An attempt is made here to examine the nature and procedure of appointments and the kind of persons, appointed as governors from a study of the actual appointments in the six Mughal Deccan provinces as this section is based on an investigation of such appointments during the second half of the reign of Aurangzeb from 1682 to 1707 A.D. Though this period is a long one yet may be considered sufficiently long to draw significant inferences from our historical records with some confidence.

This is a well established fact that only first decade of Aurangzeb's reign is covered by the detailed official chronicle, the 'Ālamgīr Nāma of Muḥammad Kāẓim whereas for the remaining nearly four decades we have to procure our information from such sources which are by no means as easily accessible or, alternatively, as reliable. The list has been compiled principally from the *A<u>kh</u>bārāt-i Darbār Mu'alla*, supplemented by the numerous chronicles, memoirs and epistolalory collections for which detailed references have been searched out to substantiate the arrangements. Through the main table of the six provinces of the Mughal Deccan containing a list of its governors, with the complete duration of their terms of office reference to the regnal years of Aurangzeb is not an exhaustive one. However, the information is virtually complete for all the six Mughal Deccan provinces. Furthermore it is also possible in regard to some Deccan provinces, where there is a blank, it can be explained by the fact that no governor was appointed or the province was being regarded as part of the superior viceroyalty of the Deccan.

Certain assumptions have been found necessary *viz*., a distinction has been made between deputies of princes, who served as governors. However, on an average, each single term of a governor lasted only a slightly more

1. For a comprehensive study of the subject, see P. Saran *Provincial Government of the Mughals* [1526-1658], Allahabad, 1941.

than 2½ years while on an average again each governor was appointed to about two terms. The Mughal court did not approve of long terms for governors as they were generally transferred or recalled after two or three years. For the Mughal Deccan provinces there are only 40 years for which appointments are known in which 19 actual appointments as governors remained which yields the duration of 2 years and 1 month.

Table – 1

Regnal Year	*Deccan*	*Bedar*	*Khandesh*	*Berar*	*Au-rang-abad*	*Bijapur*	*Golkunda*
25.	Bahādur Khān Kokā [Īrānī]		Mughal Khān [Tūrani], Lashkar Khān, Saiyid Munawwar Khān [Ind.]				
26.	Bahādur Khān Kokā [Īrānī]	Mīr Sham-suddin Mukhtār Khān Sabzwāri [Ī]					
27.	Ṣāfī Khān [Ī]		Khān-I Zamān	Īrij Khān [Ī]			
28.	Amānat Khān Mīr Muinuddīn [Ī] [d]		Mīr Khalīl [Ī]				
29.	Ḥāji Shafī' Sabzwāri [Ī]	Qūlīch Khān [T]	Prince A'zam/ Mīr Khān [Ind.] [Dy]	Īrij Khān [d] [Ī] Ḥasan 'Ali Khān Bahādur [Ī] [d]			
30.	Ḥāji Shafī' Sabzwāri [Ī]			Muḥammad Ibrāhīm, Mahābat Khān [Ī, Dy] of Prince Kām Bakhsh		Mīr Muḥammad Ḥasan Rūhullāh Khān II [Ī] 'Abdullah Khān [Ī] Lashkar Khān Munawwar Khān [Ind.]	
31.							
32.							
33.							

34.							
35.							Jān Sipāar Khān [Ī]
36.		'Abdullāh Khān [Ind.] Lashkar Khān	'Ināyat Khān II [Ī]	Nawāzish Khān Rūmi [T]			Jān Sipāar Khān [Ī]
37.		Munaw-war Khān [Ind.]	Maraḥmat Khān, Dīndār Khān [Ī]	Nawāzish Khān Rūmi [T]			Jān Nisār Khān 'Abul Makārim [Ī]
38.	Diyānat Khān, Mīr 'Abdul Qādir [Ī]	'Abdullāh Khān [Ind.]	Maraḥmat Khān, Dīndār Khān [Ī]	'Ali Mardān Khān [Deccani]		Lashkar Khān Munawwar Khān [Ind.]	Jān Nisār Khān 'Abul Makārim [Ī]
39.		Khānazād Khān Rūhlullāh Khān [Ī]	'Ināyat Khān II [Ī]	'Ali Mardān Khān [Deccani]		Lashkar Khān Munawwar Khān [Ind.]	Jān Nisār Khān 'Abul Makārim [Ī]
40.		Rūhlullāh Khān [Ī] Najābat Khān Bahrawar Khān [Ī]	'Ināyat Khān II [Ī]			Lashkar Khān Munawwar Khān [Ind.]	Rustam Dil Khān [Ī]
41.		Bahrawar Khān		Prince Kām Bakhsh			
42.	Ḥasan 'Ali Khān Bārha [Ind.]	'Ali Mardān Khān [Dec.]	Najābat Khān Bahrawar Khān [T]	'Askar Khān [I – Dec.]		Ma'mūr Khān [Af]	Jān Sipāar Khān [Ī]
43.	Najābat Khān, Bahrawar Khān [T]	'Ali Mardān Khān [Dec.]	Mu'tqid Khān, Muḥammad Qulī [T]	'Askar Khān [Ī - Dec.]		Ma'mūr Khān [Af], Lutfullah Khān [Ind.]	Jān Sipāar Khān [Ī]
44.	Najābat Khān, Bahrawar Khān [T]	Khuda Banda Khān [Ī]	Mu'tqid Khān, Muḥammad Qulī [T]	Khuda Banda Khān [Ī] 'Ali Mardān Khān			Jān Sipāar Khān [d]
45.	Najābat Khān, Bahrawar Khān [T] Lutfullāh Khān [Ind.]	Khuda Banda Khān [Ī]	Najābat Khān, Bahrawar Khān [T]	Firoz Jung [T]		Lutfullah Khān [Ind.] Chin Qilīch Khān [T]	Prince Kām Bakhsh Rustam Dil Khān [Ī] [Dy]
46.	Prince Kām Bakhsh	Khuda Banda Khān [Ī]	Najābat Khān, Bahrawar Khān [T]	Firoz Jung [T]		Chin Qilīch Khān [T]	Saiyid Mu-zaffar Khān [Ind.]

47.	Prince Kām Bak<u>h</u>sh	<u>Kh</u>uda Banda <u>Kh</u>ān [Ī]	Prince Bedar Bak<u>h</u>t	Firoz Jung [T], Tīr Andāz <u>Kh</u>ān [Dy]		Chin Qilīch <u>Kh</u>ān [T]	Prince Kām Bak<u>h</u>sh
48.	Prince Kām Bak<u>h</u>sh		Mīr Aḥmad Khān [T] Dy Prince Azam	Firoz Jung [T]		Chin Qilīch <u>Kh</u>ān [T]	Dāūd <u>Kh</u>ān Panni [Dy] [Af]
49.	Prince Azam		Najābat <u>Kh</u>ān	Firoz Jung [T]		Chin Qilīch <u>Kh</u>ān [T]	Rustam Dil <u>Kh</u>ān [Ī] [Dy]
50.			Bahrawar <u>Kh</u>ān Chin Qilīch <u>Kh</u>ān [T]	Firoz Jung [T]		Chin Qilīch <u>Kh</u>ān [T]	
51.			Bahrawar <u>Kh</u>ān Chin Qilīch <u>Kh</u>ān [T]	Firoz Jung [T]		Prince Kām Bak<u>h</u>sh	

***Source*: Deccan: [Aurangabad]**

R.Y. *Ma'āsir-i 'Ālamgīrī,* pp. 180, 205; 27 R.Y. *A<u>kh</u>bārāt* [27 R.Y.]; *Ma'āsir-i 'Ālamgīrī*, p. 243; 28 R.Y. *A<u>kh</u>bārāt*, [28 R.Y.]; 29-31 [R.Y.] *A<u>kh</u>bārāt* 28 R.Y., 30 R.Y.; [38 R.Y.] *A<u>kh</u>bārāt* 38 R.Y.; 42 [R.Y.] *A<u>kh</u>bārāt* 42 R.Y.; 43-5 [R.Y.] *A<u>kh</u>bārāt*, 43 R.Y., 44 R.Y., 45 R.Y., *Ma'āsir-i 'Ālamgīrī*, p. 441; 46-8, *Ma'āsir-i 'Ālamgīrī*, pp. 461, 476, 483, *A<u>kh</u>bārāt* 46 R.Y., 49 *Ma'āsir-i 'Ālamgīrī*, p. 496.

Bedar [Zafarabad]:

29 [R.Y.] *A<u>kh</u>bārāt* 29 R.Y.; *Ma'āsir-i 'Ālamgīrī*, p. 263; [36 R.Y.] *A<u>kh</u>bārāt* [36 R.Y.], [37 R.Y.] *A<u>kh</u>bārāt* [37 R.Y.] 38 [R.Y.] *A<u>kh</u>bārāt* [38 R.Y.]; [39-40 R.Y.] *A<u>kh</u>bārāt*, 39 R.Y., 40 R.Y.; *Ma'āsir-i 'Ālamgīrī*, pp. 384-5, [2-3 R.Y.] *A<u>kh</u>bārāt* 42, 43 R.Y.; [44-7 R.Y.] *A<u>kh</u>bārāt*, 44 R.Y., 45 R.Y. 46 RY; *Ma'āsir-i 'Ālamgīrī*, p. 432.

Khandesh:

25-26 [R.Y.] *A<u>kh</u>bārāt*, 25, R.Y., *Ma'āsir-i 'Ālamgīrī*, p. 220; [28 R.Y.], *A<u>kh</u>bārāt*, 28 R.Y., 29 [R.Y.] *Ma'āsir-i 'Ālamgīrī*, p. 262; 36 [R.Y.] *A<u>kh</u>bārāt*, 36 R.Y.; 37-8 R.Y., *A<u>kh</u>bārāt*, 37 R.Y., 38 R.Y., 39 [R.Y.] *A<u>kh</u>bārāt* 39 [R.Y.; 40-42 [R.Y.] *A<u>kh</u>bārāt* 40 R.Y.; 41 R.Y.; 43 [R.Y.]; *Ma'āsir-i 'Ālamgīrī*, p. 470, 47-8 R.Y. *A<u>kh</u>bārāt*, 47 R.Y., 48 R.Y.; *Ma'āsir-i 'Ālamgīrī*, pp. 470-480; *Ma'āsir-i 'Ālamgīrī,* p. 496; 50 R.Y. *Ma'āsir-i 'Ālamgīrī*, p. 161 [6].

Berar:

28 R.Y. *Ma'āsir-i 'Ālamgīrī,* p. 262; 29-30 *A<u>kh</u>bārāt* 30 R.Y., *Ma'āsir-i 'Ālamgīrī*, pp. 278-281; [31 R.Y.] *Ma'āsir-i 'Ālamgīrī*, p. 302; 36 R.Y. *A<u>kh</u>bārāt* 36 R.Y.; 37-9 R.Y. *A<u>kh</u>bārāt* 37 R.Y., 38 R.Y., 39 R.Y., 41

R.Y. *Ma'āsir-i 'Ālamgīrī*, pp. 390, 396; 42-3 [R.Y.] *Akhbārāt*, 42 R.Y., 43 R.Y., *Ma'āsir-i 'Ālamgīrī*, p. 396, 44-5 [R.Y.] *Akhbārāt* 44 R.Y., 45 R.Y., *Ma'āsir-i 'Ālamgīrī*, p. 432.

Bijapur [Daruzzafar]:

30 R.Y. *Ma'āsir-i 'Ālamgīrī*, pp. 282, 299, 36 R.Y. *Ma'āsir-i 'Ālamgīrī*, pp. 327, 32 R.Y., *Akhbārāt* 32 R.Y., *Ma'āsir-i 'Ālamgīrī*, pp. 329, 38-40 [R.Y.] *Akhbārāt* 38 R.Y., 39 R.Y., 40 R.Y., 40-3 [R.Y.], *Akhbārāt* 42 [R.Y.], 43 R.Y., *Ma'āsir-i 'Ālamgīrī*, p. 412, 44 [R.Y.] *Akhbārāt*, 44 R.Y., 415 R.Y., 46 R.Y. *Akhbārāt* 410 [R.Y.], 47-49 R.Y. *Ma'āsir-i 'Ālamgīrī*, pp. 441-471; 474, 479, 480, 494, 496, 498, 518, *Dilkhushā*, 157 [6]; 51 R.Y. *Dilkhushā*, 1589, *Ma'āsir-i 'Ālamgīrī*, p. 520.

Golkunda:

36-7 R.Y. *Akhbārāt*, 36 R.Y., 37 RY; 38 [R.Y.] *Akhbārāt* 38 R.Y., 39 R.Y., 40 R.Y., 42/45 R.Y. *Ma'āsir-i 'Ālamgīrī*, p. 439; *Akhbārāt* 42 R.Y., 45 R.Y., 47 [R.Y.], *Akhbārāt* 47 R.Y., 48-9 R.Y., *Ma'āsir-i 'Ālamgīrī*, pp. 483, 494, 496, 497.

[III] *Other Ṣūba Officials*

Though we find often complex pattern of revenue payments detailed in the '*awārja*'[1] or balance documents yet these list individual *jāgīr* holdings within each *pargana*. Numerous imperial, political-military elite, *amīrs* [holding 1,000 *zāt* or above which was – personal decimal rank] and predominant technical administrators for a particular point of time of almost 120 *parganas* ranging from 34th to 51st regnal years of Aurangzeb [1690-1707 AD] due to the availability of 240 *awārja* documents[2] depicting non-military role as well. We find them often serving as *faujdārs* [military commandants] *qila'dārs* [castellan or fort commanders] or sub-ordinate field commanders in prominent and responsible positions with ranks as low as 300 to 500 *zāt*.

[A] *Dīwān*

In the second phase of Aurangzeb's reign [1682-1707 AD] the most competent and successful technical professionals serving as *Dīwāns* [minister or in-charge of revenue and finance of a province], Deputy *Dīwāns* of the Mughal provinces might hold similar rank and possess

1. As defined in f. 36.
2. Inayat Jung Collection contains these āwārja papers which were generally drawn up in order to ascertain the available revenues open for reassignment to *manṣabdārs*; *Cf.*, J.F. Richards, [ed.] 'Official Revenues and Money Flows in a Mughal Province', in *Imperial Monetary System of the Mughal Empire,* OUP, Delhi, 1987, p. 209.

similar prominence and visibility who could well be known personally to the Emperor and have been recongnised by him in the court or in the Imperial camp.

Since the political and administrative assimilation into the imperial order preceded the imperial administration that also recognised the distinctiveness of the Old Deccan provinces of Aḥmadnagar, Berar, Bidar and Khandesh which experienced conquest and administrative consolidation relatively late also relatively detached from the core area of the Mughal Empire in North India by stationing a Viceroy of the four [later six] Deccan provinces at Aurangabad, who held authority over the provincial administrations as the *Dīwān* of the Deccan provinces possessed the same level of authority.

Aurangabad became the capital of the Mughal Deccan, home of the Mughal Viceroy of the Deccan, *Dīwān* of the Deccan regulation administrative structure. We frequently encounter with Diyānat Khān and Mu'tamād Khān *Dīwāns* of the Deccan[1] in our documents. Kifayat Khān was the *Dīwān* of Daulatabad.[2] Similarly Abul Makārim, *Dīwān* of *ṣūba* Bijapur.[3] Saiyid Ḥusain, was the *Dīwān* of *ṣūba* Khandesh.[4] Mīr Muḥammad Ja'far, *Dīwān* of *ṣūba* Muḥammadabad Bidar succeeded in getting approved through Emeror Aurangzeb charge of the collection of the *peshkash* [tribute and withholding] the perquisites of the *zamīndārs* of *parganas* Neola, *sarkār* Nander *ṣūba* Bidar. Accordingly he excluded Mīr Ghulam J'afar's *gumāshta* from revenue collection.

Similarly Mīr 'Ali Naqī, Deputy *Dīwān* of Aurangabad was directed to submit the receipt papers of the revenue collectors under signatures of the *zamīndārs*', seal impression of *Qāzī* and the receipt register under the seal of the clerks of the treasury w.e.f. 29th R.Y. till date along with his verification enabling him to ascertain the deposition and remission in *peshkash* to the *chaudhurīs*[5]. Muḥammad Shafī *Dīwān* of *ṣūba* Khandesh was informed that except for *Chaila* and *Khwājasara* no one should be paid in cash which was also allowed to *barqandāzān*[6]. Since Khwāṣ Khān

1. IJC, I/32/0-10-202. These documents also indicate their *jama'* and *ḥāṣil* figures assigned as *jāgīr* from different areas.
2. IJC, I/30/9-1.
3. IJC, I/32/8-1.
4. IJC, I/33/7-1. This position is confirmed from the statement of the *deshmukhs* and *deshpandiyas* of the area. Muḥammad Shafi *Dīwān* of Ḥaiderabad also implemented the Imperial order for the grant of cash of [*naqdi tankhwāh*] to the *barq-andāzān* posted at the forts.
5. IJC, I/35/2-3.
6. IJC, I/34/8-5. It seems to be a general order as its copy was also addressed to Muḥammad Ja'far, *Dīwān*. Cf IJC, I/34/8-4.

was the *Deshmukh* of headquarters [*ḥaveli*] Bijapur as well as the *jāgīrdār* Aurangzeb ordered that "Let it be communicated to the *Dīwān* that after the realisation of Rs 5,000 they should not interfere in the *jāgīr* and *rusūm* [perquisites of *deshmukhī*] in future as per Khwās Khān's *muchalka* that they should deduct ten lakh *dāms* in lieu of the installment."[1]

When 'Abdur Rahīm, *Deshmukh* of *pargana* Varval was imprisoned it was communicated by 'Ali Akbar, *Dīwān* of *ṣūba* Muḥammadabad Bidar that the *rusūm* and *in'ām* of the said *Deshmukh* shall remain suspended as his *gumāshta* [agent] shall not be permitted to seize anything[2]. Similarly 'Ali Naqī, Deputy *Dīwān* received the *parwana* of Sibghatullāh that waved off the cash perquisites to the peasantry. However, the measured land was unculturable, which was totally unproductive as the peasantry due to epidemics and famine had died and absconded owing to which cultivation of land was suspended. The *deshmukhī* and *deshpāndgī* of 27 *maḥāls* of Daulatabad etc along with Baizāpur was assigned contingent upon the *peshkash* of Rs 3,00,800 and bringing under plough seven lakh *bīghas* of uncultivable land.

The *dastūr-i deshmukhī* in 1054 A.H. [1644 A.D.] was resumed by way of trust whereafter Murshid Qulī Khān waved off the cash perquisites to the peasantry.

Since *Dīwān* used to play a crucial role in the issuance of the *farmān* it was but natural that in order to require a *farmān* a *parwana* of the *Dīwān* was essential as the petitioner could receive the *farmān* after the surrender of the fort.[3]

We are informed that 'Alī Akbar, *Dīwān* communicated that since 'Abdur Raḥīm, *Deshmukh* of *pargana* Varval had been imprisoned the perquisites and *in'ām* of the *Deshmukh* would be properly seized without allowing anything in charge of his agent [*gumāshta*].[4]

When there occurred confrontationist approach between *zamīndārs* as Saiyid Ghazanfar, *Amīn* and *Faujdār* expelled Yādwar, *Deshmukh* from *ṣūba* Bijapur notwithstanding his authority as the peasantry and the businessmen were in agreement with him. Their confrontationist approach had ruined the peasantry of the *pargana* owing to which the high road was closed as *pargana* Yādwar was *ser ḥāṣil* [full revenue paying] for

1. IJC, I/34/7-3. Khwās Khān pleaded that since in view of loss even 1/10th of the perquisites of *zamīndārī* is not received the *Dīwān* should make deduction of all *jāgīr*.
2. IJC, I/36/9-19. Mirak Ḥusain, was also the former *Dīwān* in 1095 AH [1685 AD] of *ṣūba* Berar, IJC I/40/5-9.
3. IJC, I/36/10-1.
4. IJC, I/36/9-14.

which *Dīwān* was to be communicated.[1] When five *chāwars* of land was usurped by the *zamīndārs* of Mangal Baidiyah, Abul Ḥasan *Dīwān* of *ṣūba* Khandesh was suggested to be approached so as to serve it again.[2]

We are informed that Shaikh 'Abul Ḥasan was the suspended *Dīwān* of Khandesh and Ḥaji 'Abdullāh was the present *Dīwān* thereat. Recommendations were made to approach 100 villages for which Diyānat Khān was directed to write to the provincial *Dīwān*.

Diyānat Khān, *Dīwān* of the Deccan saw to it that the *peshkash* of the state for 190 villages following the transfer of Jamāluddin *Deshmukh* of *pargana* Balapur, *ṣūba* Berar which the *mutaṣaddis* of the villages of *pargana* accepted was to be realised without depositing it in the royal treasury for which he had been directed to write to the *Dīwān* of *ṣūba* Berar[3].

Srīniwās, *Deshmukh* of *pargana* Aland *sarkār* Naldurg *ṣūba* Aurangabad represented that when Khān Muḥammad and Gobind Pandit dispatched by 'Abdur Reḥmān, the dismissed *Dīwān* of *ṣūba* Muḥammadabad [Bedar], were deputed to collect the stipulated *peshkash* and they collected Rs 1,050 without giving its acknowledgement receipt absconded in the night by listening to the news of the dismissal of *Dīwān*. Since they were staying in *ṣūba* Bijapur he solicited order for Ma'mūr Khān, Governor of *ṣūba* Bijapur which was acceded to in order to investigate the facts.[4]

Bashārat Khān, *Dīwān* of Berar commented upon the signatures of the *Deshmukh* and the *Deshpāndiya*[5], which however had become the bone of contention.[6] The matter of realisation of the installments of *peshkash* outstanding against the *Deshmukhs* were so serious that even in regard to Devdas and Baijnath, *Deshmukhs* of *pargana* Ellichpur, that when late Mūsawī Khān fixed their installments from 34th to 39th regnal year then Aurangzeb himself thus remarked about the realisation of the arears of *peshkash* from the two incumbents that:

> "Let they write to the *Dīwān* for the recovery [of *peshkash*] in accordance with the firm Imperial orders and the assessments of late Mūsawi Khān [Khān-*i Maghfirat Nishān*]"[7].

Thus, the *Dīwāns* calculations were treated as the correct one to realise the *peshkash* of arrears. The *Dīwān* of the *ṣūba* was bound to recommend the names of those who were known for extension of cultivation

1. IJC, I/41/2-10.
2. IJC, I/41/4-5.
3. IJC, I/41/4-25.
4. IJC, I/41/4-31.
5. IJC, I/41/7-7.
6. IJC, I/41/8-94.
7. IJC, I/40/8-9.

[ābādānkār] and the payment of the revenue [*mālguzār*] as such specific instructions were also issued to Bashārāt Khān, *Dīwān* of *ṣūba* Berar wherein the *Deshmukhs* had promised the cultivation of 1000 *netans* [unit of area in Berar equal to 80 *bighas* i.e.80x1000=80000 *bīghas*] yielding 9,000 *tankcha*, even which was not considered a fit case for recommending the names of Bir Bhan and Rajma etc, *Deshmukhs* of *pargana* in *sarkār* Narala *ṣūba* Berar.[1]

In view of the extension of cultivation and prosperity of the ruined villages Arshad Khān, *Dīwān* of *Khāliṣa Sharīfa* had attained special significance as he was ordered for arbitration in matters of dispute as well as remain a liaison officer in regard to financial matters of the *Khāliṣa Sharīfa*.[2] This was a common feature of the Mughal agrarian system that stress was laid on the extension of cultivation and the *zamīndārs* were also bound to execute this policy because the *Dīwāns* were responsible in such matters as well. Through such recommendations that their *sanads* were prepared thus since we come to know Muḥammad Rafi' *Dīwān* of Talkokan-i 'Ādil Khāni had written that the *sanad* that was granted to Muḥammad Ḥasan was in the office of the Deccan which was to be prepared and sent to the *Dīwān* as per the Imperial orders which was acceded to[3].

The *Dīwāns* were responsible for revenue administration. Ḥāji 'Abdullāh, the dismissed *Dīwān* of Berar complained that when he deputed Ṣafi 'Ali, *Aḥādi* [gentleman trooper] to collect the papers of the *parganas* of *sarkār* Gavil as requisitioned by the Emperor he issued *parwanas* enjoining the *zamīndārs* and letters to help the *aḥādi* by the military commandants [*faujdārān*]. But some of the *zamīndārs* due to the support of the *faujdārs* and the agents of *jāgīrdārs* and some owing to their arrogance did not respond to the *aḥādi*, instead replied to Ḥāji 'Abdullāh that he need not interfere in their matter which was to his utter dismay. Aurangzeb ordered to bring the requisite papers while others had not immediately written about the help of the present *Nāẓim* [Governor] and the *Dīwān*[4].

Dīwāns also used to report the refactory attitude of the *zamīndārs viz.*, Bashārat Khān, *Dīwān* of Berar sent Saiyid Yusuf, *manṣabdār* to collect the revenue papers of *sarkārs* Mahur and Basim yet *zamīndārs* of the majority of the *maḥāls* [fiscal units] did not respond owing to the support of the agents of the *faujdārs* and *jāgīrdārs* as the refractoriness of the *zamīndārs* of Bālāghāt was well known. Since he also commended Saiyid Yūsuf's behaviour as he had collected and sent from some of the *maḥāls* of

1. I/42/7-53.
2. I/45/11-173, I/46/2-71.
3. IJC, I/38/4-4.
4. IJC, I/38/5-8.

Ausa without any force or oppression as he had made utmost endeavours because he was quite intelligent, deserving imperial favours which was approved by the Emperor.[1]

The *Dīwān* was responsible for ascertaining the causes of loss in revenue, names of the *deshmukhs*, *deshpāndiyas*, distance of *parganas* from the surrounding townships and their direction which were to be recorded in the *mawāzana* papers as we come to know from a communication of Bashārat Khān, *Dīwān* of Berar.[2]

Aurangzeb himself relied on the potentialities of the *Dīwāns* as the Emperor commented upon the details furnished for position of *pargana* Basant Nagar's *deshmukhi* claims for seeking the Imperial orders. He observed that:

> "All these explanations and footnotes cannot be perused. Since he is the *Dīwān* and the confidante he should appoint [as *deshmukh*] taking into consideration the prosperity of the *pargana* and the consent of the peasantry".[3]

Bashārat Khān, *Dīwān* of *ṣūba* Berar also used to issue necessary instructions in regard to recording loss [*āfat*] as majority of the revenue collections of the fiscal units of the *jāgīrdārs* did not show any profit or loss to the Government.[4]

The *Dīwān* of the *ṣūba* was also approached for shifting the *zamīndārī* *viz*., Baṣālat Khān *qila'dār* [castellan] of A'zamnagar represented that the *Dīwān* of *ṣūba* Berar may kindly be ordered that *zamīndārī* of *pargana* Alsingh adjoining his *jāgīr* that belonged to refractory Bhar Karan which was to be assigned to Chandi Anthur as the *zamīndārī* of Mursi, Tenmi and Suryui situated near the said *pargana* so as to exterminate the mischief mongers which also met the imperial approbation.[5]

Aurangzeb refused to make any change in the *zamīndārī* of 'Abdul Karim, *zamīndār* of Baglāna etc because there were no such allegations against him. The emperor categorically recorded:

> "This is meant that neither the *mahāl-i zamīndārī* nor the *jāgīr-i ghair waṭan* could be granted [to anyone else]".[6]

The *Dīwān* was also responsible for bringing the waste land under plough. We are informed that during the *Dīwānī* of Makramat Khān,

1. IJC, I/41/5-9.
2. IJC, I/41/7-8.
3. IJC, I/41/8-120 & I/41/8-126.
4. IJC, I/41/9-4.
5. IJC, I/42/1-34.
6. IJC, I/42/5-13 & I/42/5-14.

Dīwān of Berar that *pargana* Devalgaon was slightly cultivated as the rest of the area was the jungle and desert where even grass did not grow that constituted almost 48,000 of *bīghas* of barren land. The *zamīndārs* thereof were summoned to the *Dīwānī* court contingent upon bringing to cultivation 2,000 *bīghas* of land. Consequent upon the completion of this process by assigning 3000 *bīghas* of barren land they would have to be granted 100 *bīghas* of barren land by way of *in'ām* to help them financially.

Though it was stipulated to bring the land under cultivation till 41st R.Y., yet by 39th R.Y. of Aurangzeb the Marathas [*Ghanīm-i laīm*] attached *pargana* Sandgali and extinguished all the *asnād* [certificates]. Since it was proved that *pargana* Devalgaon from the time of revenue administration of the Deccanis had been the abode of the miscreants, yet not a single piece of land had remained uncultivated. Accordingly they would have to be granted 150 *nītans* of land [120,000 *bīghas*] under cultivation as per the recommendation of Makramat Khān, the *Dīwān* by way of *jāgīr* side by side allocating some land to them by way of *in'ām* [to enthuse them].[1]

When Raja Neknām Singh s/o late Raja Kishan Singh *zamīndār* of Chanda solicited Imperial orders instructing Mu'tamād Khān, *Dīwān* of the Deccan to grant him his full *jāgīr* in *pargana* Parner as he was suffering heavily due to *be-jāgīrī*, which received the royal sanction as well.[2]

The *Dīwān* of the Deccan [in this case Muḥammad Khān to 'Ināyat Khān, the former *Naib Dīwān*] wrote that Satwā, *zamīndār* of *mauza* Faqirābād *pargana* Baiẓāpur *ṣūba* Aurangabad that since he had purchased 250 *bīghas* from village Ladsangwi, that could be entered in his adjoining village which however, required Imperial approbation.[3] 'Ali Naqi, s/o Diyānat Khān was the *Dīwān* of *ṣūba* Muḥammadabad [Bedar] in 1704 AD. Wizarat Khān was the *Dīwān* of *ṣūba* Muḥmmadabad [Bedar] in 45th R.Y. [IJCI/45/1-162]. The Mughals had a separate *Dīwān-i khāliṣa sharifa* which was held by Arshad Khān. [IJCI/45/4-188]. Muḥmmad Naṣeer was the *Dīwān* of Berār in 1702 [IJCI/44/6-13].

[B] Bakhshī

The *Bakhshīs*, ministers or officials supervised maintenance of military contingents and postings of commanders[4]. *Bakhshīul Mulk* Mukhliṣ

1. IJC, I/42/9-11.
2. IJC, I/46/4-4.
3. IJC, I/48/8-1, in 1704 'Ali Akbar was dismissed from the *Dīwānī* of Ḥyderabad. IJC, I/47/4-43.

574a. IJC, I/47/4-43.

4. *Cf.*, Irfan Habib, *Afrarian System,* second revised edition Delhi, 1999, p. 327. There was a *Bakhshī* of the entire Deccan [IJC, I/0/0-2021].

Khān was the *Bakhshī* while Mīr Ni'matullāh was one of the *Bakhshīs*.[1] Muḥammad Riza, s/o Ḥasan Qulī Bakhsh was the *Bakhshī* and *Wāqi'a Nigar* of *ṣūba* Bedar [IJCI/40/3-109 & I/46/3-113]. When the matter of a handicapped *manṣabdār* was brought before Aurangzeb the Emperor ordered his dismissal and the second *Bakhshī* was ordered to represent as some other dispensation was made to accommodate him.[2]

In the Mughal administration the *Bakhshīs* were also appointed at *ṣūba* level as well as Saiyid Muḥammad Ja'far s/o Saiyid Iftikhār Khān was the *Bakhshī* and *Wāqi'a-Nigār* of *Khujista-buniyad* [Aurangabad].[3]

When the matter of Imāmuddin was presented to Aurangzeb through Saiyid Iftikhār Khān *Bakhshī* and *Wāqi'a Nigār* of *ṣūba* Aurangābād, he had received *jāgīr* from the *pāibāqī* of Bīr. While he had evinced his interest in getting *jāgīr* from Ausa Fateḥābād Bir, Aurangzeb remarked that:

> "It was perused by His Majesty; it was ordered that since *jāgīr* could not be transferred for a single individual the *āwāraja* need not be submitted".[4]

Imām Qulī s/o Murshid Qulī was dismissed *Bakhshī* and the *Wāqi'a Nigār* of Tirambak as he was summoned by the Emperor.[5] In 46th R.Y. of Aurangzeb Saiyid Qulī Hāshim Beg was also the *Bakhshī*, *Wāqi'a Nigār* and *Darogha-i Dagh-o taṣḥiḥa* [Superintendent of the Branding Regulations].[6]

Muḥammad Amān Khān was the second *Bakhshī* of the gentleman troopers.[7] Mīr Muḥammad Ḥusain s/o Mīr Muḥammad Shākir was the *Bakhshī* and *Wāqi'a Nigār* of Bir in 1697 A.D.[8] Muḥammad Ashraf s/o Muḥammad Musharraf was the *Bakhshi* and *Wāqi'a Nigār* of Sulṭānpur, *sarkār* Nandurbar *ṣūba* Khandesh.[9] Muḥammad Hāshim s/o Yūsuf Beg was the *Bakhshī* and *Wāqi'a Nigār* of Baglāna.[10]

Mīr Ibrāhīm, s/o Mīr Niẓāmuddīn was the *Bakhshī-i Fauj-i Rāhdari*, [IJCI/47/3-42]. Later he became *Bakhshī* and *Wāqi'a Nigār* of Bir [IJCI/47/4-42]. Similarly Multafat Khān *alias* Muḥammad 'Alī, s/o

1. IJC, I/41/8-98.
2. IJC, I/46/12-171 & I/46/12-179.
3. IJC, I/46/2-114 & I/0/0-645.
4. IJC, I/45/2-51.
5. IJC, I/45/1-162.
6. IJC, I/46/1-100 & I/46/1-171.
7. IJC, I/0/0/0-202.
8. IJC, I/39/11-142. He was dismissed and summoned to the court in 1701 A.D. [IJC, I/45/8-50].
9. IJCI, I/42/6-14, I/41/0-17, 'Abdul Qayyūm, s/o Ḥusāmuddin Khān was the *Bakhshī and Wāqi'a Nigār* of Parenda, [*Cf.*, IJC, I/010-494].
10. IJC, I/44/6-14, IJC, I/45/2-52.

Muḥammad Ḥabib was the *Bakhshī* of the army of Prince Bedar Bakht, [*Cf.*, IJCI/47/3-42].

Bakhshīul Mulk Behramand Khān succeeded Mukhliṣ Khān in 1703-4 A.D.[1] Shaikh Ghulām Muḥammad, s/o Quṭbullah, was the *peshdasht* of the *Tan Bakhshī* of *Aḥādis*.[2] Muḥammad Ḥusain s/o Ẓiauddīn Ḥusain was the *Bakhshī* and *Wāqi'a Nigār* of Patan.[3] We are informed that Muḥammad Ja'far s/o Iftikhar Khān was the *Bakhshī* and *Wāqi'a Nigār* of the army of Khān Firuz Jung.[4] 'Ali Qulī Beg s/o Muḥammad Riza Beg was the *Bakhshī* and *Wāqi'a Nigār* of Imtiyazgarh. Ja'far Beg s/o Tarsun Beg was the *Bakhshī* and *Wāqi'a Nigār* of Bahādurgarh.[5] Muḥammad Shafī s/o Muḥammad Momin was the dismissed *Bakhshī* and *Wāqi'a Nigār* of Machhlibandar who was summoned to the Imperial court.[6] Shamsuddīn s/o Muḥammad Zamān, was the *Bakhshī* and *Wāqi'a Nigār* of Kherla etc *ṣūba* Berar, Bālāghāt[7].

We are informed that Ibrāhīm Beg s/o Ismāi'l was the *Bakhshī* and *Wāqi'a Nigār* of Aḥmadnagar.[8] Muḥammad Ḥusain, s/o Muḥammad Shafi' was the *Bakhshī* and *Wāqi'a Nigār* of Suner. He later became *Bakhshī* and *Wāqi'a Nigār* of Bir Sheogaon.[9] In the penultimate analysis we find him holding the post of *Bakhshī* and *Wāqi'a Nigār* of Sheogaon.[10]

Muḥammad Hashim s/o Yūsuf Beg was the *Bakhshī* and *Wāqi'a Nigār* of Baglāna.[11] While Mīr Muḥammad Ibrāhīm, s/o Mīr Niẓām was the *Bakhshī* and *Wāqia' Nawīs* in 1703 AD[12], Ilahwardi Beg s/o Muḥammad Beg was the *Bakhshī* and *Wāqi'a Nigār* of Kokan-i 'Adil Khāni.[13] Ja'far Beg, s/o Tarsūn Beg was the *Bakhshī* and *Wāqi'a Nigār* of Bahādurgarh. Ibrāhīm Beg s/o Ismāi'l Beg was the *Bakhshī* and *Wāqi'a Nigār* of Aḥmadnagar. [IJCI/45/9-4].

1. IJC, I/46/2-213. Jam Quli was the *Bakhshī* and *Wāqi'a Nigār* of Islamgarh Raheri [IJC, I/40/12-165].
2. IJC, I/47/3-42.
3. IJC, I/47/3-42. In 1699 he held the same post in Inderpat which was held by him in the army of Firuz Jung. He was also transferred in the same capacity to Mulher [IJC, I/45/1-16]. IJC, I/45/2-52, I/45/5-50.
4. IJC, I/47/3-42.
5. IJC, I/43/6-40.
6. IJC, I/43/6-40.
7. IJC, I/42/8-38, IJC, I/45/2-36.
8. IJC, I//47/11-105.
9. IJC, I/45/2-52; I/0/0-576.
10. IJC, I/0/0-645.
11. IJC, I/45/8-51.
12. IJC, I/45/8-51.
13. IJC, I//45/5-54.

In 1699 A.D. he held the same post as in Indapur which position was held by him in the army of Firuz Jung. He was later transferred in the same capacity to Mulher. [IJCI/45/1-16].

The Mughal administration also took care of the relatives of the deceased *K͟hānazads* as Ẓiāuddīn, maternal grandson of late Fāẓil K͟hān was appointed as the *Bak͟hshī* and *Wāqi'a Nigār* of Karnatak-i Hyderabad.[1] Mīr *Bak͟hshī* s/o Mīr Niẓāmuddīn was the *Bak͟hshī* and *Wāqi'a Nigār* of [*sarkār*] Bir, *ṣūba* Aurangabad.[2]

In 1703 A.D. Neknām K͟hān was the first *Bak͟hshī* of *Aḥādīs* and he received 3223230 *dāms* yielding Rs 39,274 from Badnera Bibi.[3] Muḥammad Ashraf s/o Muḥammad Ṣaleḥ, *Bak͟hshī* and *Wāqi'a Nigār's* payment of Sulṭānpur [Nandurbar] was cancelled from there.[4] Muḥammad Sai'd, s/o Muḥammad Qulī was the *Dīwān* of Karnatak-i Hyderabad.[5]

Muḥammad Muḥsin, s/o Abul Ḥasan Shujāi' was the *Dīwān* of Talkokan-i 'Adil K͟hāni[6] in 1702 A.D. Muḥammad Riza s/o Ḥasan Qulī was the *Bak͟hshī* and *Wāqi'a Nigār* of Muḥammadabad [Bedar][7]. Ḥusain K͟hān, s/o late Himmat K͟hān was the *Bak͟hshī* of the army of the Prince Bedar Bak͟ht. Ilahwardi Baig, s/o Muḥammad Beg was *Bak͟hshī* and *Wāqi'a Nigār* of Kokan-i 'Adil K͟hāni[8]. Muḥammad Baqir, served as the *Dīwān-i K͟hāliṣa* and *pāibāqī* of the Mulk-i Deccan[9] and Niẓāmul Mulk.

[C] *Faujdār*

Faujdār was the commandant in-charge of peace and order usually in a group of *parganas*. The *faujdār* was usually a responsible person who used to maintain law and order. In the Deccan the *faujdār* was equally important. We are informed that Dāūd K͟hān was appointed to the *faujdārī* of Bālāghāt and Pāīnghāt Karnatak-i Hyderabad[10]. Similarly Ḥasan Qulī K͟hān, was the *faujdār* of the Talkokan-i 'Ādil K͟hāni.[11]

1. IJC, I/0/0-640.
2. IJC, I/0/0-715.
3. IJC, I/45/7-84.
4. IJC, I/45/7-84.
5. IJC, I/45/2-52.
6. IJC, I/45/1-160. Imām Qulī, s/o Murshid Qulī K͟hān, who was the *Bak͟hshī* and *Wāqia' Nigār* of Tirambak was dismissed and summoned to the court. IJC, I/45/1-162.
7. IJC, I/45/5-2. In 1692 A.D. 'Abdullāh s/o Saiyid 'Ali was the *Bak͟hshī* and *Wāqia' Nigār* of Islāmgarh Raheri [IJC, I/34/7-2]; Mīr Ḥusain, s/o Mīr Niẓām was the second *Bak͟hshī* of *Aḥādīs* [IJC, I/45/1-162].
8. IJC, I/46/3-109. Ibrahīm Beg, s/o Ismāi'l Beg was the *Bak͟hshī* and *Wāqia' Nigār* of Aḥmadnagar IJC, I/47/11-105.
9. IJC, I/46/3-113, I/45/5-139, I/45/5-54, I/47/5-41.
10. IJC, I/45/2-51.
11. IJC, I/46/7-20.

We come to know that in exceptional cases the deputy military commandant was also appointed, *viz.,* Muḥammad Ṣādiq, served as *Naib-i faujadār* of Mu'tabīr Khān,[1] an influential *faujdār* like him could have two or more deputies.[2] Similarly Sazāwār Khān was the *qila'dār* of Muḥammadabad [Bedar] and Aḥmad Khān *faujdār* of *pargana* Baiẓāpur, holding the rank of 1500/200 and 1000/1000 respectively or anyone else could suffer transfer as a routine matter,[3] which was the case in regard to Naṣirullah Khān, *qila'dār* and *faujdār* of Junnar.[4] Such examples could be numerous.

Table - 2

Sl. No.	*Name of faujdār/ qila'dār*	*Name of Pargana*	*Name of sarkār*	*Name of ṣūba*	*Source: Inayat Jung collection [IJC]*
1.	Khirad, *qila'dār/ faujdār*	Dhawera	Baitalwari	Berar	I/39/11-143
2.	Shamsuddin *faujdār*	Dhawera	Baitalwari	Berar	I/41/6-49
3.	Muḥkam Singh, *qila'dār/ faujdār*	Selgarh			I/41/6-49
4.	Khajaji, *faujdār*	Nangli/ Patur			I/45/1-31
5.	Najīb Khān *alias Qāzī* Muḥammad Najib, *faujdār*	Dehari	Jalnapur	Aurangabad	I/39/11-142 I/41/10-16 I/45/1-162
6.	Khwāja Ẓafrullah	Shahgarh	[He was latter made] *faujdār* of Khargaon		I/42/2-52
7.	Muḥammad 'Alī Khān, *faujdār*	Pepari	Jalnapur	Aurangabad	I/0/0-200
8.	Zainuddin 'Alī Khān, *faujdār*	Gulshanābād [Nasik]	He became *faujdār* of Baizapur *pargana/ sarkār* Bir		I/41/0-16
9.	Muḥammad Ṣādiq, *faujdār/ qila'dār*				I/0/0-201
10.	Mu'taqid Khān, *faujdār*	Shāhgarh			I/0/0-201
11.	Purdil Khān, *faujdār*	Junnar			I/41/0-16
12.	Irādat Khān, *faujdār*	Bir	Bir	Aurangabad	I/41/0-12 I/46/2-213
13.	Sulemān Khān, *faujdār*	Balam Koban			I/45/2-51
14.	Mirza Muḥammad, *faujdār/ qila'dār*	Sira	He was transferred to Badami		I/46/2-214 I/45/2-52

1. IJC, I/45/8-15, I/0/0-616.
2. I/45/8-15.
3. I/43/1-45.
4. I/44/10-80.

15.	Wahiduddin <u>Kh</u>ān, *faujdār*	Bir	Bir	Aurangabad	I/45/2-52
16.	Dāūd <u>Kh</u>ān, *nāib faujdār*	Bālāghāt, Pāyānghāt	Karnatak Hyderabad		I/46/2-213
17.	Saiyid ‘Ali, *faujdār*	Chalisgaon			I/45/3-54 I/46/9-83
18.	Nasiruddin <u>Kh</u>ān, *faujdār*	Debalgaon			I/45/12-62 I/46/12-46
19	‘Abdul Qādir, *faujdār / qila‘dār*				I/43/6-39
20.	Kūchak <u>Kh</u>ān, *faujdār/ qila‘dār*	Satunda/ Baitala	Previously he was the *faujdār* of Mahagaon		I/44/8-4 I/46/12-46
21.	Shai<u>kh</u> Ḥabībullāh, *faujdār*	Kanhar	He was dismissed in the same year		I/45/1-16 I/45/4-79
22.	Riza Ṭalab <u>Kh</u>ān, *amīn/ faujdār*	Sangamner			I/42/6-9 I/45/1-163 I/45/5-203
23.	Amanullah, *kotwal/ faujdār*	Aurangabad	[*kotwal/ faujdār*] of Valuj		I/42/6-3 I/0/0-617
24.	Aḥmad Sai‘d <u>Kh</u>ān, *faujdār*	Sangamner		Aurangabad	I/49/8-19
25.	Burhanullah, *faujdār/ qila‘dār*				I/41/12-128 I/45/11-86
26.	Uzbek <u>Kh</u>ān, *faujdār/ qila‘dār*	Fatḥābād			I/45/5-122
27.	Ifti<u>kh</u>ār <u>Kh</u>ān, *qila‘dār/ faujdār*	Naldurg		Bijapur	I/47/1-33
28.	Mu<u>gh</u>al <u>Kh</u>ān, *qila‘dār/ faujdār*	Bahādurgarh [Pedgaon]		Aurangabad	I/45/11-188 I/47/4-44
29.	‘Ali <u>Kh</u>ān, *faujdār* of Chitapur [was replaced by Khandala]	Khandala		Aurangabad	
30.	Abul Fath, *faujdār*	Sundarwar			I/46/8-24
31.	‘Azzāmullāh, *faujdār*	Naugar/ Bayawar			I/44/8-18
32.	Muḥammad Bāqir, *faujdār*	Hoshangabad	[was transferred and summoned to the Imperial court]		I/39/11-76
33.	Saiyid Ismāi‘l, *faujdār*	Jalnapur	[In 1702 he was *faujdār* of Raver I/44/10-85, I/45/2-37]		I/42/6-9
34.	Saiyid Ḥusain, *qila‘dār/ faujdār*	Kalyan			I/42/6-9 I/42/8-38 I/46/1-20

35.	Nuruddin Muḥammad, *faujdār*	Danmarni			I/42/6-9 I/0/0-627
36.	Saiyid Ḥusain, *qila'dār/ faujdār*	Raver			I/44/2-87
37.	Saiyid Ghulām Nurud-din, *faujdār*	Bayawal	[He also served in this capacity in Nasirābād]		I/46/1-20
38.	Saifuddin Khān, *qila'dār/ faujdār*	Sholapur			I/44/10-85
39.	Muḥammad Afẓal, *faujdār*	'Adilābād	Asir	Khandesh	I/42/8-38 I/45/4-35 I/45/0-4
40.	Bakhtmand Khān, *faujdār*	Punar		Berār	I/45/8-38 I/45/12-37
41.	Yāsīn Khān, *faujdār*	Sitara Azam Tara		Bijagarh	I/45/12-34
42.	Muḥammad Mansur, *faujdār*	Parangaon			I/45/12-37
43.	Saiyid Ḥasan 'Ali Khān, *faujdār*	Sulṭānpur	Nandurbar	Khandesh	I/43/6-5
44.	Karamullāh, *faujdār*	Songīr			I/46/2-114 I/46/2-134 I/0/0-734
45.	Abūl Qāsim, *qila'dār/ faujdār*	Gama			I/45/11-154 I/45/11-106 I/46/2-125
46.	Muḥammad Farrukh, *faujdār*	Zainpur	Asīr	Khandesh	I/43/2-35
47.	Yaqut Khān, *faujdār*	Dandori			I/45/9-45 I/46/10-18 I/0/0-766
48.	Shamsuddin, *faujdār*	Zainpur	Asīr	Khandesh	I/45/4-35 I/46/5-50
49.	Kāmyāb, *faujdār*	Burhānpur	Asīr	Khandesh	I/46/5-50
50.	Fazlullāh, *qila'dār/ faujdār*	Anjari	Bijagarh	Khandesh	I/43/2-35
51.	Ẓafar Khān, *faujdār*	Paipadol			I/45/2-104
52.	Saiyid Nurullāh Khān, *qila'dār/ faujdār*	Bahādurpur			I/45/12-34
53.	Muḥammad Jamāl, *faujdār*	Miftahul Futūh			I/46/9-104
54.	Muḥammad Saleem, *faujdār*	Parangaon			I/0/0-200
55.	Saiyid Abdul Wahab, *faujdār*	'Ādilabad	Asīr	Khandesh	I/0/0-200
56.	Saiyid 'Ali Khān, *faujdār*	Jalud			I/45/4-36

57.	Saiyid Manjhle, *faujdār*	Ja'farābād *alias* Chand-aur			I/45/1-163
58.	Mu'tabir Khān, *faujdār*	Gu-lashanabad, Kalyan Bhimri			I/0/0-533 I/0/0-615
59.	Sarbarah Khān, *kotwal* and *faujdār*	[surrounding of the Imperial armies]			I/47/1-8
60.	Amānat Khān *alias* Khwāja Muḥammad, *faujdār*	Sangamner			I/47/5-23 I/47/10-25
61.	Lodi Khān *alias* Walīdād *qila'dār/ faujdār*				I/47/10-12
62.	Ghulām 'Āli Khān	Rajdhir			I/47/10-25
63.	Ḥāji Muḥammad Ma'sum, *faujdār/ qila'dār*	Dandūri			I/0/0-534 I/0/0-715
64.	Salim Beg, *qila'dār/ faujdār*	Tirambak			I/46/1-19
65.	Rozbhani Jānbāz Khān, *faujdār*	Hoshangabad [two *maḥāls*]			I/46/12-166
66.	Sheo Singh, *qila'dār / faujdār*	Islamgarh			I/44/12-110
67.	Sazāwār Khān, *qila'dār/ faujdār*			Bidar	I/44/12-110
68.	Mui'n Khān, *qila'dār/ faujdār*	Ausa	Nander	Bidar	
69.	Sarfrāz Khān, *qila'dār/ faujdār*				I/44/8-27
70.	Harchand Rao, *faujdār*	Rājdhir			I/44/6-28
71.	Muḥammad Yūsuf, *faujdār*	Ankalkot			I/44/6-28
72.	Imāji, *faujdār*	Talitkota			I/44/10-65
73.	Sazāwār Khān, *qila'dār/ faujdār*			Muahmmad-abad [Bidar]	I/41/6-158
74.	Dargah Qulī Khān, *faujdār/ qila'dār*	Sira			I/41/6-158
75.	Izzat Khān, *qila'dār, faujdār*	Qandahar	Nander	Bidar	I/45/5-38 I/45/5-39
76.	Mehdi Khān, *qila'dār/ faujdār*	Naldurg			I/0/0-540
77.	Saiyid Ḥusain, *qila'dār/ faujdār*	Kalyan			I/0/0-540
78.	Muftakhir Khān, *qila'dār/ faujdār*	Firozgarh			I/46/7-16 I/0/0-769

79.	‘Abbas Khān, *qila‘dār/ faujdār*			I/46/7-11
80.	Saibāh Khān, *kotwal/ faujdār*	Bijapur [Daruzzafar]	Bijapur	I/41/11-40
81.	Kartalab Khān, *Dīwān/ faujdār*			I/41/11-40
82.	Allah Qulī, *qila‘dār/ faujdār*	Ankola		I/46/1-58
83.	Udāji Rām, *faujdār*	Māhūr		I/37/4-7

[D] *Qila‘dārs* and *Thānadārs*

Though *qila‘dārs* have already been highlighted it would not be out of context, if we take into account 28 *thānas* surrounding the province of Daruzzafar out of which 20 *thānas* have been shown as fixed as one *thānadār* Yadgar Beg is having 500 *ẓāt* /100 *sawār*. Six *thānas* were under the command of Arshad Khān, while two *thānas* fell under the jurisdiction of Gajpat, *faujdār* and *amīn*. Similarly 8 *thānas* fell under the command of Sarbrāh Khān while four *thānas* were situated to the west of Kishna and Ganpat rivers. There appears 214 papers out of 331 documents which demonstrate the significance of *Maḥal-i Khāliṣa* in *sarkār* Baglāna in 39th regnal year [i.e. 1697 AD][1].

It became quite apparent that the contingent of the forts of Aurangabad for demanding their balance payment on 7th *Rajab* 41 R.Y. created disturbance and raised disturbance by vancat artillery. Since the demand of the group is about Rs 10,00,000. Khanazad Ali Naqi stated that Rs 2,00,000 on account of Berar and Rs 50,000 owing to Sangamner be given while the sheet of Suhail Baig, superintendent of artillery does say that if Rs 10,00,000 are there these may be distributed whereas that group plead for its arrival from North India. Likewise on 29th Rajab the Uzbeks posted at Bir accompanied with Iltifat Khān who have brought the *parwana* of *tankhwah* amounting to Rs 59,000 of Aurangabād have created disturbance. Since there is much paucity of treasury and for sometime the amount has also not reached from Chanda and Deogarh whereas the expenses of the contingent, elephants, animal foder and oxen is much owing to which there are much difficulties. Accordingly it was ordered to end it to the office of the *khaliṣa* on 10th *Shaban* 41st R.Y. it was received on 11th *Shaban* 41st R.Y.

We are given to understand that the *sanawāt* [years] pending against the *parganas* of *sarkār* Fateḥabad Dhārur begin from 1077 AH/1667 A.D. on account of the realisation of the account of Balchand, *Karorī* of the

1. I/40/0-70, I/40/0-71.

pāibāqī of *ṣūba* Aurangabad which continued with certain interruptions in 1079AH/1669 AD; 1087 AH/1677 AD; 1091 AH/1680 AD, 1102 AH/1691 AD, 1109 AH/1699 A.D. Similar type of data does emerge from *sarkār* Pattan, *ṣūba* Aurangabad commencing from 1078/1079 AH/ 1668/1669 A.D. up to 1689 A.D. during which period Balchand *Karorī* and Imām Quli[1] *Karorī of Muḥāsibat* continued to operate till 1107 AH/1697 A.D.

Similar instances can be multiplied as we are given to understand that such types of arrears were pending payment in *sarkār* and *ṣūba* Aurangabad from the year 1099 AH to 1108AD/1689-1698 A.D.[2]

However, without delving deep into the crux of the problem one has to turn back to the usual discussion which rotates round the role of the *thānadārs* and the *qila'dārs*. It would not be out of context to draw our attention to the fact that it has been an established fact that from the time of possession of this country it is obligatory on the *Chitthi* of *deh-ba dehi* that since in the *parganas Deshmukhs* and *Deshpāndiyas* are those who write in Hindi and it is also must that the register of *qānūngos* of His Majesty and the *ṣūbās* would have to be uniform. If, however, it is ordered that as per the term of revenue administration of late Murshid Qulī K͟hān, *Chitthi* in Hindi script of the *qānūngos* issued with stamp and signature of the *Dīwāns* is sent under their *signatures*.[3]

The income and expenditure of *sarkār* Talkokan-i Niẓāmul Mulki, *ṣūba* Aurangabad from Ist *Sha'ban* 40th R.Y. to 18 *Rabi* II 45th regnal year arrives at Rs 93411/11¾. There after expenses have been shown as Rs 68960/12½. Out of 21 villages of *pargana* As'adnagar *alias* Akluj, *sarkār* Akluj, *ṣūba* Bijapur on account of *K͟harif* crop of *Lui Il* and *Rabi Il* is owing to 1110 *faṣlī*. Details of every necessary item are given as well.

We also come across *mawāzna-i yak ḥarfī*, *sarkār* Sangamner, *ṣūba* Aurangabad 1105 *faṣli* from the beginning of *K͟harif* crop of *Tunguz Il* and *Rabi Sichqān Il* 1105 *fasli*, which is the *jāgīr* of 'Abdul Wāḥid Beg, *qila'dār* and a *faujdār* comprising 23 villages. Similarly Aurangzeb also ordered that 'Let it be sent to Mu'tamād K͟hān as it won't be paid in accordance with the *ẓābita* and routine [*m'amūl*] though they have taken away the *bhurti* [ears of corn] by leaving behind the grass.[4]

A *parwāngī* under the seal of Sibg͟hatullāh was received that Amānullah etc, the *ṣarraffs* and *muqaddāms* of *qaṣba* Nandurbar represented that since the said *qaṣba* is on the way to Surat Port owing to which the men plead

1. I/38/0-366, I/38/0-368.
2. IJC, I/41/0-1 to I/41/0-4.
3. IJC, I/0/0-580.
4. IJC, I/45/7-31.

for water supply. Accordingly Behroz Khān, *faujdār* thereat recommended three hundred rupees and above as *in'ām* to the *Desāī* of that *mauza'* while the *Desāī* of *pargana* Nandurbar due to dearth of water left village Dudhala's *Darra-i koh* [pass], dig the pond so as to bring the *nadi* in the *qaṣba*. Recommends the said village for digging the *band*, pond and dam of the *nadi* by way of *in'ām* then there would become abundance of water in that *zila'* as for four years Rs 4,000 shall suffice which has been agreed by Emperor Aurangzeb.[1]

Aurangzeb also ordered that in addition to *amīnship* the duty of looking after the devastation from Bangah to Mangal Bhera is assigned to Shaikh Ghulām Muḥammad as the devastation of crop by the servants of His Majesty together with the army from Bangah to Mangal Bhera should be assessed and presented to His Majesty. Written on 2nd *Rabi* II, 41st regnal year of Aurangzeb.[2]

In view of the acute necessity a *dastak* was issued on 22nd *Jumada* II, 48th R.Y. of Aurangzeb [1704-5 A.D. to Shaikh 'Ināyatullāh, *Aḥādi* [gentleman trooper] posted at the *Kachehri-i Dīwānī-i ṣūbaāt-i* Deccan to the effect that since the *mawāzna-i mufaṣṣali wa yakḥarfī*, *pargana* and *sarkār* Junnar, *ṣūba* Aurangabad from 1091 AH to 1112 *faṣli* [1682-1703 AD] in case of the measured area surrounding, south, north, east and west, distance of area, names of *deshmukhs*, *deshpāndiyas, muqaddams*, *patwaris*, *aimmadārs*, *rusūm*, *naqd-o-arāzi* and *in'ām* of that group and the *bāghāt-i* āmadnī-wa chāh wa *ghalla* in accordance with the *ẓabita* is required in the office so that the requisite paper is corrected and made worthy of deliverance in the Court.[3]

In view of the excess in revenue it was settled that from the excess in the *parganas* of *Daruzzafar* [Bijapur] and *Khujistabuniyad* [Aurangabad] it should be realised in the *sarkār* without giving it to the *jāgīrdārs* enabling the *riā'ya* to remove their grievances which was done accordingly.[4]

In view of the acute crisis Aurangzeb often used to take disciplinary action against the wrong doings. It was brought to the notice that the *rasm-i* ṣ*ibti* in the *ṣūbaāt-i* Deccan has spread in abundance, owing to the transfer of *jāgīrs* and the loss in *manṣabs* the *Wāqia'Nigārs* and *Sawāniḥ-nigārs* report to His Majesty that it is his charge to which Aurangzeb responded that: "In our time whatever has not been done has become possible like, *Haram* and *Bid'at* as it shall damage the country". [IJC, I/46/2-26]

1. IJC, I/43/1-72.
2. IJC, I/41/6-1, I/41/6-2.
3. IJC, I/48/8-4.
4. IJC, I/43/2-127.

Though the *ḥaqīqat-i ḥāl-i ḥāṣil* of the ten yearly *jāgīr* of Parshotam Dās, *mushrif-i qui Khāna*-i rikāb-i sa'adat of the *dehāt-i pargana* Kanher, *sarkār* Daulatabad from the end of 1092 A.H. / till 1103 A.H. was shown in accordance with the *Ṭūmār* under the seal of Qazi Fateḥ Muḥammad of the said 32 *jāgīrs* which were also held by some other *jāgīrdārs* in the *pargana* in question.[1] However, the Imperial order was also issued that it was intimated to all the *Dīwāns* of the *ṣūbajāt* that none should be given rent farming since 29 *Ramzan* 37th regnal year [1694 A.D.] especially to the *karorī, karkun, fotadar*, *mīr deh* and the *piyādas* of *Dīwānī* and the *quẓẓāt* otherwise they would have to suffer the Imperial wrath.[2]

When the matter of the *ta'ahhud* [agreement] of Saiyidi Aiyyub was approved by His Majesty then the *siyāha-i tappa* was to be issued; if however after the receipt of the *deh-ba-dehi* additional amount is shown then it should be re-charged. The details of the *raqimāna* of Malik 'Amber are also given therein for 85 villages.[3] Furthermore *raqimāna* of *pargana* Indapur *sarkār* Junnar *ṣūba* Aurangabad of the year 1704 A.D. is also furnished herewith excluding 14 villages.[4]

[E] *Qāzī, Ṣadr Muḥtasib*

Almost in every *pargana* we find the appointment of a *qāzī*. But as far as *ṣadr* is concerned it was at *ṣūba* level whereas the *ṣadr-i juzv* exercised a limited sway. As far as the *muḥtasib* is concerned he however had sway over a large area. Though examples can be searched out yet we would like to draw our attention to the fact that Akram Khān was the *Qāzīul Qaẓẓāt* and Muḥammad Amīn Khān was the *Ṣadrus Ṣudur*,[5] while 'Abdul Quddus was the *Ṣāḥib-i Iḥtisāb* of Aurangabad.[6]

[F] Local Administration

Though we find several examples of the *Kotwal* yet we can comprehend the capacity of such posts like *Qānūngo*, *Muqaddam* and *Chaudhurī* [counterpart of *deshmukh* and *desāī*] including *patwari*. However, if we take into consideration the details of the various significant posts available in different *ṣūbās* of the Deccan then we can easily visualise the real import of these offices. Sarbarāh Khān was the *Faujdār* and *Kotwal* of Daruzzafar Bijapur.[7]

1. IJC, I/35/4-7 to IJC, I/35/1-44.
2. IJC, I/37/11-3.
3. IJC, I/47/8-32.
4. IJC, I/0/0-861 to IJC, I//0/0-941, excluding 14 documents not found in the collection.
5. IJC, I/44/10-85.
6. IJC, I/45/8-50 & IJC, I/46/2-214.
7. IJC, I/41/11-39

The Mughal administration used to take much care about the local administration. When the matter of Rudra *Qānūngo* of *ṣūba* Bijapur was approved by His Majesty in the light of his order that "Let him personally come in the night so as to represent" which was granted with the order to report it. Accordingly from the time of the conquest of the *ṣūba* the register was submitted to the Imperial record office. Since the *sanad* of *qānūngoi* without any co-sharer was ready Fateḥ Daulat required *qaul* to order to deliver it enabling him to deposit the installment of *peshkash* in the treasury. Tama, the designated son of Jagan Nath and the nephew of Deva, *gumashta* of Jagnath and Kanha, the designated son of late Rama who was the *qānūungo* of three provinces of Aurangabad, Berar and Muḥammadabad Bedar had an *inā'm* village yielding Rs 5,000 wanted not only the *manṣab* but also to interfere in the *qānūngoi* of *Daruzzafar* Bijapur that was required to be rejected as per Rudra's request.

Although Jagnath, s/o Kanha, designated son of the late Rama, and Sunder the *qānūngos* of the old country have the register to take up the job yet Rudra brought *sanad* under the seal of Sikander Khān and has the register in the office. Since 31st R.Y. [1688-89] half of the *Qānūngoi* of Bijapur is in possession of Rudra while the other half is in-charge of Jagnath and Sunder contingent upon the payment of Rs 5,00,000 as *peshkash* and *rusūm* Re 1% per Rs 100. They paid Rs 7,700 in cash and took the *asnad.* When in 33rd R.Y. [1689-90] Jagnath died and his designated son Rama submitted the *asnad* with Rudra which was finally assigned to Rudra conditional upon payment of Rs 12,500 as the *rusūm* of *peshkash.* However it was transferred to Bābu Pandit *qānūngo* of Ḥyderabad and the matter became confused[1]. But another document of IJC does clarify that Rudra was the *qānūngo* of Bijapur since 35th RY[2].

Muqaddams used to play a quite significant role in the local administration of the Deccan provinces. There are a number of examples of their active participation. However participation in the civil administration in the event of any encroachment upon the right of *maqaddami* a thorough investigation used to be made as Saiyid Muḥammad and Saiyid 'Abdul Qādir, sons of Saiyid Imām *muqaddam* of village Malsangi *sarkār* Sholapur, *ṣūba* Aurangabad whose father was killed and burnt. Since a thorough search revealed the true facts by Diyanat Khān as per the imperial order and the right was restored[3]. Similarly 100 *nitan* [80,000 *bighas* of land] were also made subject of the resumption from the *muqaddam* of Sheogaon, *pargana* Bulapur without the *sanad*[4].

1. IJCI I/41/8-30, 31 and 32.
2. I/45/7-138.
3. IJC, I/45/9-14 & I/41/10-144.
4. IJC, I/42/3-25.

Even reports about the imprisonment and death of the *maqaddam* were also reported, *viz.,*we come to know about the imprisonment and death of Nakuji, *muqaddam* in the term of administration of Nizamuddin in the fort of Sholapur on 21 *Jumada* II 38 R.Y. during the term of administration of Mehdi Khān as *qila'dār*[1].

We find instances of the agreement in connection with a dispure of Rs 1,00,000 between Sakhuji and Raghuji, *muqaddams* of the villages of *pargana* Khandapur *sarkār* Daulatabad. There are signatures of a number of willingnesses including that of the *patwari*[2]. Similarly in the event of the abscondance of the *muqaddam* a new *muqaddam* was appointed as we come to know that in accordance with the representation of the *Desmukh* and *Deshpāndiya,* of *pargana* Neusa, *sarkār* Aḥmadabad *ṣūba* Aurangabad the *muqaddam* of Ramji Bari had resorted to flight 25 years ago owing to which the village had become desolated and ruined as without the *muqaddam* the village can not prosper. The Prince's order was issued for appointing a new *muqaddam*[3].

The *muqaddams* used to take responsibility for getting cultivated the *banjar* [uncultivated land] of *qaṣba* Bailgaon, belonging to *pargana* Ja'frabad as per the statement of Nahir Khān for which order was issued to Sanbhaji who ordered the same for a revenue of Rs 1000 by the *muqaddam* of the newly brought to cultivation *qaṣba* in favour of Ghulam Muḥiuddin s/o Sangram Khān[4].

In view of the special care taken by the Mughal administration when Saiyid Alvi the *madad-i mash* grantee represented that he may kindly be granted permission to open a *pain'th* in village Maniksar *alias* Islamabad then Aurangzeb ordered that "if there is no loss to the Government of the *jagirdar* then it [*parwana*] may be issued[5].

We are given to understand that Prince Muḥammad Kam Bakhsh communicated the Imperial order for establishing a painth entitled [Painth] Muḥiabad for which the *desmukh* and *despandayas* solicited the following:

(1) *qualnama* for *maatr-i jizya* for seven years which was allowed.

(2) The wall was to be constructed for the safety of *Painth* which was allowed from the Government expenses of 50 *bighas* to be furnished legally.

(3) A *darogha* [superintendent] for the said *mahāl* was allowed.

1. I/42/1-88.
2. I/42/8-24 & I/42/8-25.
3. I/42/4-13.
4. I/43/11-13.
5. I/41/8-21.

(4) 120 *bighas* of uncultivated land was purchased.

(5) *Sanad* of *khidmat*, *mahajan* and *patwargiri* render visit on.

(6) The local men who reside there Saturday as per rule.[1]

A local matter came to Aurangzeb's notice when it was represented to His Majesty that Ganeshgir *Sanyasi*, resident of Khataon represented that *hukkam* and *zamindars* should allow him exemption to him on account of the revenue of the orchard. It is small he is hoping that it may please be exempted by His Majesty's head. It was ordered to be exempted on *Rabi II* 47th R.Y. [Aurangzeb][2].

It was brought to His Majesty's notice that Imām Quli *Waq'ia nigār* of Junnar entered it in the dairy of events that about 350 mango-trees worthy of presentation are situated in the vicinity of *pargana* Junnar. Meanwhile the above said trees are almost ready if it is ordered that superintendentship thereof may either be given to the aforesaid person or someone else and dispatched to the supplier of fruits so as to take care in dispatching them properly as the petitioner be not deprived accordingly[3]. The subtle difference in the Mughal administration of the North as opposed to the Deccan, under Aurangzeb is well known due to the preculiar circumstances in conquering and administering the Deccan.

1. I/46/10-56.
2. I/47/6-3.
3. I/47/12-22.

VII

Land Revenue and Taxes

[I] Problem of Revenue Collection

This is an established fact that the *manṣabdārs* of the Mughal Empire used to receive their pay either in cash [*naqdi*] or in the form of assignments of areas of land from which they were entitled to collect the land revenue and all other taxes imposed by the Mughal Empire. Since the assignments were known as *jāgīr* and *tuyūl*, though sometimes the term *iqta'* used in the time of the Delhi Sulṭans, was also employed. It need not be emphasized that the officers, when paid in cash were known as *naqdi*, and were holding assignments, as *jāgīrdārs* and *tuyūldārs*. Interestingly enough, author of *Mirat-ūl-Istilah* suggests that as the term *tuyūl* was originally used for assignments held by the Princes of royal blood, but at least in the time of Aurangzeb, the term was indifferently used for all assignments.[1] It may, however, be stated that the land which was served for the income of crown was called the *Khāliṣa* or *Khāliṣa Sharifa*[2] and such areas which were to be assigned, but were for the time being managed by Imperial officers were known as *pāibāqī*.[3]

Generally speaking by far larger part of the Empire was assigned in *jāgīr*, *viz.* in the 10th reginal year of Aurangzeb, out of the total estimated revenue [*jama'dāmi*] of 924 crores of *dāms* for the whole Empire, 725 crore *dāms* were assigned to *jāgīrdārs* or placed in *pāibāqī*[4]. It may be stated that nothing like the *karorī* experiment of Akbar, when practically the whole Empire had been placed in the *Khāliṣa* was repeated in the 17th century, practically in the last years of Jahangir's reign the *Khāliṣa* shrank to 28 crores of *dāms*[5] or less than 1/20th of the total *jama'*. But

1. We are given to understand that the *jāgīr* of the Princes are usually indicated by such phrases as *jāgīr-i* or *Ināyat-Wukala-i sarkār-i Daulatmadar.*
2. *Miratu-l Istilah,* 15 [a].
3. *Khulāṣatus Siyāq*, f. 24 [b] *Waqāi-Ajmer*, pp. 7-4, 375-6, f. 156-157 [a].
4. *Miratu-l 'Alam*, f. 214[b].
5. Qazwini, p. 423, for the *jama'* of the Empire see *Majālis-i Salaṭin*, ff. 115 [a-b].

afterwards especially in the reign of Shāh Jahān, an expansion of the *Khāliṣa* had taken place. We are given to understand that its *jama'* stood at 120 crores out of the total *jama'* of 660 crores i.e. it was over 1/7th of the whole empire in Shāh Jahān's 20th years. Thus, in Aurangzeb's 10th year; it amounted to almost one-fifth of the total *jama'*.[1] However, no later information about the precise extent of the *Khāliṣa* is available.

Thus, these data show that the *Khāliṣa* covered a very large portion of the empire, but the Emperor was also in command of a commendable income collected directly by his treasury. Out of this he paid own troops, artillery men, attendants, etc and the *naqdi manṣabdārs*. However, the fact remains that no less than 4/5th of the revenue of the Empire had been alienated to the *jāgīrdārs* in Aurangzeb's tenth regnal year and the *Khāliṣa* amounted to one-fifth of the total *jama'*[2].

Although much emphasize has been laid on the land revenue and taxes yet problems of revenue collection have to be solicited in one go. Fortunately the land revenue administration in the six *ṣūbās* of the Deccan gradually began to be altered in a more systematic way especially after 1687 AD, when the whole of the Deccan came to at the high rise of conclusion. Much emphasize has been laid down on the potentialities of the capitalistic development in the economy of the Mughal empire; but equal attention on this however, has not been paid. Undoubtedly the supply of the *āwārja* of *Khāliṣa Sharifa* and the āwārja of the *jāgīrdārs* of *ṣūbās*, of Khandesh, Ḥyderabad, Berar, Aurangaabad, Bijapur and Bidar had already established the position of these provinces. However, in the last years of Aurangzeb the expenses were increasing day by day while the income was reducing gradually. It was also clarified that expenses of Aurangabad, Bijapur, Berar, Ḳhandesh were used to be met out from the *Hundwis* of Hindustan which Aurangzeb also continued including 30,000 rupees of the *piyadas* of Mawaliya etc[3].

Rūḥullāh Khān communicated the Imperial order that in the office of the Deccan the *Chiththi-Deh-ba-Dehi* is not written in Hindwi whereas the fact remains that this practice of writing in Hindwi is from the beginning of the control of the country. Since in the *pargana* the *Deshmukhs* and *Deshpandiyas* are Hindi writing ones and it is must that the register of *Qānūngos* of the Emperor and the *ṣūba* be in consonance with each other without any differentiation. If orders be issued that action should be taken in accordance with late Murshid Qulī Khān's order in the Hindwi so that

1. Lahori, *Padshahnāmā*, II, pp. 710-13.
2. *Miratu-l 'Alam, op. cit.*
3. IJC, I/46/10-65.

the *Qānūngos* should write in Hindwi without any stamp and signature of *Dīwān*[1].

We are given to understand by a *parwana* of Asad Khan to Muhammad Shafi, *Diwan* of the Deccan that it was brought to the Imperial notice that no difference of *Kharif* and *Rabi* is shown in the division of the *parganas* of the *suba* of the Deccan was maintained which division is shown in the papers of North India [Hindustan]. If this division is shown then it shall be shown in the record office. Till the requisition of the division is made in the revenue of both *khaliṣa sharifa* is related and at the time of assessment of the two crops is made with *jagirdars* who have mutual conflict so that there should remain no dispute. Accordingly the Imperial order was issued to implement in order of merit. Accordingly orders for its implementation after 7 Jumada 1090 A.H. / 1689 A.D. were issued.

According to Richards Aurangzeb retained the bulk of revenues from Golconda, retained Hyderabad province for the Imperial treasury [*khaliṣa*] or in the temporary *paibaqi* pool which remained in the pool without reassignment for extensive periods which prevailed as similar process seem to have prevailed in Bijapur and elsewhere.

Unfortunately we come to know that a crisis in the assignment system developed in the last years of Aurangzeb carried on an unending war in the Deccan, in which the concentration of the entire military power of the Deccan failed to give him ultimate success. However, during these years there was an enormous influx into the ranks of the *manṣabdārs* of the Deccan or officers from the Deccan kingdoms and the Marathas. We also come to know that the number of the *manṣabdārs*, as a result, increased to such an extent that the existing *jāgīrs* could no longer suffice for their pay.[2]

Interestingly in one of the letters, Aurangzeb himself refers to "the scarcity of *pāībāqī* and the crowds of men claiming pay" and declares that everything "flesh and bones", had been assigned no further demands for assignments could be entertained by the court"[3]. We also come to acquaint ourselves with the fact that Ma'mūri and Khāfi Khān make similar statements. "Large numbers [literally a world]" we are informed "had become *jāgīr*-less [*be-jāgīr*]". Moreover, persons appointed to *manṣabs* could not obtain *jāgīrs* for years, and if a *jāgīr* was transferred from the

1. IJC, I/0/10-580.
2. Ma'mūri, ff. 156[b]-157[a], Khāfi Khān, Add. 6574, ff. 101[b]-107[a]. Unfortunately the striking passage, inveighing against the influx of Deccanis, is omitted in the Bib. Ind. Text of Khāfi Khān. Moreover on the influx of the Deccanis see M. Athar Ali's *Mughal Nobility underAurangzeb,* 26-30.
3. *Dasturu-l 'Amal Agahi*, 1-31, Add 6574, ff. 17 [b]-18 [a].

hands of anyone, he might not get another.[1] Furthermore the older nobility [or the so-called *Khāna*-zādān] were extremely indigent at the way their claims were disregarded to provide for the Deccanis.[2] Unfortunately the real victims of the crisis were the small *manṣabdārs*, who possessed neither money nor the influence to induce the officers of the court to assign them *jāgīrs*.[3]

Much interest has been displayed in recent years in the study of Mughal revenue statistics found in contemporary records. There is abundance of such information in *arhasattha* and *ḥaqiqat-bahi* documents relating to Eastern Rajasthan, preserved in the Rajasthan State Archives, Bikaner, which provide considerable agricultural data, like crops, plough-oxen, items of taxation, village-wise revenue collections, prices of agricultural products, etc.

Attention in an equal measure is yet to be paid to the massive Mughal period records particularly 'Inayat Jang Collection' reposing in the National Archives, New Delhi.[4] This collection furnishes statistical and geographical information about various *parganas* of the *ṣūbās* of the Deccan and provides a fascinating account of the way the Mughal revenue administration was organised. Illustrative of its richness are two contemporary series of documents coming from the *parganas* of 'Ādilābād[5] and Fatḥābād [Laling], *sarkār* of Burhanpur in the *ṣūba* of Ḳhandesh both are belonging to the year *faṣli* 1104/AD 1696.

1. Ma'mūri, f. 157 [a], Khāfi Khān, Add 6574, f. 107 [a].
2. Ma'mūri, f. 182 [b]- Khāfi Khān, II, 379, 396-7.
3. Ma'mūri, ff. 156 [b]-157 [a]; Khāfi Khān, Add. 6574, 106[b]-107[a], Aurangzeb himself admitted in this condition 'great injustice is done to the small men [*reza-ha*], *Dasturul 'Amal-i Āgahi* 1-31 [a]-Add 6574, f. 107[a]. J.F. Richards, *Mughal Administration in Golconda*, 158-62. 308-9, expresses some reserve in regard to the pressure on *jagirs* developing in the late years of Aurangzeb, But however, as Athar 'Ali, *Mughal Nobility under Aurangzeb*, rev., edn. xxxxii, has demonstrated, Richards has read too much in a document containing what he assumed to be "the 1689-90 settlement" of the conquered Kingdom, and overlooked a document of 1706 [printed in *Selected Documents of Aurangzeb's Reign*, 233-5] which furnishes an entirely contrary picture, at least for the 19 *Karnatak sarkārs* of *ṣūba* Ḥaiderabad.
4. M. Athar Ali, Review of J.F. Richards, *Mughal Administration in Golconda* [OUP, 1975], *Journal of Asian* Studies, XXXV February, 1976, p.159. There are yet another incomplete series of 39 documents of Ādilābād, 1693-4 A.D.
5. I am thankful to my colleagues Miss Nighat Shigufa National Archives who has helped me in preparing a brief but comprehensive chart of the information gleaned from these documents as well as to Dr. Muḥammad Irfan for helping me in checking the relevant information from the huge plethora of over 15,000 of records of Aurangzeb's reign in the Inayat Jung Collection of the National Archives.

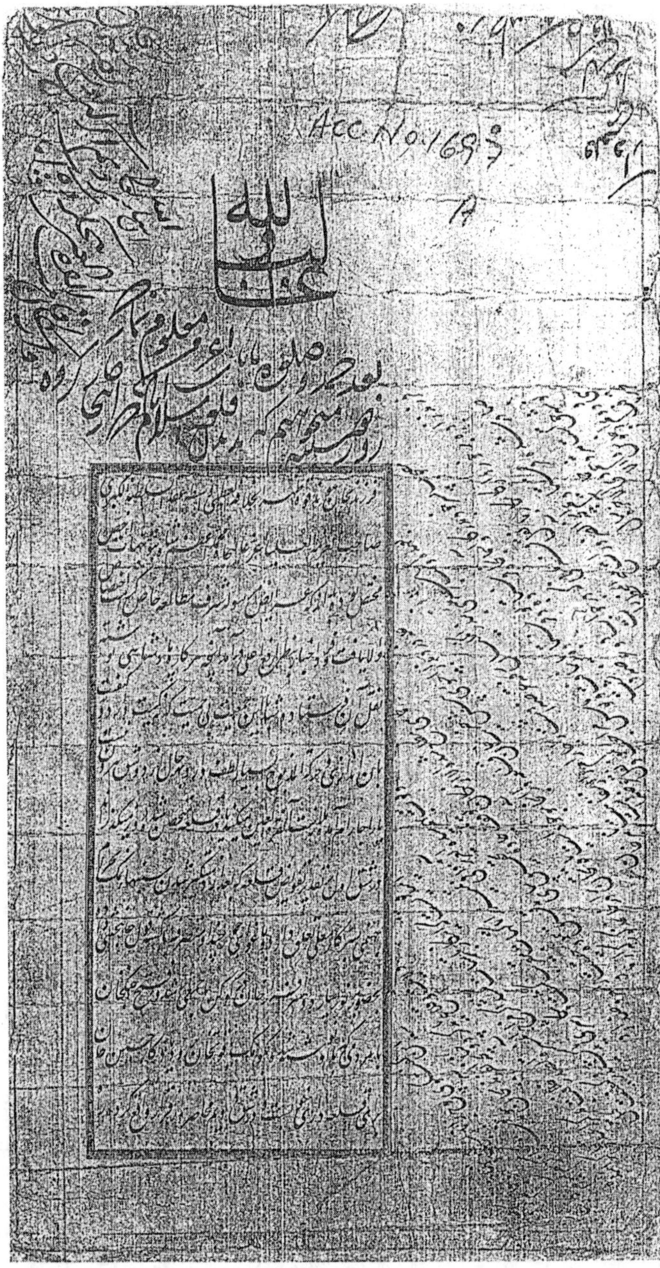

We here take for scrutiny the documents of *pargana* 'Ādilābād.[1] These furnish a village-wise report on the revenue status of the *pargana* for the closing years of the seventeenth century sent by 'Abdullāh, *Dīwān* of Khandesh to the Mughal *Dīwān* of the Deccan.[2]

Like the *arthasattha* documents the face sheet summarises the information from the report. It gives the total number for sheets as 63 and the number of villages as 135, of which 124 are classified as *aṣlī* and 11 as *dakhilī*. The revenue figures of the *aṣlī* villages are alone given, because the *dakhilī* villages were newly settled ones whose revenues were incorporated in those of older [*aṣlī*] villages.[3] The summary sheet gives the total measured area of *ai'mma* [lands alienated in revenue grants], *uftāda* [waste] and *mazrūa'* [cultivated]. The total revenues are given systematically in two units; rupees and Khandeshi *tankas* as the names of officials have also been recorded. The papers give information on a set proforma for each of 124 villages in the *pargana,* the name of the villages; its location defined in *kurohs* from the *pargana* headquarters with compass direction; the name of the principle *jāgīrdārs*, the name of the *muqaddams, patels, chaudhurīs* and the *patwārīs;* land cultivated, land fallen out of cultivation, land reserved for revenue grants, all measured in *aut* [80 *bighas*], *partan* [4 *bighas*], and *biswās*[4]; the resources of irrigation, the fixed *ḥāṣil* for the entire village; revenue collected and the balance of tax due to natural calamity [*āfat*].

1. IJC, I/40/0-1 to I/40/0-63.
2. Stewart Gordon and J.F. Richards have also analysed these documents in a joint paper 'Kinship and *Pargana* in Eighteen Century Khandesh', *IESHR*, 22, 4[1985] pp.371-3. They err, however, in treating it as a unique report coming from the Deccan during 17th century because another series of documents, though, incomplete, of the same *sarkār* and *ṣūba* of the year 1696 is to be found In the Inayat Jang Collection [IJC, I/36/0-24-45 to I/36/0-63-70]. Moreover, the 63 page report stamped with the seal of 'Abdullāh, 32/1099, which they consider to be the date of his appointment is contradicted by another seal of the same *Dīwān* which bears the date 34/1102. This series of documents supplemented by other documents cited in this chapter gives an intimate picture of 'Ādilābād's agricultural and administrative set up obtaining in the seventeenth century. Interestingly the authors have either conveniently overlooked this important piece of corroborating evidence or they had no access to such documents.
3. *Cf.*, Irfan Habib; *Agrarian Systems of Mughal India,* Bombay, 1963, p. 252n retired, 1999 AD. The Mughal administration also maintained an account of the newly settled villages [*dehat-i nāuabād*] in various *parganas*. Z.A. Shakeeb [ed.] *Mughal Archives*, A.P. State Archives, 1977, Vol. I, p. 295.
4. Khāfi Khān informs us that although in the *ṣūbas* of the Deccan the *bigha* was in use, yet most often the *aut* was used in the office [records] so that in Khandesh four *bigha-i-ra'iyatī*] made a *partan* and 20 *partans* or 80 *bighas* constituted an *aut.* [*Muntakhabul Lubab,* Biblothica Indica, Calcutta, 1869, I, p. 735]. Ṣādiq Khān also makes a passing reference to this measure. *Tawarīkh-i Shāh Jahān* Br. Mu. Or. 174 f.183 [a].

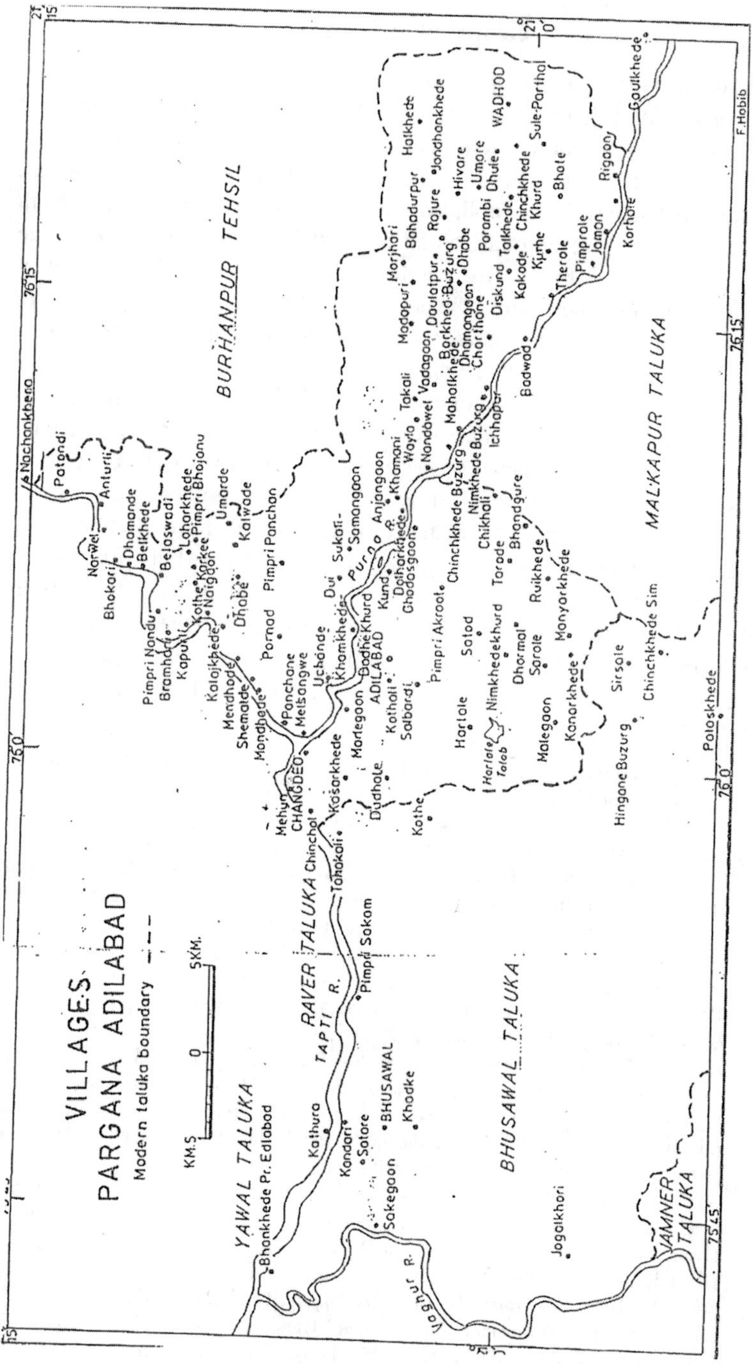
VILLAGES
PARGANA ADILABAD
Modern taluka boundary
KM.5 0 5KM.
YAWAL TALUKA
RAVER TALUKA
BHUSAWAL TALUKA
BURHANPUR TEHSIL
MALKAPUR TALUKA
JAMNER TALUKA
TAPTI R.
Purna R.
Vaghur R.
ADILABAD
CHANGDEO
BHUSAWAL
WADHOD
Nachankheda
Bhankhede Pr. Edlabad
Sakegaon
Kandari
Satore
Kathura
Khodke
Jogalkhori
Pimpri Sakom
Tahakali
Chinchol
Mehun
Kothe
Dudhale
Hingane Buzurg
Patoskhede
Chinchkhede Sim
Sirsale
Harlale Talab
Harlale
Malegaon
Kanarkhede
Satod
Pimpri Akroote
Kothali
Salbardi
Patandi
Anturli
Norwel
Bhokari
Dhamande
Belkhede
Belaswadi
Loharkhede
Pimpri Bhojanu
Umarde
Kalwade
Pimpri Panchan
Samangaon
Sukali
Anjangaon
Khamani
Nandowel
Takali
Vadagaon
Daulatpur
Barkhed Buzurg
Mahalkhede
Ichhapur
Badwad
Madapuri
Morjhari
Bahadurpur
Rajure
Dhabe
Porambi
Hivare
Umore
Dhule
Chinchkhede Khurd
Talkhede
Kakode
Kurhe
Therole
Pimprole
Jamon
Korhale
Rigaon
Bhote
Sule-Parthal
Goulkhede
Jondhankhede
Halkhede
Diskund
Charthane
Dhamangaon
Nimkhede Buzurg
Chinchkhede Buzurg
Chikhali
Bhandgure
Torade
Ruikhede
Manyarkhede
Sarole
Dhormal
Nimkhedekhurd
Kund
Dolharkhede
Ghodasgaon
Godhe Khurd
Khamkhede
Dui
Uchande
Panchane
Metsangwe
Pornad
Dhabe
Kothe
Natgaon
Karkee
Kapurl
Bramhade
Pimpri Nandu
Kalajkhede
Mendhode
Shemalde
Mandhede
Kasarkhede
Marlegaon
76°0'
76°15'
75°45'
21°0'
21°15'
F. Habib

Geographical Survey

The distance and compass directions, indicating for each village, [except for five], help us locate over 90% of the villages with the help of modern census data and one-inch maps. I have been able to plot 114 villages out of 124 villages or 92% [see map][1]. In order to re-establish the villages' names, I have collated them with *Deh ba dehi*, an eighteenth century anonymous compilation and the *District Census Handbook*[2]. The specification in *kurohs* from the *pargana* headquarters in each village sheet is fairly accurate. There is still the possibility of the existence of some more villages of the seventeenth century whose survival is obtained by changes of name or merger with other villages[3]. The accompanying map indicates that *pargana* 'Ādilābād was a rather small administrative unit [*qaṣba*] in *sarkār* Burhānpur [Asīr], *ṣūba* Ḳhandesh, whose limits coincided with those of the modern Edalabad *Maḥal* and part of Bhuswal Taluka in district Jalgaon [previously known as East Khandesh]. 'Ādilābād itself stood south-east of Burhānpur at a distance of 12 *kurohs*[4]. River Tapti formed the northern boundary of the *pargana* for a distance of about 30 miles. A tributary of Purna River constituted the southern boundary of the *pargana* and to the west it comprised only the river-irrigated villages. It was thirty *kurohs* from east to west and 10 *kurohs* from north to south. Vaghur River joined the Tapti near the village of Bhangora in the north-east. Purna river

1. I am thankful to M/s Zahoor Ali Khān and Faiz Habib who have kindly drawn the map. Survey measurement of *pargana* 'Ādilābād was begun in 1862-3 and classification in 1863-4 both finished in 1869-70, according to which, of the 114 villages 111 paid tax to Government and three alienated in revenue free grants [James, Campbell *Khandesh District Gazetteer*, 1880 p. 449]. This suggests the disappearance or amalgamation of 10 villages over two centuries as 114 villages existed in 1862, which have been shown on modern maps and plotted in our map. Of the remaining 10 villages recorded in our documents six were situated in the east and two each in west and south. In 1951 another 11 villages were marked as deserted out of 75 villages of *pargana* 'Ādilābād [*East Khandesh District Census Handbook,* 1951, Bombay, pp. 250-58] while in 1961 two villages were mentioned as deserted out of 85 villages [*Jalgaon District Census Handbook,* 1961, Bombay, p. 1].
2. *Kitab-i Deh-ba Dahi-i Ṣūbajāt-i* Deccan, A.P. State Archives Ms.373, ff 94[a]-95[b]. This work contains village-wise revenue statistics of the *parganas* of the Deccan provinces. I have used it essentially for comparative purpose and village names missing in our documents i.e. Bahadurpur [mod. Bahadurgarh] and Nachangaon [mod. Naragaon] have been located with its help.
3. Shafīq and Thākur Lal do not, provide the distance of *pargana* 'Ādilābād from the headquarters. Lachmi Narain Shafīq' *Khulāṣatu-l Hind,* Transcript Department of History, Aligarh, 1096, Thakur Lal. Ms, Br. Mu. Add. 22, 831 f. 45 [a].
4. IJC, I/40/0-1; Abū-l Faẓl, *Ā'in-i Akbarī* Nawal Kishor, 1297 AH, Lucknow, Vol. II, 108, Irfan Habib, *An Atlas of the Mughal Empire*, OUP, Delhi 1982 Map 14 A&B, Stewart Gordon, 'Burhanpur; Entreport and Hinterland, 1650-1750'. *IESHR* Vol. XXV, No. 4, p. 432 wherein he records his observations about *pargana* 'Ādilābād.

itself flowed almost through the centre of the *pargana.* The settlement pattern shows that the villages were concentrated along the bank of the rivers or laid out of this zone spread over roughly at three-quarters of a mile from another. Four villages have been specifically recorded standing on the banks of River Tapti[1]. 'Ādilābād was situated on the well-travelled route from Aurangabad to Burhānpur. The *pargana* had three towns, *viz.,* 'Ādilābād, Charthane and Wadhoda[2].

Since almost all the villages survived modem maps are traceable [see map], Gordon and Richards are in error in saying that 'there is considerable disparity in [Mughal and Maratha] village names due to which less than half the village names co-relate, even when using the additional data of geographical co-ordinates'. They consider 'Ādilābād's extensive periods of adversity responsible for this so-called disparity. A plausible explanation of this error is that their description of the village names is not often based on a direct examination of the original documents.[3] The situation in 'Ādilābād actually mirrors that of Mawar, where to the names of villages in Nainsi's record are traceable in modern toposheets up to a surprisingly high rate of 90%.[4]

Means of Irrigation

In its description of 'Ādilābād, the Ā *'in-i Akbarī* refers to the existence of an important irrigation tank:

> 'Ādilābād is a fine [*gazīn*] town near which is tank [*golabi*] a famous place of worship as the sin of Raja Jasrath [Dashrath] was atoned here.
>
> It is full throughout the year and irrigates a large agricultural tract[5]'.

Almost the entire *pargana* had access to various sources of irrigation. Except for eight villages, fields in almost every village were watered from rivers, streams, watercourses [*nālas*], tanks and wells. The chief rivers were the tributaries of the Tapti, *viz.*, the Purna and Vaghur. Forty-nine villages were watered by rivers out of which 24 received irrigation directly from Tapti and 18 from Purna. Seven villages were drained by other perennial rivers. A small river Ganga was used for irrigating 'Ādilābād town [also

1. These villages were Belaswadi, Belkhede Bhankhede and Bhokri. IJC, I/40/1-27-29.
2. Gordon and Richards have assumed 'Ādilābād and Bodva as towns while these were in fact three, and Bodva was - a village and not a town, *op. cit.*, p. 370.
3. J.F. Richards' *Mughal Administration in Golcondo* [*Preface*] wherein he refers to his caring for his inaccuracies in deciphering and transcribing the documents.
4. The north-eastern boundaries of *pargana* 'Ādilābād shown by Gordon and Richards cover a larger area than the Mughal period boundaries of 1696. The plotting of Daulatpur [represented by them Daulatpur] is also erroneous, Daulatpur is located within the modern Edalabad *Maḥal*.
5. Ā*'in-i-Akbarī,* p. 107.

supplied by wells]. The Kalinj river supplied water for villages Kothe, Kalwade and Dhabe, the Sivri irrigated Suzali, and the Vaghur, the villages of Jogukhori. Nine villages obtained water from *nullahs*. No canals are recorded.

Fifty villages have irrigation wells recorded. In 1879, the number of wells[1] was put in the vicinity of 1000 in the 'Ādilābād section of Bhusawal subdivision. Gordon and Richards argue that if the same figure held true for the 50 villages of the Mughal statistics recording wells, there must have been approximately 20 wells in each such village, meaning that 50 to 100 *bighas* could be irrigated by them in each.

The tank mentioned in the *Ā'in* has also been recorded in village Hartale as *talab* in our documents and called Hartala Talab in the lists of Shafīq and *Miscellaneous Deccan Records & C.*[2] It appears on modern maps.

Out of the total number of villages, 54.5% took water for irrigation from rivers and reservoirs and 40% from wells. For 5.5% we have no information as to irrigation.

Taxation and Settlement

Pargana 'Ādilābād was subjected to survey and brought under *ẓabt* system as a result of the revenue reforms of Murshid Qulī Khān in the middle of the 17th century, the area of cultivated *raqba,* and the total measured area [*muqarrara raqaba-i arāzi*]. Our documents give totals of the area, with further specification of revenue-free [*ai'mma*], wastes and cultivated land. The figures are given below together with totals counted by us from the individual village figures:

Table – 1

	Aimma [Land Grants]	*Uftada [Waste Land]*	*Mazrua' [Cultivated Land]*	*Total*
Total *bighas*[original] Percent	14511-16 5	180707 34	1,75,283-10= 61=	2,87,865-134 100
Total *bighas* [calculated] Percent	15987-4 5.7	95326 36.18	1,53,136= 58.75	2,63,450 100

1. Campbell, *op. cit.*, p. 144 of Gordon and Richards, *op. cit.*, p. 381; Charthane is said to have once had 700 wells and to have been a large thriving town. Campbell, *op. cit.*, p. 438.
2. Anonymous, *Miscellaneous Deccan Records & C. Br. Mu.*

The originals are given in *auts, partans, bighas* and *biswas.* I have converted them into *bighas,* taking one *aut* = 80 *bighas* and one partan = 4 *bighas.* The figures derived from totaling up village figures vary from the total as recorded for the whole *pargana.* Probably this arose because results of new village surveys were not correspondingly reflected in the *pargana* total. If the *ai'mma* land is added to the cultivated land as it too was normally under cultivation, the total cultivated areas comes to 63.83% of the total measured land. In contrast 36.17% was waste[1]. The *ai'mma* lands [5.7% of the total area] have been indicated in 40 villages out of which four villages [in entirety] were designated, as *madad-i ma'āsh,* one of which was for the upkeep of the mausoleum of Shāhnawāz Khān. Two of the *ai'mma* villages show *uftada* and *mazrua'* alongside *ai'mma* land,which suggests that some area was not assigned to the grantee here. Complete information was also called for about cropping within *ai'mma* lands.

Equally rich information about revenue is furnished in respect of all the villages. The formal assessed revenue [*jama'dāmi*] of 122 villages of *pargana* has been shown as 1,48,14,547 *dāms.*[2] The *jama'* did not indicate the exact expected revenues in a given year, and it was therefore, revised at protracted intervals [say ten years] as shown in the following table in respect of our *pargana.*

Table – 2

Sl. No.	*Name of the Source*	*Total villages*	*aṣli*	*dakhilī*	*jama'dāmi*	*ḥāṣil with year*
1.	*A'in-i Akbari*[18]	-	-	-	5,27223	1601
2.	Inayat Jung Collection[19]	135	124	11	1,48,1457 [for 122 villages]	Rs. 1,68,539/1696 A.D. 1,71,000/1702 A.D.
3.	Inayat Jung Collection[20]	-	-	-	1,55,54,539	11,71,000/1702-13 A.D.
4.	Inayat Jung Collection[21]	-	-	-	-	Rs. 1,90144/31706 A.D.
5.	Inayat Jung Collection[22]	-	-	-	-	Rs. 1,59,514/3 1715 A.D.

1. In view of our calculations, it is difficult to agree with Gordon and Richards contention that just over one-qaurter of land was actually cultivated out of the entire measured land. I have come across a single reference in a complaint of a *jāgīrdār* that the area: under cultivation in the *jāgīr* villages in 'Ādilābād was one third of the total surveyed land [IJC, I/45/0-2].
2. The summary sheet does not indicate the total *dāms* except for mentioning the head *muqarrara dam-i tankhwāhī* [fixed salary]. I have, therefore, totaled the *dāms* from the individual village sheets.

6.	*Dasturu-l Amal-i Shahanshahi*[23]	135	124	11	-	Rs. 1,76,560/9
7.	*Khulasatu-l Hind*[24]	135	124	11	-	Rs. 1,76,560/9
8.	*Dah ba Dehi-i Ṣūbājat-i Deccan*[25]	135	124	11	-	Rs. 1,76,560/1697 A.D.
9.	*Miscellaneous Deccan Records*[26]	135	124	11	-	Rs. 1,76,560/9

Ā'in furnishes the earliest *jama'* figures given in *tanka* for *pargana* 'Ādilābād. The *jama'* persisted till Aurangzeb's reign with slight modification like the introduction of Mughal *dām.*

In the above table, 1-2 mark a revision in the *jama'dami.* In sharp contrast serial numbers 6-7 give the same *jama'dāmi* figures for an unspecified period, which were, most probably compiled in the beginning of the 18th century. The *jama'* figures of individual villages also varied, as a comparison of our 1696 documents with some other documents in Inayat Jang Collection enable us to establish. The following Table may be considered as illustrative:

Table – 3[1]

Sl. No.	*Name of village*	*jama'dāmi*	*ḥāṣil*	*Year*
1 [a] [b] [c]	Bodvad " "	76,074 76,074 72,335	Rs. 874 Rs. 875	1696, 1702 1704 1705
2 [a] [b]	Khamani "	1,32,880 6,80,300	Rs. 429 Rs. 425	1696 1703
3 [a] [b]	Bhor "	37,000 28,350	Rs. 425 Rs. 648	1696 1703
4 [a] [b]	Pimpri Bhoja "	1,76,500 1,76,000	Rs. 1487 Rs. 1241	1696 1698
5 [a] [b]	Naigaon "	87,000 1,60,000	Rs. 1110 Rs. 2000	1696 1701
6 [a] [b]	Ghorasgaon "	5,50,000 6,40,000	Rs. 4710 Rs. 4720	1696 1701
7 [a] [b]	Panjana "	85,500 99,150	Rs. 849 Rs. 892	1696 1701

1. *Sources* = IJC, I/40/0-4, I/40/0-11, I/40/0-12, I/40/0-13, I/40/0-20, I/40/0-21, I/40/0-23, I/40/0-24, I/40/0-27, I/40/0-32, I/40/0-37, I/40/0-38, I/40/0-42, I/40/0-47, I/40/0-55, I/40/0-58, I/40/0-60, I/40/0-62, I/42/1-90, I/42/8-53, I/43/1-28, I/43/2-126, I/44/2-43, I/44/11-59, I/44/12-133, I/45/2-60, I/45/3-4, I/45/7-30, I/45/7-91, I/45/7-142, I/46/2-172, I/46/7-79, I/46/8-29, I/46/8-66, I/47/7-59, I/47/12-28, I/51/11-33, I/51/12-195.

8 [a] [b]	Wadhod "	- 7,69,000	Rs.7667 Rs.7804	1696 1698
9 [a] [b]	Sakegaon "	4,77,450 7,52,047	Rs.7746 -	1696 1703
10 [a] [b]	Itwa "	3,75,000 1,00,000	Rs.1790 Rs.1702	1696 1707
11 [a] [b]	Belaswadi "	1,40,000 1,70,000	Rs.1794 Rs.1761	1696 1707
12 [a]	Dhabe	25,500	Rs.516	1696, 1698
13 [a] [b]	Manegaon "	1,30,000 99,000	Rs.1421 Rs.1110	1696 1704
14 [a] [b]	Saroba "	76,000 -	Rs.843 Rs.945	1696 1704
15 [a] [b]	Khubkhera "	70,000 55,350	Rs.562 Rs.571	1696 1699
16 [a] [b]	Dhikhi "	2,67,000 23,616	Rs.322 Rs.322	1696 1702
17 [a] [b]	Badgaon "	1,82,000 1,84,000	Rs.1348 Rs.1348	1696 1707
18 [a] [b]	Pimprala "	1,49,900 1,61,000	Rs.1976 Rs.2164	1696 1702

In order to determine the magnitude of land revenue demand with exactitude the Mughal administration worked out the anticipated collection of figure known as *muqarrara ḥāṣil* which was more meaningful. The established collection of the entire *pargana* has been given both in Ḳhandesh *tanka* [*tanka-i Dandeshi*] and Mughal silver rupee in our documents. The total amounts to 2,52,809 Dandeshi Coins and 1,68,539/11 rupees respectively. The loss [*āfat*][1] and balance [*tatimma*] have also been recorded in the two units of money[2]. The fixed revenue collection is 45.78%

1. It gives an average of Rs 1369 per year for each village or town and not 1359 as calculated by Richards, 'Official Revenues and Money Flows in a Mughal Province' in *Imperial Monetary System of Mughal Indla,* OUP, 1987, p. 216.
2. Gordon and Richards erroneously designate the figure for loss [*āfat*] as receipts [*wuṣūli*], *wuṣūli* being their own term, not that of the documents. Their calculations imply 100 percent income [both receipts and arrears] which in our *pargana* seems to be next to impossible. The revenue did not even reach the established collection [*muqarrara ḥāṣil*] due to loss of revenues on account of bad harvests, destruction of cultivation owing to Maratha depredations, Mughal expeditions, passage of the *banjārās* and attack of the locusts etc See my article: 'Maratha-Mughal Conflicts --- Seen Through the Documents of the Later Years of Aurangzeb's Reign'. Cyclostyled volume of Aligarh Papers 1988, pp. 137-54]. For each year the returns were categorised thus: the fixed collections, the loss in revenues due to calamities [*āfat*] and the balance of tax [*tatimma*] or actual collection. The *āfat* and *tatimma* were equal to fixed revenues [*muqarrar-ḥāṣil*]

of the *jama'*, the actual realisation is 32.3% or roughly one-third of it. But it is 74% of the established collections [Rs 1,19,648] as a loss of 26% has been expressly entered.

Within *pargana* 'Ādilābād there were two kinds of black soils, first the rich alluvial clay found north of the town which yielded finest crops, and secondly the poorer one in the north-east[1]. Our documents do not furnish details of crops, as given in similar documents of Bijapur[2]. Irfan Habib has noted cotton and sugarcane as the economic products of *sarkār* Burhanpur and its vicinity[3]. The demand per *bigha* under cultivation in 1696 was Rs 1.40. But this relatively high imposition of taxation suggests that cash crops, including foodgrains of superior kind were being cultivated.

A checking of 14 villages out of 24 irrigated by the Tapti yields varying ratios of the actual to the standard [the income for 10 villages has not been recorded]. The actual was 73% of the established. Seventeen out of 18 villages irrigated by Purna show the percentage as 59.5%, Similarly 46 out of 50 villages irrigated from wells show the actual realisation as 54.15% of the standard. However, in several villages served by wells and the Tapti the ratio is in the vicinity of 100%.Six out of 7 villages watered from perennial rivers and the tributaries of Tapti give a low ratio of 50% but 6 villages out of 9 watered from the nullahs show the very high realisation of 77%. There seems from these and other cases to be no certain correlation between access to irrigation and the realisation.

Information on *jama'* and *ḥāṣil* is provided for the four *aimma* villages and 36 other villages which also contained revenue free grants. This raises the question weather the information about the tax income was obtained from the *patwārīs* of these villages, though this was not of any immediate use to the administration at least in the four *aimma* villages where the tax income in its entirety belonged to the grantees.

The *ḥāṣil* like *jama'* is given first in Khandesh *tanka* and then in Mughal silver rupee. The deduction [*āfat*] and then the net revenue [*tatimma*] are also given in these two money units. The universality of money tax suggests that Murshid Qulī Khān had succeeded in converting tax demand in money terms at least in this area.[4]

Administration of Jāgīrs

The 'Ādilābād documents give us considerable information about the administrative set up since they give the names of the *jāgīrdārs* in

1. Campbell, *op. cit.*, p. 349.
2. IJC, I/46/0-1 to I/46/0-46.
3. *An Atlas of the Mughal Empire,* OUP, Delhi, 1982, Sheet 14, B.
4. Ṣādiq Khān, *Shāh Jahān Nāma*, Ms.Br.Mus.Or. 174.

whose assignments each village lay and the names of the village official. The summary sheet mentions four important officials, one of whom was Muḥammad Afẓal, the Imperial *faujdār* [commandant] of the *pargana.* In 1700 he held the rank of 500 *ẓāt* 5-monthly had 250 *sawars*[1] of which 100 *ẓāt* 5-monthly and 250 *sawars* of which 200 *sawars* were conditional[2]. Though he made Zainpur to the Imperial Court, this does not necessarily mean that his jurisdiction extended to that *pargana* as well.[3] He remained *faujdār* of 'Ādilābād till 1702,[4] when he was transfered. He was dismissed subsequently and 'Abdul Wahab' was made the *faujdār* of 'Ādilābād,[5] Muḥammad Afẓal died in 1704.[6] Since 'Ādilābād town was his seat of residence, one of his relatives represented after Afẓal's death that, the fifty years old *jāgīr* is like *waṭan* [*jāgīr*]'and solicited its restoration to him.[7] He was an influential *faujdār* who firmly entrenched in the locality.[8]

Qāẓi Najmuddin and Bhakkaji Badhu [sic] held the judicial office of *qāẓi*, the former was attached to 'Ādilābād town, and 101 surrounding villages lay within his jurisdiction, while the latter's jurisdiction extended over the remaining 23 villages. Qāẓi Najmuddin had been appointed in 1681 or even earlier[9]. Muḥammad Dost was the Imperial intelligencer [*wāqia' nigār*] who submitted regular reports of the public events and official news directly to his superior in Aurangabad for transmission to the Court. Mahadev Nāyak held the offices of *deshmukh*, *deshpāndiya* and *qānūngo* who had to look after the collection of revenues and the maintenance of accurate records concerning revenue assessment and realisation. The combination of the twin offices of *deshmukh* and *deshpāndiya / qānūngo* is of some interest though it was not unique in Mughal administration. These four officials appointed by the Imperial administration attended to the executive, judicial, revenue and communication duties in *pargana* 'Ādilābād.

1. I/42/1-90
2. I/46/6-12, I/46/6-17.
3. We are told he represented the case of one 'Abdullāh, a tax-exempt grant holder of village Melgaon whose 20 *bighas* of land were being withheld by Nek Muḥammad Afghan, the newly appointed *jāgīrdār* of Zainpur. Muḥammad Afẓal, solicited the assignment of that village himself to meet the balance [*tatimma ṭalab*] of his salary so that he could transfer the disputed land to the *aimmadār* as *waqf* [IJC, I/42/1-33.].
4. IJC, I/45/4-35.
5. IJC, I/45/2-60.
6. IJC, I/46/1-12, I/46/1-17.
7. I/47/6-34.
8. Muḥammad Afẓal did not enjoy this office for 50 years, however the *jagir* was probably held for a long time by him as Badi'uzzamān was appointed the *faujdār* of 'Ādilābād on 18 January 1660. M.A. Nayeem [ed.] *Catalogue of Documents of Aurangzeb's Reign* A.P. State Archives, Hyderabad 1980, Vol. I, p. 213.
9. IJC, I/23/11-2, 3.

The village documents give us the names of the *muqaddams*, *patels*[1], *chaudhurīs* and the *patwārīs*, these officials being in a sense, subordinate to the *deshmukh*, *deshpāndiya*[2] and *qānūngo* in maintaining order and collecting revenue. In some villages the number of the *chaudhurīs* and the *patels* was astonishingly high ranging rising to as many as six in exceptional cases; and there were only a few villages having only one or two *chaudhurīs.* The names of the *patels* and *chaudhurīs* are given under the heading *muqaddam,* so that both represented village headmen [compare *chaudhurī* in north India where he was *a pargana level* official, corresponding to *deshmukh*]. In 15 villages the names *of* the *patels* have been mentioned and not of *chaudhurīs.* Two villages had the same *patel* but no *chaudhurī* or *patwārī*, which meant presumably that the *patel* here performed the *patwārī's* functions. However, the office of the *patwārī* was equally important as there were ten *patwārīs* who looked after 11 villages. Nine villages have been recorded under the jurisdiction of a single *patwārī.*

The village officials obviously belonged to *zamīndār* class but no information has been forthcoming regarding their caste affiliations. Gordon and Richards consider them as belonging to Maratha caste because their names most often end with the honorific ji [Kishnaji, Timaji]. One Sarangdhar, *zamīndār* of the *pargana* also held *jāgīr* [revenue assignment] there.

The document indicates 119 villages as assigned in *jāgīr* to more than 70 *jāgīrdārs.* This tends to suggest that due to proximity of the *pargana* to Burhanpur, the *ṣūba* headquarters, the small *jāgīrs* placed in it. Some of the *jāgīrdārs* held revenue assignments in contiguous villages. But there are instances to the contrary in that some *jāgīrdārs* had more than one village in *jāgīrs* and yet these are at some distance from each other. Ten villages have been assigned to more than one *jāgīrdar* which means that even portions of a village could also be assigned to petty *manṣabdārs.* Even some *jāgīrdārs* holding several villages have, sometimes been allotted parts of villages like Muḥammad Afẓal, the *faujdār* and Dost Muḥammad, the *wāqia'-nigār* who held 14 and 7 villages respectively. The *jāgīrdārs* did not normally reside in the assigned villages and their agents collected the revenue. They were, however, expected to make endeavour for the extension of cultivation by terms of orders of assignment.[3] They also helped

1. The *patels* were also responsible for depositing the lost goods in the treasury, as Babu, *patel* of village Mehun, *pargana* 'Ādilābād who had fetched variety of garments from the Purna sent them to the *Dīwān* in June 1644 Y.H. Khān *Selected Documents of Shahjahan's Reign, Daflar-i Dīwānī,* Hyderabad, 1950, p. 134.
2. The verification of the *deshpāndiya* was required, as has been referred to in a document of *pargana* 'Ādilābād on the current realisation of a *jāgīrdār*. M.A. Nayeem Facsimile of document, *op. cit.,* p. 60.
3. See appointment order of a *jāgīrdār* in 'Ādilābād, M.A. Nayeem, *op. cit.* p. 60.

the peasantry in numerous ways. We are told of a complaint of a *jāgīrdar* of *pargana* 'Ādilābād who was transferred elsewhere. He represented to the Imperial Court that since he had advanced *taqāvi* [*taccavi*] to the peasants and made the *jāgīr* villages prosperous and moreover had also made his *jāgīr* his seat of residence, he should not be transferred.[1]

The *āwārja* documents of *pargana* 'Ādilābād of 1702 indicate the total *jama'dāmi* and *ḥāṣil* figures for more than 70 *jāgīrdārs* and *ai'mmadārs* with their designations and postings.[2] Since transfers were an integral part of the Mughal administration, of the 70 *jāgīrdārs* listed in the *Dīwān's* report of 1696 only one-third had continued to hold their assignments by 1702. Only *ai'mma* grants remained undisturbed throughout the period [1696-1702].

Richards has prepared a table of collections by 17 *jāgīrdārs* posted outside the *ṣūba* who were drawing 20% or above of the total estimated income in our *pargana* and suggests that the same ratio was applicable to entire Ḳhandesh.[3] However, his observations require scrutiny because he has altogether ignored the other side of the picture i.e. the collections being made by various officials from other provinces of the Deccan who were posted in Khandesh which can be substantiated with the help of similar documents of other *parganas* of the Deccan provinces. The *manṣabdārs* recorded in our *pargana* include the *nāzims, Dīwāns, qāẓis, qila'dārs, thānadārs, wāqia'nigārs* and many petty officials.

Muḥammad Afẓal, son of Ja'far Beg Birloj, was the largest single *jāgīrdar* who held 14 larger villages including *qaṣba* was accommodated within 'Ādilābād annually yielding Rs 29,792 [17.8% of the total estimated income of the *pargana*].[4] The remaining *jāgīrdārs* were accommodated within 93 villages because four villages were entirely *ai'mma* and one was exclusively reserved for the imperial *k͟hāliṣa.* Gordon and Richards could count only 50 *jāgīrdārs* and resorted to the inadequate decipherment of some names. They refer to the tendency of the compilers to use the various forms of the same *jāgīrdar's* name, which, however, is not corroborated by a careful study of the documents for three villages the names of *jāgīrdārs* are not provided by our papers[5]. Since the compilers had to maintain strict

1. IJC, I/42/8-59.
2. IJC, I/45/4-35, 36.
3. J.F. Richards/Revenue Flows & C., pp.193-231.
4. He also received Rs 644 from *pargana* Zainpur in 1701 A.D., IJC, I/46/2-47, I/46/2-101.
5. The detailed table to this chapter gives the names of principal *jāgīrdārs,* the separate area of three categories of land [*ai'mma, uftada* and *mazrua'*] and the amount assessed in *tanka* and *dāms*, the established collection and the actual realisation, the number of the village officials, the distance in *Kurohs* [2.80 kms.] and the means

protocol only one form of name has been used throughout the documents because there could be no variations in official designations.

The actual *ḥāṣil* at the end of the 17th century was about one-third to the *jama'*. In the beginning of Aurangzeb's reign several villages of our *pargana* were transferred to *khāliṣa.*[1] These were probably high-yielding whereas only one village was earmarked for *khāliṣa* in 1696 which suggests a decline in the productivity of the villages previously held in *khāliṣa.* Two documents show that the conditions of *khāliṣa* villages were somewhat better than the *jāgīr* villages. Mulla Muḥammad Momin [holding the rank of 500 / 100] and others represented to the Emperor that they had to refund a large amount of loan, maintain numerous dependents and meet the cost of the contingent. Some *dāms* were allocated to them from *pargana* 'Ādilābād. But revenue realisation records of ten years *ḥāṣil-i deh sala* indicate that their *jāgīr* villages were extremely low-revenue yielding and deserted and in the best year [*sāl-i 'alā*] only one-third was cultivated. They therefore, solicited the assignment of one *khāliṣa* and three selected *jāgīr* villages which was acceded to.[2] Aurangzeb also ordered the transfer of the Deccanis not commanding any contingents in the Old Country, [*mulk-i qadīm*] in order to allow for payment of balance of salary [*tatimma-i-ṭalab*] of the above mentioned *jāgīrdārs.* There are at least 40 documents containing petitions of many *manṣabdārs* for assigning villages included in *pāibāqī* [lands temporarily in the charge of the Imperial officials pending assignment to *jāgīrdar*] in *pargana* 'Ādilābād, either due to the transfer or death or dismissal of the *jāgīrdārs* or the resumption of *ai'mma* grants[3]. This shows an unmistakable pressure upon *pāibāqī.* Gordon and Richards do not take any notice of this evidence of pressure on *pāibāqi*, which Richards has elsewhere disputed.[4] The position

of irrigation. These details demonstrate the labour and precision taken in collecting and entering the data against each village. The same format adopted by the Mughal administration was strictly followed in regard to other *parganas* of *sarkār* Burhānpur *ṣūba* Khāndesh, *viz.*, the incomplete series of *pargana* Fateḥābād [Laling].

1. IJC, I/11/0-2, I/13/0-3, I/13/10-10, I/13/0-12, I/13/0-14, I/13/0-32, I/13/0-36, I/13/0-42-43.
2. IJC, I/15/0-1, passim.
3. IJC, I/42/1-90, I/42/6-56, I/42/8-53, I/43/2-84, I/43/2-126, I/43/5-6, I/44/2-43, I/44/2-133, I/44/11-54, I/45/1-106, I/45/2-60, I/45/3-4, I/45/3-43, I/45/7-30, I/45/7-91, I/45/10-33, I/45/10-52, I/45/11-42, I/45/0-2, I/46/2-35-36, I/46/2-172, I/46/6-12, I/46/7-79, I/46/8-25, I/46/8-66, I/46/8-75, I/46/11-119, I/47/7-59, I/47/7-65, I/47/7-83, I/47/12-28, I/50/8-15, I/51/11-33, I/51/12-195, I/51/12-205 *Passim.*
4. *Mughal Administration in Golconda,* pp.104. See my article, The Working of the *Jāgīr* in the Deccan during the Last Years of Aurangzeb's Reign, *Journal of Objective Studies Delhi*, No. 2, Vol. 2, July, 1990, 71-80. In A.D. 1696 the *Dīwān* of the Deccan received a large village report on the position of 'Ādlilābād *pargana.* Interestingly for each of 124 villages in the *pargana* a separate page supplied the following

of the detailed table does further clear the matter discussed in the preceding pages.

Conclusion

The 'Ādilābād *pargana* survey shows that the Mughal administration collected considerable information about the local agrarian conditions and fiscal claims. It gives us valuable insight into the extent and nature of irrigation, variations in agrarian productivity, land revenue assessment and collection, nature of the offices of the headmen and accountants, position of *zamīndārs,* pattern of *jāgīr* assignments, state and internal administration of *ai'mma* lands etc. This basic information needs to be collated with two kinds of other materials such as of the same locality also may make possible a meaningful comparison of the extent of cultivation and irrigation across two centuries. It is very likely that 'Ādilābād surely fairly well represents the pattern of Mughal administration in the Deccan though it may have had some specific features of its own.

[II] Jizya

Aurangzeb reimposed *jizya* in 1679[1] after its final revocation by Akbar in 1580, which became a controversial issue generating considerable debate among the historians of medieval India as Rana Raj Singh of Mewar was assured of no intention to change the religious policy of his predecessors through one of his *nishāns*[2]. Though Aurangzeb imposed it after twenty one years of his ascending the throne he continued it until the end of his reign with certain exemptions. It may be specifically stated that the collection of *jizya* was a tax levied on *zimmīs* [non-Muslims] expressly as the price of protection of their lives and property in lieu of military service where women, children, beggars, monks, the elderly, the invalid, the insane, the incurably ill, retired teachers, and poor workers were exempted from its payments. A *qaulnama* under the seal of Nūr Khān s/o Kale Khān to Siwai Venkat Reddy, *Mīnwār maḥālat* [fiscal units] that the matters of the

---

data: The name of the village, its location [in *Kuroh* from the *pargana* town and headquarters in cardinal directions]; the name of the principal *jāgīrdār,* the names of the headman [or headmen and the village accountant[s]; land cultivated; land fallen out of cultivation; land in tax free grants then measured in *āut, bighas* and *biswas*], the source of irrigation, if any, the established *ḥāṣil* for the entire village, revenue collected [*wusūli*] and the balance or arrears [*tatimmat*]. Surprisingly, the Mughal administration had penetrated into the village to obtain precise information on well power and sources. Similarly the names of the village officers were known and listed.

1. Sāqī Musta'id Khān *Ma'āsir-i 'Ālamgīrī*, [Calcutta, 1871, p. 174].
2. Shyamaldas, *Vir Vinod*, Vol. II, pp. 419-20, *Cf.,* M. Athar Ali, *Mughal India:Studies in Polity, Ideas, Society and Culture*, Delhi 2006, pp. 245-6.

collection of the *jizya* of the specified *pargana* of *sarkār* Maḥammadnagar *ṣūba Darul jihād* Hyderabad amounting to Rs 1500 '*Ālamgīrī* coins of full weight in *lumpsum* for 48th and 49th R.Ys. through him concerning Shaikh Muḥammad 'Āsim, *amīn* for realising the *jizya* of Hyderabad was formed out which was to be paid in stipulated installments in the *bait* [*ul mal-i*] *jizya*[1]. Since Marathi documents published by Bharat Itihas Samshodak Mondal, Pune in their well known volumes throw very agonising light on the imposition of jizya and its severity in collection. Even Shivaji's much controversial letter to Aurangzeb has become a well established issue between Satish Chandra and S.A.I. Tirmizi. The significance of these documents are well known which have already been discussed by the historians which hardly need to be referred to by the writer as well.

It was however, made obligatory that the revenue contractor had to keep the people happy with his considerate behaviour. To crown this the *zimmīs* in service of the government and the peasantry having no means of subsistence except for agriculture were exempted from *jizya*. It was to be collected from the prosperous villages because in 1704 A.D. almost all the *parganas* had been devastated by the Marathas it was to be collected from the inhabitated villages in 1705 A.D. [which however, could not become possible since 1704 onwards].

It may be taken into consideration that the peasantry having no other source of livelihood except for agriculture was also exempted from its payment due to natural calamity. One can trace references to *jizya* in Aurangzeb's *tauqīāt,*[2]*raqāim*[3], *kalim'at*[4], *aḥkām*[5] and other documents of his reign like the Inayat Jung Collection[6] especially of Aurangzeb's reign itself.

Though J.N. Sarkar[7], S.R. Sharma[8], Zahiruddin Faruki[9],

1. *Sumasthan Documents.*
2. *Ruq'at-i 'Ālamgīrī*, Delhi, 1972.
3. Saiyid Ashraf Khān, *Raqāim-i Karāim*, ed S.M. Azizuddin Hussain, Delhi, 1990.
4. 'Ināyat Khān, *Kalimāt-i Taiyibāt*, ed S.M. Azizuddin Hussain, Delhi, 1982.
5. *Aḥkām-i 'Ālamgīrī*, Lahore, 1963.
6. Inayat Jung Collection, National Archives of India, New Delhi, Prof SM. Azizuddin Husain has cited a document of Farrukh Siyar from Inayat Jung Collection Nov/6/1/38 instead of Aurangzeb himself. *Cf.,* S.M. Azizuddin Husain *'Jizya-* Its Imposition during the Reign of Aurangzeb - An Examination, *The Indian Historical Review*, Vol. XXVI, No. x; July 2000, p. 119, n.
7. J.N. Sarkar, *History of Aurangzeb*, Delhi 1973, *Mughal Administration*, Calcutta, 1963.
8. S.R. Sharma, *Religious Policy of the Mughal Emperors*, Delhi, 1988, *Mughal Empire in India, Bombay* 1940, *The Cresent in India*, Bombay, 1966.
9. Zahiruddin Faruki, *Aurangzeb and His Times*, Delhi, 1972.

R.P. Tirpathi[1], Shibli Nomani[2], Lane Pole[3], Satish Chandra[4], Irfan Habib[5], S.A.A. Rizwi[6], M. Athar Ali[7], Muzaffar Alam[8], G.C. Dwivedi[9], J.F. Richards[10], R.C. Majūmdār[11] and H.K. Naqvi[12] have commented on Aurangzeb's religious policy including *jizya* yet Ishtiyaq Ḥusain Qureshi[13], Shaikh Muḥammad Ikrām[14], Iftikhar Aḥmad Ghori[15] and Muḥammad Aslam[16] have also expressed their views.

Aurangzeb's own inclination is duly reflected in *Ahkam-i 'Ālamgīrī* where he has quoted the Quranic injunction about *jizya*[17]. Aurangzeb issued a *farman* to the *Dīwāns* of the provinces to collect the *jizya* from *zimmīs*.[18] Isardas [Ishwardas] Nagar refers to the appointment of 'Ināyatullāh Khān to supervise the collection of *jizya*.[19] It was further endorsed by *Khulāṣtus Siyāq*[20], Khāfī Khān does highlight imposition of *jizya*.[21]

Bhim Sen's report that "*jizya* levied and collected by force in the Deccan"[22] does not stand scrutiny in the light of the above-cited *qaulnama*

1. R.P. Tirpathi, *Rise and Fall of the Mughal Empire*, Allahabad, 1987, *Some Aspects of Muslim Administration*, 1956, Allahabad.
2. Shibii Nomani, *Aurangzeb 'Ālamgīrī per ek Nazar*, [in Urdu], Azamgarh, *n.d.*
3. Lane Pole, *Rulers of India-Aurangzeb and the Decay of the Mughal Empire*, Oxford, 1901 [1707-1748].
4. Satish Chandra, *Parties and Politics at the Mughal Court*, Delhi, 2002, *Mughal Religious Policies. The Rajputs and the Deccan*, '*Jizya* and the State in India during the Seventeenth Century', *JESHO*, Vol. XII, part IV, 1959.
5. Irfan Habib, *The Agrarian System of Mughal India,* Third partly revised edition, Delhi, 2014.
6. S.A.A Rizvi, *Muslim Revivalist Movements in North India in the Sixteenth and Seventeenth Century*, Agra, 1965.
7. M. Athar Ali, *The Mughal Nobility under Aurangzeb*, Delhi, 1996, *Mughal India: Studies in Polity, Ideas, Society and Culture*, Delhi, 2006, 8th ed., 2014.
8. Muzaffar Alam, *The Crisis of Empire in Mughal North India*, Delhi, 1993.
9. G.C. Divedi, *The Jats: Their Rule in the Mughal Empire*, Delhi, 1989.
10. J.F. Richards, *The New Cambridge History of India, 1.5, The Mughal Empire*, Cambridge, 1993.
11. R.C. Majumdar, *The Mughal Empire*, Bombay, 1974.
12. H.K. Naqvi, *History of Mughal Government and Administration*, Delhi, 1970.
13. Ishtiyaq Husain Qureshi, *Ulema in Politics*, *The Administration of the Mughal Empire*, Delhi, n.d.
14. Shaikh Muḥammad Ikrām, *The Muslim Community of Indo-Pak Sub-continent,* Delhi, 1985.
15. Iftikhar Ahmad Ghori, 'Ideological Factor in the Mughal War of Succession, *Journal of Pakistan Historical Society,* 1960.
16. Muḥammad Aslam, *Aurangzeb Ki Takht Nashini mein Ulama Ka Kirdar*, Lahore, 1991.
17. *Aḥkām-i 'Ālamgīrī,* Lahore, 1963.
18. *Ma'āsir-i 'Ālamgīrī*, p. 174.
19. Ishwardas Naqar, *Futūḥat-i 'Ālamgīrī*, Delhi, 1978, p. 117.
20. MS, Centre of Advanced Study in History AMU, Aligarh, ff . 3[a] 9[b].
21. Khāfī Khān, *Muntakhabul Lubab*, Karachi, 1963, Vol. II, pp. 234-5.
22. Bhim Sen, *Nuskha-i Dilkushā*, Br. Lib., f. 139 [b].

and the Inayat Jung Collection Documents. When the word Hindu does not occur in *Fatāwā-i 'Ālamgīrī* then why Prof. Azizuddin Ḥusain is bent upon being unhistorical [*viz.*, in case of his reference to Bernier] in the garb of his criticism of Aurangzeb[1]. To his utter chagrin there is no discussion in Moinuddin Maḥmud Naqshbandi's *Al-Fatāwā-i Naqshbandi'* or Mufti Abul Barkat bin Ḥusamuddin Dehlavi's *Fatāwā-i Majma'ul Barkat* [1698 AD], about the position and status of the Hindus or the *Masail-i jizya,*[2] nor is this question discussed by historians, contemporary or modern. As stated elsewhere owing to continuous wars against the Marathas the devastation of crops or their failure led to the temporary suspension of *jizya* which was apparently realised from a limited number of the villagers as neither the employees nor the peasantry having any source of income except for agriculture nor the semi-heredity officials at village and *pargana* level were supposed to pay the *jizya*. However, Manucci's allegation of popularising Islam through the reimposition of *jizya* and fill his empty treasury is counter-productive[3], as according to Aurangzeb's estimation *jizya* was to go to *baitulmal*. Fryer does record: "Early in his reign, the puritan Emperor had reimposed the hated *jizya* on unbeliever. The impost was responsible for most of Aurangzeb's reign".[4] The same view has been expressed by Thomas Rolt, President of the English Factory at Surat.[5] Contrary to the

1. *Cf., jizya* - Its Real Position & C., p. 97.
2. Shaikh Nūr Muḥammad Lahori, M.A. Lib., AMU, p. 175.
3. N.Manucci, *Storia Do Mogor*, London, 1907, Vol. II, pp. 273, 75. A document in Inayat Jung Collection bearing accession number I/45/7-9 does indicate that any entreaty made by a neo-Muslim could partially meet the Imperial approbation as given hereunder which does show that terms and conditions apply as recorded thus: Representation of meekest of the Khānazāds [born in the house of a noble] contains orders of Aurangzeb soliciting the Holy Quran, rosary, for himself which were approved except for exemption from circumcision. He further pleaded for appointment as auditor of the Imperial claims outstanding against the *manṣabdar's* [*muṭālaba*] under Bhopal Rai, father-in-law of the applicant which Aurangzeb marked to Asad Khān. Though the penalty for absence from duty was imposed yet the previous absence was waved off. When the solicitor sought Imperial favours for his posting in Aurangabad it was marked to Asad Khān to make a recommendation. In view of his embracing the religion of Islam he pleaded for the grant of the rank so as to save him from any ignomity in the eyes of his peers leading to the conferment of 100 [*ẓāt* rank] on I *Jumada* II, 42 R.Y. He was granted five *parwāngis* for the grant of a copy of the Holy Quran, military armament, exemption from penalty and the assignment of *manṣab* [rank] etc, while two documents were issued for paying the penalty as well as to the office of the *bakhshī* [for payment of salary].
4. J.F. Fryer, *A New Account of East India being Nine years Travel*, London, 1915, Vol. II, p. 114.
5. Sir Charles Fawcett, *The English Factories in India: Bombay Surat and Malabar Coast*, Oxford, 1904, Vol. III, p. 241, wherein he alleges of 'forcing the poorer section of the population to become Muslims. Even the collection of *jizya* had become extremely difficult in Bālāghāt [IJC, I/40/1-3].

European assumption of running the poor from villages owing to payment of *jizya* Aurangzeb himself exempted them as stated initially:[1]

Contemporary and modern historians of medieval India except for Azizuddin Ḥusain call Aurangzeb as puritan which is firmly established from the impartial observation coupled with his corresponding actions. Though Aurangzeb appointed Hurjan, S/o Mansingh as *ṣadīwal* of his wife Rabiatud Durrani's mausoleum, situated in Aurangabad on the basis of a competitive bid accepting the posting of Mohan's *peshkash* [tribute] of Rs 5,000 for Begumpur equally accepted by the former contingent upon maintaining a contingent of 500, i.e. 250 for the city wall near Begumpura, 50 for the masoluem and 200 for the fort of Begumpura yet he again made a quite different dispensation[2]. He strictly ordered only the honest Muslim *mutawallī* in accordance with his orders that:

> "If any incompetent one is appointed contrary to the Islamic Law and the established usage such carelessness should not be allowed, then replace him by any other efficient Muslim [caretaker] as no Hindu can be a *mutawallī* [receiver] and the death is much close to the shoe-lace".[3]

Irfan Habib opines that, "As a tax, the *jizya* was extremely regressive and, above all, hardest on the poor". However, even poor *zimmīs* were entitled to receiving financial help from *baitulmal.* Ishwardas Nagar confirms that after the conquest of Hyderabad its *jizya* was remitted[4]. It is also mentioned in *Akhbārāt-i Durbār-i Mua'lla* that the realisation of *jizya* was stopped throughout the Mughal provinces of the Deccan on account of the difficulties caused by the Maratha raids and active famines.[5] It is also mentioned in the *Akhbārāt* that the collection of *jizya* was suspended in Devalghat for three years.[6]

1. In accordance with Francis Bernier as misstated by Prof Azizuddin Husain the *Nāẓim* of Hyderabad reported that, on account of their poverty they were unable to pay *jizya* and whenever they have to pay, they fled. He also expressed his readiness to follow the instructions issued by him. There upon the emperor orders that *jizya* of year be not collected from them and they be asked to remain in their villages and *maḥāls* and engage themselves in cultivation and their profession. *Travels in the Mughal Empire*, A.D. 1656-1668, tr. By Archibald Constable, Delhi, 1972, p. 184.
   Since the period of Francis Bernier is AD 1656-1668, there is no chance of any reference to the first decade of the eighteenth century, contrary to the assumption of S M Azizuddin Husain.
2. IJC, I/42/9-29.
3. IJC, I/45/1-41. For security purposes of the mausoleum of his wife Aurangzeb appointed a Hindu with 500 men where as he also did not like a corrupt Muslim as *mutawalli*, instead he had appointed an unblemished Muslim as per the Islamic Law. *Cf.*, IJC, I/43/1-22.
4. Ishwardas Nagar, *Futūḥat-i 'Ālamgīrī*, f . 111 [b].
5. *Akhbārāt-i Durbār-i Mua'lla*, 19 February, 1704.
6. *Ibid*, 12 November 1704.

There is no evidence to the theory of abandonment of *jizya* as suggested by Satish Chandra, as we do not come across any such reference either in Aurangzeb's *ruq'āt, tauqi'at, ahkām, raqāim, farāmīn, shuqqajāt, akhbārāt,* Inayat Jung Collection or in any contemporary Persian chronicle or European travellers accounts, instead Aurangzeb insisted on the collection of *jizya* as Bhim Sen records that "*jizya* was imposed and collected by force in the Deccan".[1] Furthermore, Khāfi Khān confirms that Amānat Khān, *Dīwān-i Deccan*, was granting remission in the arrears of *jizya* while Rashīd Khān communicated to the Emperor that he had granted the *sanads* of exemption to the Hindu population liable to pay *jizya* owing to which Aurangzeb admonished Amānat Khān for not remitting *jizya* which he had succeeded in reimposing after so many difficulties where after Amānat Khān never granted exemptions.[2]

Prof. S.M. Azizuddin Ḥusain has mis-quoted Bernier that the *Nāzim* of Hyderabad reported to the Emperor that the people on account of their poverty were unable to pay *jizya* and whenever they were to pay, they fled as Aurangzeb also expressed his readiness to follow the instructions issued by him. Thereupon the Emperor ordered that *jizya* of a year be not collected from them and they be assured by remaining in their villages and *maḥāls* and engage themselves in cultivation and their profession[3].

There are such instances of the personal deposition of *jizya viz.*, a personal assistant to the *bakhshi*, pleaded that his Muslim officer was seriously ill and that on account of his being busy with the affairs he would not be able to pay *jizya* personally and would like to send it through a deputy. His request was turned down. He was reminded that paying the *jizya* was a privilege and payment must, therefore, be made in person. The official came and paid *jizya* in person as ordered.[4]

Notwithstanding Azizuddin Ḥusain's citations from other sources he has not quoted any document of Inayat Jung collection of Aurangzeb's reign itself which is not devoid of numerous such references. Shaikh Amānullāh S/o 'Abdur Rauf, posted at the *Dīwān* of *ṣūbajāt-i Deccan*, an experienced and religious minded official well versed in financial and legal intricacies as he had excellently extracted legal *jizya* from *pargana* Rajpura as deputy *Dīwān* of *Mandavi* Begumpura etc.[5]

1. Bhim Sen, *Nuskha-i Dilkushā*, Br. Lib. F 139 [b].
2. Khāfi Khān, *op. cit.*, Vol. II, pp. 377-78.
3. *Travels in the Mughal Empire*, A.D. 1656-1668, translated by Archibald Constable, Delhi, 1972, [first published by OUP, 1891], p. 184. In fact there is no such quotation on this page.
4. *Akhbārāt-i Durbār-i Mua'llā*, 8 May 1694.
5. Inayat Jung Collection [IJC] IJC, I/41/12-148. He has realised *jizya* from 38 RY till 41 R.Y.

There are instances of their killing those who came to collect *jizya* and themselves being killed by the Mughal soldiers as is also recorded in a document.

> "*Parwangi* under the seal of Yār 'Alī Beg was received that it was learnt from the communication of Saiyid 'Abdur Raḥīm, *amīn-i jizya* of Berar that Saiyid Muḥammad Qasim, his deputy in *pargana* Tilangaon, to collect the *jizya* of Chin Qilīch Khān Bahādur had gone for house tax [*Khāna-shumari*] and count of livestock. 'Abdul Ghafūr, agent of Khān Bahādur attacked the deputy and two horsemen killed Saiyid and his brother together with fifteen infantrymen, plundered all goods and the amount of *jizya*, killed six security staff of the treasury and the deputy [i.e. Saiyid Muḥammad Qasim] who could only save his life. The Emperor ordered for the transfer of *pargana* Tilangaon, *sarkār* Kalam, *ṣūba* Berar".[1]

Though it was assigned to Sheo Singh, *qila'dār* [castellan] of Islamgarh, *alias* Raheri owing to the complaint of Saiyid 'Abdur Raḥīm, *amin-i jizya*, as the revenue collector [*'āmil*] [i.e. 'Abdul Ghafūr] killed his deputy with some persons. However, consequent upon the submission of the reinstatement order by Chin Qilīch Khān's plenipotentiary under the seal of *Bakhshiul Mulk* Mukhliṣ Khān, then Aurangzeb, subjected to his reinstatement, in favour of Sheo Singh along with order of payment of the remainder from North India [Hindustan] and the Deccan.[2]

Consequent upon the seriousness of the matter Saiyid 'Abdur Raḥīm, *amin-i jizya* of *ṣūba* Berar wrote: Yār 'Ali to represent it to the Emperor that when Saiyid Muḥammad Qāsim, his deputy, had gone to *pargana* Tilangaon, *jizya* of Chin Qilīch Khān Bahādur for house tax and head count of the live-stock. 'Abdul Ghafūr, agent of Khān Bahādur delayed him for 12 days to recall him inside the *qaṣba* [township] and communicated that it would be advisable to undertake *lumpsum* revenue-farming otherwise he would not allow. Thenceforward, when the deputy did not accept this suggestion, he instantaneously consulted with Muḥammad Siddique, the news-reporter [*wāqia' nigār*] thereat and dispatched him for one day towards Kalam in accompaniment with the *qāẓi* thereof. The next day the aforesaid deputy was communicated to settle the matter as per the Imperial order where after the said person leaving behind the [amount of] *jizya*, sent his luggage, came inside the *qaṣba* with twenty infantrymen. The said agent shut the gate, killed two Saiyid cavalrymen, his brothers along with 15 infantrymen and the said deputy, plundered the entire commodity and killed six security personnel of the treasury as the deputy ran away for life

1. IJC, I/42/7-73.
2. IJC, I/42/9-25, I/42/10-55.

so that the issue could be brought to His Majesty's notice who ordered transfer of this *pargana* to be assigned to the castellan of Islāmgarh [*alias* Rāheri].[1]

In 1702 A.D. the expenses of the Deccan provinces were gradually increasing. Even the financial position was so much alarming that all the *Khāliṣa maḥāls* of *ṣūba* Aurangabad could not yield sufficient income including the revenue of the *jizya* that the expenses of the provinces exceeded the income. Previously majority of the expenses of the *ṣūba* were being met out of the bills of exchange from North India [*hundwiyat-i Hindustan*] and the income from Indor Nimkal and the province [s] of Berar, Khandesh, tribute from the *zamīndārs* of Chanda and Islamgarh was deposited in the treasury whereas only revenue realisation from Sangamner etc there was no other source of income as out of eight *khāliṣa maḥāls* three were reserved for the men of Khān-i Jahān and Qaular Hyderabadi etc while the *Khāliṣa* of Aurangabad was in-charge of the *Dīwān-i* Deccan. The income of *ṣūba* including that of *jizya* arrived at Rs 9,10922/9½ and the stipulated income was fixed at Rs 9,61,859/12 while the expenditure of Rs 28,12,298/2, out of which the stipulated expenditure was Rs 9,61,859/2 while non-planned expenditure as per the previous year was Rs 850,439/8½ and the excess expenses were Rs 9,01,575/8½. Aurangzeb therefore observed that Parner and Sangamner are not the old *Khāliṣa* [lands]. Now, as per the previous practice the old *khāliṣa* are four provinces that shall be initially fixed for the expenses of the aforesaid *ṣūbās* and the loss [*āfat*] and the non-receipt of the tribute of Chanda and Islamgarh shall, Almighty God willing, be compensated.[2]

Though Aurangzeb does not refer to the income from *jizya* yet it is being taken into consideration for computation. Otherwise this actually formed part of *bait-i jizya*. There is a set of 23 documents which is the income and expenditure sheet of the treasury of *bait-i jizya* of *Darul Fateḥ* Muḥammadabad *alias* Zafarabad / Bidar under the seal of Kifāyat Khān and other officials for the years 1702-3 A.D. amounting to Rs 81,285/15¾.

It may be incidentally pointed out that the income from *jizya* was also deposited in the Imperial treasury by way of *dastgardan* for which receipt was obtained out of which salary of the corps posted at Firozgarh Fort was paid subject to its return. Similar dispensation was made in regard to the salary of soldiers of Ramgir Fort, Muzaffarnagar Fort, Kalyan Fort etc.[3]

1. IJC, I/42/7-51.
2. IJC, I/45/8-6, I/45/8-7.
3. IJC, I/45/10-83 to I/45/10-105 while IJC, I/45/0-94 to I/45/0-104 refer to the deposition of the *jizya* by way of *dastgardan* amounting to Rs 67290 approximately for 12 different dates of 1702 A.D.

The availability of some thirty documents of *jizya* collection of Aurangzeb's reign in the Inayat Jung Collection not only depicts the problems and prospects of *jizya* collection but also its use on loan basis for the payment of soldiers posted in the forts of *ṣūba* Bidar. Notwithstanding the limited financial resources even by making use of the *jizya* collection on loan basis the funding was most often done from the resources of North India [Hindustan].

Even Aurangzeb's extraordinary exertion for getting the *jizya* amount collected he did not take any punitive measure to bring the culprits to book while as per the cannons of law and justice except for transferring the offenders to any other place because even in one case cited above no *shari'* punishment was given to the real culprit who got assassinated fifteen infantrymen and two security guards for getting the *jizya* collected as per rule and not in *lumpsump*. It does show that contrary to the much orchestrated propaganda Aurangzeb could not initiate any punitive proceedings to streamline the machinery of the *jizya* collection, that need a second reconnaissance of Aurangzeb's position of *jizya* policy and its suspension since 1704 onwards by their killing those who came to collect *jizya* by the Mughal soldiers and revenue collectors ['*āmils*]. Though there was a separate sheet, in accordance with Aurangzeb's declaration the income derived through *jizya* was to go to *baitul mal*, *viz.*, as per *jama' o kharaj-i jizya Darul Fateḥ* Muḥammadabad [income and expenditure of the province of Bidar] according to one of the series of 23 documents of Inayat Jung Collection as mentioned above. It was not meant for the employment of Muslims as both Muslims and non-Muslims used to serve in *bait-i jizya* because one Rup Chand was the treasure in Bidar of *jizya* in the *ṣūba*.

Apparently the imposition of the *jizya*, or the pool tax on non-Muslims, by Aurangzeb in 1679 meant an important increase in the magnitude of rural taxation in *bait-i jizya* as a separate organisation of collectors [*umāna'*] was created for this purpose. Interestingly, this tax was directly collected from the individual subjects in the cities. For the villages it was first decreed that a flat rate of Rs 100 upon 1,00,000 *dāms* i.e. 4% of the *jama' dāmi*, was to be paid by the officials of the *Khāliṣa* and the holders of the *jāgīrs*, who were then to collect the tax at the authorised rates from the peasants. A manual compiled in the later years of Aurangzeb shows, however, that detailed censuses of men liable to pay this tax were prepared in both towns and villages. The specimen accounts reproduced in it shows also the incidence was not light by any means. Out of the 280 males in a village, 185 were held assessable and of these 137 paid minimum rates of Rs 3, as 2, per annum as this at the time would have meant a month's wages for an unskilled urban labourer. According to Irfan Habib, as a tax, the *jizya* was extremely regressive and bore the hardest of the poorest. However, a specimen copy of a *sanad* shows that peasants of a particular area could be granted exemption in cases of acute distress. Interestingly in 1704, in view of the famine and the Maratha war, Aurangzeb remitted *jizya* throughout the Deccan for the duration of war.[1] Nevertheless his general policy was to discourage *jizya* remissions. Moreover other authorities emphasize that the[2] collections were accompanied with the greatest oppression and most of the amount actually collected was embezzled by the officials, so that only a very small part of it is used nothing to reach the Imperial treasury[3]. Even there is an instance that a Hindu *jāgīrdār* extorting *jizya,* the theoretical purpose of which was to show the superiority of the faithful over the infidels [*Ayen yu'til jizyata ayen yadūhum sāghirūn*] in accordance with Holy Qurān. Though the *jizya was* collected in the name of *baitul mal* what the documents often show its use on loan for payment of salaries.

[III] Other Taxes

Since the Mughal administration used to look after the affairs of all classes it was but natural that Mīr Muḥammad Ja'far was asked about the complaint of the traders of *sarkār* Gavil *ṣūba* Berar that Khanna and Madhu etc traders of *Qaṣba* Karinja, complained that their clients questioned about the *jins-i abresham*, opium etc, which they have purchased from *balda* Akbarabad, Ujjain, Surat Port and Burhanpur and bring to sell them to Ḥyderabad. The *mutaṣaddis* thereat, notwithstanding collect Re 1 per Rs 100 as the forbidden imposts. Thus, instructions were issued in 1694-5 A.D. that no such forbidden imposts be collected otherwise write the fact.[4] Similar complaint was also made to Shaikh Abul Ḥusain, *Dīwān* of *ṣūba*

---

1. *Akhbārāt-i Durbār-i Mua'llā* 48/36 and A 245. *Cf., Akhbārāt* 47/323.
2. Ma'mūri, f 179 [a]. Khāfi Khān, II 377-78.
3. *Dilkushā*, f. 139 [b]; Manucci, II, 291. *Nigārnāma-i Munshī*, ed. 139, does contain a document which was published by Saiyid Suleman Nadvi in *Ma'arif* XXI [1937] no. 5, 294-6, having been extracted from a latter collection, the *Nigārnāma* of *Munshī* La'l Chand. There is a serious error in the first few lines of the *Ma'arif* text, where it reads *zamīndārān* in place of *zimmī-i nādār*, 'the indignant non-Muslim' of the original. The *sanad* is addressed to *a Dīwān* and recited that the *jizya* should not be imposed upon destitute persons. Since the poor peasants [*rezā-ri'āya*] who had to engage in cultivation were found to be in debt even for their seeds and cattle [the *Ma'arif*] text reads differently here, the cultivators were to be exempted from paying the *jizya*; but it was nevertheless, to be realised from the *ta'alluqadārs*, *chandhurīs*, *qānūngos*, *ṭarafdārs* and other inhabitants of the towns and villages.
4. IJC, I/36/3-4.

Ḳhandesh, who was rectified as well.[1]

The *muqaddams*, namely Ramji etc village Eingaon, belonging to *pargana* Varval, *sarkār* Nander, *ṣūba* Muḥammadabad [Bidar] complained against the highhandedness of 'Abdur Raḥīm, *alias* Nanaji *Deshmukh*, who not only arrested them but also expelled them from their home town. It contains the seal of Yar 'Ali, *murīd* [disciple] of Shāh 'Ālamgīr 14/1082 A.H.[2]. Similar instance can also be gauged from a representation to Muḥammad Shafī', *Dīwān* that Saiyid 'Ali, *Saudagar* complained to His Majesty about the collection of Re 1 *annas* 2 on every hundred which was however, rectified[3]. We also find such an example that Nayak etc residents of *pargana* Chimargonada that four *Chāwars* of land of Badda and Sevla contingent upon the issuance and *Nalwa Dak Chauki* and *Dali* etç belong to them which should be restricted accordingly.[4]

Though we are quite aware of the atrocities of the Marathas yet we find complaints about the atrocities being perpetuated on the *muqaddams* and *riā'ya* of Ranjini, *sarkār* Jalnapur, *ṣūba* Aurangabad due to the oppression of Zainuddin 'Ali Khān, *jāgīrdar* and *faujdār* and the crossing and staying of the Marathas and devastating of the villages. Accordingly plead for the grant of *jāgīr* to Rao Man Singh s/o Jadun Rao who is an ābādānkār[5]. The situation had become so much topsy turvy that Aurangzeb had himself observed that:

> "It was brought to the notice that *sibti* in the *ṣūbās* of the Deccan has become abundant which can be controlled by transferring the *jāgīr* and reduction in *manṣab* so long as the *wāqia' nigārs* and *sawānih navīs* report which is their duty. What has not happened despite our presence that shall happen. Crimes and innovations are causing the ruin of the country."[6]

Aurangzeb also saw to it that any other land which had been in grant of the old Deccani families should be continued unabatedly *viz.*, one *chawar* of land with seven mango and *imli* trees in the *madad-i ma'āsh* of Saiyid Nūr Muḥammad, servant of Mua'zzam Khān Deccani be continued from village Mandukan belonging to *pargana* Pandiya Bedgaon and half seer of oil expended on the light of the mosque be allowed which Aurangzeb also allowed as heretofore.[7] Aurangzeb also ordered that the excess in the

1. IJC, I/36/2-6.
2. IJC, I/36/4-10.
3. IJC, I/35/6-15.
4. IJC, I/47/3-86.
5. IJC, I/0/0-703.
6. IJC, I/0/0-735.
7. 26 *Ziqada*, I[st] R.Y. 1069 AH/IJC, I/47/1-99.

parganas of Bijapur and Aurangabad *ṣūbās* should be realised in the *sarkār* and not be given to *jāgīrdārs* so that the *riā'ya* could become satisfied.[1]

Aurangzeb ordered that 'let it be represented to Mu'tamād Khān as it shall be paid as per rules and regulations. But they have taken away the *khoshas* and left behind the *Karbi*[2]". It was but natural that anything could be borne out by the administration as we come to know through a *dastak* to Shaikh 'Ināyatullāh *Aḥādi*, posted in the *Dīwānī* of *ṣūbajāt-i* Deccan that the loss of *muwāzana-i mufaṣṣali* and *yakḥarfi* could be demanded of *pargana*, *sarkār* Junnar from 1091 to 1113 *faṣlī* in *naqd jama'dami*, *raqba* and directions of south, north, east, west, distance of way, name of *deshmukhs*, *deshpāndiyas*, *muqaddams*, *patwārīs*, *pattas*, *aimmadārs*, *rusūm-i naqd*, *arāzi*, *inā'm* of that group, *bāghāt-i* āmadnī, *chah-Khāna* etc as requisitioned which was to be deposited.[3]

Fortunately we come across āwārjas of *muwazanas* of different provinces like one of *ṣūba* Khandesh, five *sarkār* of *ṣūba* Aurangabad, some *sarkār* of *ṣūba* Berar all of which are of the *Khāliṣa* Sharifa. Thus, we come across a number of *sarkārs* which were shown included in *Khāliṣa* Sharifa.

Interestingly, the fees and perquisites of the revenue official were numerous. These perquisites [*rusūm*] are audited village account under the heading *ikhrājāt*. Besides *salāmī, qunalgha* was another prohibited tax forbidden by Akbar. Similarly *bhaint* and *bālādasti* were also the forbidden taxes. *Pattadari, balkati*, *tahsīldāri* and finally *kharj-i sadir o warid*. Such forbidden *abwāb* were prevalent in the Mughal administration. Unfortunately *begār* and *shikar* were also counted among such cases.

1. IJC, I/43/2/27.
2. IJC, I/45/7-139.
3. IJC, I/48/8-4.

VIII

Problems of the *Zamīndārs*

[I] The Different Forms of Zamīndārs

The *Deshmukh* used to be the counterpart of *Chaudhurī* [& *desāi*] in the Deccan. He used to be the *pargana* level semi-hereditary official who was concerned with revenue collection in Gujarat and Deccan.

Several studies of the position of *zamīndārs* in the Deccan have been made by the historians of Medieval India.[1] However, there is still ample justification for undertaking a similar venture concerning the status of *zamīndārs* in the six provinces of the Mughal Deccan under Aurangzeb in the light of the vast available documentation, especially the Inayat Jung Collection, preserved in the National Archives, New Delhi, which has long lain in wait for such a critical study.[2] The studies so far have been concerned rightly with the problem of assessing the strength of Imperial authority in the countryside, and the ways in which local chiefs and notables were assimilated into the Mughal administration as *zamīndārs*. It is generally admitted that the Mughal Imperial administration leaned heavily on the cooperation of the *zamīndārs* for revenue administration, military service and maintenance of law and order.[3]

The present chapter aims to study the attitude of the *zamīndārs* towards the Mughal Empire in Deccan under Aurangzeb, and conversely the policy pursued by the Mughal administration towards integrating

---

1. Irfan Habib, The *Zamīndārs* in the Āi'n, *Proc. Ind. Hist. Cong.* [*PIHC*], 1958, pp. 320-23; S. Nurul Ḥasan, Aspects of the *Zamīndāri* System in the Deccan [1695-1707], *PIHC*, 1969, pp. 262-66; Muzaffar Alam. 'The *Zamīndārs* and Mughal Power in the Deccan', *The Indian Economic and Social History Review* [*IESHR*] XI, March 1974, pp. 74-91; J.F. Richards, 'The Imperial Crisis in the Deccan', *Journal of Asian Studies* [*JAS*], Vol. XXXV, February, 1976, pp. 237-56.
2. *Cf.*, M. Athar Ali's, Review on J.F. Richards, *Mughal Administration in Golconda*, *JAS*, Feb. 1976, p. 160.
3. M. Athar Ali, *The Mughal Nobility under Aurangzeb*, Bombay, 1966, pp. 84-86; Zakir Husain, 'A *Zamīndār* Family of *Sarkār* Mandu, *Ṣūba* Malwa-Archival Evidence', *PIHC*. Warangal, 1992-93, pp. 311-20.

them in the highly centralised bureaucratic system.[1] The latter they did either by appointing them as *deshmukhs, deshpāndiyas, qānūngos, desāīs, sardeshmukhs, sardeshkhats, sardesāīs, muqaddams, patels,* etc, or confirming their old position in similar capacities, or even incorporating them as *jāgīrdārs.*

When Aurangzeb became Viceroy of the Deccan for the second term under Shāh Jahān, he endeavoured to win over the prominent *zamīndārs* as active allies of the Imperial administration,[2] which policy was continued by him in his position as Emperor as well.

It is an established dictum that an equilibrium among the Emperor, *manṣabdārs, zamīndārs* and peasants created order and stability whereas its absence resulted in disorder and anarchy as happened in the case of the Marathas, who resisted the Mughal might, because mere 'belief of the invincibility of the Mughal power' could not strike terror in their hearts in the same way as had made the *zamīndārs* submissive', as Muzaffar Alam suggests.[3] Instead, their own interests compelled the *zamīndārs* to come to terms either with the Mughals or side with the Marathas, as expediency dictated.

Aurangzeb occasionally ordered action about the Marathas:

> "Let it be transferred from the Deccani [Marathas] and be given in the *jagir* of *faujdar* who has to warn and taking the entire *yaraq* given *zamindars* to someone else and make it habituated"[4].

The Mughals since long, used to extract *peshkash* from the *zamīndārs,* without which any formal alignment with the Imperial administration was unthinkable to them. The *peshkash* was normally realised in full or in instalments as is evident from the surviving records attesting to the clearance of arrears by the *zamīndārs.* Thus, Jalu Raghunath, *Patwar,* deposited Rs 50 out of the total Rs 100 lying in arrears in 1662,[5] whereas Rs 2000 of the *peshkash* remained unrealized from the *zamīndār* of *pargana* Batlawal etc in 1670.[6]

1. For an opposite view see, Stephen P. Blake, 'The Patrimonial Bureaucratic Empire of the Mughals', in H. Kulke, [ed.] *The State in India 1000-1700,* Delhi, 1999, pp. 278-303.
2. Zakir Husain, *Calendar of Administrative Documents in Ādāb-i 'Ālamgīrī,* M.Phil Dissertation submitted at AMU, Aligarh, 1991, pp. XXXXI–XXXXV.
3. Peter Hardy, 'Commentary and Critique', *JAS,* XXXV, No. 2 [February, 1976], p. 234: Zakir Husain, 'The Mughal Maratha Conflict seen Through the Official Documents of Later Years of Aurangzeb, 'Aligarh Papers on Indian History', Dharwar, 1988, pp. 137-154.
4. IJC I/46/9-11.
5. IJC I/5/3-1.
6. IJC I/13/0-1.

We find detailed information about the arrears of *peshkash* outstanding against the *zamīndārs* [i.e. *muniwars* and *deshmukhs*] of Ḥyderabad running into millions of rupees in early 1690s. These were supposed to be realised subsequently.[1]

Since Aurangzeb paid special attention to secure the loyalties of the big *zamīndārs* to serve imperial interests, he conferred the *zamīndārī* of Ram Tek on Bhupat Singh, contingent upon his payment of Rs 50,000 as *peshkash,* out of which Rs 35,000 were paid through bankers [*sāhūkārs*], while, the remainder was recovered in unequal monthly instalments. Aurangzeb also confirmed the grant of *zamīndārī* through his *farmān* issued on his solicitation in 1674.[2]

The *peshkash* was accepted by the *zamīndārs* conditional upon the grant of the office. Rūdrājī, son of Debi Das, resident of *sarkār* Baglana received the *deshmukhi* of the *sarkār* in 1666 for which he agreed to pay Rs 15,000 by way of *peshkash,* in annual instalments of Rs 1,500, meaning thereby that the entire paymemt was to be made within a decade, while he was allowed perquisites [*rusūm*] at the rate of 1.5% of the revenue.[3] Similarly, Bhānji, the *deshmukh* of *pargana* Aurangabad [Karzmandgāon] was granted *deshmukhī* of villages Nurkara etc in *pargana* Kothli in 1669 for which he accepted to pay Rs 100 as *peshkash* over a period of five years.[4]

The *peshkash* was imposed on every *zamīndār* either big or small; Jiu *chaudhurī* of *pargana* Nandurbar agreed to pay Rs 75 as *peshkash.*[5] The payment of *peshkash* apparently followed a flexible pattern. Some of the *zamīndārs* used to promise the remittance of *peshkash* within three years whereas others assured its payment in stipulated instalments and no specific date of its full remittance was fixed.[6]

However, the appointment of *zamīndārs* as *deshmukh* or *deshpāndiya* etc was not made without enquiry. An effort was made to establish their antecedents before their confirmation. Kishnaji Bithal held the *deshmukhi* of *pargana* Aland together with 2 *chāwars* [240 *bighas*] as *in'ām* since the time of 'Alī 'Ādil Shāh allegedly through his *farmān* of 1070 AH/1660 A.D.[7] Since the Imperial administration used to scrutinise closely the claims of

1. IJC I/16/1-4 to I/16/1-10.
2. IJC I/32/2-2; I/32/3-1; I/33/3-4.
3. IJC I/9/8-1.
4. IJC I/11/1-1; I/11/1-2.
5. There are plenty of documents concerning the *peshkash* of a number of *zamīndārs* which do not only help in explaining the procedure of *peshkash* but also in understanding a many problems encountered by the *zamīndārs*.
6. IJC I/33/7-2.
7. IJC I/0/0-53.

the *zamīndārs,* it came to light that no one named Kodi Koma as *zamīndār* was appointed in any *maḥāl* during the regime of the 'Ādil Shāhs.[1] This is illustrative of the fact that the Mughals had maintained the archives of the 'Ādil Shāhi government. The *zamīndārs* were not entitled to appropriate the *rusūm* [perquisites] without securing the *sanads* [certificates] of the *Dīwānī* which were also confirmed by the *Dīwāns* of the Deccan in 1665.[2] Furthermore, the *rusūm* were co-terminus with the *peshkash,* and any laxity in remitting the *peshkash* could lead to severe punishment.[3] Thus, Shaikh Mukhdūm, the *manṣabdār* had to stand surety for payment of Rs 15,000 as *peshkash* by Naprasti [sic], *deshmukh* of *pargana* Aland, *sarkār* Naldurg, *ṣūba* Aurangabad in order to get him released.[4]

The amount of *peshkash* differed from person to person. Ūdājī Rām, *alias* Bābū Rāi, *deshmukh* of the *parganas* [23 *maḥāls*] of *sarkār* Mahur, etc, had to pay Rs 2,50,000 as *peshkash* from the time of Shāh Jahān as per his father's bond of 1635-6, which again proves that *peshkash* in the Deccan was an old phenomenon.[5] The *sardeshmukh,* was also responsible for getting the individual *deshmukhi* of the entire *sarkār* or area of his jurisdiction, as was the case with Ūdājī / Rām.[6]

Dues, which were to be collected by the state from the *zamīndārs* were termed as '*muṭāliba*'. 'Abdul Fattāḥ and other *deshmukhs* of *paragana* Ūtrān, *ṣūba Khāndesh* , had a *muṭāliba* of Rs 2716 which was ordered to be recovered from their *inā'm* in 1670.

There are numerous instances of the *peshkash* and *muṭāliba* due from the *zamīndārs.* There is a series of 41 documents of 1702-3 containing details of unrealised *peshkash* etc due from the *zamīndārs* of *ṣūba Khāndesh* [amounting to Rs 1,54,925]. These contain the demand that whosoever had executed the bond of *peshkash* was liable to pay it whereas those who did not execute the same were not to be harassed.[7]

There was a general official complaint that the *zamīdārs* used to adopt a dilatary attitude in meeting demands of the Imperial government.

"All the *deshmukhs* and *deshpāndiyas* of the *parganas* [overwhelmingly dominated by the Marathas] in the *ṣūbās* of the Deccan, from the beginning of the control of this country [i.e. Deccan] by the mighty Empire, do not

1. IJC I/20/10-1.
2. IJC I/7/7-1.
3. IJC I /26/0-12.
4. IJC I/30/10-1.
5. IJC I/30/9-1.
6. IJC I/11/5-2.
7. IJC I/46/0-44 to I/46/0-84.

pay the state dues, and without [acquiring] the *sanads* anew, they are misappropriating the *rusūm* and *inā'm*".[1]

Only a fresh settlement with the *deshmukhs* and *deshpāndiyas* was naturally felt to be a precondition to any lasting solution to the Deccan problem.[2] These terms of agreement also involved the grant of *rusūm* and *inā'm* to the *zamīndārs.* We find a detailed 121 sheet document containing a list of the *rusūm* and *inā'm* of the *deshmukhs* and *deshpāndiyas* of the *parganas* of *ṣūba* Aurangabad of 1694 A.D., comprising 10 *sarkārs* and 115 *maḥāls.*[3] Similarly another series of 95 documents from *pargana* Indapur, *sarkār* Junnar, *ṣūba* Aurangabad, furnishes detailed information in regard to perquisites of the *zamīndārs* together with the land revenue originally fixed during the term of administration of Malik 'Ambar,[4] which means that detailed *ṣūba*-wise and *pargana*-wise statistical data about the *zamīndārs* and their perquisites used to be prepared. This is in fact attested by the surviving series of *mawāzana-i-yak ḥarfi*[5] of various *parganas* which specifically mention the revenue demand of each village over a period of years as well as the names of *zamīndārs* and also give series of the *Yaddasht-i ism Nawīsī-i zamīndārān* [memorandums of the names of the *zamīndārs*].[6]

The *zamīndārs* who were anxious to secure the offices of *deshmukh* or *deshpāndiya* were required to submit written bonds conveying their consent to the *peshkash* in lieu of these offices.[7]

The rural aristocracy, having been reduced to the status of *zamīndārs,*[8] was thus not totally left unprovided for as the perquisites of their offices came to be guarded zealously as recorded in all the appointment orders of *deshmukhs* and *deshpāndiyas*. It was also stipulated that the acceptance letters of *peshkash* by the *zamīndārs* of each *maḥāl* were to be verified by the *Dīwāns* of the respective *ṣūbās* of the Deccan.

The payment of the *rusūm* of the *zamīndārs* used to be withheld till the issue of an authoritative certificate or *sanad* and those who willingly

1. IJC I/0/0-38. This complaint did not go in vain as Asad Khān ordered for resumption of all their perquisites till the settlement of the *peshkash.*
2. For details of these terms of agreement see 'Alam, *op. cit.*, p. 77.
3. IJC I/36/0-7/ to I/36/0-127.
4. IJC I/0/0-86 to I/0/0/194.
5. IJC I/32/10-81 to I/32/10-94,I/35/10-71 to I/35/10-116; I/37/0-151 to I/37/0-171, I/39/0-3 to I/39/0-14: I/41/0-33 to I/41/0-48.
6. IJC I/34/0-63 to I/34/0-87; I/35/0-1 to I/35/0-5; I/37/0-20 to I/37/0-31; I/38/0-307 to I/37/0-378. Such extensive documentation was crucial for detecting any concealment or misstatement of facts. IJC I/41/1-13.
7. IJC I/34/11-2.
8. Cf M. Athar Ali, 'Towards an Interpretation of the Mughal Empire', *Journal of Royal Asiatic Society* [*JRAS*],1978, p. 270.

accepted the *peshkash* were required to remit one-fourth of it in cash, whereas half of their *rusūm* were to be resumed till the adjustment of arrears of *peshkash.*[1]

The Mughal administration even maintained minute details of the entire *ṣūbās* as is clear from the following data of 1695 of the actual collections and arrears of *peshkash* of *zamīndārs* of *ṣūba* Bījāpur.[2]

Table - 1

Sl. No.	*Details of peshkash*	*Amount*
1.	According to the register of former *Dīwān*	Rs. 6,12,232/4
2.	Arrears remitted by Appājī etc	Rs. 30,000
3.	Arrears exempted from Hindu Rao *deshmukh* of Qamar Nagar as per reverse endorsement of the *farmān.*	Rs. 30,000
4.	Balance	Rs. 5,57,232/4
5.	Realisation by Amānat Khān, the former *Dīwān*	Rs. 41,932/8
6.	Balance	Rs. 5,15,299/12
7.	Amount of *peshkash* remitted i] In charge of Mehdi Quli, treasurer of Bījāpur. ii] In charge of Khwāja Ya'qub, treasurer of *pargana* Almala. iii] In charge of 'Abdullāh, the treasurer of...	Rs. 44,484/4 Rs. 1 0,723 Rs. 19,000 Rs. 14,761/4
8.	Total Arrears	Rs. 4,70,815/8

But as far as arrears of *peshkash* pending payment by the big *zamīndārs* were concerned, they were always given preferential treatment as compared to the intermediary *zamīndārs* even to such an extent that the *zamīndār* of Chanda paid Rs 40,65,337, whereas 1040 *asharfīs* and Rs 64,01,925 remained unpaid from 1685 to 1698.[3]

We find further details of accumulated arrears of *peshkash* etc of the *zamīndārs* of Chanda and Shāh Islāmgarh in our documents.[4] An amount of Rs 18,00,000 per annum as *peshkash* was paid by the *zamīndār* of Chanda[5] and Srirangapatam.[6] Surprisingly enough, notwithstanding the extreme step of removing Jamāluddin, *deshmukh* of 190 villages of *pargana* Balapur, *ṣūba* Berar, in 1698 and replacing him by the *mutaṣaddis* of that *pargana* by fixing one lakh *tanka-i-Berari* as *peshkash,* the *rusūm* of *deshmukhī*

1. IJC I/34/10-6; I/0/0-169.
2. IJC I/36/2-1.
3. IJC I/40/4-8.
4. IJC I/42/11-74; I/42/11-75.
5. IJC I/41/12-45; I/44/1-29.
6. IJC I/41/7-13 Jagdev Raj, *zamīndār* of Sri Rang Pattan paid 40,000 *hūns* as *peshkash* per annum.

was still realised by the *zamīndārs* without making any payment of the *peshkash*.[1]

The Imperial administration was fully aware of the *zamīndārs'* ability to help in the extension of cultivation. During the *Dīwānī* of Makramat Khān, *pargana* Devalgāon was only partly cultivated because the entire area was forest and waste infested by rebels. Makramat Khān invented the device of getting the entire *pargana* cultivated by asking the *zamīndārs* to undertake to bring under cultivation 2000 *bighas* per annum, thus bringing their entire *pargana* under cultivation comprising 48,000 *bighas* within the stipulated period [1675 to 1699], and yielding *jama'-kāmil* [maximum revenue] contingent upon granting 4800 *bighas* as incentive and 12,000 *bighas* as *rusūm*. Thus, a *pargana* which had remained desolate since the annexation became fully cultivated.[2] The *deshmukhi* of half of *pargana* Bawanbīr in *sarkār* Narnāla, *ṣūba* Berar, was given to Shankrājī conditional upon the cultivation of 1000 *nitans* or 80,000 *bighas* in 1698.[3]

When Koneri S/o Megh Shyam was represented to His Majesty then Aurangzeb saw to its assignment from the term of administration from Nizamul Mulk [*āmal-i be-nizam*] and Saiyidi 'Amber as well by ['Ala Hazrat] till his reign then he ordered 'to get it fixed as per the term of administration of Murshid Quli Khan'[4]. [from 1652-1656 AD]

The *zamīndārs* were also required to ascertain the devastation of crops on any natural calamity occurring.[5]

The *zamīndārs'* cooperation in extension of cultivation could not, however, be taken for granted. Jadun Rai, *alias* Jagdev, promised a *peshkash* of Rs 3,00,800 and cultivation of 7,00,000 *bighas* of land as *deshpāndiya* and *deshmukh* of 27 *maḥāls* of Daulatabad, etc. He did not fulfil the promise giving the excuse that it was uncultivable because the entire land was brackish, mountainous and full of nullahs, and the peasantry, due to epidemic, famine and the oppression of Marathas, had either died or run away.[6]

The *zamīndārs* were often allowed to take land on *ijāra* [or farm], which was apparently not legally forbidden. Many areas were leased out to them, e.g. the *tappas* of Sūpa, etc, belonging to *pargana* Goa, *sarkār* Muṣṭafābād or Talkokan-i-'Ādil Khāni were in the *ijāra* of the *zamīndār* of Sondha,

1. IJC I/41/4-25.
2. IJC I/42/9-11.
3. IJC I/41/6-11, I/41/6-12.
4. IJC I/42/10.
5. IJC I/40/6-11.
6. IJC I/0/0-377.

from 1698 for Rs 60,000 only [yielding him one lakh of rupees].[1] The area comprised 19 *tappas,* which was confirmed in favour of Sad Shiv Nayak, actually yielding *jama raqmāna* [i.e. *jama' raqamī*] of 1,20,000 *hūns* in lieu of an annual *peshkah* of Rs 25,000.[2] The services of the *zamīndārs* were indispensable for the revenue administration. *Zamīndārs* commonly sought to suppress the actual yield, were pointed out in Aurangzeb's order of 1701 concerning the *zamīndārs* of *ṣūbās* of the Deccan, including 12 *parganas* each of *Khāndesh* and Aurangabad and 3 *parganas* of Berar.[3] An official [probably *teḥṣīldār*] alleged that the *zamīndārs* were in the habit of usurping the land revenue.[4] Even 11 villages of the *inā'm* of 'Ālam *zamīndār*, which were not shown in the *mawāzna* of 1685, had simply to be left in the possession of the *zamīndār.*[5]

Instances of the harassment of the *jāgīrdārs* by the *zamīndārs* are numerous in our records. The *'āmil* in collusion with the *zamīndārs* usurped Rs 10,000 of the revenue of Muḥammad Khān,[6] *jāgīrdār* of Parenda. The *zamīndār* of Daruzzafar [Bījāpur] abducted and poisoned a *qila'dār* [castellan].[7] Several *jāgīrdārs* failed to collect the revenues due to the defiance of the *zamīndārs.*[8] The *zamīndārs* did not even spare the *Khāliṣa* lands due to which stringent measures had to be taken.[9] However, the nature, pattern and extent of the partnership between the Mughal Empire and *zamīndārs* requires fuller investigation as it has many implications and aspects, one of which, of course, relates to the assignment of *manṣab* and grant of military duties to the *zamīndārs.*

Thus, 'Alī, a *zamīndār,* was ordered to raise 100 matchlockmen for protecting the fort of Khandark, for which he was given a '12-monthly' *jāgīr* with abatement in 1695.[10] Narsingh, son of Neem Rao, joined Imperial service in 1696 on the condition of grant of *manṣab* and office of *deshpāndiya* of *pargana* Karkatpur, contingent upon the deduction of *peshkash* from the *ẓāt* salary,[11] holding the rank of 3000 / 1300 with a *waṭan*

1. IJC I/44/5-90, I/45/8-45; for- the *zamīndārs* of Goa see, S.Z.H. Jafri 'Mughal Relations with the Portuguese Administration in Goa, 1700-1701- Evidence of Persian Records in Lisbon Archives, *PIHC,* 1987, pp. 302-311.
2. IJC I/44/12-48.
3. IJC I/44/2-85. The *zamīndārs* of many regions, like Karnatak-i Hyderabad were creating problems. IJC I/38/2-3.
4. IJC VIII/87/422 [Inadvertently shown as the document of Muḥammad Shāh's reign].
5. IJC I/35/10-6.
6. IJC I/49/7-4.
7. IJC I/48/5-4.
8. IJC I/45/3-16.
9. IJC I/0/0-380.
10. IJC I/37/6-2.
11. IJC I/38/9-13.

jāgīr. Sripat, *zamīndār* of Juwār, who was granted *jāgīr* of Gulshanabad [Nasik], his ancestral *zamīndārī,* however, found it quite unproductive; and he was reported to be in extremely distressed condition due to the expenses of maintaining the five forts in his charge.[1]

The *zamīndārs,* as *jāgīrdārs,* anxiously yearned for actual possession of *jāgīrs.* Īsar Das, son of Rāhūjī, *zamīndār* of Hathgarh sought the balance of pay claims through assignment of a *jāgīr* vacated by another *jāgīrdār.*[2] Special significance was attached to the *zamīndārs* whose *jāgīrs* could not be easily transferred.[3] Bhim Rāo, son of Kishan Rao, *deshmukh* was granted the rank of 300/150 in 1699 A.D.[4]

Sa'ādatmand Khān *alias* Khandu, *zamīndār* of Bara Mawal was previously ordered to maintain 1000 *sawār* and 5,000 *piyādas* [infantry]. This project was abandoned subsequently because he was told by Aurangzeb that "since he is a neo-Muslim he would remain with the Imperial stirrup as he would be of no use there. Almighty God willing as soon as that territory is brought under control he would be granted its *zamīndārī*".[5] In 1702 the same *zamīndār* held the rank of 2500/1000 with the royal order for grant of *ẓāt* and 500 *sawār* salary after he obtained a branding certificate.[6]

Sachcha Rāo, *zamīndār* was assigned a large territory conditional upon the protection of the fort.[7] Mādhū Rāo, *zamīndār* of Pair, was granted the rank of 300/100 [50x2-3h].[8]

The Imperial administration maintained the separate identity of *zamīndārs* when they became *jāgīrdārs.* Their being *zamīndārs* was specifically recorded in *āwārja* documents, and even separate sheets containing the names of the *zamīndārs* in each *ṣūba* were maintained, as is evident from the following table.[9]

1. IJC I/41/6-107 It was mischievously transferred but subsequently restored to him. IJC I/44/11-48.
2. IJC I/41/6-50.
3. IJC I/41/8-84.
4. IJC I/41/8-97, I/41/8-98.
5. IJC I/45/2-87.
6. IJC I/45/12-27.
7. IJC I/42/2-5; I/42/3-44.
8. IJC I/43/2-106; I/43/12-77.
9. IJC I/0/0-824.

Table – 2: *Zamīndārs* Holding Rank

Sl. No.	*Name of Zamīndārs*	*Designation*	*No. of Maḥals*	*Name of Ṣūba*
1.	Rāo Jagdeo	*Deshmukh* and *Deshpandiaya* of *parganas* of *sarkār* Daulatabad	23	Aurangabad
2.	Nāhar Khān	*Deshmukh* of *pargana* Ashti, *sarkār* Aḥmadnagar	1	-do-
3.	Muḥammad Sai'd	*Deshmukh* of *sarkār* Talkokan-i 'Ādil Khāni	-	-do-
4.	Bhoji	*Deshmukh* of *pargana* Basi	-	-do-
5.	Ūdājī Rām	*Deshmukh* of *sarkār* Mahur, etc	23	Berar
6.	Muḥammad Ḥasan S/o Muḥammad 'Alī, grandson of KārṬalab Khān	*Deshmukh* of *pargana* Pornar; *sarkār* Gavil	1	-do-
7.	Burhānullāh Khān S/o late Sarfraz Khān	*Sardeshmukh* of *pargana* Loh-gaon, *sarkār* Nānder	-	-do-
8.	Rūdrājī	*Qānūngo* of half of *ṣūba* Bījāpur	-	Bijapur
9.	Khwāṣ Khān	*Deshmukh* of *ḥaveli* [headquarters]	19	-do-
10.	Maddaji	*Kulkarni* of the *ṣūba*.	-	-do-
11.	Murai S/o Venkat	*Sardeshmukh* of Imtiāzgarh.	-	-do-
12.	Prithi Raj S/o Bhagwat	*Deshmukh* of *pargana* Rathihalli.	-	-do-
13.	Shyām Rāj	*Nargonda* of *parganas* of Bījāpur.	-	-do-
14.	Babuji Pandit	*Qānūngo*	-	Hyderabad

'Abdul Ḥai S/o late 'Abdul Bāri, *zamīndār* of Yalgharp, was granted *manṣab* with *zamīndārī* and *faujdārī* thereof.[1] *Zamīndārs* also received other favours. On the strong recommendations of Ghairat Khān, the castellan and commandant of Parenda, Bharti, the *zamīndār* of *pargana* Kanti, who was the *deshmukh* of the *pargana,* was entrusted with the responsibility of maintaining 100 *sawārs* and directed to guard the highway and assist the *faujdār* of Parenda in escorting caravans[2] with an *inā'm* of 100 *chāwars* of land, which example was cited by Arjun g/s of Bāwā together with that of Rāno Nārū, for similar favour on similar conditions.[3]

The *zamīndārs* as *jāgīrdārs* had to fulfill all the necessary formalities like inspection of contingents: the contingent of Paddaji Jujhār Rāo, holding the rank of 2000/1000 [500x2-3h], and the *zamīndārī* of *thāna* Badda Manchgāon and Maliwāri, were found to be in full strength upon inspection.[4]

1. IJC I/42/0-59; for similar instance see I/47/4-56.
2. IJC I/42/1-39; I/42/3-16.
3. IJC I/47/4-99.
4. IJC I/45/3-29. The *zamīndār* claimed to hold it since the time of Bījāpuris and sought its permanent *deshmukhī*, *jāgīrdarī* and *faujdārī*.

The *zamīndārs* as *jāgīrdārs* were called upon to extend maximum military cooperation in various expeditions like Rūdrā, *qānūngo* of Bījāpur who had previously helped 'Ādil Khān, was directed to raise infantry for the Talkokan campaign, etc, and orders were issued to *zamīndārs* of 11 *parganas* to send 13000 *piyadas* from their *maḥāls*:[1]

> When the matter of Devya Nayak was presented to Aurangzeb about his complaint of getting written a *peshkash* it Rs 40,000 by Raja Anup Singh then the Emperor ordered him 'to come to His Majesty present before Rad Andaz Khān so that the *mansab* and *jagir* be given as per the Adil Rohani pattern'[2].

Shaikh Ibrāhīm holding the rank of 300/100 and the *zamīndāri* of Talkokan, assisted Nuṣrat Jung in the conquest of Islāmgarh [Rāherī]; his sons were also favoured with rank after his death in 1703.[3]

The *zamīndārs* and *jāgīrdārs* had tussles over the assignment of *jāgīrs*. 'Abdur Raḥīm, the *zamīndār* of *Painth* Mehja, complained against Sripat, *zamīndār* of Juwar, who had secured the former's *waṭan jāgīr*, notwithstanding his military assistance to Zainuddin 'Ali Khān in conquering Futūḥul Ḥusan fort as well as his current endeavour for capturing the fort of Lohgarh with him.[4]

The *zamīndārs* as *jāgīrdārs* served the Imperial administration in numerous ways. But their main role related to their support to the Mughal government or their antagonism against the Mughals or Marathas to suit their vested interests. A contemporary observer opined that the *zamīndārs* extended support to Shivajī enabling him to challenge Mughal power.[5] However, in the post-Shivajī era, the *zamīndārs* and the *deshmukhs* occasionally emerged as the main allies of the Mughal *faujdārs*, who were equally responsible for the oppression of the peasantry as well as usurping the land revenue. But the descriptive accounts of events in the Deccan for the period 1690-1707 indicate that the end result was the migration or flight of the peasants, followed by armed resistance, where *zamīndārs* used the distress of the peasants to augment their own armed strength.[6]

1. IJC I/45/9-68.
2. IJC I/39/11-13.
3. IJC I/47/2-18.
4. IJC I/51/11-157.
5. Bhim Sen, *Nuskha-i Dilkushā,* Ms. Br. Mus. Or 23, [Rotograph], Department of History, AMU, Aligarh, ff. 139[a]-40[b].
6. Irfan Habib, *'The Agrarian System of Mughal India.* Bombay, 1963, pp. 269-271. Irfan Habib even sees the Maratha resistance primarily one from the *zamīndār* class. *Cf.,* J.F. Richards, *'The Imperial Crisis in the Deccan. JAS.* Vol. XXXV, No.2 [Feb. 1976], p. 237.

However to suppose Shivajī to be the liberator of the peasants or friend of the *zamīndārs* is equally erroneous, because peasants merely became *bargīs* or irregular cavalry of the Maratha *sardārs*,[1] whereas Shivajī denied *inā'm* to the *deshmukhs*, and attemped to convert *peshkashi zamīndārs* into full revenue-paying ones. He thus sought to create a new class of faithful *zamīndārs*, thereby hastening the flight of the older *zamīndārs* either to 'Ādil Shāhis or the Mughals. In contrast to Shivajī the Mughal administration offered much greater privileges to the *peshkashi zamīndārs* by also granting them *rusūm* and *inā'm* lands.

In 1689, Muḥammad Ḥasan and other *zamīndārs* of Dabhol sent by Ghāziuddīn Khān Bahādur Firuz Jung, accompanied by Saiyid Luṭf, made a representation to Aurangzeb that obliged them to maintain 5000 infantrymen they had been deputed to conquer Maratha forts: now they solicited the *sanad* of *deshmukhi* as per the *sanad* of Zulfiqār Khān,[2] which was promptly accorded Imperial approval.[3] However, the above *sanad* did not mitigate the problems of Muḥammad Ḥasan, serving under 'Abdur Razzāq Lāri, who pleaded for the grant of *sanad* to him according to the Imperial order without which the *zamīndār* was totally crippled from aiding the Imperial cause. Previously the *zamīndār* had supported the Mughals in the conquest of Islāmgarh, etc, and was well acquainted with that land.[4] Notwithstanding the *zamīndār's* strenuous endeavour in bringing 5000 *piyadas* without any remuneration from the Imperial administration and capturing the forts of the Marathas including the assistance rendered in seizing Islāmgarh, the grant of a *sanad* of *zamīndārī* was kept pending till production of a guarantor [*zāmin*] and fixation of *peshkash*. It was issued only when the surety bond of Rs 10,000 which was one-fourth of the *peshkash* in cash was executed, half to be paid at the time of the receipt of the *farmān*, and the remaining half was to be deposited within the next five months. Furthermore Rs 30,000, the balance of *peshkash* was to be remitted within six years. Ẓulfiqār Khān recommended 2% *rusūm* as per the rates of the Konkan-i-Niẓāmul Mulki together with four *inā'm* villages. Ultimately the requisite *sanad* was issued to Muḥammad Ḥasan concerning the *zamīndāri* of *sarkār* Dabhol.[5]

1. Irfan Habib, *Essays in Indian History - Towards a Marxist Perception*, Delhi, 1995, p. 254. Irfan Habib even sees the Maratha resistance as primarily from the *zamīndār* class.
2. Ẓulfiqār Khān attested to the assistance given by Muḥammad Ḥasan and Ibrāhīm Ḥasan, *Adhikar* and *Chaudhurī* respectively of *pargana* Ja'farābād, *Sarkār* Dabhol, in conquering the forts of Risālgarh and Mahipatgarh and confirmed their *zamīndārī* with an addition of two *inā'm* villages. IJC I/33/12-1.
3. IJC I/31/11-1.
4. IJC I/32/0-59 [A].
5. IJC I/38/4-4.

Seth S/o Koneri, *deshpandiya* of *pargana* Baizapur *Sarkar* Daulatabad who holds the *deshpandiyagiri* since his ancestors wherein interruption was made by Babu Pandit, *qanungo* of Hyderabad. It was submitted that it would be settled as per the term of the administration of Murshid Quli Khan, which term has also been used by Aurangzeb in another document.[1]

Similar obligations were imposed on the other four *deshmukhs* of the region. Of these, Muḥammad Sai'd promised to seize the forts if [financial] assistance was given to him. He further promised to bring the *maḥāl* to maximum revenue within three years and agreed to pay Rs 10,000 in *peshkash*.[2] He was also granted a *manṣab* of 500/100 in 1698.[3]

The above was not a case in isolation as we come to know that Datta and Surya, etc, who were posted with Ẓulfiqār Khān for conquering Islāmgarh or Raheri solicited the *sanad* of the offices of *deshmukh* and *deshpāndiya* through his intercession on the strength of Sikander Khān's *sanad* and obtained orders for delay in payment of *peshkash* till the repeopling and cultivation of *pargana* Patan, *ṣūba* Bījāpur.[4]

In the hope of securing a *farmān* for *sardeskat* of *pargana* Jatapur, Ram Gonda, *desāī* stood guarantee for the conquest of Bhīmgarh fort in 1693-4; and his object was granted to him accordingly.[5] After the conquest of the fort of Khandark, 'Alī, a *zamīndār* was appointed to protect the fort with 100 matchlockmen, and nine villages were given as *inā'm* to him from *pargana* and *sarkār* Torgul, *ṣūba* Bījāpur.[6] Shambhū Dās, *deshmukh* of Nandurbar, inflicted crushing defeats on the Marathas and got released the people from the Marathas for which he was also favoured with a *manṣab* of 250 / 50.[7]

When Aurangzeb was busy in procuring funds to meet the wage bills for his field armies, help from *zamīndārs* came as a special mean of support. They not only served the Imperial cause but also mustered armies at their own cost to assist the Mughals in reducing Maratha forts. This mutual cooperation between the Mughals and the *zamīndārs* came in several ways. Such *zamīndārs* as suffered at the hands of the Marathas vehemently opposed them. When Shivajī seized the fort of Satara he expelled the *deshmukhs,* one of whom subsequently held the rank of 3000/2000 from the Mughals, along with the *deshmukhī,* when Babujī and Govind Rāi,

1. IJC I/47/11-117.
2. IJC I/35/11-1 & I/35/11-2.
3. IJC I/40/4-2.
4. IJC I/33/7-2, I/33/7-25.
5. IJC I/36/10-1.
6. IJC I/37/5-2.
7. IJC I/37/10-180.

SOUTH INDIA

POLITICAL 1707

16 A

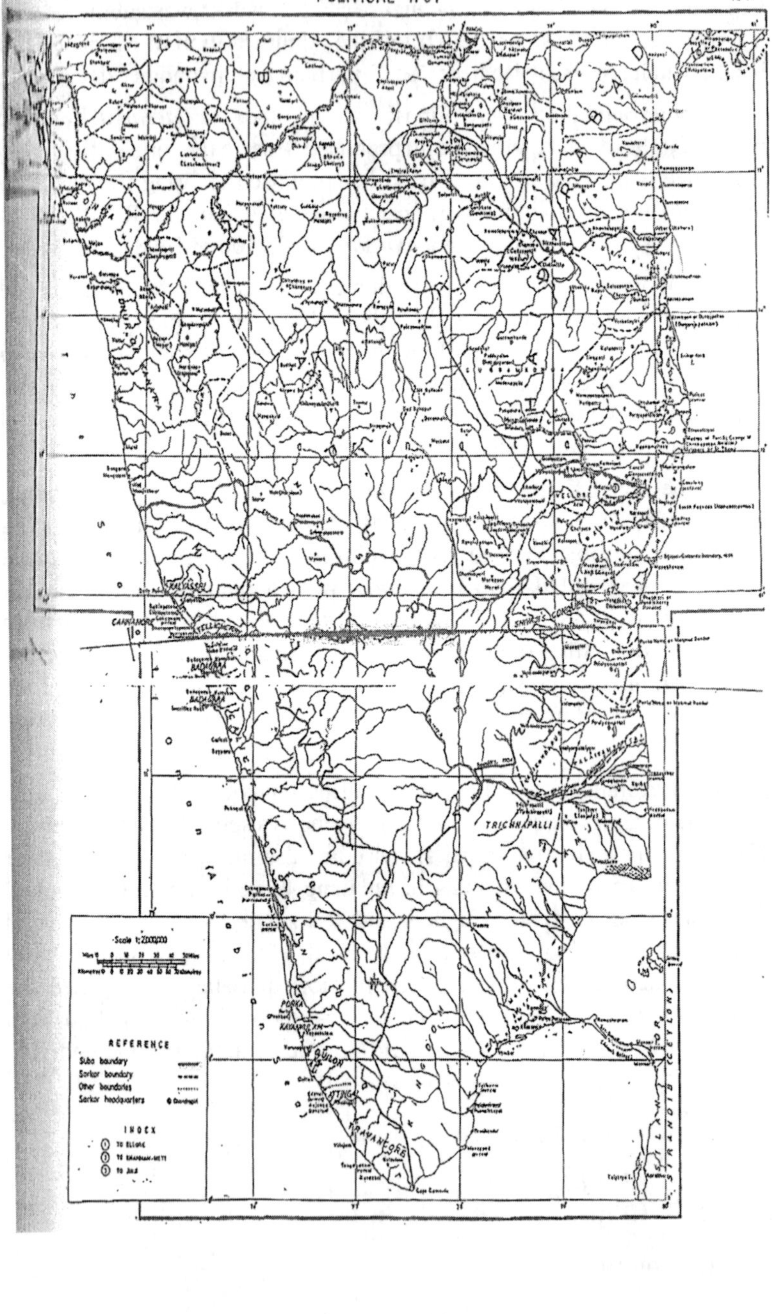

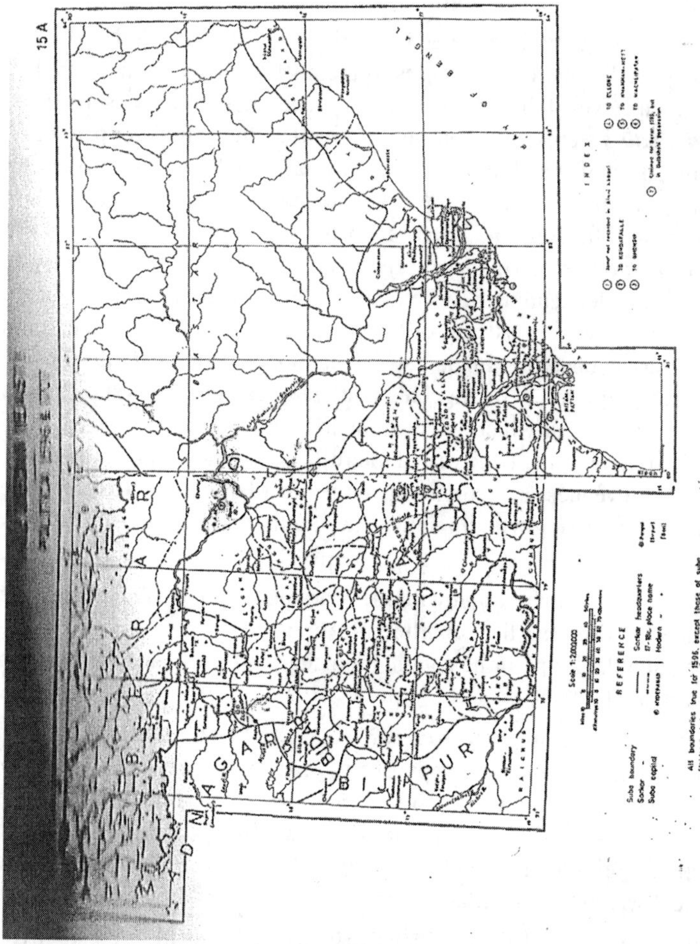
15 A
INDEX
Scale 1:2000000
REFERENCE
Suba boundary
Sarkar
Suba capital
Sarkar headquarters
All boundaries true for 1596, except those of suba Haidarabad & its sarkars which are true for 1707

deshmukhs of *pargana* Kalgi, *sarkār* Daulatabad, bordering the Maratha territory, were expelled by Sambhaji, they naturally showed resentment against him on the eve of Aurangzeb's attack upon and destruction of his power: [APPENDIX - C], they pleaded with Aurangzeb for restoration of their *deshmukhi* through an imperial *farmān* in 1689.[1]

The *deshmukhs* willingly sided with the Mughals, though the Maratha menace created numerous problems to them.[2] Despite many hurdles they exerted themselves fully in extension of cultivation.[3] Even sometimes small *zamīndārs* were engaged in self-cultivation due to flight of peasantry. The elimination of Pratap Rao, a Maratha *sardār,* by Rānū Narū, *zamīndār* of Ondargāon *sarkār*, Parenda *ṣūba,* Aurangabad, conveniently earned him a *manṣab* of 1000/700 contingent upon his maintaining 100 *sawārs* for which 100 *chāwars* of land were given as *inā'm.*[4] However, contrary to such mutual understanding between the *zamīndārs* and the Mughals, there are numerous instances as well of the *zamīndārs*' active connivance with the Marathas against the Mughals which cannot be dismissed out of hand. It was probably due to Aurangzeb's unceasing campaigns in the Deccan against the Marathas, which gave so much respite to the *zamīndārs* as to enable them to promote their vested interests by siding with their enemies, seizing the revenues and conniving with the Marathas in realising the *chauth* and plundering with impunity the country around.

Chin Qilīch Khān, the Governor of Bījāpur, complained against the Bedaris, who, in collaboration with the Marathas and the *zamīndārs,* were determined to rise after the departure of Aurangzeb. Since his entire army accompanied the Emperor he sought requisite reinforcements to deal with the *zamīndārs* [1694][5].

'Abdullāh, a refractory *zamīndār* connived with the Marathas in establishing their military camps every year in *pargana* Narsi, *sarkār* Basim, *ṣūba* Berar, due to which the *jāgīrdārs* failed to receive a single dām in revenue. Kishna, *deshpāndiya* of *sarkār* Murtazābād [Miraj], could obtain reinstatement to his ancestral office on the plea that the new incumbent was not only a Maratha but also a patron of the Marathas.[6]

Even the agent of Chin Qilīch Khān was alleged to have connived with six *deshmukhs* of *pargana* and *sarkār* Pathri, *ṣūba* Berar, in seizing Rs 70,000 from the small *zamīndārs* and peasants. Together with 1000

1. IJC I/39/11-121, I/39/11-172.
2. IJC I/42/12-2.
3. IJC I/43/4-4.
4. IJC I/45/5-46.
5. IJC I/36/8-6, I/51/12-123.
6. IJC I/42/3-26

sawārs he collaborated with the Maratha *sardārs* in devastating the *pargana* and even paid *chauth* to them in 1700.[1] Conflict among the *zamīndārs* was a recurring feature and they even sought the intervention of the Marathas in settling their scores. It is related that Gorkhoji, *deshmukh,* posted at Jinjī with Ẕulfiqār Khān served the Mughals with a rank of 1000/900, with *waṭan-jāgīr.* But due to the dirty machinations of some co-sharers like Madhu, who sided with the Marathas, his agent was dismissed and imprisoned.[2]

The *zamīndārs* even plundered the *parganas* in collaboration with the Marathas.[3] The Marathas by consent of the *zamīndārs* of Ankola had become so much emboldened that they penetrated into Kalyani hills in 1701.[4] The *zamīndārs* of some villages of *pargana* Dehari, due to the support of the *jāgīrdārs*, had established a rapport with the Marathas. Furthermore, the fortress of the *deshpāndiya* of *pargana* Bhokran became the abode of the Marathas where from they attacked that *pargana.*[5] It was reported that the Marathas had established the military camps in *pargana* Malwari, *ṣūba* Bījāpur, because of Tolajī, brother of Maddajī, *deshmukh,* who was a Maratha *sardār:* Madda seized the revenues in 1702.[6]

The Marathas even killed the men of loyal *zamīndārs*[7]. The men of Maratha *jāgīrdārs* and of the Marathas used to become indistinguishable from each other due to their racial affinity[8].

The *zamīndārs* who endeavoured to promote cultivation, were unable to provide safety to the peasantry against the Maratha onslaught. Occasionally, due to the Maratha devastation and mischievousness of the *deshmukhs,* the *parganas* became ruined.[9] Nay, even the agents of the *deshpāndiyas* and *kulkarnis* used to indulge in conspiracy as they even seized 1230 *hūns* which they delivered to the Marathas in 1702.[10]

In view of the damage caused by the Marathas in weakening Mughal hold over the *zamīndārs* and other sections of agrarian society, Aurangzeb strictly opined that "to show pity to the Marathas was wrong".[11]

---

1. IJC I/43/4-1, I/46/1-105.
2. IJC I/41/4-2.
3. IJC I/41/8-126.
4. IJC I/44/4-73.
5. IJC I/45/6-11.
6. IJC I/45/7-116.
7. IJC I/45/7-46.
8. IJC I/45/12-142.
9. IJC I/46/5-52, I/46/5-53.
10. IJC I/46/9-91.
11. IJC I/46/11-64.

The *zamīndārs* were frequently reported to assist the Marathas.[1] They had become so subservient to them that even the *zamīndārs* of *pargana Peinth* Pala had fixed Rs 1000 as *sibti* of the Marathas and whatever was realised was given to them.[2]

The *zamīndārī* rights were saleable: half of the *deshmukhī* of *pargana* Oepari [sic] was sold, though the proceeds might be from the connivance of a relative in 1706.[3] The *deshmukh* of *pargana* Naldurg seized the stores of the fort in collaboration with the Marathas in 1706.[4]The situation had worsened to such an extent that the *zamīndārs* became active allies of the Marathas. It was reported that Rājmal, *deshmukh* of *pargana* Kalgi, had been collaborating with the Marathas since long. As and when the Maratha army came there, the *deshmukh* sent his contingent under his nephew's command, which already had an enviable record. Still the *deshmukh's* plenipotentiary sought full *deshmukhī* instead of half of the *deshmukhī* of *pargana*, as a result, manipulation and mis-statement denying his client's involvement in any conspiracy with the Marathas.[5] To crown all, "they no longer fulfilled their obligations but assumed strength, joined the Marathas, enlisted in the armies, and laid the hand of oppression on the country."[6] This had become a totally changed situation because the very intermediaries who [*zamīndārs*] were allowed to retain a minor share of formal revenue demand, became the potential rivals of the Empire.

In the light of the above Muzaffar Alam's assertion about the role of the *zamīndārs* as the Mughal collaborators[7] is quite untenable because only a few of them did not refrain from supporting the Mughal cause. But the majority of them emerged as the potential opponents of the Mughals in the Deccan. The position of the *zamīndārs* in the Deccan under Aurangzeb remained quite strong. There were *zamīndārs*, who were loyal to the Mughals, whereas there were disloyal ones too, who harmed the Imperial interests beyond redemption. Furthermore, the *zamīndārs* promoted agriculture and assisted in revenue collection, while they also placed hurdles in proper realisation of revenues. There were also *zamīndārs* on whom were conferred higher ranks. The presence of loyal *zamīndārs* who supported the Mughals and received *jāgīrs* and those who opposed them bitterly, demonstrate a unique phenomenon of the *zamīndāri* system in the

1. IJC I/47/4-89.
2. IJC I/50/8-5.
3. IJC I/50/11-173.
4. IJC I/51/11-36.
5. IJC I/0/0-522.
6. Bhim Sen, *Nuskha-i Dilkushā,* 139 [b].
7. Alam, *op.cit,* p. 79.

Deccan, *viz.,* the multiple support the people of Berar were to give to the Marathas.

[II] *Pālīgārs* and Marathas

Notwithstanding a cursory study these documents demonstrate numerous complaints about the dearth of *pāibāqī* and that owing to *be-jāgīri* [lack of *jāgīrs*] people were dying gradually. Unfortunately these complaints seem to be particularly numerous after 1696-7.[1] Fortunately M. Athar Ali has also drawn our attention to a document of the year 1117/ 1706 relating to Ḥyderabadi-Karnatak, included in *Selected Documents of Aurangzeb's Reign* [ed. Yusuf Ḥusain Khān] showing that the area under the *Khāliṣa* accounted for only 6 percent of the *jama'*; the *pāibāqī* accounted for 20 percent of which 16 percent was in the hands of Pālīgārs, thus leaving very small areas for assignment, amounting to a little above 4 percent as we have good testimony for the intense pleasure for *jāgīr*, which contemporaries were speaking of.

Dāūd Khān Panni, the new *faujdār* campaigned actively against the various Pālīgārs and the *rajas* of the area in a firm effort to compel them to recognize the imperial authority of Aurangzeb. Before it neither 'Ali 'Askar, *faujdār* and *Dīwān* of the Karnatak from 1687 to 1688 nor Bashārat Khān, *Dīwān* [1688-1690] succeeded in prying satisfactory collections out of the Pālīgārs in the area. However, in 1706 much of the remainder *pāibāqī* nominally under the central treasury, was of uncertain status recorded as under the control of Pālīgārs [9 percent]. However, *peshkash* from Pālīgārs added another seven hundred thousand rupees. Moreover Dāūd Khā Panni's vigorous campaigns against the Pālīgārs probably brought collections close to the normative demand.

Anyhow even this does not provide us is a clear picture of the situation because a recent study of the Inayat Jung Collection documents shows that there was a large amount of *pāibāqī* in the Hyderabadi and Bījāpur areas which was called *mulk-i jadīd* or new areas.[2] Bijapur also proposed the *Paligārs* as it is who is evident from the summary for the representation. "Previously it was written to Rustam Chak, *Diwan* of Karnatak Daruzzafar that *parwangi* under the seal of Manṣūr Khān was received that in accordance with represention of Namdar S/o late Fattaḥ Khān, *qiladār* of

1. S.M. Azizuddin Husain, 'Scarcity of *Pāibāqī* Lands during Aurangzeb's Reign in the Light of Inayat Jung Collection Documents', *PIHC*, XXXIX, 1978, 426-30.
2. Zakir Husain, 'Problems of the Deccan Administration in the Last Decade of Aurangzeb's Reign- based on Explorations in the Inayat Jung Collection of the National Archives, mimeographed paper presented to the 61th Session of *Indian History Congress* Calcutta', 2000-2001, in *Papers from the Aligarh Historians Society*.

Kautar it was reported to His Majesty that his client for the safety of the frontier fort maintained contingent beyond rule. The *jagir* of the dismissed was distributed among the *Paligārs* owing to which not a single *dām* is received. Since this is the rule that the *qasba* and *panith* are allotted to the castellan who should be granted 50% abetment. Since the register of *dah-ba-dehi* of Karnatak is not before His Majesty the person concerned should send in writing the true facts of the *qasba* and the *painth* with the current rates which he did accordingly to grant the *jagir* thus[1]. In a statement addressed to Aurangzeb it is stated that in the *mulk-i jadīd* Bījāpur and Ḥaiderabad the *pāibāqī* is considerable, since owing to its low income the [claimants] representatives with the *jama'* are also in abundence.

We are given to understand that by the end of the 1700 A.D. the problems of the *Paligarh* was increasing particularly in Ḥyderabad. As such the *Pāligārs* had become such a danger that as per the *parwangi* of Manṣūr Khān in accordance with the writing of Amānullah, *qila'dar* of Bhongi in the vicinity of *suba Darul Jihad* was brought to the august notice of His Majesty that majority of the tumultuous *Pāligārs* in view of the fact that since the office of *faujdari* [*ḳhidmat-i faujdari*] of this *sarkar* as the supplement of *qila'dari* as heretofor is not fixed on him owing to which they [*Pāligārs*] are busy in gathering the contingent and constructing the small fortresses and the mischievous plans. Since in view of the fact of the non-repair of the fort the supplicant is not with full peace of mind (i) the jury of *faujdari* of the *sarkar* is made the supplement of the *qila'dari* as per the previous from years to the supplement then he would properly make proper arrangement for the chastisement of the miscreants [*Pāligār*]. Accordingly the Imperial order was issued to the *Dīwāniyān-i uzzām* to represent the matter[2].

There are instances of the *jagir* distribution among *Poligars* as previously it was written to Rustam, *Diwan* of Karnatak Daruzzafar it was communicated that under the seal of Manṣūr Khān it was received that as per the representation of Namdar S/o late Fatah Khan. *Qila'dar* of Kolar it was represented to His Majesty that the client for the partition of the frontier fort had the contingent beyond the regulation. The *jāgīr* of the dismissed has divided the army and to the *Pāligārs* not a single *dām* is received[3].

Fortunately the background to this situation is clear from the documents. The *mulk-i qadīm* or the country was the area in the Deccan conquered upto the time of Shāh Jahān i.e. Ḳhandesh, Aḥmadnagar, and Berar while

1. IJC I/47/7-94.
2. IJC I/43/4-8.
3. IJC I/47/7-44.

mulk-i jadīd or the new country contained Bījāpur and Ḥaiderabad including the Karnataka and parts of Daulatabad and Bider provinces.[1] Large ports of the *mulk-i jadīd* were disturbed and unsettled, and were called *g͟hair-'amli*. This was particularly so in the Karnataka where the Pālīgārs were very powerful, and no settlement had been made with them so that position was better in the old Ḥaiderabad state, but in Bījāpur had deteriorated due to Maratha depredation.[2]

The Inayat Jung Collection at the National Archives, New Delhi, has over 15,000 official Mughal documents relating to Aurangzeb's reign. All of them are concerned with Deccan, and arranged in connected series, from the 28th regnal year of Aurangzeb. These documents have not been utilised for various aspects of the political and administrative history of Deccan. Prof S Nurul Ḥasan, J F Richards, Muzaffar Alam and this writer have used these documents to clarify matters regarding relations of the Mughal administration with *zamīndārs* and problems of the *jāgīr* system in Deccan.[3] But, despite showing keen interest in the contemporary Maratha history, there has been no earnest effort to use this enormously rich documentary material for establishing facts and elucidating the factors behind them.

This chapter is also an effort to exhibit the kind of information on Mughal Maratha relations that these documents contain. Since the documents were composed with the official Mughal point of view, it has been thought best to proceed by examining how the Mughals looked at Marathas. That perception might have been partly self-serving and incorrect; but this is always the case; when too hostile sides leave behind different evidences for the same events. The information from both sides has to be subject to critical scrutiny to arrive at the truth.

Before we begin, we may note that by an officially sanctioned usage, the Marathas opposed to the Mughals, appear concealed under opprobrious terms, like robbers, rebels etc.[4] Satish Chandra in his essay on 'The Deccan

1. IJC I/46/12-167 & I/46/12-178.
2. J.F. Richards, *Mughal Administration in Golconda, op. cit.*, 111-34.
3. S.N. Ḥasan, 'Aspects of the *Zamīndāri* System in the Deccan' [1696-1707] *PIHC*, 1969 pp. 265-70; J F Richards, *Mughal Administration* in *Golconda OUP*, 1975; Muzaffar Alam, 'The *Zamīndārs* and the Mughal Power in the Deccan - 1685-1712', *IESHR*, Vol. 11, No. 1, 1974, pp. 74-91; Zakir Husain, 'The Working of the *jāgīr* system in the Deccan during the Last Years of Aurangzeb, *Aligarh Vol. of Papers on Indian History'*.
4. According to an Imperial '*farmān*' orders, were issued for calling refractory Marathas '*ashqiya*' and '*nasardārān*'. But we come across some generic terms analogous, to official terminology like '*nasardaran-i g͟hanīm-i-laīm, maqhūr; duzdān, mufsidān, mak͟hāzil, Ṭabqa-i-wajibut tafarqa, firqa-i zalla, kafra fajra, jahannumi*' etc [*Cf.*, Muzaffar Alam, "The *Zamīndārs* and the Mughal Power in the Deccan, *IESHR*, 1974,

Policy of the Mughals' has convincingly argued in detail the salient features of the Mughal Deccan Policy is quite significant as it is a new breeze which has opened new vistas of research in this field[1] as he has made refreshing departure when he argued that there were complex factors responsible for the Deccan policy of the Mughals.

However, it would not be out of context if we take into consideration a brief account of the other points of views about the Marathas and Shivajī and his successors activities till Aurangzeb's death. Although a cursory view of the Deccan policy of the Mughals from Akbar to Shāh Jahān has been taken by taking into account that if the Marathas were a nation than Malik Amber was the father of the nation as he taught them the hit and run tactics yet we have taken into account the Deccan policy of the Mughals under Aurangzeb taking into consideration the Mughal civil war, Shivajī conquered Purandhar, seized north Konkan, including Kalyan and Bhiwandi, defeated Afẓal Khān and captured Panhala.

There was a tussle of Aurangzeb with Shivajī as is borne by the advice Aurangzeb gave to his deputies, Naṣīrī Khān and to the 'Ādil Shāh on the eve of his departure to north India to fight in the civil war. He therefore, asked Naṣīrī Khān to watch the Imperial territories, 'as the son of a dog [Shiva] is waiting for his opportunity'. He wrote to 'Ādil Shāh, 'Expel Shiva who has sneaked into the possession of some forts of the land. If you wish to entertain his services, give him *jāgīrs* in Karnataka far away from Imperial dominions, so that he may not disturb them.[2] It was like Shāh Jahān's peace treaty of 1636 with Bijapur which he adopted towards Shāhji.

Shivajī's night attack on Shāista Khān's camp in 1660, and the discredit it brought on Mughal arms, led to the appointment of Mirza Rāja Jai Singh who decided a policy of divide and rule. In 1665, Jai Singh in his forward policy of Shivajī to surrender his 23 forts out of his 35 forts in the Deccan and attached territory worth four crore *hūns*. In exchange, equivalent territory was awarded to him at the expenses of Bijapur as well as Jai Singh

pp. 741-91]. Other refractory elements have been mentioned by their caste names, *viz.,* Gond, Bhil, Afghā*n,* Jat and Koli etc.

1. Satish Chandra, *Essays on Medieval Indian History,* OUP, Delhi, 5th reprint, 2008, pp. 446-84. Moreover it is also recorded in *Tarikh-i Meo Mehr*, publisher, Mewat Development Agency, Nuh, 2009, pp. 404-5, that Shivajī was secretly freed by the 35 Muslim Meo Community from Mughal Agra prison of Aurangzeb silently taken to Maharashtra in 1666 A.D. which was however blindly believed by Sardar Patel in 1947 A.D.
2. *Ādāb-i 'Ālamgīrī*, MS, Abdus Salam Collection, 326/96, Maulana Azad Library, AMUL, Aligarh, ff. 92 [a] 163 [a]. Jadunath Sarkar, *Shivajī and His Times*, 4th ed. Calcutta, 1948, pp. 53-4.

visualised a joint Mughal-Maratha campaign against Bijapur. He wrote to Aurangzeb, 'The conquest of Bijapur is the preface to the conquest of all the Deccan and Karnataka.[1]

Although Aurangzeb reluctantly agreed to campaign against Bijapur yet he rejected to come personally to the Deccan in order to take charge of the operations there and carry them to completion.[2] However, in 1664 Shivajī had accomplished the sack of Surat. Consequent upon the death of Mīr Jumla, Karnataka was allowed to be absorbed into the Golcunda Kingdom.[3] Aurangzeb also succeeded in realizing his early objective in the Deccan when in 1668 he obtained Sholapur, the last Nizamshāhi outpost, in Bijapur.

To conquer Bijapur and subdue Shivajī was an impossible task in 1672 for Bahādur Khān. Aurangzeb was however, dissatisfied with these limited successes and replaced Bahādur Khān by his lieutenant, Diler Khān, who replaced former's policy who listened to Bahlol Khān's grandiloquent plea for a joint expedition against Golcunda and then jointly crushing Shivajī. However, his invasion failed ignominuously in 1677 A.D. and furthered the policy of Madanna and Akanna in building the united front of the Deccani powers against the Mughals. However this particular diplomatic struggle of Madana and Akanna in the Deccan politics and their efforts to build an alliance of the Deccani states including Shivajī had far reaching consequences. It was also agreed that Shivajī would be confined to the Konkan.[4] In 1676, Aurangzeb neither succeeded in repeating Jai Singh nor was able to win over the Deccani states to an alliance against the Marathas.

Consequently the arrival of Aurangzeb in pursuit of Prince Akbar in 1681-82 did not lead to any immediate change in the Mughal policy towards the Deccani states. We are given to understand that by 1684 prince Akbar had been virtually bottled up in Shivajī's *swarajya* and even the scale of Maratha depredations in Mughal territories had declined.[5] Aurangzeb in his *farmān* to QuṬb Shāh alleged handing over the entire control of affairs of the kingdom to infidels, the brothers Madanna and Akanna.[6] In 1683,

1. *Haft Anjuman*, compiled by Udairaj, secretary of Rustam Dil Khān and Mirza Rāja Singh, Bib. Nat. Paris, No. 37, a fragment, f. 90 [a], Satish Chandra, Deccan Policy of Mirza Rāja Jai Singh, *Pros. Raj. His. Cong*; [Jodhpur, 1966], pp. 76-84.
2. *Haft Anjuman*, ff 179 [b], 194 [a].
3. *'Ādāb-i 'Ālamgīrī*, ff. 66 [b]-67 [a], Jagdish Narayan Sarkar, *The Life of Mīr Jumla*, Calcutta, 1951, pp. 110-13.
4. *Basātinus Salātīn*, litho, p. 456, *History of Aurangzeb*, IV, pp. 172-3, *Shivajī and His Times*, p. 302.
5. *History of Aurangzeb*, IV, 335-58.
6. Khāfi Khān, *Muntakhabu-l Lubāb*, II, p. 328.

Aurangzeb wanted to return north India after the rain and wanted to leave prince Shah 'Ālam who refused to budge.[1]

Instead of about a quarter Aurangzeb had decided about 20 years later than the treaty of Purandhaur the annexation of the two Deccani states of Bijapur and Golcunda in which he succeeded. The capture and execution of Shambhaji on 11th March 1689 appeared to be a coping stone to his success. In 1686, the *ṣūbadārs* of Golcunda and Bijapur had been instructed to bring together a train of transport animals for the Emperor's return to Agra where preparations were set afoot for welcoming the Emperor.[2] However, Aurangzeb's inflexibility and the turn of events made the Emperor's return to north India an ever receding mirage. Thus, a Muslim Meo poet wrote: *wa din sabhi sukhi ho jayengen; ja din aa jayen 'Alamgir* [on that day all men shall become happy when 'Alamgir shall return to north India]"

Aurangzeb suffered many problems after the annexation of the Deccani states and in Karnataka in and around Shivajī's old *swarajya* after 1693.[3] Aurangzeb failed to understand the nature of the Maratha movement by his surprise raid and execution of Shambhaji in 1689, his failure to come to terms with Tara Bai widow of Rāja Rām in 1700 and with Shahu in 1703.[4]

The Marathas had intimate relations with other non-Maratha *zamīndār* caste like Reddis, the Berads, the Velamas etc. The Mughal attempt to introduce into the Deccan the system of administration from their north Indian Mughal system which implied a reduction of their perquisites of the *deshmukhs*, *zamīndārs*, *munīwārs*, *muqaddams* etc also weakening of the administrative control over the countryside. The distribution of the revenue and administrative duties between the *jāgīrdārs* and *faujdārs* weakend the ability of the former to realise their allocated dues from the *jāgīrs*, to maintain even the reduced quota of *sawārs* prescribed in the month scale.

Aurangzeb however, recklessly extended the Mughal line of communication to Jinji, without first winning over the Marathas, or dealing with the Maratha roving bands which regularly gained strength and striking capacity taking advantage of local disgruntled elements and absorbing many disbanded [Muslim] soldiers of the erstwhile Deccani states. However, it was only in 1703 that Auranzgeb offered to treat with the Marathas by restoring to Shivajī's *swarajya* to the captive prince Shahu and the grant of *sardeshmukhī* of the Deccan to him. But these efforts

1. '*Arzdāsht* of Kanwal Sen, dated 18 *Rajab*, 1094/14 July 1683 [Jaipur Records, *Wakil's* Reports, p. 4615].
2. Amber *wakil's* report dated *Ramazan*, RY 32/23 June 1688 [Akbarabad].
3. *Akhabārāt*, 27 *Zil*, RY 36/30 July 1693.
4. Aurangzeb could have become successful if he would not have attached so much importance to Jinji till its conquest in 1698 A.D.

THE DECCAN, 1689

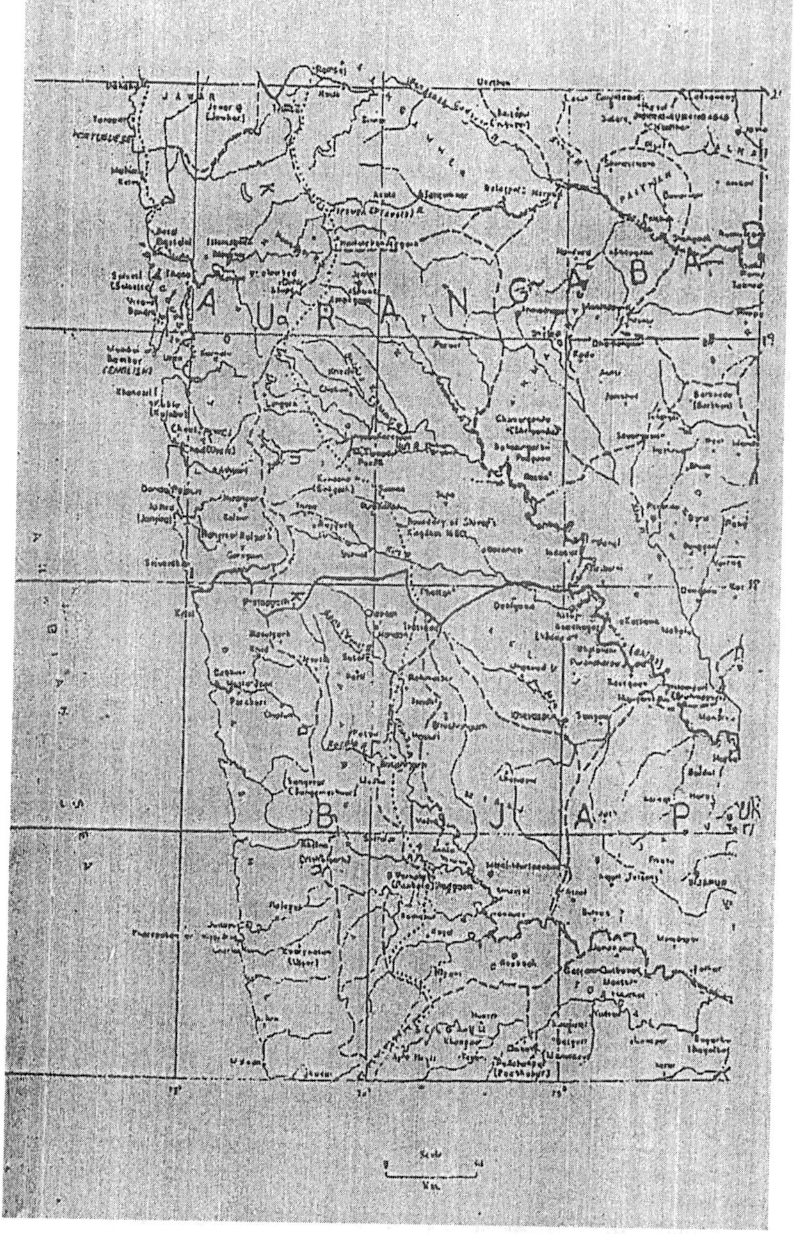

collapsed, largely due to unacceptable Maratha demand of *chauth* for the six provinces of the Deccan and Aurangzeb's lack of sense in the Marathas.

Such are the results of Henry Grant Duff's *History of the Marathas*, [2 vols.] M.N. Pearson,[1] Peter Hardy,[2] Jadunath Sarkar's *Shivajī and His Times, History of Aurangzeb*, 5 vols, J.F. Richards,[3] Satish Chandra,[4] Muzaffar 'Ālam[5] and several other stanchant critics who have carefully studied the Mughal-Maratha conflict from their point of view. But it would also be outside the purview of the historiography of Mughal India if we take into account the Mughal point of view which seems to be different as given here under because before his death in 1680 A.D. Shivajī had, according to Pearson controlled an area of about 50,000 square miles or 4.1% of the area of the whole subcontinent. His revenue was one-fifth and one-sixth of that of Aurangzeb. Moreover in his territory he had set up comparatively elaborate administrative apparatus.[6]

Moreover Shivajī's second and most astounding attack was his first seizure and sack of Surat in January 1664. After this two more attacks of 1670 and 1677 were more ferocious and dangerous. In 1666, Shāh Abbas of Iran taunted of Shivajī not to be suppressed by Aurangzeb.

By the end of Aurangzeb's reign, the Marathas were spread over the entire Deccan. The *parganas* of the three *ṣūbās* of Berar, Aurangabad and Bidar became especially vulnerable to the Maratha inroads.[7]

Najābat Khān, a 17th century Mughal official, claimed that, "The hell traversing robbers [*ashqiyā-i-jahannum paimā*] scattered everywhere in groups, have attacked, destroyed, sacked, ravaged and depopulated the entire country; except a few towns having strong fortifications [*qila'jāt-i-mustaḥkam*], they have left no signs of habitation. They have forcibly seized from the [Mughal] tax-collectors the revenues of both the crops in the Prince's [name not mentioned] 'conditional' *jāgīr*, six months need now to pass before the revenue realisation can be undertaken again.

1. M.N. Pearson, 'Shivajī and the Decline of the Mughal Empire' in Symposium; *Decline of the Mughal Empire*, *Journal of Asian Studies*, XXXV, No. 2, pp. 220-36.
2. Peter Hardy, Commentary and Critique, Symposium: *Decline of the Mughal Empire*, *op. cit*, pp. 257-63.
3. JF Richards, The Imperial Crisis in the Deccan, Symposium: '*Decline of the Mughal Empire*', JAS, XXXV, No. 2, pp. 237-56, Feb. 1976.
4. Satish Chandra, The Deccan Policy of the Mughals under Aurangzeb, *op. cit.*, pp. 461-84; *idem*, Religious Policy of Aurangzeb during the Later Part of His Reign-Some Considerations, *Essays in Medieval Indian History*, OUP, Delhi 2008 [5th ed.] pp. 324-45.
5. Muzaffar 'Ālam, The *Zamīndārs* and the Mughal Power in the Deccan 1685-1712, *IESHR*, Vol. XI, No.1.
6. A.R. Kularni, *Maharastra in the Age of Shivaji*, Poona, 1969.
7. IJC I/47/5-56.

The accursed [*maqhūrān*] want to establish military camps [*chhāonīs*] in Khāndesh like the previous year...[1]

The Marathas oppressed the peasantry and demanded one-fourth of the revenue known as *chauth.* It had begun to be demanded in the early phase of Aurangzeb's reign. In 42nd regnal year, it was reported that Nigon Bakht, [in collusion with the Marathas], collected Rs 31,000 as *chauth* from *pargana* Nandgaon, *ṣūba* Berar and posted his men at Malkapur and Mehkar.[2]

In 42nd R.Y., *muqaddams* and the peasantry of 135 villages of *pargana* and *sarkār* Pathri, *ṣūba* Berar Bālāghāt reported that six *deshmukhs* of the *pargana* collected more than the stipulated *rusūm* [perquisites] with the support of the *gumāshta* [agent] of Chin Qilīch Khān, exacted, Rs 70,000 unlawfully, constructed fortresses in their assigned villages, maintained the retainers, indulged in robbery and during the time of the Maratha raids 1,000 of their men joined hands with them and attacked and ravaged the villages and delivered *chauth* to them. They did not allow the revenue paying peasantry to undertake cultivation peacefully.[3]

In 45th R.Y., Naqī Khān reported that the peasantry of *parganas* Baizāpur and Komhāri, *sarkār* Daulatabad, complained against the *faujdār* of the area, who failed to chastise the Marathas [*kāfir*]. Instead, he collected money from the *pargana* and paid it to them [*makkār*] as *chauth,* while he retained some with him.[4]

Thus, instead of getting support of the peasantry in their bid to oppose the Mughal armies, the Marathas started plundering and impoverishing them by demanding one-fourth of their revenue. They wrought awe and terror in the hearts of the peasantry that it had no option against the Maratha onslaught, except to run away-a fact frequently recorded in the documents. These phenomena further accentuated the crisis in the *jāgīr* system, because the Mughal *jāgīrdārs* found it difficult to realise the revenue due to non-cultivation and flight of the peasantry.

'Iwaz Khān, *qila'dār* of Biswapatan represented that the peasantry of *pargana* Dhar Dharwah, which lay in his *jāgīr,* fled away due to Maratha attacks so that his *jāgīr* had become desolated.[5]

1. IJC I/50/5-15.
2. In 1671, Shivaji demanded '*chauth*' from Suhrab Khān, *commandant of Udgir fort. Selected Documents of Aurangzeb's Reign*, p. 87.
3. IJC I/42/10-36 & I/42/10-81.
4. IJC I/45/1-127.
5. IJC I/41/10-150, I/41/10-/151, I/43/2-79, I/47/8-13. Village Kokara, *pargana* Sulṭānpur, *ṣūba* Khāndesh, situated in the foot-hills could not prosper due to the ravages of the Marathas, [I/42/4-5]. The peasantry and the *zamīndārs* of *pargana*

The *deshmukh* and the peasantry of *pargana* Thalner petitioned the court that the Marathas [*mufsidān*] tortured the revenue paying peasantry.[1] Raghujī received the *deshpāndiya* rights of 27 *maḥāls* of *sarkār* Daulatabad on the condition of bringing seven lakh *bighas* of virgin land under the plough and deposit its revenues. Subsequently, he wrote to Sibghatullāh that the said land was not worth cultivation as it was barren [*shor*] and due to epidemic and famine the peasantry had taken to flight. However, orders were issued for investigation and it was revealed that due to the unprecedented Maratha activities, the peasantry of the said *parganas* had scattered. It was hoped that when the rainy season commenced, the peasantry would be safe from the enemy and return to their native places.[2]

Similarly, in 51 R.Y., Muṣāḥib Khān reported that he had been granted *jāgīr* in *pargana* Phulambari. But, the peasantry of most of his *jāgīr* villages ran away to village Malungaon due to Maratha disturbances and became *pāhīkāsht* [non-resident cultivators].[3]

A sheet under the seal of Yar 'Ali Baig was received that Muta'bir Khān had written that in *pargana* Angola there are almost ten forts while the trust of the contingents of the aforesaid forts failed owing to excessive demand and lack of salary. Meanwhile most of the *dehat* of aforesaid *pargana* were assigned to Satwa Daflia owing to which the Marathas, his retainers would continue their to and fro in that *pargana*. It should be taken care that in the guise of his retainers might harm the fort. He therefore hopes that the Marathas entire *jagir* assigned to Satwa be assigned to them while Satwa would be granted *jagir* where there would be no fort[4].

An interesting case has been recorded in a document of 45th R.Y. One 'Abdur Reḥmān, *muqaddam* of village Balor, *pargana* Qandahar, *ṣūba* Bidar, reported that he had one hundred dependents. The peasantry ran away due to Maratha disturbances and as such his dependents were compelled to cultivate the land themselves for their maintenance.[5]

The Marathas were also responsible for the destruction of the standing crops. We find recurring incidents of the destruction of crops, non-cultivation of the agricultural land and plunder of grain[6] for making

Burdapur, *sarkār* Fateḥābād, *ṣūba* Aurangabad, petitioned that they had become tired of the Maratha raids], [I/47/4-41].

1. IJC I/41/11-12.
2. IJC I/42/12-77.
3. IJC I/51/11-40 & I/51/11-41.
4. IJC I/47/11-43.
5. IJC I/45/5-46.
6. Khandu and other Marathas were reported to have plundered of a *jāgīrdar* holding *jāgīr* in *qaṣba* Ankola. Moreover, the deputy of the *faujdār* of the area forcibly collected Rs 13,000 from the peasantry. [IJC I/50/2-8].

the peasantry destitute. Nāhir Khān wrote to Asad Khān [43rd RY] that 1,500 *bighas* of land of his *jāgīr* in *pargana* Ja'farābād [Chandor], *sarkār* Sangamner, *ṣūba* Aurangabad, remained uncultivated due to the turmoil of the Marathas and the Bhils.[1] Ḥāji Suhail reported about the destruction of the standing crops of his *jāgīr* in *pargana* Parner due to the passage of the Marathas and the Banjaras.[2] Village Norgi, *pargana* Almala, *ṣūba* Bījāpur, yielding Rs 2,200 was deserted due to the perpetual disturbances of the Maratha armies.[3]

Occasionally, the Mughal officers destroyed the crops on the pretext of chastising the Marathas. This was alleged against Uzbek Khān, due to whose action 13 villages remained uncultivated and the peasantry fled away.[4]

Mehda, *gumashta* [agent] of *deshmukh* and Manku *deshpāndiya* of *pargana* Baramati, *jāgīr* territory of Suleman Khān, disappeared on the pretext of *lāwani* due to arrears of two years, scarcity of rains and the destruction of standing crops due to the passage of the Imperial armies.[5]

The statement of revenues of various areas duly records the loss of revenues due to the disturbance of the Marathas [*ba sabab-i futūr-i ghanīm-i laīm*].[6]

The Marathas, sometimes incited the peasantry of certain villagers to rebel. Neknām Khān submitted that due to the turmoil of the Marathas and the rebellion [*chirāghi*] of the peasantry, little amount was received in *pargana* Dhongi.[7]

In view of the mounting pressure of the Marathas on the peasantry, the latter generally sought imperial help. Aurangzeb wrote on the *āwārja* of *pargana* Muḥīābād [Poona] that since the said town was to be assigned to the Prince [unnamed], efforts should be made for its settlement, by constructing fortresses, advance of *taqāvi* [loan] and the appointment of

1. IJC I/43/4-4.
2. IJC I/47/8-2.
3. IJC I/43/2-64.
4. IJC I/44/11-19. *Pargana* Kadak was ruined due to the march of the Marathas and the Imperial armies [I/43/1-32].
5. IJC I/49/10-12.
6. IJC I/44/11-63 & I/48//0-78. Towards the closing years of Aurangzeb's reign, there is a massive amount of evidence relating to the Marathas in all kinds of official Mughal records because they occupied a central position for the Mughal policy. The Inayat Jung Collection containing as it does, a very large amount of material from Mughal official archives of the Deccan furnishes wealth of information about the Maratha devastation. I am greatful to my colleague Miss Nighat Shagufa, at the National Archives, for letting me use copies of some documents made by her.
7. IJC I/50/8-7.

the *faujdār, deshmukh* and *deshpāndiya.* The peasantry also petitioned for the settlement of the entire *pargana* by the following means:

Fortresses should be built in five deserted villages, so that the peasantry of the adjoining villages could take shelter in the event of Maratha raids and the *faujdār* should post a reliable deputy in the *thāna.*

Jizya should be remitted for five years.

Promise was made to bring *jama'* of the *pargana* up to the maximum assessed [*jama'-kamīl*] within five years and it should be assessed according to *hast-o būd* [actuals] every year.

The *jāgīrs* of Shaikh Jamāl and others be transferred, since they were oppressive. All these demands were approved by the Emperor.[1]

The peasantry of *pargana* Ankalkot, [Akalkot / Akot] *sarkār* Naldurg, petitioned that the *faujdārī* of the said *pargana* was attached with the *faujdār* of Naldurg, who should depute his *nāib* for chastising the Marathas and the miscreants who come there and seize the money and cattle. The *gumāshta* [agent] of Ṣadruddin Khān was suitable for the purpose in question.[2] Similarly, Najābat Khān stated that Jagdīsh Rāo was an efficient servant and aware of the qualities of the region and the peasantry and the *zamīndārs* were happy with his considerate behaviour as he had properly chastised the enemy and was aware of the customary crossing places of the Marathas [*ghāthāi-'ubūr-i ashqiyā*]. As such, he posted him at *thāna*,of Pipla and Dang.[3]

An interesting incident has been described about village Karanjkhera, *pargana* Antur, *jāgīr* of one 'Abdur Razzāq Khān, which happened to be adjacent to settlements of the Bhils and Marathas [*duzdān*]. Its *faujdār* had made no arrangements to protect the peasantry. It was stated that in the absence of any fortification [*iḥāta*], the peasantry could not settle and without Imperial orders such fortification was not possible. Accordingly, he solicited permission for erecting the fortification, so that it could protect the way and the poor peasantry, which was acceded to.[4] Ghiyāsuddīn Khān had established the fort and mart of Rasūlpur at village Bhondi, *pargana* Raver, which was now in *Khāliṣa.* The peasants kept their belongings [*asbāb-o ashiyā*] during the disturbances caused by the Marathas. But, now Ghiyāsuddīn Khān's nephews were refusing to permit the peasants to do this and such action would ruin village Bhondi.[5]

1. IJC I/47/2-90.
2. IJC I/47/12-129.
3. IJC I/51/12-3.
4. IJC I/51/11-162.
5. IJC I/50/10-11, I/50/10-12 &I/50/10-13.

The peasantry suffered badly at the hands of the *zamīndārs* due to the active connivance of the Marathas. Naval Singh, *zamīndār* of *sarkār* Kalam extremely tortured the peasantry in collusion with the Marathas.[1] The peasantry of Tirambak fort, *sarkār* Sangamner, *ṣūba* Aurangabad, complained that the *deshmukhs* of the area were in league with the Marathas and so the former *qila'dārs* had to imprison them. However, Salīm Beg the present *qila'dār* released them. But, their internment was helpful in encouraging the peasantry, while their release was the cause of their ruin.[2]

The above incidents do not mean that the *zamīndārs* all the time harassed the peasantry and did not protect them. They could also join hands with the peasantry in redressing their grievances against the Marathas as we see often in our documents. They also cooperated with the Mughal administration in resisting the Marathas and seizing their strongholds. The last years of Aurangzeb's reign witnessed both the unprecedented concentration of Mughal might in Deccan and yet the ever-increasing Maratha raids. We find that due to considerable concessions given to the *zamīndārs*, the Mughals were able to muster their support against the victorious Marathas.

The myth of the invincibility of the Mughal power was the most important factor, which made the peasantry submissive to Mughals, and which led the majority of the big *zamīndārs* into joining Mughal service. But, as Mughal power seemed more and more vulnerable to Maratha onslaught, the *zamīndārs* developed a peculiar tendency of vacillating between the Mughals and the Marathas and utilised their position to serve their own interest.

Muḥammad Ḥasan and other *zamīndārs* of *sarkār* Dabhol were sent by G͟hāziuddin K͟hān Firūz Jung to the court with Saiyid Luṭf and posted for the conquest of the forts of the Marathas on the condition of maintaining 5,000 infantry. They asked for *sanad* of *deshmukhi* according to the terms of the *sanad of* Zulfiqār K͟hān.[3] He obtained the requisite *parwāna,* but without '*arz* [Imperial confirmation], he remained idle. 'Abdul Razzāq K͟hān Lāri, therefore, recommended his case that he was an efficient person, who did a lot [*maṣdar-i-taraddudāt*] at the time of the conquest of Islāmgarh fort. He, therefore, hoped for an early grant of *saranjam* [pay] so that he could perform his assigned duties efficiently and strive for the welfare of the

1. IJC I/42/5-21.
2. IJC I/47/11-83. Under the corrupting influence of the Marathas even the *zamīndārs* of *sarkār* Raichūr used to demand *chauth* from the peasants with the active connivance of Gonds.
3. IJC I/31/11-1.

government.[1] According to the *parwāna* of Zulfiqār Khān [6 *Shwwal* 33rd RY], Muḥammad Ḥasan and Ibrāhīm Ḥasan, *adhikar* and *chaudhurī* of *pargana* Ja'farabad, *sarkār* Dabhol helped in the conquest of Rasālgarh and Mahipatgarh forts and hence the *zamīndāri* of the said *pargana* with the *rusūm* [perquisites] of two villages amounting to Rs 2,000 was granted as *inā'm*.[2] It was also recorded that the said *zamīndār* was present in the army with 5,000 unpaid infantry and captured the forts of the Marathas and many Maratha leaders [*nāsardārān-i 'umda-i-maqhūr*] of Udai Singh. Therefore, in view of his meritorious services and the habitation of the area, the *deshmukhī-zamīndāri* was recommended for him on the condition of bringing the revenues to the maximum.[3]

Shambhu Das, *deshmukh* of Nandurbar, was assigned [rank of] 200/50 on account of his repulsing the Marathas and releasing his men.[4] At the time of the conquest of Khandrug fort, Saiyid 'Abdullāh Khān assigned nine villages, including Badnekoi, *pargana* and *sarkār* Torgul, *ṣūba* Bījāpur as *inā'm* to 'Alī, *zamīndār* on the condition of maintaining 100 matchlockmen for the protection of the said fort.[5] Twenty *sawārs* were added to the rank of Rāo s/o Mehdaji for establishing *thāna* at Mahur, *pargana* Bir, the main passage of the Marathas.[6]

Ranū Narū, *zamīndār* of *pargana* Undargaon, *sarkār* Parenda, killed Pratap Rāo, Maratha in 39th R.Y. and for this reason he was recommended a *manṣab* of 1000/700 by Muṭālib Khān. He requested that 100 *chāwars* of land held by him at village Maligaon could be granted to him as *inā'm*, enabling him to serve with Manṣur Khān with 100 *sawārs,* establish the *thāna* and contain the Marathas. This too was sanctioned.[7] Since he fulfilled the obligations, he continued to enjoy the concession even after five years [i.e. 44th RY].[8] But in the same year, a complaint was lodged by Mun'im Khān that Ranū did not maintain the contingent, but retained the said *inā'm*.[9] However, the Emperor declined saying that, "There could be some possibility [*gunjāish*] which should be explored."[10] His example was imitated by Phar, *deshmukh* of *pargana* Kānti, who requested that since he was unaware of the Imperial regulations [*zawābit-i bādshāhi*], he also

1. IJC I/32/0-59 A.
2. IJC I/33/12-1.
3. IJC I/35/11-1, I/35/11-7 & I/36/9-9.
4. IJC I/37/15-4.
5. IJC I/371/5-2.
6. IJC I/42/3-34.
7. IJC I/39/11-121 &I/39/11-122.
8. IJC I/44/2-88.
9. IJC I/47/11-63.
10. IJC I/47/3-72.

expected the grant of village Kothli, *pargana* Wāluj, yielding revenues of Rs 5,000 [his *zamīndāri* area] on the condition of establishing *thāna* and serving the *faujdār* with 100 *sawār,* which was accepted *in-toto*. He fought against the Marathas with the *faujdār* and many of his men were killed or wounded in the warfare and even his son was captured by the Marathas.[1]

Since the *deshmukhs* also maintained peace and were supposed to guard the peasantry against Maratha encroachments the Mughal administration took a lenient view of their shortcomings. The *wakīls* of Ghaziuddīn Khān Firūz Jung and other *jāgīrdārs* of *pargana* Varval represented that since 'Abdur Raḥim *alias* Subhānji was interned for the last 1½ years, the *'āmils* of *pargana* wrote again that the said *pargana* was completely ruined and the Marathas ravaged the entire *pargana,* established *thānas* everywhere and nothing was received by the *jāgīrdārs* and no settlement was visible. They, therefore, solicited his release so that he could increase local prosperity and chastise the Marathas.[2]

The *zamīndārs* and the peasantry of *pargana* Burdapur, *sarkār* Fateḥābād, *ṣūba* Aurangabad, joined in pleading that they were distressed due to the Maratha attacks and requested the assignment of *faujdārī* to the *jāgīrdār* thereof, so that they could be no more in trouble.[3]

Despite these exhibitions of loyalty to the Mughals, the *zamīndārs* were a disgruntled class who also fomented troubles in unison with the Marathas. It was communicated that in view of the vastness of *ṣūba* Bījāpur, known to the Emperor, the Bedars having evil designs, were determined to rise into full rebellion [*bahujūm-i-tamām shorish numāyand*] with the cooperation of the Marathas and the *zamīndārs* just after the departure of the Emperor from there.[4]

'Abdur Rasūl Khān complained that the Marathas encamped in *pargana* Narsi, [his *jāgīr*] every year due to the cooperation of 'Abdullāh, the recalcitrant *zamīndār* of the area and nothing was procured from there. Any carelessness would result into his annihilation [*kār bajān wa kārad ba istikhwān rasīda*].[5]

Reports of the ravages of the *jāgīrs* by the *zamīndārs* in cooperation with the Marathas were made on several occasions. Shāh Muḥammad *qila'dār* of Rai Huwalli complained of the complete ruin of his *jāgīr* due to Maratha raids and the tumult of the *zamīndārs*.[6] The Marathas were

1. IJC I/41/10-186, I/41/10-187, I/44/9-15 &I/45/4-34.
2. IJC I/0/0-218.
3. IJC I/47/4-103.
4. IJC I/36/8-6.
5. IJC I/37/0-180.
6. IJC I/43/11-7.

reported to have reached Kalyāni hills due to the support of the *zamīndārs*.[1]

The Mughal officials, sometimes, also encouraged the *zamīndārs* in their activities in league with the Marathas. The *zamīndārs* of some villages in *pargana* Dehari used to cooperate with the Marathas due to the support of the *jāgīrdār.* Moreover, the fortress [*gadhi*] of the *deshpāndiya* of *pargana* Bhokran was atop the Imperial fortress [*qila'cha*] and the Marathas due to its shelter used to ravage the said town. It was, therefore, suggested either to demolish it or establish an Imperial *thāna* there, for maintaining peace.[2]

The Maratha *zamīndārs-deshmukhs* also created lawlessness in the areas of other *jāgīrdārs.* Qādir Dād Khān reported that Baddā deputed his agent for collecting *rāhdārī* [road toll] in *pargana* Melwari. Since the said *pargana* was held in *jāgīr* and *faujdārī* by him, he sought the grant of the *sanad* of *jāgīr* and *faujdāri* in order to expel the *deshmukh* thereof, a brother of Baddājī, Maratha [*nasardār-i ashqiyā*]. This proposal was further supported by Yāsīn Khān, who reported that the Marathas [*duzdān*], encamped at *pargana* Melwari and Tolaji, *deshmukh* of the area was the brother of Baddājī, Maratha, who seized the revenues of the town and the villages of Melwari, which were included in *pāibāqī* and adjoined to Baddā Machangaon. He also recommended grant of favours to Qādir Dād Khān, who would not allow a single *sawār* of Baddaji to remain there.[3]

The Marathas even instigated the agents of the *zamīndārs* to defy Imperial orders. Khandu and other agents of Amrit Rao, *deshpāndiya* and *kulkarni* of Nauras Tara fort *alias* Parli, hatched a conspiracy against him in complicity with the Marathas and claiming to be the *deshpāndiya* themselves allowed the Marathas to capture their master's *waṭan* [*jāgīr*] did not pay him the revenues and forcibly collected 1,230 *hūns*. Furthermore, Shivajī Nirmal and Nimajī Narsu, his agents, also sold 15 of his villages to the Marathas and received Rs 1,700. Therefore, official intervention was solicited for recovering the amount from the imposters and expelling them for the habitation of the *pargana* and eradication of their oppression.[4]

'Alī Naqī Khān reported that *pargana* Partur, *sarkār* Jalnapur, was included in *pāibāqī* and the *zamīndārs* of the area, at the instigation of the agents of the *faujdār,* [the Maratha Achlūjī] who was in league with the Marathas [*ashqiyā*] did not pay the revenues. Since the *faujdārī* of the area was assigned to the Marathas, the enemy could encamp there and disturbance was created. Hence, the transfer of the *pargana* from its Maratha assignees was recommended. It was also learnt from the reports

1. IJC I/44/4-73.
2. IJC I/45/6-11. The Marathas also blocked the passage IJC 5/42/12-2.
3. IJC I/45/7-116.
4. IJC I/46/11-37.

of Aurangabad that the agent of Achlu supplied lead [*sarab*], gunpowder [*bārūt*] and iron rockets [bān] to the Marathas.[1] Dhanna Jadav and other Marathas were reported to have requisitioned lead and gunpowder from the agents of Achlu, the Maratha *jāgīrdār*, who had contacts with the notorious Marathas, who sent him the following items.

Lead [*sarab*]	gunpowder [*bārūt*]	iron-rocket [*bān*]
2 *mans*	5 *mans*	100

The *harkāra* of *sarkār* Pāthrī also reported that formerly he held *jāgīr* in *pargana* of Koneri. Since he allowed the Marathas to establish the cantonment there that *maḥāl* was transferred from him. Subsequently, he obtained *jāgīr* in *pargana* Partur but he maintained contacts with them [*duzdān*].[2]

The *zamīndārs,* sometimes, paid lumpsums to the Marathas. The *zamīndārs* of *Painth* Pala were reported by the *harkāra* posted at Chandor fort on 12 *Jumada II,* 50th R.Y. to have fixed Rs 1,000 as *rātib* [provisions] of the Marathas [*ashqiā*] and whatever was collected was delivered to them [*maqāhīr*].[3] Kāmyāb Khān reported that the *deshmukh* of Naldrug having seized upon the stores of the fort [*ijnās-i zakhīra-i qila'mutaṣarrif shuda*] joined hands with the Marathas and indulged in uncalled-for-acts unworthy of him; and the *deshmukh* seized control of the fort and the area from Muhṭashim Khān.[4]

Muzaffar Alam could trace in these documents only two instances of the defiance by the *deshmukhs* of the Mughal authority during the last two years of Aurangzeb's reign whereas the incidents of such defiance are quite numerous, during this very period, often pointing to the connivance of the Marathas.[5] Rival claimants sought the help of the Marathas for usurping the *deshmukhī-muqaddamī* rights.[6]

The Maratha depradations resulted in large-scale devastation of the

1. IJC I/50/5-13.
2. IJC I/50/2-12.
3. IJC I/50/8-5.
4. IJC I/51/11-36.
5. The *muqaddam* of Maligaon claimed the *muqaddami* of *qaṣba* Nander; *pargana* Chandor due to the support of the Marathas and collected Rs 10,000 from the inhabitants. [I/47/4-102]. *Deshmukhs* of Tirambak also supported the Marathas [I/47/11-83], also see I/50/11-2; M. Alam, p. 79 n.
6. Dharma *deshmukh* of *pargana* Dehāri, petitioned that he had purchased half *deshmukhi* of *pargana* Dehāri and *muqaddamī* of *qaṣba* Ḥasanābād and Chinkhili. However, Ankoji, his nephew, had cooperated with the Marathas and ravaged Dehāri. Dharma and his father fought and killed some Marathas. But Ankoji managed to have him arrested in league with Zābita Khān, plundered his house and obtained *lādāwā-i-deshmukhī* [I/50/11-173].

Imperial territories, considerable loss to the standing crops and failure of the administrative set-up. They received encouragement and active support, even from the Mughal officers, particularly the Maratha *manṣabdārs,* who most often tried to frustrate the efforts of the administration to dislodge the Marathas.

K͟hudāyār K͟hān reported that Dakni Rām held *jāgīr* in village Chaundi, *pargana* Chimargonda, his *faujdārī* area, which became the abode of Maratha tribe due to the support of Dakni's agents. Whenever any effort was made to expel them, they created disturbances.[1] The *qila'dār* complained of the failure in his getting a *jāgīr* in the foothills of the fort according to established rule, since these territories were assigned to the Deccanis who were difficult to distinguish from the turbulent Marathas on account of their belonging to the same caste.[2]

Firūz Jung reported to the Emperor that Darko and other Marathas held *jāgīr* in village Rāmrāi etc in *pargana* Wāluj, *sarkār* Daulatabad, situated on the highway and the [tumultuous] Marathas stayed there with their fellow-Maratha [*jāgīrdār*] and plundered the traders.[3] Qāsim K͟hān *qila'dār* of Naldrug also stated that Īma Nibālkar, a Maratha was granted the *faujdārī* of that territory and he provided shelter to the Maratha hostiles.[4] A similar complaint was made about Dattājī and other Marathas, who received *jāgīr* assignment in *pargana* Shivgaon which became refuge of the Marathas [*duzdān*] due to their having the same caste and the names [*ba dastāwez ism-i jāgīr-i Marhataha tafrīq namī tawānad kard*] due to which the peasantry and travellers suffered and no prosperity was possible.[5]

Their presence in the Imperial dominions created many problems, some of which were recounted by one Ḥusāmuddin, *qila'dār* of Ūdgir. The Marathas [*mufsidān*] created disturbance just two *kurohs* from the fort. Since the majority of the villages in the vicinity of the fort were held by the Deccanis and its *faujdārī* was assigned to them, the Marathas slipped into these villages as and when they were chastised. After the departure of the army, they returned to their own places due to which they could not be banished, Even an Afg͟hān also created disturbance and joining hands with the Marathas blocked the highway.[6]

The Maratha *jāgīrdārs* promoted insurgency of their rebellious

1. IJC I/41/10-138, I/41/10-139.
2. IJC I/45/2-56, I/45/12-42.
3. IJC I/47/12-54.
4. IJC I/48/8-6.
5. IJC I/46/9-62.
6. IJC I/46/10-1, see also IJC I/42/12-12. The Marathas even killed the messenger of Shankra, *deshpāndiya* of Ellichpur, IJC I/45/7-46.

compatriots. One Santājī, Maratha, was granted village Karkanjī [as *jāgīr*], in *pargana* Aḥsanābād, who gathered a group of the Marathas and their men [*mardum-i ashqiyā*], visited there and during the disturbances they kept the property [*amta'*] of the Imperial territory with the miscreant Marathas in the said village and shared it with them as well in addition to committing other oppressions.[1]

The Marathas often concealed their presence in the royal territories even in the guise of the peasantry owing to the support of the Mughal officials and it was impossible to flush them out from villages assigned to neighbouring *jāgīrdārs*. They freely committed robbery and even plundered the cattle of the villages held by other *jāgīrdārs*.[2] They also caused loss to revenues of [non-Maratha] *jāgīrdārs* by taking undue advantage of their presence in a Maratha *jāgīr*.[3] The retainers of Nayyā Rāo, Maratha *faujdār* of *pargana* Manglor, joined hands with the Marathas [*maqhūrān*] who lived in the said *qaṣba* and plundered the adjoining villages.[4]

The religious centres also became the halting places of the Marathas. They were reported to take shelter in *thāna* Nema Devhra, situated in the middle of Sangamner, Parner and Neusa wherein a temple sprang up. The Emperor, therefore, remarked that "Nema Devhra was named after an idol and the temple was demolished as it was made the place of worship by the chief [*rais'*] thereof due to the ignorance of the *'āmils*".[5]

The bands of the Marathas were found spread like 'ants and locusts' in the Imperial territories. We find much information about their presence in different regions *viz.*, 1,000 *sawār* and infantry stayed in village Donga, *pargana* Ūdgīr.[6] They [*ashqiyā*] came out from the *katl* [pass] of *pargana* Un, Gulshanābād [Nasik] with the cooperation of the Kolis and fomented trouble in Khandesh. Kannad and other mountains and hilly districts proved a bone to them as they frequently attacked and plundered the adjoining *jāgīrs* and rushed to their dwellings in the hilly areas.[7]

The pressure of the Marathas compelled many Mughal officials to surrender their forts to them. The news sent from Gulshanābād by Saiyid Jān Muḥammad on 8 *Safar* 49th R.Y. was related to the capture of the fort of Raj Manji by the Marathas [*duzdan*]. Meanwhile, news was received on

1. IJC I/46/6-97; I/46/6/99; I/47/3-101; I/47/3-102.
2. IJC I/47/6-71. They were also found involved in highway robbery in *pargana* Komhāri, *sarkār* Daulatābād in a Maratha *jāgīr*. [I/47/10-54].
3. IJC I/47/7-90.
4. IJC I/47/8-44.
5. IJC I/48/10-11.
6. IJC I/47/6-36.
7. The Marathas were reported to have entered from Vargi Ghat 12 *kurohs* away from Komhāri and plundered the Imperial dominions. [I/45/1-127].

5 *Shawwal* 49th R.Y. that Saiyidi Aḥmad, deputy of Zainuddin ʻAlī Khān had negotiated with the Marathas [*az duzdān qaul girifta*], surrendered the fort to them and came out with the infantry.[1]

The above incidents make us believe that even Aurangzeb's famous policy of *qila'giri* vs *mulkgiri* was foiled by his own officials, who settled terms for surrendering the forts. Therefore, the ambitious claims made by some officials regarding the conquest of certain forts appear to be exaggerated. Moreover, these were often conditional. Mutmin Khān, *mutaṣaddi* of *Bandar* [Port] Chaul wrote that Tājuddīn ʻAlī, *qila'dār* of Madangarh, who had been his deputy in the *Dīwānī* of Talkokan-i ʻĀdil Khāni, was sent either to conquer the said fort or die in this effort. Moreover, the contingent of ʻAbdur Reḥmān also arrived which circumscribed the Marathas and it was hoped that the fort would be conquered and its *qila'dāri* could be restored to him, as before.[2]

There is no dearth of examples of Maratha marauding activities and the cooperation they sometimes received from the official quarters. However, we are mainly concerned with the attitude of the Mughal Court towards their rebellion and the punitive measures initiated to curb their activities. The administration encouraged the *manṣabdārs* to lead punitive expeditions and granted promotions in rank, enhancement of the *manṣab* and the assignment of conditional *manṣab* and land grants etc.

Uzbek Khān was awarded the rank of 100/50 on the condition of dislodging the Marathas from the frontiers of *sarkār* Fateḥābād etc[3]. Miftāḥ Khān requested that Manak Dona was ten *kurohs* from Aḥmadnagar in the hills and the Marathas lived there. He promised to expel them from there, if he was granted the said area as pay of 100 *ẓāt*.[4] A similar offer was made by ʻAbdul Ghafūr, who pleaded that since a large army was demoralised without any commandar, he could crush the Marathas with half of the army.[5] Ikhlāṣ Khān was sanctioned *jāgīr* and *faujdārī* of *pargana* Neusa for exterminating the Marathas.[6] Likewise Randola Khān received *faujdārī* rights over his *jāgīr* for not allowing notorious Marathas to stay there.[7]

The Marathas also fully benefited from the difficulties encountered by the Mughal officers on account of distance. Muʻtaqid Khān submitted that

1. IJC I/49/4-1.
2. IJC I/51/11-81.
3. IJC I/40/9-10.
4. IJC I/50/6-11.
5. IJC I/43/1-113, I/43/1-114.
6. IJC I/47/1-52 Mohan Singh *qila'dār* of Tirankalwari who served in Bālāghāt, a frontier also received grant of *faujdārī* to curb the Maratha uprising [IJC I/44/11-4].
7. IJC I/45/12-54.

the villages in the environs of Shāhgarh *pargana* Bir, were neglected by the *faujdārs* thereof, due to long distance and the Marathas [*ashqiyā*] engaged in plundering with impunity. He suggested precautionary measures for protecting the said *qaṣba*, so that the news of the arrival of the Marathas could reach there in time.[1]

The Marathas caused great loss of revenues to the Mughal *jāgīrdārs*. Numerous instances have been recorded of the loss in revenues due to which the *jāgīrdārs* invariably demanded *faujdārī* rights over their *jāgīr* for combating the Maratha depredations.[2]

Amānat Khān wrote that last days of *Rajab* 45th R.Y. while the *Kharif* crop due to termination of the *'āmil* and the *karorīs* most of the peasantry ran away except for small numbers while the seeding of *Kharif* crop could not be done in full while now due to the presence of the *muqaddams* the assessment has begun. There is much disturbance in this region. The writer marched five *kurohs* towards the west to beat 1,500 of the Marathas [*firqa-i zalla*] from the order of *parana* Barodara and the villages of Baizapur which has their abode while the cattle seized were delivered to the contingent. The surrounding *faujdars* do not move at all while the deputy of Ikhlas Khān, *faujdar* of Neusa has given it to the Marathas who have buil their adode in it. The village of Khandpur and Neusa are close to each other. Whenever the Marathas are chastlised they in the *pargana* while during their stay they allege that the deputy of Ikhlās Khān on the *faujdāri* of the said Khān is not out in that *pargana* is not suitable. Accordingly Aurangzeb is ordered that 'Let the *faujdārī* of Neusa be given to Amānul Khan. If he want *jāgīr* then it be given elsewhere in Berar and Khāndesh'[3].

Khudāyār Khān stated that he incurred loss in his *jāgīr* due to the raids of Santa as tabulated below:

Ḥāṣil

1097 A.H. according to salary	1105 A.H. according to *Ṭūmār* of Āatish Khān	1106 A.H. [in accordance with Āatish Khān's *Ṭūmār*]
Rs 31,562	Rs 31,548 Loss=Rs 12,300 Remainder = Rs 19,154/8	Rs 31, 248 Loss=Rs 14,101/8 Remainder = Rs 17,147/8[27]

Tarbiyat Khān had the common grievance of not receiving half of the revenues. He was sanctioned Rs 44,041 out of which he could realise

1. IJC I/50/9-11.
2. IJC I/47/10-33, I/48/10-3, I/50/7-9, I/51/12-63.
3. IJC I/45/10-71.

Rs 22,364/5. He had incurred a net loss of Rs 21,676/12 due to Maratha raids.[1] Such circumstances led the *jāgīrdārs* frequently to request abatement in *jama'* and the grant of *taufīr* [addition to their pay].[2]

The kind of activity that was expected of Mughal officials in dealing with the Marathas is illustrated by the commendatory report made about Muḥammad Ibrāhīm, *faujdār* of Kannad [Kanhar]:

> "He undertook regular patrolling in the mountains and killed many [hostiles]. Firstly, he expelled 'Umar Afghan. Subsequently, he caught alive Chāuji at the gate of Wakla on 9 *Zulqada* 41 R.Y. and sent him to Aurangabad to Muḥtashim Khān, the *nāzim.* Meanwhile, the Marathas arrived and he killed some of them. Four Maratha leaders [*nāsardārān*] from amongst them were captured and despatched to Aurangabad to the *nāzim,* he hanged the rest of them on the road to Surat. Then, he sought Gondiya Bhīl and combed the entire valley from Kalili to Rajdhir; spies brought the news that Gondiya had fled the said mountains with some followers. There remained no miscreant in the hills and the administration of Khāndesh was streamlined as the inhabitants submitted an agreement [*rāzīnāma*] regarding the extermination of the miscreants."[3]

Similar expeditions were led by various Mughal officers who made claims of having routed the enemy. One Nasīruddīn Khān, *faujdār* of Devalghat, chastised Sankarā Rām who had plundered certain [revenue free] villages of Shāh Burhānuddīn, killed many of the Marathas and did not pay a single dām as *chauth* to them.[4]

Mughal officers, placed in critical positions sometimes abetted the Marathas. Village Sirki, *pargana* Gulbarga, was attacked by Rāno, Hanwant and Hindu Rāo, Marathas and Yashwant Rāo, *thānadār*, fought against them. The Marathas, however, cornered him, and captured the fort in addition to plunding elephants, horses etc. It was reported that since he became helpless, he sought for mercy through Hanwant Rāo and joined the Marathas. Finally, this news was confirmed.[5]

The inactivity of many Mughal *manṣabdārs* also resulted in the worsening of the situation. We are told that Amānat Khān drove off 1,500 Marathas 15 *kurohs* from *pargana* Kandapur. But, the *faujdārs* of the surrounding areas did not move at all and the deputy of Ikhlāṣ Khān,

1. IJC I/46/6-109, I/48/0-3, I/50/6-17.
2. IJC I/45/4-46, I/47/6-33.
3. IJC I/41/4-15, Chāuji was sent to the court with Uchap his accomplice [IJC 1/41/6-19].
4. IJC I/42/1-34.
5. IJC I/4517-26.

faujdār of Neusa, surrendered the entire *pargana* to the Marathas who resided into the foothills. They slipped into Kandapur and even the *faujdār* came to their assistance.[1]

Our documents are replete with descriptions of military expeditions against the Marathas and the problems created by them, including *Pāibāqī / Khāliṣa.*[2] The Mughal administration was compelled to recognise that a large area had passed under Maratha control by designating it *pāibāqī* i.e. not assignable in *jāgīr.* Thus, when the fort of Rāj Mānji was captured it was marked as *pāibāqī*[3] and a *maḥāl-i ghair 'amli* [non-tax-paying territory] as *pargana* Mandan also fell into the same category.

The most daring bid of the Marathas was the plunder of Imperial treasury and the royal *kārkhānās* while these were being shifted from one place to another.[4] Khān Firūz Jung reported that the treasury and the *kārkhānās* of Prince Muḥammad Kām Bakhsh were being moved to Murtazābād. It was reported by the *harkāras* that Mādhu Rāo and other Marathas numbering 3,000 intercepted them 17 *kurohs* from Murtazābād. He [Mu'tamād Khān] rushed there with Khān [Firūz Jung] killed many of them, seized 200 horses and 500 bullocks.

Some Marathas willing to join the Mughals received extraordinary favours from the Mughal court. The moves initiated from time to time by Aurangzeb to persuade Shivajī, Sambhājī, Sahujī and Rāja Rām to join the imperial service are too well-known to be repeated. Many of the Maratha officers controlled *jāgīrs* without maintaining the contingent on the basis of several years old *dāghnāmas* [branding certificates] and received their salary without inspection of *maujudāt* [present troops], which caused loss to the government. Therefore, orders were issued for transfer of such men.[5]

In view of their changing loyalties, some strict measures were also adopted in assigning or transferring their *jāgīrs.* Aurangzeb granted *jāgīrs* to the wife of Shivajī's brother [in all ten Deccanis and Marathas]. However, they did not maintain the contingents and received the stipulated salary for the *tābīnān* [contingents]. Therefore, their *jāgīrs* were transferred as a remedial measure.[6]

Specific orders were issued banning the grant of *jāgīr* to the Marathas in the 'Old Country' [pre-1686 Mughal Deccan] and until the Muslims

1. IJC I/45/0-77.
2. IJC I/43/4-7, I/43/7-7, I/43/10-6, I/43/11-27, IJC I/44/6-140, I/46/10-9.
3. IJC I/50/12-6.
4. IJC I/46/1-105, Aurangzeb, therefore, condemned to show any leniency to such Marathas [1/46/11-64].
5. IJC I/45/11-127. These branding certificates were 10-12 years old [I/46/3-81].
6. IJC I/0/0-2029.

had any claims [to *jāgīr*] the Marathas [*kāfirs*] should not be assigned the same.[1] However, the *jāgīrs* of old Marathas were not generally transferred probably to save them from any disillusionment.[2] Imperial orders were promulgated denying them assignment of *jāgīrs* in Khāndesh because they created much disturbance there.[3]

Loyal Marathas were looked at with suspicion.[4] Mu'tabir Khān wrote that *pargana* Ankola, which had 10 forts, had been assigned to Satwa Daflea. It was possible that the Marathas might harm the forts in the guise of Satwa Daflea's retainers. He, therefore, should be granted *jāgīr* in a *pargana* having no forts.[5] Since Satwa Daflea's son joined the service of Rama [Rāja Rām] his credentials were not so good. However, he again joined the Imperialists and it was observed that he could be granted *jāgīr* on the other side of the fort of *pargana* Bagwāri, *ṣūba* Bījāpur.[6] Both father and son [Babaji] were allowed to rejoin the Mughal service.[7]

The *jāgīrs* of the Marathas were often transferred owing to such suspicion. Niẓām Rāo wrote that on the representation of Lodi Khān's *wakīl* orders for transfer of his *jāgīr* had been issued in view of his being a Maratha. He pleaded that since Tikona fort was conquered before schedule his *jāgīr* should not be transferred which was acceded to.[8] Niẓām Rāo enjoined some influence at the Mughal Court because we are informed that 18 persons suspected of being in league with the Marathas were released at his surety.[9]

The above constitute illustrative material from the Inayat Jung documents. Obviously, they do not lend themselves to a single consistent interpretation. There were, from the Mughal point of view, loyal as well as disloyal Marathas, territories to protect as well as turbulent areas to sack, a pressure for revenue in a situation of erosion of revenues, in a word, the dilemma of a crisis. It is this critical situation, which our documents portray, along with the varying reactions of many classes that mattered *zamīndārs*, local chieftains, notables and, not the least, the peasantry.

1. IJC I/47/5-54.
2. IJC I/47/5-70.
3. IJC I/47/12-89.
4. Forged letters were written in the names of loyal Marathas and allegations were also made about their matrimonial relation and Babū Pandit and Rūdra *qānūngos* of *ṣūbas* of Hyderabad and Bījāpur were suspected of having secret correspondence with the Marathas, IJC I/43/9-5, IJC I/45/4-21, IJC I/45/7-138.
5. IJC I/147/11-43.
6. IJC I/42/5-17, I/42/7-46.
7. IJC I/42/6-29, *Akhbārāt*, 10 *Zilqada*, 43 RY, 11 *Zilqada*, 43 R.Y.
8. IJC I/47/5-67.
9. IJC I/41/12-38.

[III] Others

As far as the others are concerned their number is large in number. However if we go through the Inayat Jung Collection and other sources than their number can be taken into active consideration because so far we have restricted our treatment to those *zamīndārs* who survived within the territories under the direct Imperial administration. But he had certain lines which he had in common with men of greater power, with chiefs, and kinglets, the so called *rājas, rānās, rāos, rāwats* etc. Fortunately, like them, he held some territory which could be designated his own, like them he was no creature, generally, of the Imperial government; and like them he had armed retainers to defend his possessions as occasionally lines between the two could not be rigidly drawn. Normally we encounter a person calling himself a *rāja* selling his right to a village like any other *zamīndār*. In the Deccan a *deshmukh* [equivalent to North Indian *chaudhurī*] could develop into a chief as happened in case of Chananeri *Deshmukh*, Chief of Indor in Telangana, [referred to in the A'in, I, 477] as one of the chiefs of Indor.[1] The descendents of a powerful chief might be curtailed into *deshmukhs* as happened to the descendent of Ūdājī Rām the chief of Mahur.[2]

Abū-l Faẓl does not speak of any contemporary Indian ruler as "king, but generally as *marzbān*, "chief over a territory" as the Mughals insisted on calling "'Ādil Shāh", 'Ādil Khān, and Quṭb Shāh "*Quṭbul* Mulk". From Akbar's time onwards both of them were styled *duniyadaran*, [men of the world suggesting them as only glorified *zamīndārs* who had not firm in faith, being worldly men].

Interestingly enough the Imperial territories in the provinces of Malwa and Sorath [Saurashtra] in Gujarat were ringed by a belt of states which included in the South the chieftaincy of Baglana, which was annexed in 1638 to the Mughal Empire. Moreover there was a large block of states down to Indor in Telangana. From the available records of Shāh Jahān's reign we can judge that western Berar, Khāndesh and Aurangābād provinces did not contain any large or significant tributary states.

1. The financial obligations of his decendents, all called Chananeri *Deshmukhs* constitute the subject of a letter from Aurangzeb when he was viceroy of the Deccan during his second Viceroyalty. *Ādāb-i 'Ālamgīrī,* Vol. I, pp. 630-9.
2. *Maāsiru-l Umarā* I, 42-45.

IX

The Question of *Jāgīr* Crisis

[I] *Pāibāqī* and *Khālişa*

Pāibāqī:

Interestingly enough the *pāibāqī* comprising the lands earmarked for re-assignment to *jāgīrdars*, was fundamentally a part of the *khālişa*, though for administrative convenience was kept a separate charge as its administration follow the same pattern as that of the *khālişa*. Fortunately the same three principal officials, *amīn*, *karorī* and *foṭadār*, were appointed and the regulations of the *khālişa* were followed in preparing all records and accounts. Furthermore, the entire administration of the *pāibāqī* was under the control of the central *diwan-i khālişa*. Fortunately areas due for assignment, but not yet assigned in *jāgīr*, were called *pāibāqī* because *pāibāqī* is an accountant's word for the balance at the bottom of the account. Accordingly from this, apparently, it derived the peculiar sense of territory held in reserve for assignment defined in an administrative manual of "a *jāgīr*", which has been taken from a person and whose revenues; till its assignment to another person are appropriated by the Imperial government.[1]

Khālişa

We are given to understand that in the last years of Shāh Jahān a reform was introduced in the revenue administration of the Deccan, the change-over to crop-sharing was enforced not only in the *khālişa*, but also in the assignment of *jāgīrdārs*.[2] Surprisingly no *khālişa* figures are provided for the six Deccan provinces; but there exists a summary statement of the assignment in the 19 *sarkārs* of the Karnataka [*şūba* Ḥaiderabad] in 1706

1. *Khulāştus Siyāq*, f. 89 [a]-90 [a]; Or 2026, f. 51 [a]-52 [b]. See *Waqāi' Ajmer*, 74, 375-6, *Akhbārāt-i Durbār Mua'lla* 47/107, *Dastūru-l 'Amal-i Āgahi*, f. 31[a], and Ma'mūri, ff. 156[b]-157[a], 182 [b], and Khāfi Khān, Add. 6574, f. 107[a], Bib. Ind. ed. II 396-7 for use of term in this sense.
2. *'Ādāb-i 'Ālamgīrī*, f. 118 [a], [letter not published in the printed text].

[*Selected Documents of Aurangzeb's Reign*, 233-35]. This does naturally show that the *Khālisa Sharīfa* accounted for just 6.3% of the total *jama' kāmil*, and the *pāibāqī*, after deducting the share of the *Pālīgārs*, accounted for another 4.2%. So in this area, *khālisa* was by no means much extensive. Fortunately in the early years of Aurangzeb [1667-8] its *jama'* rose to almost one-fifth of total empire[1] for this up to the 10th R.Y.

There was the scarcity of *pāibāqī* and the crowds of men claiming pay, in Aurangzeb's words, who declares that everything, "flesh and bones had been assigned and no further demand could be entertained by the court".

In accordance with the standard formula employed in the assignment orders, the *chaudhurīs* [or *deshmukhs*], the *qānūngos* [or *deshpāndiās*] and *muqaddams* [or *patels*] and the peasants and cultivators were answerable also for the whole of the *māl-i wājib* [revenue] and *huqūq-i Dīwānī* [fiscal demands].[2]

Moreover, it seems to have been an accepted policy to keep for the *khālisa* the most fertile and conveniently administered territories.[3] Furthermore, certain *parganas* were, therefore, kept almost permanently attached to it. Since the extent of the *khālisa* differed from time to time in 1574-5. Akbar brought the whole of his Empire, with the exception of Bengal, Bihar and Gujarat, under the *khālisa* for five years which however again reached to one-fifth in 10th R.Y. of Aurangzeb [1667-68 A.D.]. Under Shāh Jahān it was nearly one-seventh by the 20th year [1646-47].

The statistical tables of data belonged from 1701-02. Though no *Khālisa* figures are provided in these tables for the six Deccan provinces, but there exists summary statement of the assignments in 19 *sarkārs* of Karnatak *sūba* Haiderabad in 1705-6.[4]

We are given to understand that in the late years of Shāh Jahān a reform was introduced in the revenue system of the *Khālisa*, as well as in the assignments of *jāgīrdārs*.[5] Moreover we find detailed information in respect of officials of *Khālisa*.[6]

---

1. *Miratu-l 'Ālam*, Add. 7657, f. 445[b].
2. See Harkaran, 53, 54. *Selected Documents of Aurangzeb's Reign*, 4, 5, 17, 18, 21, 23, 147, 151, 158, 171, 175-6; *Nigārnāma Munshī*, ed. 91-2, Aurangzeb's *farmān*, 37th RY, in *Nāma-i Muzaffarī*, I, 288. The state tax and other documents are classified into *māl-o-jihāt* [land tax and related taxes] and *sāir-jihāt* [transit and other taxes].
3. *Khulasatus Siyāq*; 89 [a-b], or 2026, ff. 51 [a-b], *Waqāi 'Ajmer*, 35-6.
4. This naturally shows that the *Khālisa Sharīfa* accounted for first 6.3% of the total *jama' kāmil*, and the *paibaqi*, after deducting the share of *Pālīgārs*, accounted for another 4.2%. Thus in this area, too, the *Khālisa Sharīfa* was by no means extensive.
5. This is found in *'Ādāb-i 'Ālamgīrī*, f. 118 [a], letter not published in printed text.
6. See Irfan Habib, *Agrarian System*, Delhi 2014, pp. 318.24.

[II] Income from *Jāgīr* Assignments

The Inayat Jung Collection[1] in the National Archives, New Delhi, contains a large number of documents from Aurangzeb's reign which throw much light on the problems of Mughal administration in the Deccan. These also tell us how the Mughal administrative system functioned in the Deccan. The core of this system may be said to be the mode of assignment of *jāgīr* or territorial revenue-charges.

At the time of the assignment of *jāgīr* care was taken for so limiting it that the *jama'dāmi* [or *jama' raqamī*] fixed on it in the Imperial registers equalled the net pay claim due to the assignee. Where it seemed that the *jama'* had been understated [where, i.e., the *jāgīr* would be *sair ḥāṣil*,bearing high ratio of revenue-income to *jama'*, in this case the territory was 8-monthly] the *jama' raqmī* was ordered to be increased. Orders were enforced by increasing the *dāms* according to the *māhwār* [ratio of *ḥāṣil* to *jama'* in terms of months of the year] of the *manṣabdārs*,who were on the 5 and 6 monthly scales. It is stated that "in the Deccan provinces it is customary that the *jama'* is increased or diminished according to the *māhwār* of the person concerned [assignee], but there cannot be any pay above the 12 monthly scale".[2]

Another document shows that some *jāgīrs* of princes [e.g., Kām Bakhsh in this case] and high nobles [Asad Khān] could be treated as "12 monthly" and the *jama'*,fixed accordingly.[3]

In the Deccan *manṣabdārs* with ordinary [*barāwardi*] ranks [or rather in respect of pay claims on ordinary *sawār* ranks] were placed on a '6-monthly' scale. This had been reduced to "5-monthly"; but on a plea of Saiyid Ḥasan Khān, Governor of *ṣūba* Muḥammadabad [Bidar], the "6-monthly" scale was restored in his case.[4] Likewise, the *manṣabdārs* serving under Prince Muḥammad Mua'zzam and Faẓāil Khān were granted five-monthly *jāgīrs* in the Deccan. However, some of them obtained six-monthly *jāgīrs* under the seal of the Imperial *bakhshīs* [*bakhshiyān-i 'uzzām*].[5]

1. National Archives of India, New Delhi. Thus in IJC, I/47/11-43, 'I' indicates Aurangzeb, '47' the 47th regnal year, 'II' the 11th regnal month, and '43', serial No. 43 among documents belonging to the particular month. Documents from this collection are cited by the abbreviation IJC, followed by the serial number assigned by the National Archives.
2. IJC, I/47/12-16.
3. IJC, I/37/1-4.
4. IJC, I/40/10-28.
5. IJC, I/45/1-183.

As the salary was stated in terms of month scales [*māhwār*] the *bakhshīs* did not check the cavalry without the fixation of *māhwār.*[1]

The *jama'* of the *jāgīrs* were generally subject either to deduction [*takhfīf*] or increase [*izāfa*] and certain rules were formulated for the purpose. It was proclaimed by the Emperor that the newly appointed *manṣabdārs* should obtain *jāgīr* with the abatements of '10-20' as usual, otherwise they will be dismissed. But this did not solve the problem because no one was ready to accept it on account of its being *ghair' amli.* Therefore, fresh orders were issued that the grant of *manṣab* of 80 may be made from old *pāibāqī* but from 100 to 150 half each from the *pāibāqī* of the old and new [country] may be granted.[2]

Jama' could be reduced or increased but there were some routine limits to reduction. The reduction could be granted generally '10-15' but no more than '10-20' and if more than that was required it had to be submitted to the royal perusal. Muhṭashim Khān represented that he had been assigned *jāgīr* in *pargana* Mahindri, *sarkār* Naldurg apparently with a reduction in *jama'* of 'ten-to-twenty', i.e., by 50% to accord with his high month-scale. But the 'clerks of the office' did not issue the certificate [*sanad*] on the ground that a reduction of more than 'ten-to-fifteen, i.e., by 33.3%, was not permissible. He, therefore, solicited special Imperial dispensation. The following actual figures are furnished:

Total *jama' ḥāṣil* 51,50,000 [*dāms*][3]

ḥāṣil 49,583 [rupees]

Reduction according to *māhwār* 25,50,000 [*dāms*]

Reduction as per '10-15' rule 17,00,000 [*dāms*]

Excess over '10-15' reduction 8,50,000 [*dāms*]

The *jama'* fixed on his *jāgīr* according to '10-15' rule. 34,00,000 [*dāms*][4]

It was also ordained that no more abatement could be given after abatement [*takhfīf dar takhfīf*].[5] If *ḥal-i ḥāṣil* was equal to *māhwār* it was given without reduction.[6] It was also not must that reduction was given to everyone. Yaḥya Khān, *faujdār* and *amīn* of Mangal [Baidyā] requested [through his *wakīl*] that *pargana* Sawai assigned to him was previously held

1. IJC, I/45/1-135.
2. IJC, I/50/2-4.
3. This figure has been recorded as 59,50,000 *dāms* in the original document, but this is apparently a transcriptional mistake because this does not conform to other details [as per the rules discussed above].
4. IJC, I/45/4-26.
5. IJC, I/44/2-2.
6. IJC, I/45/5-73.

by K͟huda Banda K͟hān, Multafat K͟hān and Neknām K͟hān with abatements so he should also be granted the same *takhfif* [reduction in *jama'*]. But his request was turned down.[1] It was ordered that Firuz Jung may be granted 8-10 monthly *jāgīr* in lieu of the *naqdī jāgīr* and no abatement should be given.[2]

The actual *jama'dāmi* of *pargana* Ankot was one crore *dāms* when it was held by Aurangzeb during his Fisrt Viceroyalty [1635-1644 A.D.] but with the passage of time it rose to 1,52,55,000 *dāms* in his 42nd R.Y. He issued orders that the abatement of 20 lakh could be given but not more than that.[3]

If anyone's *jāgīr* was transferred, he could not be placed on a month-scale double his previous one.[4] If anyone surrendered his *jāgīr*, he was to be granted *jāgīr* elsewhere according to his original *māhwār*, but if he was transferred by the Imperial Government on its own, he received the new *jāgīr* on the previous ratio of its *ḥāṣil* [to *jama'*].[5] If anyone realised revenue [*ḥāṣil*] in his *jāgīr* by his own endeavour beyond the *ḥāṣil* fixed by his month-scale, it was to be left with him so long as it did not exceed '10-months', otherwise resumed.[6]

The *jāgīrdārs* were subjected to certain deductions under items like the *muṭāliba, taṣarruf, chaharrum-ḥiṣṣa, muḥāsiba-i-jāgīrdārī*, etc The documents contain an interesting exchange between two officials recorded on 16 *Shawwal,* 42nd R.Y. of Aurangzeb, regarding the implementation of such deductions:

> "From the reports of the *kachehri,* it has been conveyed to His Majesty that Arshad K͟hān told Mihr Chand that when the Imperial claims upon the *jama'dāmi* ["*dāms*"] have to be realised on account of *taṣarruf* [recovery] of wrongful appropriation by *jāgīrdār* and *muṭāliba* [Imperial claims],the territory to be resumed should be good-and-bad ['meat-and-bone'] and not simply the territory [*maḥāl*] that the *manṣabdār* of his own wishes to part with. Mihr Chand replied that Diyānat K͟hān had so fixed that one may accept whatever the *manṣabdār* surrendered. Arshad K͟hān [however] maintained that it is

1. *Ibid,* We are told that a new incumbent sought on three occasions assignment with abatement of land previously held by Siyam Raj without any *tak͟hfīf*. It was ordered that if he submits again without demanding the abatement, the request may be acceded. [IJC, I/0/0-499].
2. IJC, I/46/12-49 & IJC, I/0/0-707.
3. IJC, I/42/1-124.
4. IJC, I/39/3-9.
5. IJC, I/40/11-31 & IJC, I/45/5-138.
6. IJC, I/42/10-138& IJC, I/45/5-138.

proper that good-and-bad should be taken [and not the bad territory only]. His Majesty has ordered that good-and-bad ['meat and bone'] should be taken".[1]

The transfer of *jāgīr* was an essential feature of the *manṣabdārī / jāgīrdārī* systems, it was fairly rigorously enforced in the Deccan as well. However, *jāgīrdārs* who had entrenched themselves in particular regions did not like their transfer. They were only interested in transfers when either the land assignment was not *sai'r-ḥāṣil* or he could not realise the revenues or the *jāgīr* was scattered.[2] Transfers, however, did not come smoothly. One officer Muḥammad Muqīm complained to the court that he surrendered his earlier waste [*kharāba*] *jāgīr*, but could not take charge of the new one in Jawar, *sarkār* Pathri, because Muḥammad Taqī, *faujdār* of that area expelled his men and seized the revenues.[3]

Sometimes, as a favour and for other reasons, particular *jāgīrs* were exempted from transfer. Aurangzeb issued orders for retaining the old *jāgīr* of Muḥammad Jawān Bakht who had accompanied Prince Muḥammad Mu'azzam with the remark that "transfer of *jāgīr* is the cause of ruin of the *jāgīrdār* and the peasantry [*ri'āya*] and should be avoided, so far as possible".[4] In another document, a *jāgīr* in *pargana* Asīrgarh was restored after its transfer, on the ground that the assignee had held it for 17 years, and a transfer would cause him distress. In the same document it is also observed that "Transfers should not be made 'without need,' or they should be fewer, two or three times… [illegible]. The peasants are ruined and there are short-sighted expectant ones who repeatedly petition for transfers".[5] Sometimes the transfers of the *jāgīrdārs* were sought by other *manṣabdārs* in their own interest. The transfer orders were also solicited due to certain grievances. A complaint was made by 'Amber *Dārogha* of *baghāt-i-Ḥyderabad,* against the encroachment by 'Ālam and Mīran, *manṣabdārs,* upon the lands of the gardeners and the Imperial gardens adjacent to their *jāgīrs.* Orders were issued for the transfer of their *jāgīr* villages into the *khāliṣa* in the charge of 'Amber on the condition of realising maximum *jama'* [*jama'-kāmil*].[6]

Previously the position of the excessive expenditure and the complaints of the demand holders of *suba Khjista buniyad* [Aurangabad]

1. IJC, I/42/3-27.
2. Ḥāziq Khān wanted transfer of his *sai'r-ḥāṣil jāgīr* as it was granted in six-*maḥāls*, while he wanted *jāgīr* in a single *maḥāl*. [IJC, I/46/7-21A].
3. IJC, I/26/0-11.
4. IJC, I/45/5-63.
5. IJC, I/45/7-9.
6. IJC, I/38/9-10.

was represented to His Majesty. It was ordered that the *mahsul* [revenue] of Aindur and Yamkal and the treasury of Berar with the *peshkash* of Chānda etc *suba* Khandesh as per the former practice would have been coming in the treasury of Aurangabad. Since the *mutasaddis* of *khaliṣa*, most often draw the salary from the revenue of Zafarabad [Bidar], Berar and Khāndesh which after the aforesaid expenses does not suffice so as to reach at Auragabad and suffice the expanses thereof. Meanwhile one piece of *parwana* comprising Rs 30,000 of the total demand of the Mavaliya infantry accompanied with Abdul Karim and secondly in regard to the cost of 200 camels which the *buyūtat-i sūba* do purchase are received in the name of the *Khānazad* and similarly other *parwānas* for other unfixed expenses are always paid from the said treasury. In view of the fact that amount is not available in the treasury or the *naib* Diwan does face the extremely from demand holders. Previously the unspecified expenses from His Majesty were paid from the treasury of Aurangabad were paid from the treasury amount of North India. What are the orders in the matter. Aurangzeb ordered them it, should now be extracted from the treasury of North India etc as this amount should be expeditiously given"[1].

The peasantry of *qaṣba* Tirambak, *sarkār* Sangamner, protested against the atrocities of Sulaiman Beg, *qila'dār* and *jāgīrdār* of the said *qaṣba*, like exaction of Rs 4000 from the peasantry [*ri'āya*], unlawful detention and the murder of a Brahmin and demanded that either the said *qaṣba* should be transferred to another *qila'* of that *ta'alluqa* or they be permitted to reside elsewhere.[2] Some of the *jāgīrdārs* were that transferred without any fault on their part. Aḥmad Khān, *qila'dār* of Miftāḥul Futūḥ resigned in protest against the unjust [*be-taqṣīr*] transfer of his conditional *jāgīr*. However, his *jāgīr* was restored subsequently.[3] If anyone's *jāgīr* was transferred but the new assignee could obtain the *parwāna*, the orders for the restoration of the *jāgīr* of the former *jāgīrdār* were issued, so that it remained in his [former *jāgīrdār's*] possession.[4]

It was common that the majority of the *faujdārs* and *thānadārs* obtained *jāgīrs* on the submission of undertaking [*muchalka*] for procuring the *parwāna-i-sibti*, but they did not submit the same. It was, not therefore, ordered, that their *jāgīrs* should be resumed [contrary to the practice in north India].[5] However, it was necessary to obtain orders for transfering

1. IJC I/46/10-65.
2. IJC, I/46/8-33.
3. IJC, I/46/1-86.
4. IJC, I/42/2-54.
5. IJC, I/46/12-180.

jāgīr in lieu of the *muṭāliba* due from the [*ahl-i-khidmat*].[1] Likewise, many of the Marathas occupied *jāgīrs* without the contingents [*jami' at*] on the strength of several years old *dāghnāmās*, hence, orders were issued for their transfer.[2]

It is also interesting to note that many of the *manṣabdārs* took advantage of the activities of the Marathas. A *manṣabdār* who possessed no *jāgīr* complained that a *jāgīr* held by Māyājī in *pargana* Komhari, *sarkār* Daulatabad, had become the abode of thieves who committed highway robbery there. He, therefore, requested the transfer of the *jāgīr* in his favour which was acceded to.[3] Achla son-in-law of Shivajī was transferred from *pargana* Partur on the charge of providing shelter to robbers and inciting them to commit robbery.[4]

Transfer orders were obtained for Satwa, a Maratha, who held a *jāgīr* in *pargana* Ankola with ten *qila's* to *maḥāl-i-ghair-'amlī* [*maḥāls* not paying revenue] in the *pāibāqī* [unassigned *maḥāls*] on the pretext that the infidels [Marathas] may raid the fort in the guise of his Maratha retainers [*naukarān*].[5]

Mahābat Jung *sawāniḥ-nigār* of *sarkārs* Firuzgarh and Muzaffarnagar reported that village Basantpur, *pargana* Firuzgarh was held in assignment by Kanhuji Maratha and as the Marathas have been ordered to be granted assignment in *mulk-i-jadīd*, he petitioned that the said village should be granted to Muftakhar Khān with prescribed abatement [of the *jama'*].[6]

Since the Deccanis were not allowed to hold *jāgīrs* in Khāndesh, Fazlullāh succeeded in getting back his *jāgīr* in *pargana* Bir which was transferred inadvertently to Bharji.[7]

The exchange or transfer of some portions of *jāgīrs* could, sometimes, be done by mutual agreement among the *jāgīrdārs*.[8] But this, of course, had to be put into writing for official use. Sometimes again, transfer of a particular village was sought to eliminate confusion from a 'mixed' *jāgīr* [i.e. where the *jāgīrs* of two officials were found intermixed].[9] If a *manṣabdār* held *jāgīr* in a distant area he tried to surrender it in favour of

1. IJC, I/42/10-138.
2. IJC, I/45/1-127.
3. IJC, I/47/10-54.
4. IJC, I/50/3-11.
5. IJC, I/47/11-43.
6. IJC, I/50/1-1.
7. IJC, I/46/9-28.
8. IJC, I/45/1-39 & IJC, I/45/1-41.
9. IJC, I/45/1-60.

another adjacent *jāgīr.* Shihabuddin who was posted in Deccan held *jāgīr* in Punjab which he surrendered on the ground of delay in receipt of *hundis* [bills] therefrom.[1]

Many of the *jāgīrdārs* were unable to maintain the requisite contingents so their *jāgīrs* were transferred.[2] A general order seems to have been issued that Hindu *manṣabdārs* were not to be given *jāgīrs* relinquished by the Muslims,[3] but, if necessary, assigned *jāgīrs* out of *pāibāqī.* But our own documents contain an exception; though there the transfer was cancelled.[4]

The *pāibāqī* constituted the reserve territory from which *jāgīrs* could be assigned. So long as fair, revenue-yielding lands were available in *pāibāqī,* the *jāgīr* system could function fairly smoothly. But during the later years of Aurangzeb there seem to have been developed a severe restriction of *pāibāqī* in many regions of the Deccan and the Inayat Jung Collection is replete with complaints of non-availability of suitable *pāibāqī.* It may be recalled that J.F. Richards has argued that there was an abundance of *pāibāqī* lands in the *ṣūbās* of the Deccan, but in this argument he seems to over-look the kind of *pāibāqī* lands that were available; though on the basis of his 'discovery' he has contested the theory of the 'crisis in *jāgīr*'.[5]Apparently, he builds up his theory on the basis of such statements as there is much *pāibāqī* land in the *ṣūbās,*[6]or 'there is abundance of *pāibāqī* land in *ṣūba* Bijapur which has neither been granted to anyone nor anything has been realised by the government, so the *pāibāqī* should be cared for:[7] But the real issue was that these *pāibāqī* territories existed more or less in theory only, being often territories not yet fully subjugated with little prospect of revenue collection, so that *manṣabdārs* could not be brought to accept them in *jāgīr.* The *manṣabdārs* were always anxious to acquire *sai'r-ḥāṣil jāgīrs.* Aurangzeb in view of this issued orders that due to holding of *manṣab* undue desires could not be fulfilled. They may

1. IJC, I/44/10-90. An interesting situation arose when Mu'taqid Khān, *nāzim* of Burhanpur was dismissed and Ṣadruddin was appointed in his place. According to the rule, the *jāgīr* of the previous *manṣabdar* was resumed from the date of issue of the order and the conditional rank attached to *ṣūbadāri* continued for the duration of the performance of the duties of the said office. Accordingly, Mu'taqid Khān's *wakīl* requested that said office should remain with him till the new incumbent assumed his duties and the *jāgīr* for the *ẓāt* and *sawār* rank should also be retained till that date. [IJC, I/44/10-117].
2. IJC, I/46/11-4.
3. IJC, I/44/6-9.
4. IJC, I/51/11-82.
5. J.F. Richards, *Mughal Administration in Golconda,* Oxford, 1975, p. 158.
6. IJC, I/42/6-30 & IJC, I/46/6-60.
7. IJC, I/47/7-73.

be granted in *pāibāqī* of old and new country with necessary abatements [in *jama'*][1].

We find many reports, complaints, petitions, indicating since the *pāibāqī* lands were more or less low revenue yielding [*kam-ḥāṣil*], the assignee did not show willingness to accept *pāibāqī* in Deccan even with abatement.[2] Therefore, sometimes, a mixed grant [from *k͟hāliṣa* and *pāibāqī*] was made; the *k͟hāliṣa* territory being usually high revenue-yielding. The newly recruited Deccanis were ordered for the grant of *jāgīr* from the *pāibāqī* of *mulk-i jadīd* with abatement or as *inā'm* and not from the *mulk-i qadīm*. They generally held assignment for *ẓāt* in *mulk-i qadīm* [Old country] while for that of *sawār* in *mulk-i-jadīd* [newly Conquered Territory] and some of them also succeeded in getting salary for contingents in *mulk-i qadīm*. They were also not ready to accept salary from *mulk-i jadīd* in lieu of *mulk-i qadīm*.[3]

This was, of course, due to the paucity of revenues in *pāibāqī* of *mulk-i jadīd*. Transfer from *mulk-i qadīm* was not accepted easily. Not a single dām could be realised from some of the *maḥāls* which were included in *pāibāqī*.[4] The crisis in *jāgīr* in the Deccan had become so acute that in *ṣūbās* of Bijapur and Hyderabad though there was a theoritical abundance of *pāibāqī* the *manṣabdārs* were not ready to accept assignment on the basis of original *jama'* as it was *kam-ḥāṣil*. Therefore, orders were issued that they should be granted from the *pāibāqī* of the subjugated Old Country [*mulk-i qadīm-i ' amlī*] or from the *k͟hāliṣa-i g͟hair-muqarrarī* [land not permanently reserved for *K͟hāliṣa*?].[5]

The grant of *jāgīr* from the *g͟hair- 'amlī* territory was constantly declined.[6] In order to induce acceptance the Emperor even granted exemption from the '1/4th Part'- Deduction in some areas.[7] A petition of K͟hān 'Alam's *wakīl* states that Bak͟ht Buland collected Rs 31,000 from *pargana* Nandgaon and posted his supporters at Malkapur and Mehkar. Therefore his client was disturbed on account of non-payment of *tank͟hwah* and ruin [*k͟harāba*] of his *jāgīr*. Hence, orders were issued for grant of *jāgīr* from *k͟hāliṣa-i g͟hair-muqarrarī*, or *pāibāqī* within the Old Country; but even neither kind of lands was available.[8]

1. IJC, I/42/1-69.
2. IJC, I/45/11-47.
3. *ibid.*
4. IJC, I/0/0-505.
5. IJC, I/42/8-115 & IJC, I/0/0-486.
6. IJC, I/42/3-35.
7. IJC, I/0/0-597.
8. IJC, I/42/10-36.

The *manṣabdārs* appointed on the recommendations of Firūz Jung and Nuṣrat Jung could only be granted *jāgīrs* from the ghair- *'amlī* land *of mulk-i jadīd.*[1]

Moreover, many of the *manṣabdārs* whose *jāgīrs* were transferred were unable to get *jāgīrs* anywhere due to the non-availability of suitable *pāibāqī* land.[2] Saiyid Ḥaidar and Saiyid Mīrān, *manṣabdārs* petitioned that they had got their horses branded two years earlier, but without the *jāgīr* for their *sawār* rank [*tabīnān*] they were in debt, so they requested grant of *pāibāqī* made available by Shakir Khān's transfer.[3] The old horses of Badiuzzamān died because he had been assigned no *jāgīrs* [*be-jāgīri*].[4] The crisis was so deep-rooted that Mīr Muḥammad did not occupy his *jāgīr* and his contingents attacked his son to press their demand for salary. He, therefore, requested immediate grant of *jāgīr,* otherwise he would be killed.[5] This problem of *be-jāgīrī* was so acute that many of the assignees complained about it.[6]

Due to the scarcity of *pāibāqī,* care was taken that no land should remain *pāibāqī*, instead it should be assigned to the Deccanis or the *qila'dārs* and *thānadārs* of the area.[7]

In contrast, Richards believes that there was much *pāibāqī* land and even the *jāgīrdārs* had a right to refuse assignments of their disliking. In support of this assumption he cites a document[8] from Inayat Jung Collection. The document under reference states that despite the abatements on the scale of '10-15' or '10-20' no one was willing [*raghbat*] to accept assignment from the *pāibāqī.* This shows that a *manṣabdār* could complain against the assignment of any territory which was not likely to give him much net income. But he could not refuse the grant as such. He could, however, explain his problems in order to convince the Emperor.[9] But refusal might mean that one could be deprieved from holding any assignment for ever. Moreover, we find numerous examples of how the *manṣabdārs* kept an eye on the *pāibāqī* land, and got it alloted. The *wakīls* of Anil Singh Bajgoti, *qila'dār* and *faujdār* of Lohgarh, Ibrāhīm, *faujdār* of Kanehar and 'Abdul Karīm sought the assignment of land in *pargana* Dhanda which

1. IJC, I/48/2-1 & IJC, I/48/12-3.
2. IJC, I/47/7-124.
3. IJC, I/42/12-104.
4. IJC, I/45/4-91.
5. IJC, I/46/11-36.
6. IJC, I/45/1-18 & IJC, I/46/6-9.
7. IJC, I/41/6-59.
8. J.F. Richards; *Mughal Administration in Golcunda,* p. 202.
9. IJC, I/46/12-178.

had become *pāibāqī* due to the transfer of Abū Tūrab.[1] Such heavy pressure was there on the *pāibāqī* that the same area might be demanded by three *manṣabdārs* simultaneously; the *jāgīr* was granted in proportion to their claims [the actual amount held in *jāgīr* by Abu Turab is not mentioned].[2]

A *manṣabdār* petitioned that he had been assigned *jāgīr* from the *pāibāqī* of *ṣūba* Muḥmmadabad [Bidar], but since the *pāibāqī* in the said *ṣūba* was so much waste [*kharāba*] that no one was willing to accept it. There was alleged to be no land in *pāibāqī* left except wasteland.[3]

It is, therefore, clear that [A] there was a shortage of real *pāibāqī* in the Deccan, i.e., reserved territory out of which *jāgīrs* could be assigned; and [B] such *pāibāqī* as there really was available contained so much unsubjugated and low revenue-yielding territory that it was *pāibāqī* only in name; in other words, it was practically unassignable.

We are given to understand that J.F. Richards in his important book *Mughal Administration in Golconda,* Oxford, 1975, pp. 158, 160, 161, 308-9; argues that the theory of *jāgīr*-crisis had been greatly overstated with regard to the Deccan, and especially *ṣūba* of Golcunda/ Ḥaiderabad. He particularly based his case on a document from the Inayat Jung Collection, which showed that after annexation there was a large area of *pāibāqī* [land held by treasury but assignable in *jāgīr*] available in the province of Golkunda, and since this could have been given away in *jāgīrs,* if-there was really, a pressure for them, no such pressure in fact existed.

When the representation of Abdul Muhammad etc sons of the late Abdur Rasul Khan then Aurangzeb critically commented that. If there does not occur clear discrepancy than the meat be given to them and bones without meat be assigned to other is easy otherwise not whereas the *faujdari* [military] command and be given to the major party *jagirdars* who is having *jagir* from 28 villages listed market because still he does stipulate the assignment from the good and bad *jagir* as given while the reminder be given to Abdul Muhammad[4].

When it was represented by the *Wakil* of Ishaq etc *jāgirdārs* of Gulshanabad that during the term of administration of the late Murshid Quli Khan no income could be made due to it. It was however ordered by Aurangzeb, "Let it be represented in detail, give in accordance to his

1. IJC, I/36/2-7.
2. IJC, I/41/4-12, IJC, I/41/4-13 & IJC, I/41/4-14.
3. IJC, I/38/10-13.
4. IJC I/45/12-132.

demand and not to transfer Ranjini except for reducing as it would be restored[1].

When Dostam Baig S/o Uzbek Khān which was inadvertantly handed over to Mutaqid Khān, then Aurangzeb ordered that the matter was not properly understood, Dostam and Muḥsin should represent it to the *Bakhshī*[2].

Muhammad Momin made a representation in regard to the assignment of *jāgir* to the writer who due to excess expenditure and the tribe and expenses of the victorious contingent he is yearning for original and additional *jagir* which may be granted owing to transfer of Muhammad Murad from *pargana* Nasirabad. Accordingly Aurangzeb ordered Mutamād Khan to hand over all the demand including in Adilabad from the *Khaliṣa* and required villages.

There was shortage of *jagir* while Aurangzeb commented that the *āwarja* be intentionally sent as the claiments are much in this *maḥāl* it should be given with original *jama*'[3].

Though Aurangzeb accepted *jāgir* for Rs 48,601 for the whole year in lieu of cash he ordered that 'Let it be given from the *pāibāqī* of *pargana* [Pandiya Bedgaon] and *sarkar* Junnar yet exchange and recompensation is not possible as all are busy in official assignments it is not possible as he is sitting in the fort:

> Though Ankot and Ashti were fixed as the stipulated *Khaliṣa* used it was ordered that let it be given from Ramgir with abatement if the *pāibāqī* is there then it should be sent otherwise[4]. When Aurangzeb ordered that 'Let the *taujih* of Murtaza Khān, his sons and brothers be sent as no share in *Khaliṣa* is possible they should be given the *mahāl* in entirety[5].

When Ḥasan Ali Khān from the army of Khān Firoz Jung arrived for the work in *jagir* etc in the Imperial presence as all the *jagirdars* and *sawars* have received Rs 4,000 while assignment to some other *mutasaddis* was ordered from the *pāibāqī* which become less while the remainder of the *paibaqi* is under. Accordingly *jagir* specially of the *zat* be given from *mulk-i qadim* which was allotted by Aurangzeb[6].

---

1. IJC I/45/12-131.
2. IJC I/45/12-130.
3. IJC I/45/12-128.
   IJC I/45/12-113.
4. IJC I/45/12-108.
5. IJC I/45/12-102.
6. IJC I/45/12-18.

What Richards seems to have overlooked is that the *manṣabdārs* wanted income; they had little use for areas formally claimed, but really *g͟hair ʻamlī* [not under administration] from which little revenue could be hoped to be obtained.

I accordingly present below excerpts from some documents from the Inayat Jung Collection [IJC], which might be taken to indicate the actual situation.

IJC, I/41/8-102; "Note from the *Daftar-i K͟hāliṣa:* letter from Brindaban [*amīn* of *K͟hāliṣa*, Ḥaidarabad] received to the effect that some of the *maḥāls* of the *K͟hāliṣa* in *sarkār* Medak have been assigned to *jāgīrdārs,* but these produce surplus revenues [*sair-ḥāṣil*]. These should not be assigned to *jāgīrdārs.* In *pāibāqī* of this *ṣūba,* there is great deficit in the *jama' tank͟hwāhi* [officially assumed income], let these be assigned in *jāgīr* with a small reduction in *jama*'." Dated 10 *Jumāda*, I 41 R.Y.

IJC I/48/2-1: "Paper [*fard*] received with seal of Muḥammad Ik͟hlāṣ. It had been ordered on the proposals of K͟hān Firūz Jung and K͟hān Bahādur Nuṣrat Jung, that in the Deccan, the *tank͟hwāh* [*jāgīrs*] should be assigned in the New Territory is still not administered [*mulk-i jadīd-i g͟hair ʻamlī*]. But a set of persons who are K͟hānazāds [old nobility] or Deccanis whose fathers were in service have been newly appointed. What are the orders about them. 'Ināyatullāh secretary, wrote on it: let it be recorded in the *Wāqi'a kachehri.* The Emperor ordered thereupon: the same orders [as for others] issued on 3 *Zihijj* 48 R.Y." Dated 4 *Zihijj* 48 R.Y.

IJC I/49/6-4:"Imperial order has been issued: As to the persons for whom have come from K͟hān Nuṣrat and Firūz Jung, let *tank͟hwāh* be assigned out of New Territories not yet administered. Most of these persons have been officers for a long time and received *jāgīrs.* Now they come for *jāgīrs* to meet the balance due to them and for addition becoming due on promotion. Orders had been sought as to where their *tank͟hwāh* should be assigned: Old territories, New Territories or those not yet administered. Now that the candidates are to be assigned *tank͟hwāh* from New Territories not yet administered from which date is to be done? Order from the date of the order. Let them implement the order to assign *tank͟hwāh* in the New Territories not yet administered. As for what was assigned before the issue of this order on the proposals of the above two nobles, let these remain unchanged; nor should they change [orders for] the K͟hānazāds. Let the K͟hānazāds not be put to trouble". Dated: 5 *Rabi*' II, R.Y. 49.

IJC I/50/11-4: "Petition of Muḥammad Mahdi with Emperor's endorsement: It is four years since this *K͟hānazād* and his sons have not received one dām in *jāgīr.* For this reason distress has reached its acme.

I have many dependants, and have no place to keep them. These days, even without any *jāgīr* [*be-jāgīrī*], I have kept a large contingent and kept order in a frontier. If I do not have *jāgīr* now, I will be totally undone…" Dated *Ramazan* R.Y. 50.

IJC I/50/2-9: "It has been ordered that the new appointees [*nau-sar afrāz*] shall receive *jāgīr* against half their pay-claims [*ṭalab*] in the Old Territory and half in the New Territory. Otherwise, they shall be dismissed." Dated 22 *Zihijj* R.Y. 50.

These documents show that the *jāgīr* crisis was, in fact, quite grave and many *jāgīr*-assignments were in effect being given in tracts not yet subdued. Richards 'refutation' of the earlier scholars' inference about the growing crisis of *jāgīrs* needs therefore, to be itself reviewed.

X

The Great Famine and Mughal Administration

Although terrible famines began at the tail end of 1554-55 and 1555-56 yet the great famine of 1630-32 which affected Gujarat and most of the Deccan as in the Deccan draught seems to have continued. Qazwīnī records that though there was a deficiency of rain in 1630 in "most of the *maḥāls* of Bālāghāt, especially the region around Daulatābād" the draught was much wide spread in 1631. Both Qazwīnī and Ṣādiq Khān had personal experience only of conditions in the Deccan where it is possible that the famine continued there in 1631 owing to the cause directly opposite to Gujarat. In the third year Ṣādiq Khān adds, mice and locusts caused great damage to the crops. However, the transportation of grain by the *banjārās* to Gujarat from Malwa and beyond was hampered in 1630 by the assignment of feeding Shāh Jahān's army encamped at Burhānpur. But the prices remained prohibitive in the next year. Interestingly enough unprecedented gains accrued to the Imperial treasury in Malwa by the sale of grain for supply to the Deccan. Unfortunately the villages could hardly have fared much better as Ṣādiq Khān declares that the *parganas* of Sulṭānpur, Nandur, Māndu, Aḥmadabad and indeed the [entire] province of Khāndesh and some *parganas* of Bālāghāt were rendered utterly desolate. 'Abdul Ḥamīd Lahori, II, 711-2 writing in 1646-47 declares that Gujarat and the Deccan provinces were adversely affected by the famine.

Moreover, in 1665 the *Kharīf* crops in parts of Bālāghāt region of Mughal Deccan was damaged by late and heavy rains.[1] Unfortunately draught was also experienced in the Deccan, where plague began to rage in the towns from 1682 A.D.[2] Similarly, draught was also experienced in the Deccan, where plague began to rage in the town from this year.

1. *Ādāb-i 'Ālamgīrī*, II 54 [b]-55 [a], ed; II, 213, 217.
2. Ma'murī, ff. 155[b]-156[a], Khāfī Khān, Add. 6574, f. 105[a-b].

Surprisingly the draught extended to the whole of the Deccan in 1686. So that what happened to the poor and indigent cannot be recorded."[1]

However, this is an established fact that a great famine began in the Deccan in 1702 A.D. Surprisingly enough in February 1702 it was brought to His Majesty's notice from Sangamner [Aurangabad Province] that due to draught "most of the villages" had been desolated,[2] "as in the whole year" in the entire Deccan no rain fell that was in keeping with the interests of cultivation.[3] Practically the rains were so prodigious as to devastate the *kharīf* harvest. Great scarcity spread everywhere south of the Narmada, and people were compelled to migrate from their ancestral homes.[4] Unfortunately the next year brought no relief, as owing to the excessive winter rains the *Rabī* crop was also damaged, wheat suffering from plight.[5] Naturally a historian speaks of it as the year for Maharashtra, of "famine and scarcity owing to draught, mortality of the poor and the wail of the weak."[6] Furthermore draught with its close companion, plague continued into 1704.[7] Unluckily within two years i.e. from 1702 to 1704 in the Deccan there expired over millions of souls, fathers compelled by hunger, offering to sell their children for a quarter or a half of a rupee, and yet forced to go without food, finding no one to buy them."[8]

During the last years of Aurangzeb's reign the situation had become so much topsy turvy that corruption had become rampant especially in judiciary system as shall be evident from the content of a letter written by a person of Sandila family of *qāzīs* from the Deccan to Sandila in Awadh. Furthermore it shall explain the scarcity of the food grains and other food items and rampant corruption which had made the life difficult in the Deccan.

Ṣāḥeb [sir] of courteous orientation, beneficent, a great lord, Ḥaẓrat Ṣāḥeb, [a title by which great men are addressed], may the Almighty God keep him with peace. After giving precedence to the particulars of humble submission and supplication, represents that great certificate in writing and the excellent letter from a superior to an inferior [*muq'āwama-i-girāmī*], which was issued in response to earnest supplication, was received in the most happy change of time, which made [the writer] dignified and

1. Khāfi Khān, II, 236-7. Qani, *Tahfatu-l Kiram,* III, p. 97.
2. *Akhābārt-i Durbar-i Mua'lla,* 46/12.
3. *Dilkushā*, f 146 [a].
4. Mannu chi, p. 423; Abul Faẓl Ma'murī, f. 202 [b], Khāfi Khān, II, p. 510.
5. Ma'murī, f 202 [b], Khāfi Khān, 510-11.
6. *Ma'asir-i'Ālamgīrī*, p. 477.
7. *Akhbārāt* A, 245 [July 1, 1704] for refrence to scarcity of grain and lack of rain throughout the Deccan.
8. Manucci, IV, 97.

eminent. When the news about the current occurrences of the good ending circumstances of that dignified great lord was learnt, it gave tremendous satisfaction. Yearns that till the time of attainment of the visit, marked with auspiciousness, the addressee would remember him. Whatever was uttered is that Shaikh Naẓrullāh, *Ṣadr-e Juzv* [ecclesiastical officer] has enmity with the writer. If the revered one writes any complaint to the officials *Ṣadr -i* [*Mutaṣaddiyān*] that officials pay heed to this servant, then by his writing they would issue order for looking into the result of the affair and by forbidding the disorderly affairs, effort should be made that certificate is procured from His Majesty. May the dignified great lord remain in peace. The supplicant with his maximum possible limit is attentive with the chief ecclesiastical office [*daftar ṣadāratu-l 'āliya*] and the matter of *Ṣadr-eJuzv* was divulged to Khwaja Mūsa and Mehta Ishar Das. Since owing to the refuge of sublimity, Qaẓi Shaikh 'Abdur Raḥīm, who is now posted to the office of *qaẓiship* of Burhanpur, [the writer] has abundance of servitude with the chief ecclesiastical officer [*Ṣadrus Ṣudūr*] and Khwaja Mūsa. Due to the grace of God he is extremely hopeful, that the writing of the *Ṣadr-e Juzv* unjustly recommended an order concerning that dignified of orientation [point]. But it is incumbent on that courteous one to follow the rule, so as to endeavour that whatever is written from there, should not be written except for describing elegance and considerate treatment because the behaviour of the addressee is quite clear to that person which does not require any entreaty and in order to forbidding disorderly conduct without any document which is a newly produced one, except for offering a thing to the *Ṣadrus Ṣudūr*. Procurement of certification is impossible. Until I had communicated through Mehta Ishar Das that how much 200 rupees would suffice for the staff [*'amla-o-fa'ila*] so as to say anything according to requital so that it should be accomplished by them. Accordingly I cannot dare to say without any information to that dignified one and they also want documentary proof. If any written recommendation is issued from there and the expenses in amount if communicated in writing, then Almighty God willing by considering auspicious the assignment of the addressee, the official should make an endeavour and the *farmān* of the land grant which accompanied with a paper was dispatched as due to inaction he could not prepare the *farmān* at that time. Now that *farmān* owing to lack of signature is not being issued and the writers of another *shiqq* [part/clause] also utter that as soon as the certificate [*sanad*] of the duty of *qaẓiship* is prepared afresh by the *Daftar-i-Dīwānī* [Finance / Revenue Department] etc where after another *farmān* is written that is passed through the offices. This *farmān* would not be issued from the offices. Accordingly copy of the stipulated *farmān* was sent to the addressee. If the land grant of the aforesaid *farmān* would be in possession of that orientation point [Ṣāḥib-o-Qibla] then what is the need of the *farmān* except that whatever would be your orders that would be complied with.

The servants of His Majesty by decamping from the places of village Kāras for subduing the stronghold of Wakinkira are attentive in travelling one after another. Although the group of the accursed [*Maqāhir* / vanquished ones i.e. Marathas] on the way indulge in imprudence on *pesh-khana* [Imperial tent of the state sent in advance when travelling] and also plundered the goods of the attendants of the royal army who had accompanied the tent equipage and the month of *Ramazan* of 49th regnal year [1117 AH/December 1705 – January 1706], commenced on the way. Despite suffocation, His Majesty used to observe the fast. But he did not halt anywhere since the time of the [march of the army] till the day of writing of the representation of the supplicant three months have passed away that they are marching to Almela [Almala]. In another month they would reach to the foothills of the aforesaid fort, from here that an order [*ḥukm-i-farmān*] has been issued that practically the camp of the victorious army has arrived at Almela.[1] Chin Qilīch Khān[2], the *Nāzim* [governor] of Bijapur has forwarded to the fort of Wakinkira and has inspected the place of an entrenchment for besiezing the fortified place [*jāi morchāl*] and the place of the Imperial camp [*makān-i daulat khāna*-i bādshāhi] and has recommended to arrive at Almela so as to serve there from here as His Majesty would stay here. From Almela to Wakinkira there is a distance of 12 *kuroh-i jaribi* [about 34 kms]. There is abundance of contingents in the fort. It is related that four of infantrymen would accompany the fort commandant [*qila'dār*]. Let it should be observed that what should be done that owing to travelling one after another the army men are not being hard and strong. The daily rent of camel is up to Rs 5 and that of the oxen is procured up to Rs 2. It should be imagined that how much costly is daily *kirāya* [price paid for the labour of conveyance]. In this army and in this expedition there is nothing except for worry and the dearness of food stuff and straw/hay for the last two years which the polite, civilised men are suffering. He who used to spend five rupees *per diem* is unable to sustain even in Rs 10. Let the Almighty show His favour so that the creatures of God should overcome the embarrassment [*kashāla* rectified *kasala*] so that servants of His Majesty may turn towards North India [Hindustan]. What else should be written as the empire may prosper. He should be excused for

1. Almel [spelt Almala] in our sources *Cf.*, *An Atlas of Mughal Empire*, 1983, Sheet 14-A.
2. Chin Qilīch Khān, son of Ghāziuddīn Khān Firūz Jung held the rank of 5000/5000. Mir Qamruddīn, *Maasir-i-'Ālamgīrī*, p. 506.

writing this letter in a hurry. Let greetings and servitude [*salām-o bandgi*] be accepted by courteous Miyan Moi'nuddin Jiv, Miyan Muḥammad Zakariya[1].

Under such circumstances Bhimsen turns to the second reason and finds a connection between the rise of the Maratha power and the oppression of the peasants in the Imperial territories because the Mughal commanders were not maintaining their contingents up to the standard required by the regulations. Accordingly the Maratha "malefactors" did not entertain any fear of the Mughal *faujdārs* and so "those regions that have been assigned in pay to the *manṣabdārs* cannot be compelled to pay the revenue". "The *zamīndārs* also having obtained power, have allied themselves with the Marathas". Until the crisis of Deccan wars, the Empire was self-financing which did not depend upon the private sector for capital. Moreover, nearly after two decades of uneasy drain on the liquid reserve necessary to support the Maratha campaigns in the south the Mughals were far from entirely depleted.

Unfortunately as the country has been divided into the *k͟hāliṣa* and pay-assignments of the *jāgīrdārs*, so the Marathas too have distributed the very same country among their own "pseudo-chiefs".[2] Naturally they had to live by plunder only for Shivajī's reputed maxim was "No plunder, No pay".

When Dāūd K͟hān Panni an Afg͟hān *amīr* on Zulfiqār K͟hān's staff, became deputy *faujdār* of Ḥyderabad Karnatak and subsequently of recently conquered Bijapur Karnatak then Dāūd K͟hān began the first phase of Imperial pressure on the Karnatak as the new *faujdār* between 1700-1704 campaigned actively against the various *Pālīgārs* and *rājas* of the area in a determined effort to force them to acknowledge the Emperor's authority. Before 1700 A.D. in 43rd R.Y. of Aurangzeb it was reported that Decument under the seal of Fazail Khan was received that from the communication of Zulfiqar Khan Bahadur it was brought to His Majesty's notice it was fixed to the former *faujdars* [military commandants] that 7,70,000 *huns* were fixed as *seh-bandi* while at the time of its assignment the duty for two years a sum of 10,30,000 *huns* were fixed on the *parganas* of the *sarkar*. But owing to less yield and desolation even one-third of the revenue is not received. The true facts of the disturbance of the *zamindars* of this district is crystal clear. To keep the contingent more than the prescribed limit and

1. He also served as *Qāẓi* of *pargana* Sandila [1734-1754 AD]. *Cf.,* Zakir Husain, 'Some Original Tughluq Documents and Their Significance', *Proc. Ind, Hist. Cong.*, 1989, p. 221 [Genealogical table].
2. *Na-Sardārān*. This is also the official term used for the Maratha commanders in Mughal documents.

to make the arrangement while the contingent and army of the fort and the *jagirs* of the *zamindars* and *Pāligārs* does not become less hence *sih-bandi* should not be reduced. Previously 7,70,000 *huns* were fixed for the *faujdars* while now 10,00,000 *huns* for one year have been fixed under Ali Mardan Khān Bahadur which was again assigned to Zulfiqar Khān for two years which was also confirmed on the *farman*[1].

When there occurred famine in 46th R.Y. of Aurangzeb then Amānat Khān, *amin* and *faujdār* of *pargana* Kandapur, *sarkār* Sangamner etc wrote to Mu'tamād Khān so as to convey it to His Majesty, who has fixed Rs 2,10, 000 as the *jama' bandi*. However, he has also collected signatures of 270 *muqaddams* whereas the rest have turned away elsewhere. On this Emperor has naturally asked from the dismissed officials [*nā-sardārān*] where after he has ordered Shaikh Sa'dullāh Khān to investigate about the dismissed ones and has also ordered for the collection accordingly.

When there began to occur dearth then Aurangzeb first asked to meet out the expenses from the *Khāliṣa* especially due to famine. However, it was finally ordered that since reserve source from *parganas* of Aurangabad do not suffice Aurangzeb ordered that, "Now these cannot be transferred from the people but it can be given by transfer to the *pāibāqī* so that expenditure should reach regularly. The *peshkash* of Chāndā, Islāmgarh and Ḥaiderabad, which were in the income as these, has not been received till date."[2]

Under such adverse circumstances of the great famine the transfer application of the *qila'dar* of an area was denied by Aurangzeb as he himself ordered that "no transfer could be effected without any need and without any statecraft."[3] It was settled on the orders of Aurangzeb that ten lakh *huns* from the date of fixation till the next two years be fixed as they should not insist for one year for the *dāgh* and *chehra* should be accomplished in collaboration of the *mutaṣaddis* for the *sih-bandi* of Ḥaiderabad.[4] However, nothing could be given out of which the total amount of 10,00,000 *hūns* were refixed for the next two years.[5]

Aurangzeb confessed in his last year that "there is no province or district where the infidels have raised a tumult and since they are not chastised, they have established themselves everywhere. Most of the country has been rendered desolate and if any place is inhabited, the peasants there

1. IJC I/38/2-3; I/32/5-2.
2. IJC I/45/1-44.
3. IJC I/37/11-15.
4. IJC I/39/11-74.
5. IJC I/47/12-55.

have come to terms with the 'Robbers' [*Ashiqa*, official Mughal name for the Marathas].[1]

When, in view of the famine, a matter of undisputed nature came to light then it was reported that on 4th *Ramazan* 47th R.Y. Aurangzeb wrote that Paithan became *jāgīr* of that son who should send the men known as excellent and ābādānkār as *qaṣba* and *qita'* be given. Wizārat Khān be told that let him send in the *fard* with *manṣab* as no more the *Bakhshī* should report.[2]

What had been happening in the period of great famine and the Mughal administration's responsibilities towards it is a deep rooted question as Aurangzeb had himself admitted and wrote to Bidār Bakht that since his departure from Ajmer he had spent twenty-five years, shake the holy wars in the Deccan,[3] the result of which proved devastating in the long run".

Even in the year 1700, Bhimsen, while writing his memoirs, set himself to explain the reasons for the success of these "malefactors and Marathas". Unfortunately the Mughal commanders were not maintaining their contingent up to standards required by the regulations. Not only the "malfactors did entertain any fear of the Mughal *faujdars* but "the *zamīndārs* also, having obtained power, have allied themselves with the Marathas". It came to be represented [at the Imperial court] that the Marathas obtain collaboration from the peasants of Imperial dominions. It was, thereupon, ordered that the horses and weapons found in every village should be confiscated. When this happened in most villages, the peasantry providing themselves with horses and arms joined the Marathas.

Unfortunately "the troops of the [Maratha] leaders who come in for the sake of plundering the country, export money from every *pargana* and all places, in accordance with their desire, and let [their horses] graze and trample upon the cultivated field. Order has disappeared. Now things have gone beyond limit. The produce and the field does not reach the grainary. They [the peasants] are totally ruined.

In view of the famine and the Maratha War in 1704, Aurangzeb naturally remitted the *jizya* throughout the Deccan for the duration of War.[4] Inspite of this his general policy was to discourage *jizya* remissions.[5]

Unfortunately a crisis in the assignment system developed in the last years of Aurangzeb. Surprisingly enough from 1682 to his death

1. *Aḥkām-i'Ālamgīrī*, f. 61 [b].
2. IJC I/47/11-34.
3. M. Athar Ali, *Mughal India: Studies in Polity, Ideas, Society and Culture*, OUP, Delhi, 2006, p. 390.
4. *Akhbārāt* 48/36 and A 245, cf also *Akhbārāt* 47/323.
5. *Cf.*, Ma'mūrī, f. 179 [a] Khāfi Khān, II, 377-78.

in 1707 Aurangzeb carried on unending war in the Deccan in which the concentration of the entire military power of the Deccan failed to give him ultimate success. During these last years there was an enormous influx into the ranks of the *manṣabdārs* of the Deccanis or officials of the Deccan Kingdoms and the Marathas. However, the number of Marathas, as a result, increased to such an extent that the existing *jāgīrs* could no longer suffice for their pay.[1]

Aurangzeb himself, in one of his letters refers to the "scarcity of *pāibāqī* and the crowds of men claiming pay" and unequivocally declares that everything "flesh and bone" had been assigned and no further demands for assignment could be entertained by the court. Similar statements are made by Ma'murī and K͟hāfi K͟hān. We are told that "large numbers [lit a world] had become *jāgīr* less [*be-jāgīr*]" as persons appointed to *manṣab* could not obtain *jāgīr* for years and if a *jāgīr* was transferred from the hands of any one, he might not get another. Unfortunately the older nobility or the so called K͟hānazādān were extremely indigent at the way their claims were disregarded to provide for the Deccanis. However, the real victims of the crisis were the small *manṣabdārs* who possessed neither money nor the influence to induce the officer of the court to assign them *jāgīrs*.[2]

Though J.F. Richards, *Mughal Administration in Golconda* 158-02, 308-9 expresses some reserve in regard to the pressure on *jāgīr* developing in the late years of Aurangzeb, yet Athar Ali has demonstrated in *Mughal Nobility under Aurangzeb*, rev. edn. XX-XXII, that Richards has read too much in a document consisting what he assumed to be "the 1689-90 settlement" of the conquered kingdom, and totally ignoring a document of 1706 [printed in *Selected Documents of Aurangzeb's Reign* [233-35] which gives an entirely different picture at least for the 19 Karnatak *sarkārs* of *ṣūba* Ḥaiderabad.

We take into consideration those commanded by Maratha or Bedar nobles were staffed solely Marathas or Bedar *manṣabdārs* and subordinate commanders, many being specifically identified as brothers or sons of the leaders in the late 17th century because in the last quarter of this century, larger number of Deccanis like former Golcunda, Bijapur and Maratha officers were enrolled in the Mughal service for political reasons.

---

1. Ma'mūrī, ff. 156 [b]-157 [a]; K͟hāfi K͟hān, Add 6574, ff. 106[b] - 107[a]. Unluckily this striking passage, inveighing against the influx of the Deccanis, is omitted in the Bib. Ind. Text of K͟hāfi K͟hān. On such an influx of Deccanis, see M. Athar Ali, *Mughal Nobility under Aurangzeb*, rev. edn, 26-30.
2. Ma'mūrī, ff. 156 [b]-157 [a], K͟hāfi K͟hān, Add.6574, ff 106[b]-107[b]. Aurangzeb himself naturally admitted that "great injustice is done to the small men [*reza-hā*], *Dastūrul 'Amal-i Āgahī,* f 31 [a] Add, 6574, 107[a].

Bhimsen's account also becomes much more sober as he describes the steady demoralisation, the general devastation and disarray of the Imperial territories in the Deccan as the endless wars against the rebellious Marathas dragged on. Intensified Imperial military responses increased the burden on the Deccan military administration. In 1706, food grain became scare in the Deccan. The Marathas, as well as lawless men of all sorts had rebelled and plundered the country side, *zamīndārs* no longer kept their obligations but assumed strength, joined the Marathas, enlisted armies, and laid the hands of oppression on the country "The peasants themselves procured horses and arms and joined the Marathas".[1] Moreover, in Aurangzeb's last year the entire *pargana* of Ellichpur became desolated due to famine.[2]

The Emperor seized with a passion for capturing first [*qila'gīrī* v/s *mulkgīrī*] has not attending to the happiness of the subjects[3]. The Mughal India continued to decline and display those symptoms of a general crisis noticed as early as the Deccan famines of 1702-4. It is also likely that funds from the Karnatak did support many of the troops which Aurangzeb threw into the sieze of Wakinkira in 1706 against the Bedar Chief Pidiyah Nayak. Before him in February 1703 Riza Khān, a former Mughal officer, turned bandit chief, came right to the gates of Machilipatnam with a force of 9,000 or 10,000 men as his plundering and burning virtually closed the Machilipatnam - Hyderabad trade route[4].

Unfortunately the Deccan provinces experienced several terrible years in the early 1700's as we find a wider pattern of shortage and mortality in the Deccan. However, during the last two to three decades of Aurangzeb the Imperial treasures were fully stocked.

Unfortunately Aurangzeb's attempt to coopt the services of large numbers of former nobles from Bijapur, Golcunda and the Maratha Kingdom added a defty increase to the Deccanis for *jagirs* as Aurangzeb retained the bulk of revenues from Golcunda renamed of Hyderabad for the Imperial treasury [*khaliṣa*] or in the temporary *pāibāqī* pool as similar policies seem to have preserved in Bijapur and Maratha lands for extended periods of time.

Incidently a draught and failure of crops encouraged a number of smaller chief and middlemen to support the rebel. When they endeavoured then they could not make their required revenue payments.

Similarly the short-fall in *jagirs* in the Deccan became to be more than an artificially treated problem. Since the Maratha wars continued year after

1. Bhimsen, *Nuskha-i Dilkushā,* p. 230, text f. 139[b].
2. IJC, I/51/1-26.
3. Bhimsen, p. 240, text fol. 146[b].
4. K.A., 1570 [10.10.1703], Second Part + 28.

year, the Maratha by their predatory raiding the Mughal reapprisals drove greater numbers of peasants off the land. Moreover burnt villages and towns and traders and caravans hindered production while the embittered men joined the Marathas or the group of the band as public order declined[1]. Naturally under such conditions *jagīrdārs* holding lands in the Deccan found it more difficult to collect even reduced revenue.

Before Aurangzeb's death in the early 1700's many Mughal officers suffered heavily to obtain paying *jagirs*.

The K͟hānazāds naturally blamed the newcomers from the Deccan Kingdoms for their troubles, the ensuing widespread conflict and demoralisation among the Mughal nobility was thus an unanticipated effect of the Deccan conquests. Moreover the resulting increased demand for *jāgīrs* [salary assignments] exhausted the reserve [*pāibāqī*] lands usually available for that purpose, owing to which many K͟hānazāds lost heavily.

Pidiyah Nayak who began to control Wakinkira from 1688 to 1691 was little more than a bandit or robber chief who solely rose through illegitimate and indiscriminate force. Between 1696 and 1706 Pidiyah Nayak was free to develop his various enterprises, until Aurangzeb himself directed his last personally led campaign against Wakinkira which has been referred to in detail as stated in the beginning of this chapter.

In the late 1690s the Deccan came under steadily increasing military pressure as the Marathas, Bedars, Gonds and others raided deep into the Imperial provinces of the Deccan while the bandit whose power and number had swollen also raided and looted freely. Unfortunately dislocation caused by these events was enhanced by a disastrous drought, famine and epidemic affecting nearly the entire Deccan between the years 1700 and 1704. Moreover agricultural and industrial production dwindled. Similarly in unfortified cities, the expectation or the actuality of the raids disturbed the urban population. However, in the country side, peasants starvation and disease frequently lost their livestock, tools and sometimes their lives to raiders. Unfortunately peasants who survived often migrated in search of safety, or joined one of the bands of raiders or bandits.

Precipitous declines in collections from even the most productive *jāgīrs* must have contributed to the troubles of the Mughal officers serving in the Deccan under such prevalent conditions. Furthermore, after 1700 the Emperor sent reinforcements only under the most desperate circumstances. Aurangzeb could not however take up similar steps like Shahjahan who did it in 1632 in Gujarat as we are not in a much better condition about the government help in the Deccan famines.

1. J.F. Richards, *Mughal Administration in Golconda*, Oxford, 1975, pp. 157-62.

When these circumstances were prevailing then Rustam Dil Khān without resisting 50,000 Maratha cavalry stayed in Golcunda fort allowing undisputed plunder for three full days which he however succeeded in stopping by offering 7,00,000 silver rupees by illegally taking it from the treasury. Although Dāūd Khān Panni replaced Rustam Dil Khān for less than one year he was called back by Aurangzeb to assist the Emperor in his sieze of the Bedar fort at Wakinkira in 1706. Though Dāūd Khān Panni's vigorous campaigns against the *Pālīgārs* probably brought the collections reasonably close to the normative demand yet it is also likely that funds from the Karnatak supported many of the troops which Aurangzeb threw into the sieze of Wakinkira in 1706 against the Bedar chief Pidiyah Nayak. Thereafter assisted by the intervention of Asad Khān, the Imperial *wazīr* Rustam Dil Khān returned to the deputy Governorship of Hyderabad which came to an end in 1708 by his execution through Prince Kām Bakhsh.

However, of equal importance was the precipitous loss of confidence on the part of these groups whose support and cooperation was equally essential for the Imperial system. Furthermore, Muslim urban notables, Telgu and Maratha *deshmukhs* and *zamīndārs* and tributary chiefs of all descriptions, not fully integrated by Aurangzeb into the empire, in effect declared a moratorium on participation in the Empire which was equally dangerous as the droughts and famines in the Deccan.

During Aurangzeb's closing years after 1700 A.D. an analysis of contemporary Mughal official documents and news reports from both Bijapur and Hyderabad support the view that the *deshmukhs* did not engage in widespread sustained revolts. Moreover they did not supply willing assistance to raiders attacking from outside the provincial boundaries notwithstanding the fact that in Hyderabad, bandits like Rizā Khān whose forces were augmented by deserted soldiers and uprooted peasants, had begun to challenge the local power of the *deshmukhs* and *zamīndārs* [whose outright defence was not common] seriously threatened their security.

Whether a similar explanation of the Deccan provinces hold for the remaining territories of the vast empire is a billion dollar question as we can apparently suggest same indices of declinc found in the Deccan provinces also existed in other provinces as incomplete administrative and political consolidation in Bijapur and Golcunda after 1686-87 and commitment of best military and administrative resources of the Empire to continue expansion in the Deccan brought about a crisis of public order and public confidence. But as far as Mughal decline is concerned there are several theories which need to be discussed and analysed here as these do not fall outside the preview of our discussion, [though it was also enhanced by a disastrous draught and famine, and epidemic affecting the entire Deccan]

ranging from Irvine's *harem* theory to Athar Ali's cultural failure over a dozen one about the decline of the Mughal Empire. To present an artificial theoritical interpretation does not seem sound yet a sound interpretation in a more exhaustive manner is still a thing to be taken into consideration. The affirmation of prevailing position needs to be proved by the documentary evidence which can however be slightly modified as the Mughal sovereignty was well established in early modern period.

Furthermore, in the debate on the fall of the Mughal Empire and the role of the 'Deccan Factor', the economic significance of the Mughal expansion has largely escaped notice. Moreover the fall of the Mughal Empire came close at the heels upon the annexation of the Deccan by Aurangzeb gave further impetus to the criticism of the Mughal Deccan Policy. Under Aurangzeb the *jama'* of the Mughal Empire rose from less than 21% in 1640 and 1656 to over 32% of the Empire in 1667 A.D. as this 'artificial inflation, raised by Akbar in a single stroke of pen by 50% seems to have continued throughout the seventeenth century.

The increase in the Deccan nobility was thus even disproportionate to the rise in the *jama'* of the Deccan i.e. 20.3% as compared to 290% which automatically created the crisis of *jāgīr* among the Mughal nobility thereby weakening the very basis of the empire as the Mughals thus met with political failure along with their military difficulties. Consequent upon Aurangzeb's reaching the Deccan with large armies, the compulsion towards aggrandizement increased with still large strain on the resources. Undoubtedly the presence of the Marathas was a factor in the further expansion into the Deccan, but it seems to be secondary to the economic considerations.

The drain of resources was caused by the burden of continuous Deccan campaigns almost till the end of Aurangzeb's reign. Moreover Bhimsen's famous passage brings out the unending cycle of agrarian depredations, fall in revenues, increase in revenue pressure, internal disturbances and further agrarian depredation of which the Maratha *sardars* were the main beneficiaries, with the peasant *bargīs* as their instruments.

More substantial amounts of revenues were required in the Deccan for the Imperial treasury due to the prolonged stay of Aurangzeb and the need to finance his own khāṣṣā troops and artillery which had to be paid out of the revenues collected for the Imperial treasury for which large areas of the Deccan needed to be kept unassigned as revenues from the *pāibāqī* were practically no different from those of the Khāliṣā being collected for the Imperial administration.

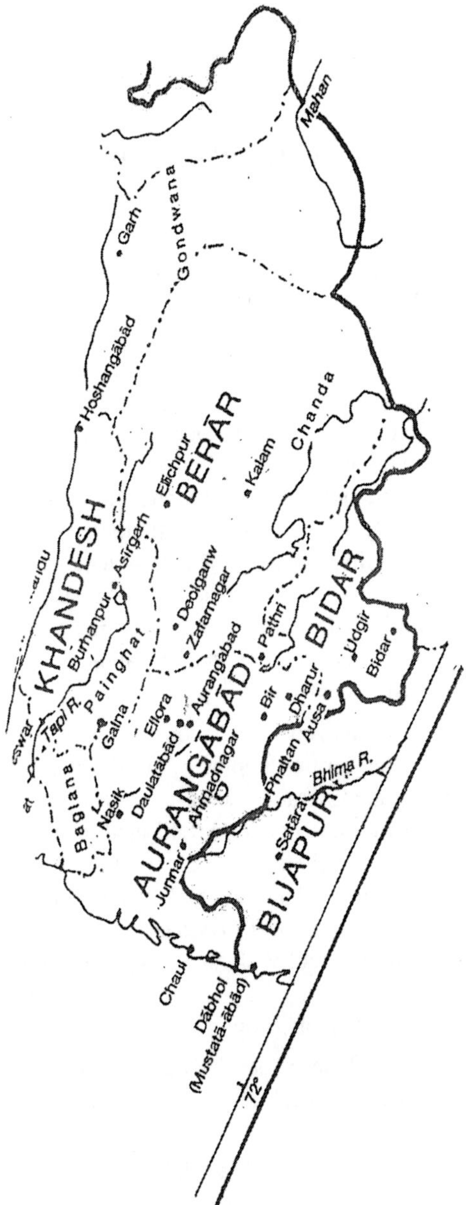
KHANDESH
BERĀR
AURANGĀBĀD
BIDAR
BIJAPUR
Gondwana
Chanda
Baglana
Painghat
Mahan
Garh
Hoshangābād
Ellichpur
Kalam
Asirgarh
Burhanpur
Deolganw
Zafarnagar
Pathri
Udgir
Bidar
Tapi R.
Galna
Ellora
Aurangabad
Bir
Dharur
Ausa
Daulatābād
Ahmadnagar
Phaltan
Bhima R.
Nasik
Junnar
Satara
Chaul
Dābhol
(Mustafā-ābād)
72°

XI

Conclusion

Practically the Mughal *jāgīr* was an accentuated version of the older *iqta* system or administrative fief used by the early thirteenth-fourteenth century Delhi Sultanate. However, *jāgīr* shortage began to appear during the Deccan wars in the first half of Shahjahan's and second half of Aurangzeb's lengthy reigns while Aurangzeb who in 1681 had led the household, and grand army personally into the Deccan, had actually conquered and annexed the Sultanats of Bijapur, Golcunda and the Maratha Kingdom by 1689, whereafter Aurangzeb's armies taunched a protracted sieze, of the great stronghold at Jinji which was the far southern refuge of Raja Ram, the new Maratha ruler. Ultimately over the next seventeenth years the emperor directed expensive, campaigns against the Maratha forces in the Deccan. We can argue that it is in the context of these campaigns that the number of claimants for the *jāgīrs* began to exceed the lands in the temporary pool or *pāibāqī* availing assignment[1].

To argue that Aurangzeb's endeavour to coopt the territories of the larger number of the former nobles from Bijapur, Golcunda and the Maratha Kingdom a considerable increase to the actual demand for *jāgīrs*. Naturally the most obvious course would have been for the emperor to assign the most productive lands to meet their requirements. Contrary to it what appears to have been a deliberate policy decision, Aurangzeb retained the bulk of the Imperial treasury or *khaliṣa* in the temporary *paībāqī* pool as there remained in that pool without reassignment for extended periods of time[2]. Naturally similar policies seem to have been prevalent in Bijapur Kingdom and the Maratha territories.

Under the circumstances the shortfall in the *jāgīrs* in the Deccan proved to be more than an artificially created problem because the Deccan wars continued continuously as the Maratha style of predatory raiding and the Mughals represents to drove larger and larger number of peasants off

1. M. Athar Ali, *Mughal Nobility*, pp. 42-4.
2. J.F. Richards, *Mughal Administration in Golconda*, OUP, 1975, pp. 157-60.

the land. Unfortunately burnt villages and towns and traders and caravans hindered production. Moreover embittered traders and the Marathas or group of the bandits lands as public order deteriorated[1]. Naturally under these circumstances *jāgīrdārs* holding the lands in the Deccan provinces found it more cumbersome to collect the even reduced revenues. Moreover Mughal officers fighting with one another over *jāgīrs* to these tracts of land years before Aurangzeb's death, many Mughal officers suffered real impoverishment as they failed to obtain paying *jāgīrs*.

Richard does argue that had Bahadur Shah lived longer and the Emperor not been subject to even bloody wars of succession in 1712-13 and had Farrukhsiyar [1713-19] been able to control, his king makers, the Saiyid brother, revenues would have resumed their inward journey. How any authority in its outward movements from Delhi, then the situation would have been much better. Instead, all the reserves of the Emperor's central treasuries were consumed by the time of Farrukhniyar's reign. We are given to understand that the six-years were occupied by the bitter political struggle which ended with the execution of Farrukhniyar allowed the Marathas to consolidate their supremacy over much of the Deccan. By 1724 during Muhammad Shah's initial years, the empire no longer functioned as the centralised entity that it had been in the previous century.

Surprisingly the Mughal Empire continued to decline and to divide those symptoms of general crisis noticed as early as the Deccan Famines of 1702-4. Under the circumstances one may well argue that the eighteenth century crisis was the by product of new forces, of new connections to which the Indian subcontinent had become subject, which may be the most plausible exploration for the rapidity with which the empire broke apart and political order diminished. Surely we must point to the potent effect of the conjecture established between India and Europe under the Mughals, mentioned above. We should naturally recall the potentiality of disruptive effects of continued Imperial military and administration consolidation for well over a century. One may naturally question whether the symptoms of the crisis in the eighteenth century did not mark a profound structural change in Indian society concern.

We are well acquainted with the fact that after taking the reins of government in his hands [1560] Jalaluddin Muhammad Akbar [r. 1556-1605] took the responsibility of putting his hand in order in right earnest. It is also a well established fact that since agricultural tax [*māl or mālguzāri*] was the chief source of the state income, he made sincere efforts to recognize the land revenue administration in the first instance. Naturally the

1. *ibid*, 215-35.

subjugation of unconquered areas and suppression of the recalcitrant nobles was taken up almost simultaneously. Thereafter creation of an advanced and elaborate administrative structure was taken up next. We are given to understand that the Emperor began to build new administrative apparatus at the central, provincial and local level. The Empire was subdivided into 12 homogenous units called *subas* in 1581 which reached upto 15 under Akbar. Moreover each unit was further subdivided into smaller units of administration designated as *sarkārs* and *parganas*. Moreover for each unit that Emperor appointed a set of officials of practically equal status and rank to look after the administration. Similarly several other measures were adopted by the Emperor to improve the working and efficiency of the officials. Fortunately historians of Mughal India have of late taken up the detailed study of Mughal *subas* in order to comprehend the intricacies and complexities of the working of Mughal administrations. However, an exclusive and comprehensice study of the Deccan as an administrative unit, notwithstanding John F. Richard's path breaking study of *Mughal Administration in Golconda*, a [1975] has not been done so far.

Shahjahan had initiated the policy of appointing a Viceroy in the Deccan with headquarters at Aurangabad, who exercised overall control over the governors of Aurangabad. Berar, Bidar and Khāndesh and that policy was continued by Aurangzeb. A similar policy was adopted in case of the base of *Diwan* and *Bakhshi* who supervised the work of the *Diwans* and *Bakhshis* of the four Deccan provinces. The deficiency in the collection of revenue in the Deccan has started during the reign of Shahjahan and that there is no evidence to suggest an improvement in the situation of the reign of Aurangzeb.

Though the Mughal administration was quite organised in the Deccan as the Mughal documents lead us to show yet the Maratha problem failed the Mughals in the Deccan. As far as J.F. Richards is concerned he has been dismissed outright in the light of the documentary evidence. Similarly the Mughal expedition in the Deccan despite environment and ecology could become possible by the Mughal endeavours. As far as the Deccan is concerned every rise has a natural decline in history. Aurangzeb due to his policy failed to restrain the Marathas well in time. But as far as Andre Wink's theory of fitnais concerned it does not fit in this context.

We are given to understand that the expansion in the Deccan naturally added considerable to the administrative led to burden on the Mughal government that contributed to the crisis in the Deccan which then eventually led to the decline of the Mughal Empire. The continuous drought conditions coupled with never ending wars with the Marathas devastated the entire Deccan in which more than a million people died. The Emperor's prolonged stay in the Deccan in the last 25 years and deployment of practically all the resources of the Empire in the Deccan had a debilitating effect on Northern India and consequently hastened the decline of the Mughal Empire should be well taken. However, the Mughal response to the Deccan famine by exempting it from the payment of *jizya* and steps taken by the government to tackle the problem and see the situation is however not much clear yet we can critically analyse of the ways and means of handling the problems and to its effect on the immediate course of events.

Appendix – A

Aurangzeb's First Viceroyalty of the Deccan

The *Ādāb-i 'Ālamgīrī*[1] is the correspondence concerning Aurangzeb's Second Viceroyalty of the Deccan [1652-1657]; we are still not much acquainted with his first Viceroyalty of the Deccan [1635-1644] which period is also not unimportant. When Aurangzeb was initially appointed as Viceroy of the Deccan he successfully conducted the administration of the large *ṣūba,* with its considerable financial problems of which we come to know from the availability of numerous documents[2] and newly discovered records[3]. Aurangzeb was initially tutored in the intricacies of the Mughal administration as he even referred to this period during his holding the Imperial authority.

The date of a *nishān* of Aurangzeb issued on 18 Āzur 9th RY/ 2nd *Rajab* 1045 A.H. corresponding to 3rd December 1635 A.D. clearly stipulated that Aurangzeb was appointed to his first Viceroyalty of the Deccan just before this date. When Amān Beg[4], the castellan of the fortress of Qandahar in the Deccan which was conquered

1. *Ādāb-i 'Ālamgīrī* is a collection of letters drafted on behalf of Aurangzeb before his accession by Munshi Abul Fateḥ Qābil Khān, along with a collection of letters of Prince Akbar *c.* 1680 by Muḥammad Ṣādiq Khān who edited the entire collection in 1703-04, [ed.] 'Abdul Ghafūr Chaudhuri, Punjab University, Lahore, 1971, 2 Volumes, *Cf.,* Zakir Husain, *Calendar of Administrative Documents in Ādāab-i 'Ālamgīrī,* Dissertation submitted at the Centre of Advanced Study in History, AMU, Aligarh, 1991 for the award of M. Phil. Degree.
2. *Cf.,* M.Z.A. Shakeeb, *Mughal Archives,* Andhra Pradesh State Archives, Hyderabad, 1977, Volume 1, containing durbar papers and a miscellany of singular documents.
3. *Blochet Supplement Persian,* Bib. Nat. Paris, 482, and a collection of documents in possession of Mr. Kabir of Bhopal [Madhya Pradesh], out of which I have already presented a paper entitled 'Sai'd Khān and the Conquest of Qandahar -1638, a Unique *Farmān* of Shāh Jahān, *Aligarh Papers on Indian History, Indian History Congress,* 1997. Since the owner belongs to the family of Sai'd Khān, a *nishān* of Prince Aurangzeb on the eve of his dismissal from the Deccan to Rashīd Khān who was probably a son or a near relative of Sai'd Khān, is also available.
4. Amān Beg, Tūrani, 1000/1000 is reported to holding the castellan of Qandahar in 1636 A.D. with the increase of 300/430 ['Abdul Ḥamīd Lahori, *Padshahnama,* 1[b] 216. *Cf.,* Andhra Pradesh State Archives, Hyderabad, 60]. In 1644-45 he held the rank of 1500/1000, Hyderabad, 426. He was promoted to the rank of 1500/1500 on the same post [Lahori, II, p. 417]. In 1646-47 A.D. he was conferred the title of Qipchāq Khān [Lahori, II, p. 612]. In 1647-48 he held the rank of 2000/1000 [Lahori, II, p. 680]. He also held this rank in 1656-58 as well [Waris, p. 262[b], Ṣaliḥ, III, p. 459].

in 1631 A.D. sought instructions regarding the disposal of spoilt food-grain and repairs of the fort he was directed to distribute the same as *'alūfa* [salary] among the soldiers [aḥshām] of that place and purchase and store up the fresh food-grain by taking action in consonance with Sunder Das, the *Dīwān* of Telingana *ṣūba* which province had been carved out in 8th R.Y. of Shāh Jahān. He was instructed to avail of the services of Jahān, the architect and submit the bill to Aurangzeb in agreement with both the officials, maintain the *roznāmcha* [daily report] and forward it with necessary verification to the cashier for disbursing the amount[1]. Since the food-grains were much spoilt that soldiers of the fort declined to accept it. Accordingly a new princely order [*nishān*] was issued on 20th *Bahman* 9th R.Y. [31 January 1636] for supplying food-grains for a period up to *Isfandyar.* While for the current claim they were to be paid in kind for one month and in cash for the remaining period whereas the residual food-grain was to be sold out expeditiously at prevalent market rate[2].

Since Amān Beg had made a representation regarding the repair of one of the turrets of the fort of Qandahar Aurangzeb through his *nishān* of 10th *Jumāda II* 1046 A.H. [30th October 1636] allowed the same. Aurangzeb kept in view the population of *pargana* Qandahar which was reported to have increased as compared to that of the last year. The report resulted in favour of Aurangzeb who encouraged him to restore it to its original state of prosperity[3]. When Amān Beg represented about the completion of the repairs of the fort of Qandahar it made the Prince extremely happy as is confirmed by his *nishān* of 4th *Shaban* 1047 corresponding to 12th December 1637. Since Aurangzeb had been continuously keeping a vigilant eye on the day to day developments in the Deccan he ordered Amān Beg to look into the administration of the fort with utmost care as its *qila'dār* [castellan] as the fort being the best in Telingana. Since Aurangzeb was aware of the sincerity of the castellan he instructed him not to move to the [Prince's] court and remain busy in the assigned work as it was inadvisable for him to be away from the fort[4].

Aurangzeb issued a *nishān* on 29th *Ramazān* 1048 [23rd January 1639] granting 3,01,005 *dāms* from *pargana* Sarbar, *ṣūba* Telingana to Qalandar Beg[5] S/o Amān Beg in place of Sa'adat Bhakkari besides his present emoluments of 4,10,000 *dāms* from *pargana* Saroon [Murtazapur], *sarkār* Gavil, *ṣūba* Berar, bringing his *jāgīr* to 7,11,005 *dāms.* Aurangzeb also instructed the *deshmukhs, despāndiyas, muqaddams* and the peasantry to recognize him as their *jāgīrdār,* honestly co-operate with him for the *māl-i wajibī* [land tax] and specified state fiscal imposts [*huqūq-i Dīwānī*]. Qalandar Beg like his father was also encouraged to strive for the increase of the prosperity as well as the extension of cultivation.[6]

When Amān Beg, the castellan of Qandahar made a representation ['arzdāsht] to Prince Murād Ba<u>kh</u>sh complaining against the oppression of the son of Amar Singh and others for unjustified payments from his *jāgīr* the Prince directed Rao Roop, through his *nishān* of 24th *Rajab* 1049

1. Ḥusain 'Alī <u>Kh</u>ān Collection, No.5. [Shakeeb, p. 16].
2. *Ibid.*, [Shakeeb, p. 17].
3. *Ibid.*, No. 7.
4. *Ibid.*, [Shakeeb, p. 18].
5. *Ibid.*, [Shakeeb, p. 18].
6. Qalandar Beg S/o Amān Beg who is reported to hold the rank of 200/50 [Hyderabad 40].

[10th November 1639] that whenever the agent of the said person would request him for help it should be given to him according to his entitlements and accounts.[1]

Since Aurangzeb appreciated the appropriate action taken by his officials *viz.*, Amān Beg's information to him regarding the punishment meted out to notorious Hathkaran, the Prince approvingly cited this fact in his *nishān* of 9th *Zilhijja* 1049 [22nd March 1640]. Aurangzeb encouraged him to suppress the refractoriness of such persons of the *pargana* and also assured him of his favour.[2]

Aurangzeb seemed to take care to make officials appointment on certain conditions *viz.,* in one of his *nishān* of post-1638 A.D. which he had addressed to the big and the small *zamīndārs,* [āzim-o asā<u>gh</u>ir *zamīndārān*] – ignoring the so-called intermediary *zamīndārs, deshmukh* and the peasantry of *sarkār* Bijagarh who aspired to the Prince's favours that he had assigned the office of the *faujdār* [commandant of a territory, in-charge of law and order] of the said *sarkār* to a particular official. They were, however, specifically instructed that the said appointee was to be treated as their permanent *faujdār* and that they had not to deviate from his utterances and decisions which were aimed at the extension of cultivation and prosperity, welfare of the condition of peasantry, extermination of the evil-doers and the suppression of the disturbances and tumult of the mischief mongers. However, the incumbent was simultaneously directed that he was supposed to remain engaged whole heartedly in considerate behaviour with the peasantry, and the safety of the highways without leaving any stone unturned by considering it as his duty. He was issued injunctions not allowing any deviation in the matter.[3] This practice was also adopted in all other appointments as we come to know through Aurangzeb's order [post-1638 AD] wherein it is stated that "the brave, worthy of kindness and courtesy Usmān <u>Kh</u>ān who was distinguished by princely favour that he should know that we have appointed him to the office of *ba<u>kh</u>shī* and *wāqia' navīsī* so that they should consider the said duty attached to him and they should strengthen his hand in this matter so that he should consider himself responsible in the matter.[4]

Side by side looking after the administrative matters of the various *sarkārs* of the Deccan provinces Aurangzeb paid attention to preserve existing charity grants. Confirming the *sanads* of the former local potentates issued in favour of one Shai<u>kh</u> Ibrāhīm for 170 *bighas* as the *madad-i ma'āsh* along with 1/4 seer of oil for the mosque, Aurangzeb confirmed this land grant in *Gaz-i Ilahi* with 1/8 seer of oil [*per diem*] in village Dewla, *pargana* Bir with usual instructions for demarcation and consolidation of the grant without any obstruction on the pretext of fiscal imposts and state demands.[5]

In response to the entreaty of Amān Beg soliciting permission to visit to his court, Aurangzeb, through his *nishān* of 22nd *Rabi* I, 1052 [20th June 1642] confirmed that he had already reached at Burhanpur by 19th *Rabi* I, 1052 [17th June 1642].[6]

1. Ḥusain 'Alī <u>Kh</u>ān Collection No. 10, [Shakeeb, p. 19]. Prince Murād Ba<u>kh</u>sh who received a fresh appointment of 10000/4000 in 1638-39 [Lahori, II, p. 133] held the rank of 10000/5000 in 1639-40 [Lahori, II, p. 176].
2. Ḥusain 'Alī <u>Kh</u>ān Collection No. l, [Shakeeb].
3. *Bloch Supp. Pers.,* 482, ff. 82[b]-83[a].
4. *Bloch. Supp. Pers.,* 482, ff. 83[a-b].
5. Ḥusain 'Alī <u>Kh</u>ān Collection No. 2, [Shakeeb, p. 20].
6. *Ibid.*, [Shakeeb, pp. 19-20].

He had enjoined Amān Beg to look after his duties of protecting the fort and its district. Since the Prince was pleased he had bestowed on him an *'alam* [banner, standard] which was being dispatched through Sāqi Beg, an imperial servant.[1]

Since the emperor very well knew the importance of trade and commerce he encouraged the merchants and traders by abolishing trade tax, transit duties and forbidden imposts throughout the Mughal empire which fact was also endorsed by Prince Aurangzeb during his first viceroyalty of the Deccan as is evident from his following *nishān* which was definitely issued after the transfer of Baglana to *ṣūba* Khandesh in 1638 A.D.

"Let it be known to the potentates [*ḥukkām*] and *jāgīrdārs* from Burhanpur city to the frontier of Baglana who were dignified by the Imperial favours and the princely courtesies that since the visit of traders and merchants is the cause of increase of goods and abundance of commodities in the towns and the cities and keeping in consideration the welfare of that group is the cause of plentitude and the availability of abundant commodities. In accordance with the Imperial order the traders should not be harassed at all throughout the Imperial dominions for the *zakāt* [tax on trade], transit dues [*rāhdāri*] and the forbidden taxes and they should not hover around them on any pretext. They should make endeavours for their welfare and they should abstain from harassing that group so that by remaining free from any worry they should continue visiting the [Imperial] dominions. He announced that he had appointed Mehrāb Beg for forbidding *zakāt* and *rāhdāri.* They should consider strict injunction in the matter and not to act against the order".[2]

An interesting *wājibu-l-'arz* of Amān Beg is a note submitted by an inferior to a superior seeking orders [5th *Zilqada* 11th RY] regarding the repair of *fasīl-i khandaq* [ditch] with lime mortar for about 3000 yards as it was previously built of mud. Aurangzeb allowed the repair [i.e. by mud plaster only]. Thenceforward it was done. When orders regarding the repairs of certain turrets were sought Aurangzeb sanctioned accordingly. Since Aurangzeb was well aware of the availability of the timber of the required quality in the suburbs of Qandahar he ordered the acquisition of the same for all 31 turrets of the fort of Qandahar. Thereafter Aurangzeb's attention was drawn to the expeditious procurement of food grains in the grainary to replace the old stock due to non-passage of *banjaras* [grain carriers] and *beoparis* [traders] he ordered that the same be obtained from the villages of the *pargana* on payment. The Prince also ordered purchase of 6500 maunds of gun powder.[3]

Shāh Jahān as an Emperor regularly took stock of the situation in the Deccan. He instructed Aurangzeb by the following Imperial *farmān* in regard to the implementation of branding and muster regulations in the Deccan:

> "Let it be known to the fortunate son, the renowned seeker of the [Imperial] willingness, the supporter, the victorious, the auspicious, the illuminated eye of the Empire, the commendable forehead of auspiciousness, the new plant of the garden of the Empire, the light of the garden of grandeur, the illumination of the orchard of grandiloquence, prince of the world and the people, of high

1. Ḥusain 'Alī Khān Collection No. 12, [Shakeeb, p. 2]. Sāqi Beg held the rank of 150/20 in 1636-37 [Hyderabad 36].
2. *Bloch Suppl. Pers.*, 24[a]-25[a].
3. Ḥusain 'Alī Khān Collection No. 31, [Shakeeb, pp. 94-98] which produces Persian text.

progeny, grandiloquent, of high caste, of sublime status as the sea of the fame is dignified by the pearl of Sulṭan Muḥammad Aurangzeb Bahadur that due to special Imperial attention and favours he became dignified, that meanwhile from the contents of the events of the Deccan it was brought to the sublime notice of His Majesty that due to low yield of the *jāgīrs* of that *ṣūba*, since the time of his arrival, [the *manṣabdārs*] out of their own consent and inclination have got the branding done for the [horses of the] soldiers [aḥshām] and obtain 1/4th of the salary. When that fact has been known by that celebrated son seeking the Imperial willingness through Luṭfullah *bakhshī* and *wāqia' Nawīs,* he [voluntarily] has instructed him to enter the fact in the diary of events [*wāqia'*] and solicit its elucidation. Accordingly, the said person has brought it to the sublime notice of His Majesty that the regulation of branding and verification [*dāgh-o taṣḥīḥ'a*] is not prevalent in this *ṣūba,* if the *dastūru-l 'amal* [schedule] is received from the sky high vestibule then branding and certification can be done accordingly. The sublime Imperial order is issued that we are sending the regulation of branding and verification along with this sublime Imperial order. Among the nobles whose entire *jāgīr* is in North India [Hindustan], is Rai Satarsāl. It is most probable that before the promulgation of this schedule he used to keep and is still keeping the contingent with himself and in this event the auspicious son surely knows about Rai Satarsāl [Hāḍā] and some others that they maintain the contingent in accordance with the regulation and demand [*ṭalab*] accordingly and in regard to other persons who do not care for this [regulation] whosoever has his entire *jāgīr* in North India shall get increase or decrease in *jāgīr* as per the schedule in North India and the reminder as in the Deccan. He should have the *jāgīr* in North India in accordance with the regulations of North [India] and get share of the *jāgīr* according to the actual realisation thereat contingent upon getting the branding done according to the stipulated [regulations]. Whosoever has his entire *jāgīr* there the actual yield of his entire *jāgīr* should be inspected, demand the branding claim [*ṭalab-i dāgh*] according to it and consider this regulation perpetual, get it verified year to year and consider our sublime favours increasing upon him. Written on 2nd *Sha'hān* 14th R.Y. [of Shāh Jahān] [1641]".[1]

Aurangzeb issued a *nishān* on 8th *Ramazan* 1052 [20th November 1642] sanctioning the continuation of Kanhoji S/o Baisaji as *deshmukh* of *pargana* Pāthri in place of his father on the same terms and conditions on which his father was granted the office of *deshmukh.* The *jāgīrdārs, karorīs, zamīndārs, deshpāndiyās, muqaddams,* and the cultivators were instructed to recognize him as the *deshmukh* contingent upon the *inā'm* and *rusūm-i desmukhi,* prevalent in that *pargana* and the *desmukh* on his part was to endeavour for the increase in its prosperity and the extension of cultivation as per the established rates, and assured that no change or alternation would be effected in it.[2]

Aurangzeb issued a *nishān* on 19th *Ramazān* 1053 A.H. [21st November 1643] wherein he divulged his plan of moving his forces to capture Deogarh after *Ramazān.* Accordingly Aurangzeb asked Amān Beg to leave his son as his duty for the protection

1. Mīr 'Abdul Salām Mashhadi, Ikhtiṣaṣ Khān, Islām Khān, Tūrani, became the *Dīwān-i Kul* with the rank of 5000/5000 [4000x2-3 h], Bloch. Suppl. Per., ff. 46[a]-47[a].
2. Ḥusain 'Alī Khān, Collection No. 13, [Shakeeb, p. 22].

of the fort of [Qandahar] and start for Ellchipur immediately on the receipt of this *nishān.* He was instructed to join Shāh Beg Khān to participate in the campaign.[1]

When Amān Beg made a representation to the Prince that Sevanthi [?] village, under *pargana* Qiyampur that was assigned to him in *jāgīr* was thoroughly plundered and ruined, then on 14th *Safar* 1054 [12 April 1644] Aurangzeb issued a *nishān* to recompense Amān Beg for the loss with strict injunctions and that none should disturb him unjustifiably and that these orders were to be strictly adhered to.[2]

The divergence between the *jama'* [paper amount of expected receipts for salary-payment] and *ḥāṣil* [actual revenue] was sought to be met out by the introduction of the institution of month scale which first appeared in Shāh Jahān's reign. The *farmān* of Shāh Jahān issued to Aurangzeb in his 14th R.Y. does suggest that conditions seem to have been better in North India which definitely meant that any transfer from there to Deccan entailed a *jāgīr* on a lower month scale. Aurangzeb says that Firuz Khān Decanni 500/250 had claims for a *jāgīr* of 20,62,500 *dāms,* out of which he was already enjoying 1,20,000 *dāms* from *pargana* Chitkhali, *sarkār* Baitalwādi, *ṣūba* Berar, the balance of present additional assignment of 9,42,500 *dām* was now granted to him consequent upon the transfer of Muḥammad Shāh from *Kharīf Lui II* as recorded in a *parwāncha* of 9th *Jumada* I, 1052 [26th July 1642].[3] In compliance with the Imperial orders Aurangzeb through a *parwāncha* of 27th August 1642 got implemented the *jāgīr* assignment to Khande Rai out of which he was already availing 50,25,000 *dāms* from the *parganas* of *ḥavelī* Basim in partnership with Ūdāji Rām while he was assigned an additional grant of 16,75,000 *dāms* from the revenues of *pargana* Chincholi, *sarkār,* Mahūr, *ṣūba* Berar after transfer of Aḥmad Khān Ghori and others from *Kharīf Yūnt II* as recorded on the reverse of the *parwāncha* of 29th *Jumāda II* 1052 [14th September 1642].[4]

Other instances of Aurangeb's orders regarding the enforcement of the Imperial orders of *jāgīrs* are found *viz.,* a *parwāncha* of *Safar* 1054 [18th April 1644] regarding the Prince's order for enforcing Imperial order of *jāgīr* to 'Abdullāh Beg S/o Āqā Muḥammad Rūmi from *pargana* Balapur, *sarkār* Narnala, *ṣūba* Berar amounting to 9,00,000 *dāms* out of which, 7,25,200 *dāms* were continued as before while, 1,74,800 *dāms* as additional amount were made following the transfer of Muḥammad Ḥusain and others from the beginning of the middle of *Kharīf Yūnt II.*[5]

From a personal collection at Bhopal comes an order of Aurangzeb to Rashīd Khān, issued on 10 *Rajab*, R.Y. 17 of Shāh Jahān, assuring him of his patronage while the Prince was on his way from Deccan upon his recall, terminating his first viceroyalty of the Deccan.[6]

1. *Ibid.*, No. 13, [Shakeeb, pp. 22-23].
2. *Ibid.*, No. 243, [Shakeeb, p. 62].
3. *Ibid.*, No. 306, [Shakeeb, p. 65].
4. *Ibid.*, No. 333, [Shakeeb, p. 66].
5. *Ibid.*, No. 350A, [Shakeeb, p. 67].
6. Private family collection of Mr. Kabir who has kindly allowed me to retain a copy of his entire collection. Rashīd Khān Ansāri held the rank of 3000/1500 in 1627- 8 [Lahori, I, p. 183]. In 1630-1 his *manṣab* was raised to 3000/2000 [*ibid.*, p. 364]. In 1631-2 he was the *faujdār* of Agra [West of Yumna] [*ibid.*, p. 411; Qazwīnī 251[b]]. In 1634-5 he was promoted to the rank of 3000/3000 [Lahori, I[b], p. 60]. In 1636-7 he was raised to the

This is a unique *nishān* exposing the critical circumstances in which Aurangzeb was proceeding to the Imperial court. However, despite all these trials and turbulations which Aurangzeb had to undergo in the Deccan he not only learnt the techniques of administering such a deficit province spread over a vast region, in fact, controlling four provinces but also in order to cope with the emerging situation he personally looked into the matters, issued orders [*nishāns*] received important *farmāns* [Imperial orders] in regard to the administration of the Deccan as well as cultivated relations with important subordinate officials.

---

manṣab of 4000/3000 [*ibid.*, p. 257] Rashīd Khān Ansāri was the *ḥākim* of Telingana in 1637-8 [Lahori, II, p. 41. In 1638-9 he was the *ṣūbedār* of Burhānpur [Lahori, II, p. 98].

Appendix – B

Farmān of Aurangzeb

Sarnāma: Invocation not forthcoming due to wear and tear.

Sigillum: Abul Muzaffar Muḥiuddīn Muḥammad Aurangzeb Bahādur ʻĀlamgīr Badshāh Ghāzi, [3rd Regnal Year, 1660 A.D.], son of Shāh Jahān Badshāh Ghāzi, son of Jahāngir Badshāh Ghāzi, son of Akbar Badshāh Ghāzi, son of Humayūn Badshāh Ghāzi, son of Babur Badshāh Ghāzi, son of ʻUmar Shaikh Shāh, son of Sulṭān Abū Saʻid Shāh, son of SulṬān Muḥammad Shāh, son of Mirān Shāh, son of Amīr Taimur Sahīb Qirān.

Tughrā: *Farmān* of Abul Muzaffar Muḥiuddīn Muḥammad Aurangzeb Bahādur ʻĀlamgīr Badshāh Ghāzi.

Translation: Best of the intelligent well wishers, cream of the bravely dedicated ones, convalescent cheerful devotee, model of the well wishing dedicated ones, worthy of the limitless Imperial courtesies, deserving unlimited Imperial favours, purest and the best of the devotedly sincere Rajas, obedient to Islam, Mirzā Raja Jai Singh[1], who was glorious and exalted by the Imperial attentions, should know that the representation which he has sent in accompaniment of the keys of the fort of Kohaj and nine other forts in addition to other earlier acquisitions out of the remaining total 23 forts of Siva [Shivajī] that have come under the control of the friends of this mighty Empire and his petition that was brought through Muḥammad and Ḥājī Badi'uzzamān to the vestibule of dignity and majesty was brought to the august Imperial perusal. It was represented that the sublime Imperial order was issued from the court of caliphate and governance in regard to the appointment of troopers as per the requirements of each fort from the aforesaid forts.

In view of the fact that the Imperial *sanad* [certificate] received concerning the recruitment of 10,000 infantrymen, as according to the regulations of the Deccan, the former Governors thereat and when the supplicant arrived here, where out of the total, 5,500 persons were present over there, out of whom, 1,700 Infantrymen, who were the residents of the villages and *Maḥāl-i-*Talkokan were maintained by Lodī Khān[2], in accordance with the *sanad* of the arm of the great caliphate, pillar of the great

1. Mirzā Raja Jai Singh in 1665 concluded a successful campaign against Shivajī by the treaty of Purandhar. Though the Mughals in 1665 had launched a big attack on Bījāpur, yet Mirzā Raja Jai Singh was made the Viceroy of the Deccan in 1665 A.D., *ʻĀlamgīr Nāmā,* pp. 903-04, 913, 998 *passim.*
2. Muzaffar Lodī, Lodī Khān, Afghan held the rank of 3000/2000 Muḥammad Kāzim. *ʻĀlamgīr Nāmā*, pp. 51, 76, 291.

Empire, confiding in the excellent empire, trustworthy of His Majesty, model of the great nobles of high status, reserved for abundant favours and obligations, 'Umdatu-l Mulk[1] [best of the country] Amīru-l Umara [chief of the nobles], that the posting of all these *qaṣbati* [men of the surrounding townships] is not justified in the conquered forts, it was decided that those may be dismissed, and if the remainder of the footmen are found sufficient for the said forts, that would be better, otherwise represent to the fortunate, renowned, of illustrious house, splendour of the house of grandeur, lamp of august house of magnificence, new plant of the garden of Caliphate and good fortune, fruit of the genealogical tree of grandeur and majesty, of laudable manners, [and] auspicious qualities, Prince Muḥammad Mu'azzam[2] that the contingents for the protection of the aforesaid forts should be drawn from the old forts and dispatched. These intending steps were evidence of adoration by His Majesty, who approvingly ordered that whatever is thought expedient should be implemented.

Representation was made in regard to the appointment of some experienced persons for accomplishing the expedition, which is undertaken according to this law-regulation by demolisher like Sirājuddin, who is in Aurangabad, *Khujista Buniyād* [happy foundation] and is practically without any assignment. According to the request of the aforesaid purest of the well wishing, devoted ones [i.e., Mirzā Raja Jai Singh] the above named person [i.e. Sirājuddin] and Abul Ḥasan, who was previously the plenipotentiary of [Shāh] Shujā' and the old timer 'Alī Rizā because three of whom were appointed to the service in that province [i.e. Aurangabad] were posted accompanied with that undoubtedly best of the selected sincere ones [i.e. Jai Singh] and like this group some others shall be deputed as well. It was represented to His Majesty that Angad, son of Champat Bundela[3], Jam, his uncle and Satar Sāl [Chhatr Sal][4] is younger brother, by encouraging them to yearn for the service of the world asylum vestibule, had brought them along with him. Since they had exerted the utmost in the siege of Purandhar fort[5] they are expecting for the grant of ranks while other devotees whose reports of the true circumstances of their endeavour, also communicated separately, received enhancement [in their ranks] from the Imperial court of dignity and beneficence. According to the representation of that cream of the bold and the brave, the first of them [i.e. Angad] with the *manṣab* [rank] of 800/600, the second [i.e. Jam] with the rank of 400/300 and the third [i.e. Satar Sāl] with the *manṣab* of 250/100 were honoured, while other devotees, who had also exerted [the utmost] were promoted to higher ranks as their real circumstances shall be known from the separate sheets.

---

1. Umdatu-l Mulk, Amīru-l Umara Ja'far Khān, who previously held the post of *Dīwān*, considered to carry the highest authority, *Cf.*, Athar Ali, *Mughal Nobility under Aurangzeb*, Bombay, 1966, p. 148. 2nd reviced edition, 1996, OUP, Delhi.
2. Prince Muḥammad Mua'zzam was the Viceroy of the Deccan prior to Mirza Raja Jai Singh in 1665 A.D. He was charged for culpable negligence in crushing the Marathas and was replaced by Jai Singh as Viceroy of the Deccan. However, Jai Singh's success against Shivajī proved a fiasco due to Shivajī's flight from Agra in 1666 while Jai Singh's invasion of Bījāpur failed owing to which he hopelessly died in 1667.
3. Champat Bundela, Rajput, held the rank of 5000, *Nuskha-i-Dilkushā*, 15 [b], *'Ālamgīr Nāmā*, pp. 78, 92, 163, 207, 217.
4. Satar Sāl Rāthore, the Rajput *zamīndār* in 1679 A.D. received the rank of 4000.
5. Purandhar fort 18+77 is situated in *sarkār* Junnar, *ṣuba* Aurangabad. *Cf.*, *An Atlas of the Mughal Empire,* Sheet 14 [A].

It was brought to the ears of the joyful tidings of the congregations that if forty cannons are not required in Bījāpur expedition then these should be left at Purandhar, fetch seven cannons with him, while five cannons which were granted from the royal army [*az rikāb-i- daulat*] would arrive shortly and five other cannons, which Ṣaf Shikan Khān[1] has brought from the forts of Daulatabad[2] etc, has decided to dispatch them, and after the accomplishment of the campaign against Siva, has suspended their supply and 6-7 cannons that are at Burhanpur[3], whose transportation is assigned to the men of Dāūd Khān[4], *Nāzim* [Governor] thereof, and their total number would a be either 22 or 23. He is yearning that a *miṣāl* [royal mandate], coupled with auspiciousness, is issued to Ṣaf Shikan Khān, so that he could make arrangement of '*rahaklās*' [carriage for the cannons] and other accessories of the aforesaid cannons together with some other cannons that would be in the forts of the provinces of the Deccan, and the cannon-balls, lead, gunpowder and other necessaries as per the requirements so as to dispatch them expeditiously; and that he should exert his utmost in regularly supplying food provisions to the army guiding to victory. This fact was evident in the affectionate Imperial opinion and the sublime Imperial order received the dignity of issuance in the name of the aforesaid Khān, earmarked in regard to dispatch of five cannons from the fort of Daulatabad to the embodiment of victorious army. And the cannons that Zainul 'Abidīn[5], meanwhile, as per the august Imperial order, has to dispatch from Burhānpur to Aurangabad, *Khujista Buniyād* [happy foundation]; should not show any delay and carelessness in transportation, to that prop of the well wishing sincere ones, [i.e. Mirzā Raja Jai Singh], in view of the fact that we have fixed 20 cannons in the forts of the Deccan, as we have stipulated, and cannons that would be concerning this regulation, so that the clerks of the artillery accompanying the victorious stirrup from the Imperial headquarters, should send cannons in lieu of that, and as soon as six cannons reach Aurangabad, the aforesaid Khān would send *them to the victorious army, together with the cannon balls,* lead, gunpowder and other accessories in agreement with the *Dīwān* and *Buyūtāt* thereof since the Imperial order was issued to them in this matter that by providing necessaries, the aforesaid cannons would be transported to the victorious army as well as supply provisions to the victorious army with utmost endeavours so that sufficient grain could reach there.

It was brought to His Majesty's notice that there is still scope, if further contingents are appointed there, as the riding musketeers have been recruited in

1. Muḥammad Ṭahir Ṣaf Shikan Khān was holding the rank of 2000/1000. '*Ālamgīr Nāmā*, pp. 53, 68.
2. Daulatabad is in *sarkār* Koilkunda, *ṣūba* Ḥaiderabad, *An Atlas of the Mughal Empire,* Sheet 14[A].
3. Burhanpur *pargana* with the fort was situated in *sarkār* Asir, *ṣūba* Khāndesh, *An Atlas of the Mughal Empire,* 14 [A] [21 + 76].
4. Dāūd Khān Qureshī was the Governor of Khāndesh in 1664-66 A.D. '*Ālamgīr Nāmā* pp. 873, 972. We are informed that since Dāūd Khān Qureshī was openly opposed to Jai Singh's campaign against 'Ādil Shāh and endeavoured to discourage the Muslim soldiery by asserting that it was against the dictates of the Holy Quran [*Cf., Haft Anjuman*]. This fact is also endorsed by Qureshī's condition of issuance of a *farmān* to Ṣaf Shikan Khān. Furthermore the Afghan *manṣab*-holders in the Deccan probably developed a soft corner for Bijapur owing to the presence of a number of their compatriots at the court of Bījāpur.
5. Zainul 'Abidīn Bukhari, a Turānī held the rank of 1000/300, Muḥammad Kāzim, *'Ālamgīr Nāmā,* pp. 52, 62, 92, Asiatic Society, Calcutta, Shāhnawāz Khān *Maasiru-l Umara,* Vol. I, pp. 584-87.

an inadequate number in the victorious army. Let it be known to the best of the sincere Rajas that 1000 mounted musketeers are posted in the Deccan province, as out of them 500 are in the campaign, while the other 500 serve in Aurangabad. Two hundred men were posted by His Majesty in the auspicious army and the Imperial order was issued to Ṣaf Shikan Khān that 300 men out of the total matchlockmen thereat should be dispatched to that recipient of innumerable favours so that from the preceding and the supplementary, 1000 men [matchlockmen] could be deployed in the campaign.

It was represented to His Majesty that consequent upon the receipt of the most exalted Imperial order in regard to the campaign, by summoning Mulla Khurram, *Ḥajib* it was told to him that for diagnosing the matters thereof, the sublime Imperial order received the honour of issuance by His Majesty, that it is suitable that 'Ādil Khān[1] should send Mulla Aḥmad,[2] who is an old timer of that region along with a confidante of him [or another person of his trust] so as to make his matter crystal clear. If not, it has become evident from the report of the couriers [*harkārās*] that the aforesaid Khān has not recognized the value of the tremendous favours and the august Imperial courtesies and by closing again his eyes from the rights of favours of tranquility and serenity of mind has made arrangements for the causes of this failure and misfortune. It is incumbent and obligatory on the devotees of the eternal empire to bring him to the point of punishment so as to awaken him from deep slumber of carelessness and pride as the purpose of the arrival of Mulla Aḥmad in the matter is also to acquaint the above named Mulla [from true facts]. It is said that if the Khān dispatch him then the aforesaid person would be kept under observation and if any delay is occurred then this very pernicious thing would become the cause of desolation and military action [against him] and with the representatives [envoys] of the aforesaid Khān the matter of assessment would come into focus regarding the remittance of the amount of tribute [*zar-i-perkash*] in one installment and the cessation of the fort of Sholapur and other *Maḥāls* [fiscal units] of Niẓāmu-l Mulk [i.e. forming the so called Talkokan-i Niẓāmu-l Mulki] and Chincholi[3] etc, that would relate to Zafarabad[4]. The world-subduing Imperial order is issued that whatever has been represented in regard to Mulla Aḥmad would prove extremely commendable and reasonable from the brilliant thoughts of action and balance of the *peshkash* [tribute] of Bījāpur is not in the interest of that worthy of miscellaneous favours. If 'Ādil Khān would dispatch the aforesaid person then by considering him attached with the string of the devotees of the sky like vestibule, he could represent the true facts and if the said Khān would not send the message with that descending place of unlimited favour, Mulla Aḥmad, then the Imperial matters are not to be discussed with the aforesaid Mulla and he cannot interfere in these affairs and whatever is thought

1. 'Alī 'Ādil Shāh, II of Bījāpur.
2. Mullah Aḥmad Naitha who was won over by Jai Singh was a leading noble of Bījāpur and on the Raja's recommendation after 4th September 1665 when this *farmān* was received; he was given the rank of 6000/6000, *'Ālamgīr Nāmā,* pp. 919-920. *Futuḥāt-i-'Ālamgīrī, Cf.,* 103.
3. *Pargana* Chincholi [*sarkār* Māhur] *Cf.,* Irfan Habib, *An Atlas of the Mughal Empire,* OUP, Delhi 1982, Sheet 14[A], 20 + 77.
4. *Ṣūba* Bidar also known as *ṣuba* of Ẓafarabad, was the former seat of the Bahmanis which was annexed from Bījāpur in 1657. It was then given the name of Ẓafarabad. Muḥammad Ṣalih Kumboh, *'Amal-i-Ṣālih.*

in each matter in a particular manner and the appropriateness is seen there than act accordingly otherwise these very matters would become the cause of drawing armies against Bījāpur.

It was represented that *Sarrishta* [register] of *kaghzāt-i-jama'* [papers of revenue assessment], *wāsil-o-bāqi* [collection available here and arrears] and it was known from the agent [*qumāshta*] of Pratīt Rāi that about 7,00,000 rupees in cash from the *Tilangi hūns* and six boxes of ornamented weapons are in the custody of Muḥammad Ṣādiq, *Ḥajib* thereof. In this matter it was represented to the Prince of the elevated family [i.e. Muḥammad Mu'azzam][1] that either he should summon him to Aurangabad or he should order that the aforesaid Muḥammad Ṣādiq should send it to the meekest [Jai Singh] because keeping such objects there is not advisable. It is hereby ordered that following receipt of this exalted Imperial order the aforesaid boxes of the ornamented weapons that would not have much value should be requisitioned by him accompanied with the stipulated cash and the true facts of the stipulated *peshkash* that are known from the Imperial record office [*daftar khana-i mu'alla*] and its details that are recorded on separate sheets are ascertained from the above mentioned sheets. Besides this, its detailed register should be procured from Shafī Khān[2], *Dīwān* thereof so as to become well acquainted with the true circumstances.

It was brought to His Majesty's notice that a reduction of 100/20 was made from the rank of Muḥammad Ibrāhīm, who was sent to Bījāpur and his default is not known as no omission was committed by him in regard to his duties of embassy, and moreover anything, represented to His Majesty, did not occur at all and in totality. If, anything apparently alleged, was relating to his departure, accompanied with his companions, then the sublime princely order is hereby issued that since it was represented by the acquainted of the sky-high-threshold that owing to the honour of this everlasting Empire, negligence was shown that by demotion was reprimanded in rank. In view of the fact that since there is complete trust on the report of that model of the sincerely devoted well wishers, in accordance with the representation of that cream of the sincerely devoted ones, we have restored the reduction in rank. It was represented to His Majesty that as to what are orders in regard to Muḥammad Ṣadiq[3], Muḥammad Ibrāhīm and the Brahmin *harkārās* etc, who are in Bījāpur. Whether before his departure to Bījāpur he should summon them or allow them there or in exchange keep the plenipotentiaries of 'Ādil Khān under his [direct] surveillance or allow them to depart? The world subduing Imperial order receives the honour of enforcement that as soon as the best of the sincere well wishers knowing the Imperial temperament, turn towards the stipulated destination, he should summon Muḥammad Ṣadiq, *Ḥajib,* along with his own envoys to himself, otherwise the agent who would always have to remain there, should not allow Mulla Khurram to proceed to Bījāpur,

1. Consequent upon Jai Singh's death Muḥammad Mua'zzam was appointed Viceroy of the Deccan in 1667 A.D. on whose recommendation Shivajī was pardoned and his son Shambhājī was granted the rank of 5000/5000 while Shivajī was permitted to conquer as much territory of Bījāpur as per his resources or confine only to his territory and comply the Viceroy of Deccan's orders.
2. Shafī Khān, remained Ḥāji Muḥammad Shafī, [I], held the rank of 1000/300 *Akhbārāt-i-Durbār-i-Mu'allā,* 22nd *Safar*, 20th R.Y. He was promoted to the rank of 1500 *zat.*
3. Muḥammad Ṣādiq, who held the rank of 1000/300 was a Turānī, *'Ālamgīr Nāmā,* pp. 55, 92, 206.

before the arrival of the aforesaid group. The true condition of recording a will and testament, which that most sincere of the well-wishers had made with Siva, and the heavily strengthened swearing in like that of the Hindus that Siva took for binding the same, while recalling and allowing twelve small and big forts to him and the *Maḥal* [fiscal unit] whose revenue yield [*ḥāṣil*] is one lakh *hūns,* belonging to the territory of Niẓāmu-l Mulk, to his control and other entreaties contingent upon his treading the straight path of submission and obedience and performing the duties of servitude and compliance of the sky-high Imperial vestibule, and the presence of his son Shambhu[1] and Bebu [wife] before the Governor of the *ṣūba* [province] of the Deccan, in the state of being known, was brought to His Majesty's notice. In view of the complete reliance that we have reposed in on the sincerity, well wishing, prudence [good management] and soundness of imagination of the best of the well wishing Rajas, and the covenant and agreement which that worthy of miscellaneous favours has made with Siva, and the solicitations that he had made about him, that we agreed to accept for the grant of the title of Raja which we have entrusted to the confidante of the sublime Empire, trustworthy of the excellent Empire, best of the magnificent ministers, cream of the sublime Khāns, the administrator of the country and the treasury, the finder of the path of Empire and the good fortune, worthy of numerous favours, deserving miscellaneous kinds of benevolence, the auspicious Khān, substance of the country [*jumlatu-l mulki*], Prime Minister [*madraul-muhami*] Ja'far Khān[2], as the true facts shall be known from the report of the cream of the most excellent of the sublime status. The august Imperial order having title of benevolence that was issued to him owing, to pardoning the sins and suppressing the errors, was adorned with the auspicious palm impression. A robe of honour that we have sent with this *miṣāl* [Imperial order] coupled, with auspiciousness for his pre-eminence and exaltation, by sending them to through him, to him [Shivajī], so as to make him glorified and exalted. It is hereby ordained that he shall permanently remain strict and firm in following the path of submission, as well as remain actively culminate in performing the Imperial duties. The matter of the grant of the fiscal unit [*Maḥāl*] whose revenue realisation would be four lakh *hūns,* shall be assigned from the Talkokan-i-Bījāpur[3] and a territory whose revenue collection would be five lakh *hūns,* that would be given from the Bālāghāt-i 'Ādil Khāniya[4], to Siva as recorded in the sublime Imperial order, that would have been known from its copy that is [also] being sent accompanied with the favourably treasured *Manshur* [Imperial order], having the descending place of abundant favours.

It was brought to the august notice that the sublime Imperial order was enforced regarding the extraction of *Shukrānā* [thanksgiving ceremonial fees] from Siva, Ram Singh[5] *Khānazād* [son of a noble] of the court would represent this matter to

1. This correct rendering is 'also his son with his bride [*babaraya*] to present themselves before the *nāzim* of the Decccan', G.T. Kulkarni, p. 278.
2. *Zawābit-i 'Ālamgīrī,* ff. 82[a-b]. The noble of the first rank like Ja'far Khān was appointed to the post of central *diwān,* which was considered to carry the highest authority.
3. Talkokan-i Bījāpur was most probably known as Takokan-i 'Ādil Khāniya which comprised 7 *maḥāls*, *Cf., An Atlas of the Mughal Empire,* Notes, p. 57.
4. Bālāghāt-i 'Ādil Khāniya was probably given to Siva or it was known as Karnātak-i Bījāpur.
5. Kunwar Ram Singh Kachhwaha held the rank of 3000/2000, '*Ālamgīr Nāmā,* p. 96. He was promoted to the rank of 5000/5000 [2-3h]. He was the Indian Rajput *zamīndār* and was granted the title of Raja, *Akhbārāt* 19th RY, *Rabi* II, *Maasiru-l Umara,* Vol. II, pp. 301-303.

His Majesty. Kunwar Ram Singh represented the circumstances of the aforesaid matter to His Majesty. The Imperial order is issued that let that worthy of miscellaneous favours, by applying his mind act accordingly, and he should not personally disturb Siva regarding performing as *Shukrānā* and a *harkāra* should be deputed for the purpose of depositing the *Shukrānā*. Let it be stipulated that he should accompany with a suitable contingent, to perform the Imperial service in a commendable manner, as his paying respects lies herein. Written on 4th *Rabi* [8th auspicious R.Y. corresponding to 4th August 1665 A.D.].

[On the right hand below the round lineal seal of Aurangzeb is a note in Aurangzeb's hand that reads:]

'He is Overpowering'

Let it be known to the best of the sincerely well-wishing experienced Raja, that whatever has been recorded in that sublime Imperial order, is in accordance with the world subduing command, which should be complied with accordingly, [while] Muḥammad 'Azim[1] [Aurangzeb also called Muḥammad Mu'azzam[2] thus] should consider himself busy in the conquest of Bījāpur and recognize special Imperial attentions increasing towards him day by day.

---

1. Muḥammad Mu'azzam was the Viceroy of the Deccan in 1665. *'Ālamgīr Nāmā,* pp. 819, 854, 869, 874, 879, 903, 904, 907, 913 *Ma'asir-i-Ālamgīrī,* pp. 45, 52.
2. Prince Azimushshan was another son of Aurangzeb who also used to indulge in private trade in 1703 A.D. practicising plunder of the people. *Cf., Mughal Nobility Under Aurangzeb,* p. 156.

APPENDIX- C

Details of *Pargana* ʻĀdilābād, *sarkār*, Burhanpur, *ṣūba* Khandesh, 1104 *faṣlī* [A.D. 1696]

SNo 1.	Name of Village / *Qaṣba* 2.	Total amount in *dāms* [Rs.] 3.	Total measured area [*bighās* / *biswas*] 4.	Aimma land [*bighās* / *biswas*] 5.	Uncultivated land [*bighās* / *biswas*] 6.	Cultivated land [*bighās* / *biswas*] 7.	Estimated income in *tankas* / Rupees 8.	Loss in *tankas* / Rupees 9.	Remainder Tatimma *tankas*/ Rupees 10.	Name of *Jāgīrdār* / *aimmadār* / *khāliṣa* 11.	Total No. of Mughal *dāms*/ *Patwārīs* 12.	Distance/ direction/ Means of Irrigation 13.
1.	*Qaṣba* ʻĀdilābād	647357 [16184]	10097-3	784	4127-19	5185-4	14790/ 7527-1	6930 / 4620-3	5860/ 3306-14	Muḥammad Afẓal *faujdār*	4/1	12 K South, Baknai R & well
2.	Anturli	931534 [23288]	11224-11	4451-19	916-15	5855-17	13430/ 8953-12	4414 / 2943-5	9015/ 6010-7	Ya'qūb Khān	5/2	7 K North Tapti
3.	Anjangaon	62650 [1566]	1360-10	42	474-6	844-4	917/ 611-14	527 / 351-15	389/ 259-15	Saiyid Mukhtār uddin	2/1	3 K North Well
4.	[Narengaon]	60000 [1500]	708-2	-	212	492-14	1024/ 683-4	-	-	Dost Beg	3/1	6 K North Tapti
5.	Itwa	375000	2142 19½	70	228	1844-9	4035 / 2690-8	1210 / 806-13	2825/ 1883-12	Malik Jan Muhammad	3/1	2 K West
6.	Unchande	-	4338-4	714	1222-10	2401-14	3979/ 2652-8	1499/ 999-11	2479/ 1652-13	Shaikh Darya & Others	4/2	1 K North Purna
7.	Umarde	30000 [750]	560	28	121	411	542/ 361-12	341/ 227-12	201/ 134	*Khāliṣa*	1/1	5 K North Well
8.	Kandari	405000 [10125]	6770-16	593	3124-3	3053-13	5426/ 3617-13	1775/ 1183-11	3651/ 2434-2	Sharīf & Others	1/2	10 k West Tapti
9.	Kathūra	152900 [3822]	1288-2	-	331-6	956-16	1644/ 1096-1	459/ 306-3	1184/ 789-11	Muḥammad Ismāʻīl *Faujdār* of Raver	1/1	6 K West Tapti
10.	Kasar Khera	30000 [750]	803-13	-	391-6	412-7	797/ 731-11	230/ 153-14	566/ 377-13	Muḥammad Afẓal	1/1	3 K West Well
11.	Kalaj Khera	10000 [250]	1208	140	696-3	372	250/ 140	80/ 26-11	170/ 113-5	Ya'qūb Khān	1/1	4 K North Stream

12.	Kothle	125000 [3125]	2015-14	48	399	1568-14	3540/ 2360-3	-	-	Aimma	-/1	1/ 4 K
13.	Kanar Khera	114900 [2872]	1605-4	-	1002	603-4	1055/ 703-15	453/ 302-9½	602/ 401-8	Muḥamamd Afẕal	2/1	3 K South Well
14.	Karki	30000 [750]	811-2	-	221-16	589-6	582/ 388-4	320/ 218-10	254/ 169-10	Mīr 'Alī Akbar	2/1	5 K North Nullah
15.	Kothe	65000 [1625]	768-5	-	200-2	568-3	671/ 447-8	421/ 280-13	250/ 166-11	Muḥammad Bāqir	2/1	4 K North Kalinj
16.	Kalwara	66000 [1650]	912-6	-	306-16	605-10	892/ 595-5	757/ 505-5	135/ 90	Mīr Kalān	2/-	5 K North Kalinj
17.	Kund	33334 [833]	651-10	-	191-11	459-19	500/ 334	-	-	Ghiyāṣuddin	1/1	2 K East Purna
18.	Konhi	44000 [1100]	544-17	-	229-10	315-7	675/ 450	-	-	Bahlol posted at Aurangabad	3/1	7 K North Tapti
19.	Kham Khera	86000 [2150]	1664	-	1002-5	661-15	999/ 666-3	485/ 323-9	513/ 342-9	Saiyid Sharafuddin	3/1	1 K North Purna
20.	Khob Khera	70000 [1750]	858-10	-	572-16	285-14	855/ 570-9	342/ 228-10	512/ 341-15	'Azmatullāh	1/1	3 K West Tapti
21.	Khamni	136780 [3419]	1228	14	606-5	607-15	629/ 419-12	209/ 139-10	420/ 280-2½	Saiyid Mukhtāruddin	2/1	3 K North Well
22.	Kharka	120200 [3005]	2997-10	175	1560-8	1262-2	2603/ 1735-6	1247/ 831-12	1355/ 903-10	Muḥammad Ḥusain *Wāqia' nigār* of Raver & Naṣirābād	3/2	9 K West Well
23.	Gondan Khera	181000 [4525]	1802-11	175	833-11	794	1154/ 763-14	799/ 532-12	346/ 231-2	Sarangdhar *zamīndār* of Nūn Khānī	3/1	5 K North Stream
24.	Ghoras Gaon	550000 [13750]	8616-14	1421-17	2578-17	4616	7064/ 4709-13	1308/ 872-5	5756/ 3831-8	Khandari Beg	5/3	3 K East Purna
25.	Chinch Khera	30300 [757-8]	1760	140	841	789	1015/ 676-12	-	-	Amānullāh	3/1	4 K South Well
26.	Changdev	240000 [6000]	4034-11	-	1372	2662-12	3696/ 2464-1	703/ 469-5	2992/ 1994-12	Muḥammad Shafī & others	4/1	2 K West Tapti

27.	Chincholi	73000 [1825]	1231-14	-	576-14	655	1122/ 748-5½	-	-	Muḥammad Ismāʻīl	2/1	3 K West Tapti
28.	Chikhli	90300 [2257-8]	984	-	292-13	691-7	1400/ 933-13	199/ 133-2	1201/ 800-11	Muḥammad Kāẓim	2/1	4 K East Nullah
29.	Jogul Khora	19350 [484]	871-9	-	336-9	535	487/ 325-13	-	-	Tumānjī	1/1	13 K West Vaghur
30.	Daular Khera	21762 [544]	640-4	70	111-1	459-7	666/ 440-10	196/ 130-13	470/ 313-13	Shai<u>kh</u> Ṭāhir	1/1	3 K North Well
31.	Dhurmal	108000 [2700]	1462-18	-	761-6	701-12	1500/ 1000	917/ 611-13	582/ 388-3	Muḥammad Nasir	2/1	2 K South Well
32.	Tarode	265000 [6625]	2504-6	-	148-10	2355-18	5172/ 3448-10	3123/ 2082-1	2049/ 1366-9	Muḥammad Afẓal	3/1	3 K East Well
33.	Dolvi [Dui]	61330 [1532]	1200	-	562-8	637-12	932/ 621-6	710/ 473-7	221/ 147-15	Dost Beg & others	3/1	3 K East Well
34.	Dodhad Buzurg	66000 [1650]	1040	-	283-8	756-12	1357/ 905	307/ 205	1050/ 700	Munim, posted at Burhānpur	2/1	1 K East Purna
35.	Dodhad <u>Kh</u>urd	40000 [1000]	720	-	424	296	405/ 270-3	196/ 130-11	209/ 139-14	ʻAlī Akbar	1/1	1 K North Purna
36.	Dudhale	90000 [2250]	1936	140	893-10	910-10	1427/ 949-3	831/ 556-2	582/ 393-1	Asadullāh Beg	2/1	2 K West Well
37.	Dhamande	73500 [1825]	920-15	-	300-15	620	1170/ 780/2	158/ 105	1012/ 675-2	ʻAbdur Raḥīm Mushrif	2/1	7 K North Tapti
38.	Dhabe	25500 [625-8]	815-6	-	355-6	460	324/ 216-4	276/ 184-7	47/ 31-9	ʻAbdur Raḥīm	2/1	5 K North Tapti
39.	Naigaon	87000 [2175]	2452-8	-	994-9	1387-14	1664/ 1109-14			*Jāgīr*	2/1	5 K North Tapti
40.	Narwel	281000 [7025]	-	560	486-9	1846-5	3717/ 2478-6	960/ 640-5	2757/ 1837-1	*Jāgīr*	4/1	
41.	Haibat Khera Khurd	23100 [575]	1040	140	590	310	320/ 213-13	125/ 83-13	195/ 130	Saiyid Rājī Muhammad	1/1	2 K South Nulluh
42.	Palas Khera	15000 [375]	921-8	28	692-8	201	161/ 107-13	-	-	Shai<u>kh</u> Daryā	1/1	4 K South
43.	Panjane	85500 [2137-5]	1419-19	-	679-19	740	1341/ 894-13	-	-	Sayyid Raji Muḥammad	2/1	3 K West Tapti

44.	Pepri Sanjam	155800 [3895]	2702-19	168	1355-14	1179-5	1827/ 1218-8	204/ 136-3	1623/ 1082-5	Muḥammad posted at Burhānpur	2/1	7 K West Tapti
45.	Pepri Bhojana	176500 [4412-8]	1556-17	-	306-11	1260-5	2240/ 1486-15	841/ 561-1	1388/ 925-14	Imjī	2/1	5 K North Stream & Well
46.	Pepri Akarawat	90000 [2250]	2560	-	814	1746	2687/ 1791-13	586/ 391-2	2101/ 1401-11	Madad-i Ma'āsh	2/1	1 K East Well
47.	Pepri Nandu	110927 [2773]	1152-5	-	481-13	670-12	1063/ 908-15	-	-	Malik Fatḥ Muḥammad	2/1	7 K North Tapti
48.	Purnari	150500 [3762-8]	3004-6	140	1568-13	1285-13	2497/ 1664-11	1097/ 731-5½	1400/ 933-5½	Sairzad	2/1	2 K North Well
49.	Pepri Panjam	27807 [695]	912	210	339	363	300/ 200	217/ 145-3	82/ 54-13	Rozīna of Karamatullāh etc	2/1	5 K North Well
50.	Patondi	95850 [2396]	1242-8	-	211-1	1031-7	1800/ 1200	-	-	Rustam Beg, Amīn-i Ijnas of Burhanpur.	2/1	7 K North Tapti
51.	Bahmani	39000 [975]	543-17	-	236-5	307-12	551/ 367-8	-	-	Muḥammad Afẓal	1/1	7 K North Tapti
52.	Belaswārī	140000 [3500]	2213	327	144-14	1741-6	2691/ 1794-1	890/ 593-6	1801/ 1200-11	Dost Beg	3/1	5 K North Bank of Tapti
53.	Bel Khera	44750 [1119]	579	-	152-19	436-1	800/ 533	298/ 199-1	501/ 334-4	Ya'qūb Khān	2/1	6 K North Bank of Tapti
54.	Bhan Khera	36000 [900]	1200	-	704-4	495-16	470/ 313-5	-	-	Muḥammad Kāẓim	3/1	4 K West Bank of Tapti
55.	Bhokari	182500 [4562-8]	1055	-	202	853	1354/ 903	50/ 33-12	1303/ 869-4	Muḥammad Saī'd, *dīwān-i* Karnātak Ḥyderābād	4/1	6 K North Bank of Tapti
56.	Bhandgora	55000 [1375]	960-10	84	458-16	418-14	1009/ 673-3	633/ 422-5	376/ 250-14	Ghulām Raẓā posted at Burhānpur	1/1	4 K East Nulluh

57.	Bhor	38000 [950]	2400	-	1680	720	638/ 425-7	143/ 95-6	495/ 330-1	‘Alī Beg	3/1	2 K North Well
58.	Bhusāwal	245000 [6125]	5827-12	-	3283	2544-12	4344/ 2896-5	-	-	Muḥammad Kāẓim	4/2	11 K West Well
59.	Manyar Khera	167000 [417-8]	883	-	719-5	163-15	327/ 218	-	-	Amānullāh	2/1	3 K South Well & Nulluh
60.	Melsangoh	93500 [2325]	250 [sic]	-	778-13	1404-10	17781185-7	477/ 318-2	1301/ 867-5	Dost Beg	3/1	3 K North Tapti
61.	Manegaon	130000 [3250]	238	98	977-17	1305-8	2131/ 1421-1	771/ 514-6½	1360/ 900-10½	Muḥammad Afẓal	2/1	1 K West Purna
62.	Mondhudha	105200 [2630]	971-14	-	154-1	817-13	1038/ 691-11	838/ 558-13	200/ 133-11	Shaikh Faẓlullāh Posted with Nuṣratjūng	3/1	3 K North Tapti
63.	Mandhudha	26000 [650]	582-2	-	249-11	333	337/ 225-3	182/ 121-13½	155/ 103-5½	Muḥammad Bāqir	3/1	3 K North Tapti
64.	Malegaon	45000 [1125]	1424-9	-	1077-4	347-5	559/ 373-3	174/ 116-8	385/ 256-11	Yādgār	2/1	3 K South Well & Nulluh
65.	Salbard	72736 [1818]	1155-14	-	340-17	814-17	2212/ 808-2	175/ 117	2036/ 691-2	Ya‘qūb Khān	2/1	3 K South Well & Nulluh
66.	Sokli	66000 [1650]	3340-6	-	2055-6	1285	1399/ 926-8	388/ 259-3	1010/ 677-5	Muḥammad Afẓal	2/1	3 K North Shivri
67.	Rokholi [Kapurli]	40000 [1000]	800	-	177-10	622-10	952/ 635-3½	552/ 368-9	400/ 266-10½	For Shāh Nawāz Khān's Masoelum	2/1	3 K North Well
68.	Lohar Khera	152500 [3812-8]	1723-16	-	396-10	1327-6	2270/ 1513-5	830/ 559-8	1430/ 953-13	Dost Beg	2/1	5 K North Stream
69.	Mehūn	290784 [7268]	2138-4	-	583-9	1554-15	3312/ 2208-6	1174/ 783	2138/ 1425-6	Ḥātim Beg S/o Safī Qulī Khān	6/2	3 K South Tapti
70.	Rūī Khera	218941 [5472]	2525-5	-	972-18	1552-7	3069/ 2046-7	1876/ 1250-11	1193/ 795-12	Haziq Beg	2/1	3 K East Well

71.	Sakigaon	497450 [127680]	10320	-	3956-18	6363-2	11619/ 7746-6	120/ 80-5	11449/ 7666-1	'Ināyat Khān	4/2	12 K West Vaghur
72.	Satāra	72000 [1800]	2160	-	1116-12	1043-8	1688/ 1125-13	-	-	Muḥammad Afẓal	1/1	12 K West Well
73.	Sarola	76000 [1900]	1863-15	364	799-2	700-13	1265/ 843-10	-	-	Muḥammad Muqīm	2/1	3 K South Well
74.	Satod	217500 [5437-8]	4480-14	56	2636-1	1788-13	3406/ 2270-11	801/ 534-8	2604/ 1786-3	Fakhruddin	1/1	3 K South Well
75.	Semalde	93600 [2340]	1967-3	238	759-5	969-18	1249/ 832-14	-	-	Ḥātim Beg	2/1	3 K North Tapti
76.	Sarsoti	158000 [3950]	2522	98	1264-2	1159-18	2516/ 1677-8	424/ 282-13	2092/ 1394-11	Muḥammad Afẓal	1/1	-
77.	Soman Gaon	713330 [1775]	1280	-	399-10	880-10	1037/ 691-2	320/ 213-13	716/ 477-15	Muḥammad Afẓal	2/1	3 K East Purna
78.	Hingne Buzurg	36000 [900]	1536-10	-	829-16	666-14	656/ 437-10	105/ 70-4	551/ 367-6	Amānullāh	2/ 1	1 K North Purna
79.	Hingne Khurd & Bharmanga	13000 [325]	400	-	290	110	201/ 134-6	86/ 57-11	115/ 76-11	Saiyid Ghiyāṣudddin	2/1	1 K South
80.	Hingne Chahrrum	55000 [1375]	840	-	342-17	6	861/ 574-13	513/ 342-9	348/ 232-4	*Jāgīr*	2/1	4 K East Well
81.	Ha[r]tāla	615000 [15250]	9525-5	1414	2122-15	2988-6	8724/ 5818-9	4888/ 3259-4	3835/ 2559-5	Saiyid Murād *Qila'dār* of Baitnl	2/2	2 K South *Tālāb* Stream
82.	___sh	-	11096	280	3916-16	6899-4	11500/ 7667-4	1065/ 710-5	10435/ 6956-15	Mansingh & others *Qila'dār* of Dond	4/1	14 K East Well
83.	[Bahādurpūra]	125000 [3125]	1314-19	-	458-8	856-11	1256/ 837-12	728/ 485-9	528/ 352-3	Shaikh Tājuddin psoted at Bijapur	4/1	12 K East Stream
84.	Kolhara	60000 [1500]	2720	-	512	2208	3656/ 2237-9	888/ 592-11	2467/ 1644-14	Muḥamamd Ḥanīf	4/1	4 K East Purna
85.	Golkhera	20000 [500]	1376	-	970	406	330/ 220-6	28/ 18-15	302/ 201-7	Muḥibullāh	1/1	
86.	Chinch Khera Khurd	61000 [1525]	1272-19	140	479-15	653-4	942/ 628-5	192/ 128-5	750/ 500	Mir Fakhruddin	2/1	13 K East Well

87.	Jodhan Khera	120260 [3006-8]	1272-19	140	479-15	653-4	950/ 633-7	548/ 365-5	401/ 267-12	Saiyid Mukhtār Uddīn	3/1	12 K East Well
88.	Halkhera	65000 [1625]	1809-18	-	555-18	1254	1251/ 834-7	11/ 7-12	1240/ 825-11	Saiyid Mukhtār Uddīn	3/1	12 K East Well
89.	Diskund	60350 [1508-9]	1072-6	-	200-6	872	1426/ 950-13	619/ 413-4	806/ 537-9	Saiyid Mukhtār Uddīn	3/1	10 K East Stream
90.	Dhule	47350 [1183-8]	2049-2	-	1199-5	849-7	1238/ 825-9	61/ 41-2	1176/ 784-7	Saiyid Mukhtār Uddīn	2/1	11 K East Well
91.	Dhaman Gaon	214952 [5374]	2580	182	802-15	1595-5	1864/ 1213-4	341/ 227-14	1523/ 1015-6	Saiyid Mukhtār Uddīn	2/1	16 K East Well
92.	Pimprale	149700 [3742-8]	2685-5	-	627-2	1991-3	2963/ 1975-9	411/ 274-1	2552/ 1701-8	Saiyid Mukhtār Uddīn	2/1	17 K East Well
93.	Parambani	140000 [3500]	2168-14	-	27-9	2140-15	3335/ 2223-12	516/ 344-2	2819/ 1879-10	Bahlol	1/2	12 K East Well
94.	Patod	41000 [1025]	1085-18	-	345-9	739-8	811/ 540-13	210/ 140-6	600/ 400-7	'Abdul Karim *Amīne Ijnās* of *Manṣabdārs*	2/1	12 K East Stream
95.	Parthal	19000 [475]	380-6	-	188-6	192	209/ 139-3	45/ 30-9	163/ 108-14	Saiyid Mukhtār Uddīn	1/1	14 K East Well
96.	Borkhera Buzurg	128100 [3202-5]	2201-4	140	568-10	1492-14	2370/ 1580-8	768/ 512-2½	1602/ 1068-5½	Muḥammad Afẓal	3/1	9 K East Well
97.	Borkhera Khurd	112000 [2800]	1643-18	56	784-5	803-3	1755/ 1170-2	-	-	'Alī Murad	2/1	10 K East Well
98.	Bhote	278800 [6950]	4112	-	1767-13	2344-7	3433/ 1322-7	-	-	Behram Beg *Wāqia' nigār* of Jalnāpur	1/1	14 K East Well
99.	Mardi	27140 [678-5]	998-18	-	308-8	690-10	586/ 390-11	69/ 46-4	516/ 344-7	Saiyid Mukhtār Uddīn	1/1	14 K East Well

100.	Raigaon	120000 [3000]	1602-19	-	384-7	1218-12	1967/ 1311-5	400/ 266-14	1566/ 1044-7	Dost Beg	5/1	14 K East Well
101.	Rajura	105000 [2625]	2604-15	-	1361-13	1243-2	1914/ 1276	803/ 535-9	1110/ 740-7	Muhibb *Amīn-i Filān*	4/1	14 K East Well
102.	Sula	140000 [3500]	2028-4	-	602-7	1425-17	2449/ 1632-13	235/ 157-3	2213/ 1475-10	Abdul Ali posted at Dīwānī-e Deccan	4/1	14 K East Well
103.	Henura [Hivare]	60000 [1500]	1897-3	252	910-6	734-17	1082/ 721-9	31/ 20-11	1051/ 700-14	Saiyid Muhibullāh	4/1	-
104.	Talkhera	43500 [1087-5]	844-5	-	471-5	373	356/ 237-6	214/ 142-15	141/ 94-7	Saiyid Mukhtār Uddīn	4/2	-
105.	*Qaṣba* Chōrthōne	450000 [11250]	8065-17	404	1849-16	5812-1	10145/ 6763-11	2143/ 1429-3	8001/ 5334-8	Muḥammad Afẓal	2/1	8 K East Well
106.	Īsāpur [Ichhāpur]	42000 [1050]	722-13	-	214-13	508	804/ 536	387/ 258-4	416/ 277-12	Dāwūd Beg	4/1	8 K East Purna
107.	Kakora		2720	-	323-5	2396-15	4295/ 2863-5	939/ 626-1	3355/ 2237-4	Muḥammad Aslam posted at Khandesh	3/1	11 K East Well
108.	Korah [kurha]	100000 [2500]	2133-6	-	327-12	1805-14	2331/ 1554-7	-	-	Saiyid Mukhtār Uddīn	3/1	11 K East Nulluh
109.	Chinch Khera [Buzurg]	152230 [3805-12]	2478-9	-	658-2	1821-2	2367/ 1578-5	788/ 458-12½	1579/ 1119-8½	Ghulūm Muḥammad	2/1	7 K East Purna
110.	Jamni		460	-	169-18	290-2	443/ 295-8	259/ 173-4½	183/ 122-3½	Dost Beg	1/1	11 K East Purna
111.	Talki	108000 [2700]	1196-16	-	284-2	912-14	1741/ 1161-1	1417/ 951-6	324/ 209-11	Saiyid Sharfuddin	2/1	7 K East Well
112.	Hilora	136200 [3405]	1683-2	-	308-11	1374-11	2568/ 1712-8	886/ 457-10	1882/ 1254-10	Nūruddīn Muḥammad posted at Burhānpur	2/1	11 K East Purna
113.	Dikhi	26700 [667]	585-17	-	221-19	363-18	482/ 321-12	180/ 120-4½	302/ 201-7½	Saiyid Yāsīn	1/1	11 K East Nulluh
114.	Dom Tek	5000 [125]	248	-	94	154	86/ 57-10	-	-	Ya'qūb Khān	1/1	10 K East Nulluh

115.	Daulat Pura	98000 [2450]	1220	-	749-14	470-6	738/ 492-5	174/ 116-1	564/ 376-4	Shaikh Fazlullāh	1/1	10 K East Well
116.	Nandawel	102000 [2550]	1696-19	-	798	898-19	1724/ 1149-8	582/ 388-6	1141/ 761-2	Muḥammad Afẓal	2/1	8 K East Purna
117.	Haibat Khera Buzurg	170200 [4255]	2460	-	1061-5	1398-15	2365/ 1577-4	372/ 248-6	1793/ 1328-14	Muḥammad Afẓal	4/1	6 K East Purna
118.	Bodvar	17674 [1767]	1125	-	286-7	838-13	1322/ 875-1	465/ 310-5	847/ 564-12	Khalīl Beg	3/1	10 K East Purna
119.	Madhapuri	36000 [900]	696-15	-	305-3	388-12	453/ 302-9	238/ 159	215/ 143-9	Shaikh Shahbaz	1/1	9 K East Well
120.	Moranhera [Morghari]	16000 [400]	780	-	391-19	388-1	436/ 291-1	201/ 134-6	235/ 156-11	Noor & others in Rakāb-i Sa'adat	-	9 K East Well
121.	Mahal Khera	39740 [993-8]	959-18	-	487-8	472-10	613/ 408-13	212/ 141-11	401/ 267	Saiyid Imamuddin posted at Aurangābād	2/1	9 K East Purna
122.	[Dhaman] Gaon	182000 [4550]	1994-18	-	727-16	1267-2	2021/ 1347-8	879/ 586-6	1141/ 761-2	Aftab Muḥammad	1/1	9 K East Well
123.	Wayla	21000 [343]	884-5	56	567-5	260-15	338/ 225-5	285/ 180-7	52/ 34-14	Saiyid Ghiyāṣuddīn	1/1	7 K East Nulluh
124.	Hingne Sivam	20000 [500]	760	-	424-14	335-6	364/ 243-5	-	-	Khwāja 'Abdul Karīm posted at Khandesh	-	10 K East Well

Appendix – D

An Openning to Rājarām: A *Farmān* of Aurangzeb, 1689

I wish to draw attention to a *farmān* of Aurangzeb, which was issued in late March 1689, from the vicinity of Chākan [Islamābād] soon after Sambhajī's capture and execution, which last event took place on 11th March 1689. His brother Rāja Rām, who had been practically a prisoner of his, was proclaimed ruler at Raigarh, on 8th February 1689. The present *farmān* was issued to Prince Muḥammad A'zam Shāh, Aurangzeb's third son, regarding the position to be taken in relation to Rāja Rām. The *farmān* has been acquired by the National Archives, No. NAI - 1697, and a photograph of it is annexed to this [APPENDIX - D]. It is interesting that when in private hands, a photograph [apparently a bad one] of it was brought to the notice of Sir Jadunath Sarkar, who, in a letter dated 9th February 1932 AD, pronounced the document to be genuine and pointed out briefly its context and occasion. He held [rightly, of course] that the lines in "thick running hand" written at the top and top left was "Aurangzeb's autograph".

I append a translation of the text of the *farmān* with a minimum of annotation, while a photograph of the document is also annexed: some parts of the text are not clear in the photograph are still legible in the original paper. Sir Jadunath, it may be mentioned, was able to decipher only bits of the text, because of the bad quality of the photograph supplied to him.[1]

Reading the *farmān* it is clear that Aurangzeb wished to leave the door open for negotiations, with Rāja Rām though not for useless parleys. It would seem, at first reading, that having gained the military advantage by the destruction of Sambhajī, Aurangzeb was, in fact, demanding total surrender from Rāja Rām, the only concession to be made was with regard to his personal safety. Yet the concern at the fiasco in the negotiations at Mumbai, caused by the unspecified "folly" of Nāhar Khān, or the failure of Yāqūt Khān's son to return from the court, suggests that the failure to respond to Rāja Rām's petition, however caused, was not intentional; and the copy of a *farmān* was now being sent to Prince A'zam in reply to two petitions sent [by Rāja Rām?]. Unfortunately, there is no clue as to what it contained; indeed, we also do not know what Rāja Rām's proposals were in his "petition" sent from Mumbai. These are dark corners that may hopefully be illumined one day by further discoveries of documents.

1. Photograph, courtesy my friend Qazi Jauhar.

Farmān of Aurangzeb
To Prince A'zam

[Invocation]: And Allah hath full power and control[1]

Let it be known to the son, attached to my soul; giving great strength to the caliphate, the pearl of the great Empire, endowed with exalted determination, dearest of the high station, Muḥammad A'zam Shāh, having been chosen for special attention, that the representations dispatched by him, have received the honour of special perusal, of miraculous effect, and the single sheet [*fard*] of the news report [*akhbār*], has also been seen by His Majesty. Whatever the Imperial courier [*harkāra-i bādshāhī*] had written, its copy has been sent [to the Prince]. In dealing this group, which has no sense of honour, is possessed neither of numbers or quality, being much addicted to rocketry [*bān-andāzi*] and constant [?] mobility, there are two alternatives: Either Rāja Rām comes to offer service to that pupil of the eye [Prince A'zam] or retires to a stronghold [*qila'*] and passes his time there. In the first case, upon his surrender of the fort [of Raigarh], which after the capture of Shambha, the faithless, and resident of Hell, belongs to the exalted Imperial government, but which, due to the action of some negligent ones, he has seized, he should be brought to His Majesty's presence after grant of a promise [*qaul*] of personal safety. Sarfrāz Khān[2] would remain in Konkan, with a contingent and Fateḥ Jung Khān[3], with the troops assigned to him should reinforce Yāqūt Khān[4]. Yādgār Ḥusain Khān[5] is good enough to be the castellan. In the second case, the fort [of Raigarh] should be effectively besiezed, a stop put to useless negotiations, and [proper occupation of] the country and forts achieved by establishing military posts. According to what that the dear son has written, [paper torn in Sarkar's bad photograph], the hope is strong that, with the favour of the Benevolent God, this work should not stretch up to the rainy season. If the inclination of that scion of the Caliphate is turned towards the happy mean, and the [required] power is attained, then that dear, discerning one should proceed up to the Ghat, as if engaged in tour and hunt, and become acquainted with the true position of the passes, or otherwise from his stationary position, he should undertake full enquiry and report the facts [to the Emperor]. Grain in Dhanda Rajpuri is available with Khairiyat Khān[6], fort commandant [*qila'dār*] thereof. Yāqūt Khān, brother of the aforesaid Khān, who has the charge of Armau [armada], went to Mumbai, the port held by the English, and sent the petition ['*arzdāsht*] of Rāja Rām, through the folly of Nāhar Khān[7], carried by his [Yāqūt Khān's?] son, to this sky-high court. Since he did not receive back what he had sent, he returned disappointed. We have [now] sent copies of the petition of our happy, fortunate grandson [A'zam's son], along with the *farmān* in response to

1. Quran, Chapter XII, Section 3, Verse 21.
2. Sarfarāz Khān Deccani, held the rank of 5000/4000 [1000x2-3h] [*Selected Documents of Aurangzeb's Reign* [*SDAR*], ed. Yusuf Ḥusain Khān, Hyderabad, 1958, p. 48, Ṣamṣamud Daulah Shāhnawāz Khān, *Ma'asirul Umara,* Vol. II, pp. 469- 73].
3. Fateḥ Jung Khān held the *manṣab* of 3000/2000, [*'Ālamgīr nāma,* pp. 79, 93, 126]. He was promoted to the rank of 3500/3000 [*ibid.*, 290, *Ma'asirul Umara,* Vol. III, pp. 22-26].
4. Yāqūt Khān held the *manṣab* of 2000/700 [100x2-3h], *SDAR,* p. 10.
5. Yādgār Beg, probably Yadgar Husain Beg, had the rank of 1000/500 [Ṣaliḥ Kambūh *'Amal-i Ṣāliḥ,* III, p. 465; *'Ālamgīr nāma,* p. 68].
6. For details of Khairiyat Khān, see *SDAR*.
7. Sangrām Khān Ghor *alias* Nāhar Khān held the rank of 3000/1000 [*Akhbārāt,* II *Muḥarram*, 40th RY of Aurangzeb; *Nuskha-i Dilkushā*, f. 91[a].

the two petitions [of Rāja Rām]. Whatever has been written above, about the action, necessary to face all difficulties [*azzarūrātu yantijul makhtūrāt*] is right [*haqq*].

Written on 16th *Jumāda II*, 32nd R.Y. [27th – 28th March 1689 AD]

[Lines in Aurangzeb's writing at the top and top left]:

After returning thanks to God and supplication for forgiveness to Him, my dearest son should know that on Monday, we would, Almighty God willing, like to see the fort of Islāmābād [Chākan][1], which is four *kurohs* [over 15½ kms] away from here and five *kurohs* [12½ kms] away from the camp of that pupil of the eye [A'zam]. If that light of the eye also … [Text damaged][2].

1. As Sir Jadunath Sarkar noted in his letter Islamabad is to be identified with Chākan, which was so renamed by Aurangzeb. It belonged to the Mughal *sarkār* of Junnar of *ṣūba* Aurangabad. See Irfan Habib, *Atlas of the Mughal Empire*, Delhi, 1982, p. 55, col. [c].
2. The writing, in fact continues at the top [upside down] extending to top right corner, most of it torn away, ending with the word *qila'dāri*.

Bibliography

The source material concerning the process of the formation of an early modern Mughal state has been carefully studies and several new sources have been studied much alternatively. The catagorisation of the source material in six sections has been made. We have taken into consideration the most prominent but less used Inayat Jung Collection which contains some documents of Shah Jahan's reign as well as Mughal Archives five volumes as the last four are still unpublished. Thirty two historical works have been carefully studied and used where necessary. Moreover documents and *insha* collection numbering 25 have been properly utilised. Similarly six biographies and Persian dictionaries have also been carefully used.

We have also laid stress on modern works based on original contemporary and near contemporary source to integrate the prevailing situation in the by gone era which are quite significant. We have also taken into consideration 12 important historical journals and well known historical proceedings for a better understanding of our subject in a most comprehensive manner. Although there is much need for a detailed analysis of the bibliographical study of the source material yet this brief summary would give a brief picture of the material to some extent *viz.*, on important source material Blochet Supplement Persian in Bibliotheque Nationale Paris No. 482, is also quite important.

[I] Inayat Jung Collection, *National Archives, New Delhi:* This is a rich collection of official Mughal documents. Interestingly enough reports, memoranda and accounts were regularly sent to the *Dīwāns* of the Deccan or to the *bakhshīs* from the provincial *Dīwāns* and *bakhshīs* in each of the six Deccan provinces which were kept in the Imperial chancery at Aurangabad. The entire collection totals 1,35,000 documents from 1658 to 1774 A.D. beginning in regular series from circa 1680 of Aurangzeb to 1774. Unfortunately a large number of documents of Aurangzeb's reign destroyed at Aurangabad due to the pond situated there. However, prior to 1724, these are Mughal Imperial records; after 1724, they are archives sources for Hyderabad state under first Nizam and his two immediate successors till 1774. In 1961 the National Archives, New Delhi purchased it from 'Abbās Ali Khān, a successor of Inayat Jung, whose ancestor Nawab Majdud Daulah had served Nizam Ali Khān as chief Minister from 1761 to 1775 in the late eighteenth century. These papers had remained in family's possession for two centuries and in 1924-25 the seal of Inayat Jung was fixed on each document which are gratifyingly authentic and exact, once deciphered. Majority of these documents represent cases or problems are clearly middle-level administrative memoranda, testimony to the complexity and sophistication of the Imperial bureaucracy. These have been digitized as well by Iran Culture House, New Delhi.

[II] HISTORICAL WORKS

1. Abū-l Faẓl Ma'muri, *Tarikh-i Aurangzeb*, Br. Mu. Or. 1671.
2. Abū-l Faẓl, *Akbarnama*, Bib. Ind. 3 vols., Calcutta 1873-87.
3. Abū-l Faẓl, *A'in-i Akbari*, Nawal Kishor, Lucknow, 1273 AH. Tr. Jarrett, Calcutta, 1944, Vol. I-i.
4. 'Ali Muḥammad Khān, *Mirat-i Aḥmadī*, ed. Syed Nawwab Ali, Baroda, Vol. I, 1927-28.
5. Anonymous: Collection of Deccan Records & C. Br. Mus. M/F Department of History Aligarh Muslim University.
6. 'Āqil Khān Rāzi, *Wāqiā't-i 'Ālamgīrī*, ed. Zafar Hasan, Aligarh, 1945.
7. Bhimsen Burhanpuri, *Nuskha-i Dilkushā*, Br. Mus. Or. 23 [Rotograph in the Department of History Library, Aligarh, No. 43].
8. Brij Rai, *Dastūru-l 'Amal-i Shahanshāhi*, revised and enlarged by Thakur Lal, MS Br. Mus., Add. 23831 [Rotograph in the Department of History Library, Aligarh, No. 52].
9. *Dastūru-l 'Āmal Āgahī.*
10. *Dastūru-l 'Amal-i 'Ālamgīrī* [1659] Ms. Br. Mus. Add. 6598.
11. Hātim Khān, *'Ālamgirnāma*, MS Br. Mus. Add. 2633 [Rotograph in the Department of History Library, Aligarh, No. 37].
12. Ishwardas Nagar, *Futuḥat-i 'Ālamgīrī*, Delhi, 1978.
13. Jahangir, *Tuzuk-i Jahangiri*, ed. Blochmann., ed. Syud Ahmad, Ghazipur, 1862.
14. *Khulāṣat-ul Siyāq*, AMU, Aligarh.
15. *Kitāb-i Deh-ba Dahī Ṣūbajāt-i Deccan*, A.P. State Archives, Hyderabad, MS 373.
16. Lachhmi Nara'in 'Shafiq', *Khulaṣatu-l Hind*, transcript from Āsafiya [MS No.768/492] in the Department of History, Aligarh.
17. Lāhorī, 'Abdul Ḥamid, *Pādshāhnāma*, Bib. Ind. Calcutta, Vol. II.
18. *Mirātu-l 'Ālam*, Bakhtwar Khān, [ed] Sajid Alvi, 1979.
19. Muhammad Amīn Qazwini, *Pādshāhnāma*, transcript, Riza Library, Rampur, Department of History, AMU, Aligarh.
20. Muḥammad Hashim Khwāfi Khān, *Muntakhab-al Lubāb*, ed. K.D. Ahmad & Haig, Bib. Ind., Calcutta, 1866-74, 1909-25.
21. Muḥammad Ṣādiq Khān, *Shāh Jahān Nāma*, Br. Mus. Or. 174 [Rotograph in the Department of History Library, Aligarh, No. 39].
22. Muḥammad Ṣādiq Khān, *Tawarikh-i Shāh Jahān o Aurangzeb*, MS, Br. Mus., Or. 174 [Rotograph in the Department of History Library, Aligarh, No. 45].
23. Muḥammad Ṣāliḥ Kambūh Lāhorī, *'Amal-i Ṣāliḥ,* ed. G. Yazdāni, 4 vols., [Vol. IV, Index]. Bib. Ind., Calcutta, 1923-46.
24. Muḥammad Wāris, *Pādshāhnāma*, transcript of Riza Library [Rampur], MS in the Department of History Library, Aligarh, Nos. 86-87. India Office, Ethe, 329.
25. Saiyid Ashraf Khān, S.M. Azizuddin Husain [ed.] *Raqāim-i Karaīm.*
26. Saqi' Mustai'd Khān, *Ma'asir-i 'Ālamgīrī*, Calcutta, 1871, tr. Jadunath Sarkar, Calcutta, 1947.

27. Sharif Najafi, *Majālis-i Salāṭin*, Ms. Br. Mus. Or. 1903.
28. Sundhari La'l, *Tuḥfa-i Shāh Jahāni*, India Office, Ms No. 339 [Rotograph in the Department of History Library, Aligarh No. 91].
29. S.M. Azizuddin Husain [ed.] *Kalimāt-i Taiybāt*.
30. *Waqā'i Ajmer*, transcript, Department of History, Library, Aligarh from Asafia Library, Ḥaiderabad, 1078-88.
31. *Wāqi'āt-i 'Ālamgīr*.

[III] DOCUMENTS, INSHA COLLECTIONS

1. Abul Fath Qabil Khān, *Ādāb-i 'Ālamgīrī*, ed. Abdul Ghafūr Chaudhurī, 2 vols., Punjab [Pakistan], 1971, MS Department of History Library, No. 20 [bound with MS No. 50]; MS National Archives of India, Oriental Records Division, Acc. No. 2019.
2. *Aḥkām-i 'Ālamgīri*. ed. Sir Jadunath Sarkar, as *Anecdotes of Aurangzeb*.
3. *Akhbārāt-i Durbār-i Mua'lla*, Sitamau Transcript, Department of History Library.
4. Blochet Suppl. Pers., 482 Bibliotheque Nationale, Paris [Microfilm in Department of History, Aligarh, No. 470].
5. B.N. Goswamy & J.S. Grewal, *The Mughals and the Jogis of Jakhbar: Some Madad-i Ma'ash and other Documents*.
6. Francis Bernier, *Travels in the Mughal Empire* 1656-1668, by Archibald Constable Delhi, 1972.
7. Harkaran, *Insha-i Harkaran*.
8. Isardas Nagar, *Futuḥāt-i 'Ālamgīrī*.
9. John Fryer, *A New Account of East India and Persia being Nine years Travels 1672-81*. II Edited by William Crooke, London, 1912.
10. *Makatibat-i Haẓrat Saḥib Qirāni*, Abdus Salām, MS No. 288/58.
11. Mannuci, *Storia do Magor*, Vol. IV.
12. *Miratu-l Iṣtilāh*.
13. Munshi Malikzada, *Nigar Nama-i Munshi*, Nawal Kishore, Lucknow, 1882.
14. M.A. Nayeem, *Mughal Documents: Catalogue of Aurangzeb's Reign*, A.P. State Archives, Hyderabad, 1981, Vol. I, part I.
15. *Nama-i Muzaffari*, Hardoi, 1917.
16. National Archives of India, Acquired Documents, NAI-1697.
17. Saiyid Najib Ashraf Nadvi, *Ruqa't-i 'Ālamgīr*, Vol. I, Azamgarh, 1930.
18. *Samsthan Documents*, A.P. State Archives, Hyderabad.
19. Sir Charles Fawcet, Oxford, 1906-27. *The English Factories in India*: *Bombay, Surat and Malabur Coast*, Oxford, 1904, Vol. III.
20. Yusuf Husain Khān, *Selected Documents of Aurangzeb's Reign*, 1958.
21. Yusuf Husain Khān, *Selected Documents of Shāh Jahān's Reign*, Daftar-i Diwani Deccan, Hyderabad, 1950.

22. Yusuf Husain Khān, *Selected Waqā'i of the Deccan*, 1660-1671, Hyderabad, 1953.
23. W. Foster, *The English Factories in India*, 1618-19, 13 vols.
24. *Zawābit-i 'Ālamgīrī*, MS, Br. Lib, Or, 1641.
25. Z.A. Shakeeb [ed.], *Mughal Archives*, A.P. State Archives, 1977, Vol. I.

[IV] BIOGRAPHIES AND DICTIONARIES

1. F. Steingass, *Persian-English Dictionary*, Delhi, 1973.
2. H.H. Wilson, *Glossary of Judicial and Revenue Terms*, Delhi, 1968.
3. Khwaja Yasin, *Glossary of Technical Terms* [Rotograph, Department of History Library, Aligarh, No. 244].
4. Shah Nawaz Khān, *Ma'asiru-l Umara*, ed. Maulwi Abur Raḥim, Bib. Ind., 3 vols, 1888.
5. Shaikh Farīd Bhakkari, *Zakhiratū-l Khwānīn*, ed. S. Moinul Haq, 3 vols, Karachi, 1961-74.
6. Tek Chand Bahar, *Bahar-i 'Ajam*, Nawal Kishore, Lucknow, 1916.

[V] MODERN WORKS

1. Abha Singh, Jhujhar Singh's Rebellion: A Reappraisal, *PIHC*, 1990, pp. 230-40.
2. Anees Jahan Syed, *Aurangzeb in Muntakhab-al Lubab*, Bombay, 1977.
3. A.A. Beg, Aurangzeb's Second Viceroyalty of the Deccan and His Relations with Bijapur', *Isl. Cul.*, XLVIII, I, 1974.
4. A.J. Qaisar, 'Note on the Date of Institution of *Manṣab* under Akbar', *PIHC*, 1961.
5. A.R. Kulkarni, *Maharashtra in the Age of Shivajī*, Poona, 1969.
6. B.R. Grover, 'Raqba Bandi Documents Under Akbar', *IHRC*, Pt. II, 1960.
7. *East Khandesh District Census Hand Book*, Bombay.
8. Ghulam Yazdāni, *Jahanara*, Hyderabad, 1937.
9. G.C. Divedi, *The Jats, Their Role in the Mughal Empire*, Delhi, 1989.
10. G.T. Kulkarni, A Note on Mirza Raja Jai Singh's Purandhar and Bijapur Campaigns: An unpublished *Farmān* of Aurangzeb [1665], *PIHC*, 2010, Calcutta, pp. 274-83.
11. G.T. Kulkarni, *The Mughal-Maratha Relations: Twenty – Five Fateful Years* [1682-1707], Pune, 1983.
12. Haroon Khān Sherwani, *History of the Quṭb Shāhi Dynasty,* Delhi, 1974.
13. H.K. Naqvi, *History of Mughal Government and Administration*, Allahabad, 1974.
14. H.K. Sherwani & P.M. Joshi, *History of Medieval Deccan*, 1974.
15. Ibn-i Hasan, *The Central Structure of the Mughal Empire and its Practical Working Up to the Year 1657*, Oxford, 1936.
16. Iftikhar A. Khān: Ideological Factor in the Mughal Empire, *Journal of Pakistan Historical Society*, 75 [A], 1960.
17. Irfan Habib, *An Atlas of the Mughal Empire: Political and Economic Maps with Detailed Notes, Bibliography and Index*, OUP, Ist 1982, IInd 1984 and IIIrd 1986.

18. Irfan Habib, *Essays in Indian History – Towards a Marxist Perception*, Delhi, 1995, 1996, 14th reprint 2016.

19. Irfan Habib, 'Evidence for Sixteenth Century Agrarian Conditions in Guru Granth Sahib', *IESHR*, Vol. I, No. 3, 1964.

20. Irfan Habib, '*Manṣab* and Salary Scales Under Jahangir and Shahjahan', *Isl. Cul.*, Vol. LIX, No. 3, 1985.

21. Irfan Habib, '*Manṣab* System, 1597-1637', *PIHC*, 1967.

22. Irfan Habib, [ed] *Medieval India*, 1992, 2014 [16th ed].

23. Irfan Habib, 'Postal Communication in Mughal India', *PIHC*, 1985.

24. Irfan Habib, *The Agrarian System of Mughal India, Bombay*, Ist 1963, IInd 1999 & IIIrd 2014.

25. Irfan Habib, 'The Social Distribution of the Landed Property in Pre-British India', Enquiry, N.S., Vol. II, No. 3, 1969.

26. Irfan Habib, *The Zamīndārs in the A'in, PIHC*, 1958, pp. 320-23.

27. Irfan Habib, 'Usury in Medieval India', *CSSH*, 1964.

28. I.H. Qureshi, *Ulema in Politics*, New Delhi, 1985.

29. I.H. Qureshi, R.V. Ranade, *Feudal Content of the Maharashtra Dharma, IHR*, Delhi, pp. 40-50, I, 1977.

30. Jadunath Sarkar, *A Short History of Aurangzeb*, 1972.

31. Jadunath Sarkar, *Fall of the Mughal Empire*, 4 vols.

32. Jadunath Sarkar, *History of Aurangzeb: Mainly Based on Persian Sources*, Vol. 5, Delhi, 1972.

33. Jadunath Sarkar, *House of Shivajī*, 3rd edn., Calcutta, 1960.

34. Jadunath Sarkar, *Shivajī and His Times*, 5th edn., Calcutta, 1952.

35. Jadunath Sarkar, *Studies in Aurangzeb's Reign*, Calcutta, 1933.

36. Jagdish Narain Sarkar, Military Dispatches of a Seventeenth Century General, translation Mirza Raja Jai Singh's, correspondence *Haft Anjuman*, MS of Udairaj.

37. Jagdish Narain Sarkar, *The Life of Mir Jumla, the General of Aurangzeb*, 2nd edn., Delhi, 1979.

38. *Jalgaon District Census Handbook*, 1961, Bombay.

39. John Campbel: *Khandesh District Gazeteer*, 1880.

40. J.F. Richards and Velcheru Naraina Rao, Bandatry in Mughal India, Historical and Folklore Perceptions, *IESHR*, XVII, 1980.

41. J.F. Richards, *Document Forms of Official Orders of Appointment of the Mughal Empire*, Cambridge, 1986.

42. J.F. Richards, Revenue Flows and Money Supplies in a Mughal Province in [ed.], *Imperial Monetary System of Mughal India*, OUP, 1987.

43. J.F. Richards, J.F. Richards with Stewart Gordon, 'Kingship and *Pargana* in Eighteenth Century Khandesh', *IESHR*, 22 [4], 1985.

44. J.F. Richards, *Mughal Administration in Golconda*, OUP, 1975.

45. J.F. Richards, Mughal Retreat from Coastal Andhra, *Journal of Royal Asiatic Society*, Great Britan and Ireland, 1978.

46. J.F. Richards, Mughal State Form and the World Economy in *CSSH* [*Comparative Studies in Society and History*, Hangne].

47. J.F. Richards, *The Mughal Empire*, 1993 in the *New Cambridge History of India*.

48. J.F. Richards, The Hyderabad Karnatak, 1687-1707 *Modern Asian Studies*, 1979.

49. Kavi Shymaldas, *Vīr Vīrnod*, Vol. 2 [out of 4 vols.].

50. Lane Pole, *Rulers of India, Aurangzeb and Decay of the Mughal Empire* [1707-1748], Oxford, 1901.

51. Momin Mohiuddin, *The Chancellory and Epistolography Under the Mughals*, Calcutta, 1971.

52. Muḥammad Ṣaliḥ Athar, *Tarikh-i Meo Mehr*, District NUH [Haryana], 2009.

53. Muzaffar Alam, *The Crisis of Empire in Mughal North India*, Delhi, 1987.

54. Muzaffar Alam, 'The *Zamīndārs* and the Mughal Power in the Deccan', *IESHR*, XI, [March, 1974], pp. 74-91.

55. M. Aslam, *Aurangzeb ki Takht Nashini Mein Ulema ka Kirdār*, Lahore, 1991.

56. M. Athar 'Ali, '*Manṣab* and Imperial Policy under Shahjahan', *PHIC*, 1975.

57. M. Athar 'Ali, *Mughal India, Studies in Policy, Ideas, Society and Culture*, Delhi, [8th ed.] 2014.

58. M. Athar 'Ali, Review on Richards', *Mughal Administration in Golcunda*, in JAS, XXXV, February, 1976, p. 160.

59. M. Athar 'Ali, *The Apparatus of Empire, Awards of Ranks Offices and Titles to the Mughal Nobility*. [*1574-1658*], OUP, Delhi, 1985.

60. M. Athar 'Ali, *The Mughal Nobility Under Aurangzeb*, Bombay, 1966.

61. M. Athar 'Ali, 'Towards an Interpretation of the Mughal Empire', *JRAS*, No. 1, 1978.

62. M.N. Pearson, Shivajī and the Decline of Mughal Empire, *Journal of Asian Studies*, *XXXV*, Vol. 2, Feb., 1976.

63. M.Z. Siddiqui, 'The *Muhtasib* Under Aurangzeb', *Medieval India Quarterly*, 5, 1963, 113-19.

64. Noman Ahmed Siddiqi, '*Implications of the Month Scale in the Manṣabdāri System*', *PIHC*, 1961.

65. Noman Ahmed Siddiqi, *Land Revenue Administration under the Mughals*, [1700-1750], Delhi, 1989 [reprint].

66. Riazu-l Islam, *Indo-Iran Relations, A study of the Political and Diplomatic Relations Between the Mughal Empire and Iran*, Tehran, 1970.

67. R.A. Alvi, 'Mughal Geographical Accounts of Khandesh', *Medieval India. A Miscellany*, Vol. III, Bombay.

68. R.C. Majumdar, *The Mughal Empire*, Bombay 1974.

69. R.P. Tripathi, *Some Aspects of Muslim Administration*, Allahabad, 1936.

70. R.P. Tripathi, *The Rise and Fall of the Mughal Empire*, Allahabad, 1987.

71. [Saiyid] Najib Ashraf Nadvi, *Muqaddama-i Ruqa't 'Ālamgīr*, 2nd edn., Azamgarh, 1981.

72. Shaikh Muḥammad Ikrām, *The Muslim Community of Indo-Pak Sub-Continent.*

73. Satish Chandra, *Jizya and State in India during the 17th Century*, *JESHO*, Vol. 12, Part IV, 1959.

74. Satish Chandra, *Parties and Politics at the Mughal Court*, 3rd edn., Delhi, 1979, 4th ed., OUP, 2002.

75. Satish Chandra, 'Social Background to the Rise of the Maratha Movement during the Seventeenth Century', *IESHR*, 3, 1973, pp. 207-17.

76. Satish Chandra, *Studies in Medieval Indian History*, 5th ed, OUP, 2008.

77. Satish Chandra, 'The Deccan Policy of the Mughals- Reappraisal', *IHR*, 1978-9.

78. Seema Singh, 'The Golkunda Tribute', Aligarh Papers on Indian History Congress, 1986.

79. Shibli Nomani, *Aurangzeb Alamgir Par ek Nazar.*

80. Shireen Moosvi, Aurangzeb's *Farmān* to Rasikdas on Problems of Revenue Administration 1665 in *Medieval India*, [ed.] Irfan Habib, OUP, Delhi, 1992 till 2014 [16th ed.].

81. Shireen Moosvi, *Economy of the Mughal Empire*, c. 1595 - *A Statistical Study*, OUP, 1994, 2016.

82. Shireen Moosvi, 'Evolution of the *Manṣab* System Under Akbar Until 1596-7', *JRAS*, 1981.

83. Shireen Moosvi, 'The Economic Consequences of the Deccan Policy', *PIHC*, 1982.

84. Shireen Moosvi, 'The *Zamīndārs*' Share in the Peasant Surplus in the Mughal Empire-Evidence of the *A'in-i Akbari* Statistics', *IESHR*, XV, No. 3, 1978.

85. Stephen P. Black, 'The Patrimonial Bureaucratic Empire of the Mughals, in H. Kulke, *The State in India, 1000-1700*, Delhi, 1999, pp. 278-303.

86. S. Moinul Haq, *Prince Awrangzib: A Study*, Karachi, 1962.

87. S.M. Azizuddin Husain, *Jizya* - It's Imposition during the Reign of Aurangzeb, An Examination, *IHR*, XXVI No. II, July 2000.

88. S.M. Azizuddin Husain, Scarcity of *Pāibāqī* Lands during Aurangzeb's Reign in the Light of Inayat Jung Collection Documents, *PIHC, XXXIX*, 1978, pp. 426-30.

89. S.M. Jaffar, *Some Cultural Aspects of Muslim Rule in India.*

90. S.R. Sharma, *Crescent in India*, Bombay, 1960.

91. S.R. Sharma, *Mughal Empire in India*, Bombay, 1940.

92. S.R. Sharma, *Religious Policy of the Mughal Emperors*, 1988.

93. S.A.A. Rizvi, *Muslim Religious Movements in Mughal North India in the 16th and 17th centuries*, Delhi, 1965.

94. S.A.I. Tirmizi, '*Studies in Islam*', Delhi, I [3], 1964, pp. 174-84.

95. S.Z.H. Jafri, *Agrarian Systems of Awadh under the Mughals and the Nawab Wazirs*, 1595-1856 A.D., Ph. D. submitted at AMU, Aligarh, in 1986.

96. S.Z.H. Jafri, 'Mughal Relation with the Portuguese Administration in Goa, 1701-Evidence from Persian Records in Lisbon Archives', *PHIC*, 1987, pp. 302-311.

97. S.Z.H. Jafri, *Sarkar Qanungos*: 16th – 17th Century Documents, *PHIC*, 1985.

98. Tapan Raychaudhurī & Irfan Habib, *The Cambridge Economic History of India* [1200-1750], Cambridge, 1982.

99. T. Rama Rao, *Biographical Sketches of the Rajas of Venkatagiri*, Mandu, 1875.

100. William Irvine, *The Army of the Indian Mughals*, Delhi, 1962.

101. W.H. Moreland, '*Manṣab* [Rank] in the Mogul State Service', *JARS*, 1936.

102. Yusuf Husain Khān, 'The Deccan Policy of Mughal', *Isl. Cul.*, 1944.

103. Zahiuddin Faruqui, *Aurangzeb and His Times*, Delhi, 1972.

104. Zahoor Ali Khān, 'The Mughal Campaigns' in Bijapur - Geographical Interpretation Dharwad, 1988.

105. Zakir Husain, A *Zamīndār* Family of *Sarkār* Māndu - *Ṣūba* Malwa- Archival Evidence, *PIHC*, 1992-93, pp. 311-20.

106. Zakir Husain, 'Agrarian Survey of *Pargana* 'Ādilabad, 1696- A Second Reconnaisance', Aligarh Papers on Indian History, 1987.

107. Zakir Husain, *Calendar of Administration Documents in Ādāb-i 'Ālamgīrī*, M. Phil Dissertation submitted at AMU, Aligarh, 1991.

108. Zakir Husain, '*Jāgīr* System in the Deccan During the Last Years of Aurangzeb', JOS, Delhi, Vol. II, No. 2, 1990.

109. Zakir Husain, 'The Maratha-Mughal Conflict - Seen Through Official Documents of the Later Years of Aurangzeb's Reign' [mimeograph].

110. Z.U. Malik, *The Reign of Muḥammad Shah*, [1719-48], Bombay, 1977.

[VI] JOURNALS & PROCEEDINGS

1. *Comparative Studies in Society and History.*
2. *Cyclostyled Volume of Aligarh Papers on Indian History.*
3. *Indian Economic & Social History Review.*
4. *Indian Historical Review.*
5. *Indian Historical Record Commission.*
6. *Islamic Culture.*
7. *Journal of Asian Studies.*
8. *Journal of Objective Studies.*
9. *Journal of the Royal Asiatic Society of Great Britain and Ireland.*
10. *Medieval India – A Miscellany*, Vol. III.
11. *Medieval India*, 1992 – 2014 [16th ed.].
12. *Proceedings of the Indian History Congress.*

Glossary

ABWĀB:	Exaction of officials in addition to the *jama' Agrarian System,* pp. 175, 284 & n. 288.
AFRĀD-I DEHSĀLA:	Comparative revenue statements of past ten years giving the jama' [assessed revenue] and area or estimation of net revenue yielding capacity of different territories on the basis of which these were assigned in *jāgīr*. Irfan Habib, 'A System of Trimetallism & C!, in J.F. Richards' [ed.] *The Imperial Monetary System of Mughal India,* Delhi, 1987, 144.
'AHDNĀMA:	Treaty, for detail see Momin, *Epistolography and Chancellory under the Mughals,* Calcutta, 53.
AUT:	Measure of Area [Deccan].
'AMAL:	Revenue collection to the period when a person has been revenue collector so that an event may be described as happening during the *'amal* of a particular official. Irfan Habib, 'Evidence for Sixteenth Century Agrarian Conditions in Guru Granth Sahib', *IESHR,* Vol. I, No. 3, 1964, 72n.
'AMAL GUZĀR:	Revenue collector = *'amil, 'amal-i jarīb*, revenue assessment by measurement *Agrarian System*, p. 240 & n.
'ĀMIL:	Official in-charge of both the assessment and collection of the revenue. Goswami & Grewal, *The Mughals and the Jogis of Jakhbar,* 1967, 63.
AMĪĪN:	Revenue collector = *munsif,* head of measuring party, imperial officer concerning conformity in the *Khāliṣa* and *jāgīr, Agrarian System*, 2014, pp. 212, 218n, 262n, 295, 318-20 & nn, 321, 323 & nn, 324, 325n, 327 & n, 333, 334, n, 338 & n, 339.
'ARZDĀSHT:	Supplication, a petition or an official communication addressed by a subordinate to his superiors. N.A. *Siddiqi, Land Revenue C.,* 5n.
ASHRAFI:	[I] Mughal gold coin [*muhr*].
ĀWĀRJA:	Balance document listing individual *jāgīr* holdings within each *pargana* for a particular point in time. These documents were usually drawn up in order to ascertain the available revenues open for reassignment to *manṣabdārs*. J.F. Richards 'Official Revenues and Money Flows in a Mughal Province', ed. *The Imperial Monetary System of Mughal India,* 1987, 209.
BĀLĀDASTI:	"High-handedness", fines and bribes exacted by the officials.
BALKATI:	Exaction for granting permission to have the crop & cut. *Agrarian System*, 288, & n.,

BĀGHĀT:	Fields, irrigated by wells [Deccan].
BAITULMĀL:	Public treasury.
BAKHSHIUL MAMĀLIK/ MĪR BAKHSHĪ:	In charge of awarding *manṣab* and checking *manṣabdārs'* contingents through the dāgh system; and controller of intelligence, *Apparatus of Empire,* XXV.
BĀJ:	Impost trade, *zakat, Agrarian System*, p. 72.
BAKSARIYA:	Infantry soldiers and "Clubmen of *Zamīndārs*" Cf. William Irvince, *The Army of the Indian Mughals,* 1907, 168.
BARĀWARDI:	Ordinary *sawār* rank, I. Habib, *'Manṣab System',* IHC, 1967.
BATĀĪ:	Crop sharing = *ghalla bakhshi, Agrarian System,* 237, 238 b, 265.
BHENT:	Customary or compulsory gift to superior [*Cf., salāmi*].
BIGHA:	Measure of area, *Agrarian System*, 2, 233, 249-250 & nn.
BI-L MAQTA':	[Revenue etc.] fixed at the same figure rate indefinitely or for fixed period, *Agrarian System*, 215, 274 & n.
	Lumpsum, at the same figure permanently, *Agarian System*, 175.
BISWA:	One-twentieth of bigha, 407n, one-twentieth share of *zamīndār* or other rights [e,g. *muqaddami*] of village, *Agrarian System*, 165-6, 174 & A, 191 n.
CHĀCHER:	Land kept follow for previous three or four years, *Agrarian System,* 261, 293 n.
CHAKLA:	Territorial unit between *ṣūba* and *pargana* but not necessarily identical with *sarkār, Agrarian System*, p. 320 & n.
CHAUDHURĪ:	The hereditary *zamīndār* held responsible for the collection of revenue in each *pargana, CEHI,* I, 58.
CHAUDHURĪ:	Officer or area of Jurisdiction or perquisites of *chaudhurī, Agrarian System,* p. 336 n.
CHHINT:	*Chhint* [Hindi] *Chit* [Pers]. Any cotton cloth [usually calico] with floral or other patterns printed [by block-stamping of resists or mordents and subsequent dyeing or painted [by brush or pencil called *qalam*] *Atlas*, 69.
CHAUKI:	Toll and guard post. *Agrarian System*, 74 n.
CHAUTH:	One-fourth revenue, claimed by chief of *zamīndār* [Maharashtra]. *Agrarian System*, p. 335.
C<u>HA</u>VAR:	Measure of area 120 bighas [Deccan], *Agrarian System,* 345 n].
DĀ<u>GH</u>:	Branding of horses for checking the contingents of *manṣabdārs* at muster or identification as ispector, *Agrarian System*, 381 &n.
DĀK CHAUKI:	The official postal organisation, *dak* being the word for post and *chauki* signifying relay stations for runner and horses, I. Habib 'Postal Communication in Mughal India, *Cyclostyled Volume of Aligarh Papers on Indian History,* 1985, p. 54.

DĀKHILI:	New village still shown under on [*aṣli* village] for revenue purpose, *Agrarian System*, 295 n].
DĀROGHA:	Superintendent of any department, Steingass, *A Comprehensive Persian-English Dictionary,* 497.
DĀROGHA-I PESHKASH:	Officer-in-charge of receiving *peshkash* [gift] made to the Emperor. The *peshkash* included ceremonial offerings as well as the levy or annual tribute paid by the chiefs and subordinate rulers. *Cf., Apparatus*, XXV.
DAROGHA-I TOPKHANA:	Corresponding to *Mīr-i Ātish*, Chief of the Artillery, *Apparatus*, XXV.
DASTURU-L 'AMAL:	Schedule of cash revenue rates. Shireen Moosvi, 'The *Zamīndārs*' Share in the Peasants' Surplus & C', *IESHR*, Vol. XV, No. 3, 1978, 359; *idem*: 'The Evolution of the *Manṣab', JARS*, 1981, 173.
DECCANI:	Nobles and officers recruited from the Deccan, *Agrarian System*, 312 & n.
DESĀĪ:	*Pargana* level Semi-hereditary official concerned with revenue collection [Gujarat & Deccan], *Chaudhurī, Agrarian System,* pp. 87, 90, 161n, 175, 223n, 306n, 332 D, 33 A, 337 n, 386, 401n 402 n.
DAUL-I JĀGĪR:	*Jama'* of *jāgīr, Cf., Agrarian System*, 222n.
DAUL:	Papers containing revenue assessment for season or year, *Agrarian System.*
DESHMUKH:	A hereditary revenue village officer. He was to maintain an armed body of retainers and assist in the collection of land-tax. Richards' *Mughal Administration*, 27. Counterpart of *chaudhurī* [& *desāī*] in the Deccan, *Agrarian System*, 186, n, 295, 335 & n, 402.
DEHNĪMĪ [DAHNĪM]	'Five percent charge on revenue [process equal to it] divided between the *muqaddam* and *chaudhurī, Agrarian System,* pp. 162 & n, 163n.
DESKULKARNI:	*Pargana*-level accountant = *deshpāndiya Agrarian System*, p. 85.
DESHMUKHI:	It was a kind of *in'ām* which was hereditary in character and peculiar to Maharashtra and Deccan only and it was made in terms of the *dāms* of the income of certain *parganas* in consideration of a stipulated *peshkash* presented to the Emperor. The right implied a share in the revenue amounting to 9 to 10 percent. *Mughal Chancellary,* 99; *Agrarian System,* 349n.
DESHPĀNDIYA:	Counter of *qanūngo* in the Deccan, see also *Deshkulkarnī, Agrarian System*, 33.
DĪWĀN or WAZIR:	*Wazir-i Kul* or *Diwan-i Kul*. Minister in charge of Imperial finance, *jāgīr* assignment and revenue collection. *Apparatus*, XXV.
DIWANIAN'-I 'UZZAM:	Imperial finance ministry, its official, *Agrarian System*, 326n.

DU_ASPA SIH_ ASPA: A trooper with two horses receiving higher pay then the ordinary [*barawardi*]. This additional *do-aspa sih-aspa* came into use under Jahangir for the first time and theoretically it was a part of the *sawar* rank. Apparatus, XIII.

DUNIYADĀR: 'Men of the World'. The Mughals always insisted on calling "Ādil Shāh" "Ādil Khān" and Quṭb Shāh "Quṭubūl Mulk" and from Akbar's time onwards both of them were styled *duniya-dars*, being worldly men, *Agrarian System*, 183.

FARMĀN: This term is applied to every royal missive that issued from the sovereign on the chancellery bearing the Imperial *tughra* and seal. S.A.I. Tirmizi, Medieval Indian Diplomatics, *PIHC*, 1982, 3-4.

FAUJDĀR: Commandant of a territory. In-charge of law and order. *Apparatus*, XXI, XXV. Commandant in charge of peace and order usually in a group as *parganas*, *Agrarian System*, 320 & n, 334, 337.

FOṬADĀR: Treasurer = *Khizānadār faujdārī* jurisdiction of or cess levied by a *faujdār*.

FAUJDĀRĪ: Military command, *Agrarian System*, 181.

GAU SHUMARI: Tax on cattle, *Agrarian System*, 284 & n.

GIRASYA: Originally he had been servant of the state, holding a revenue assignment similar to the *jāgīrs* of the Mughal period, but later indistinguishable from that of the *bhūmia* [allodial proprietor]. *Agrarian System*, 143.

GUMĀSHTAS: Agents of revenue officials, revenue collectors of *jāgīrdārs, Agrarian System*, p. 326.

ḤĀL-I ḤĀṢIL: The actual realisation of the revenues. Shireen Moosvi, *IESHR,* No. 3, 1980, 331. *Agrarian System*, 178n.

ḤĀṢIL- SANN-I KĀMIL: Revenue realised in year of maximum collection, *Agrarian System*, pp. 306, 465 & n, 466n.

HANGĀM-I KHĀM: Case or occasion when revenue was assessed on, or collected directly from, peasants [& not through intermediaries], *Agrarian System*, p. 183.

ḤAOQ-I MILKIYAT: Claim to share of produce based on ownership [of superior or rights], *Agrarian System*, p. 179.

HARKARA: Spy; an attendant upon men of rank, also employed to go on errands; a messenger, Steingass, 1496.

ḤASBŪL AMR: Order issued on behalf of the princes, *Agrarian System*, 282; *Cf.*, Momin, *Chancellery and Epistolography Under the Mughals*. 98.

HASBŪL ḤUKM: Imperial orders issued through court officials or Minister's order on oral instructions of the Emperor, *Agrarian System*, 282n.

ḤĀṢIL: [plural *ḥaṣilāt*, revenue, actually collected]. *Cf., Jama'*.

ḤĀṢṢIL-I KĀMIL or ḤĀṢIL SAN-I KĀMIL: Revenue realised in year of maximum collection, Agrarian System, 306, 465 & n 466n.

HAST-O-BUD:	Summary assessment upon casual inspection of state of harvest *Agrarian System*, p. 238 & n.
ḤUBŪBĀT:	Exaction of officials, zamīndārs, etc, in addition to the jama' = abwab, *Agrarian System*, p. 284.
ḤUQŪQ-I DĪWĀNĪ:	Fiscal claims of government. *Agrarian System*, pp. 300 n 343.
ḤUQŪQ-I ZAMĪNDĀRĪ:	*Zamīndārs* claim on produce of land, *Agrarian System*, p 179.
IJĀRADĀR/ MUSTĀJIR:	Revenue farmer/contractor, *Agrarian System*, 235.
IKHRĀJAT:	Extortion of officials professed to meet their "expenses" [*Cf.*, *malba*] *Agrarian System*, pp. 288 n, 343.
IN'ĀM:	When a *jāgīr* is assigned not against a rank, but as in'ām, free bestowal, without placing the assignee under any obligation. I. Habib, 'The Social Distribution of Landed Property in Medieval India', 124.
IN'ĀM-I ALTAMGHĀ:	Land assigned as *altamghā*, in addition to *jāgīr* assigned against *Manṣab* pay or without grantee holding any *manṣab, Agrarian System*, p. 358 n.
JĀGĪR:	Transferrable territorial revenue assignment to the *manṣabdār*. A tract of land which the king grants to *manṣabdārs* and persons of that kind, they might take its revenue [*maḥṣul*] from cultivation, whatever it be, *Bahar-i 'Ajam*', Nawal Kishore, 283, as cited in *Agrarian System*, 257; cf. Shireen Moosvi, *The Economy of the Mughal Empire* & c., 196.
JAMA':	Literally meaning 'gathered together, aggregate, total, the estimation of tax income or the expected net revenue, i.e. the gross realisation less charges of collection and other allowances for subordinate right holders. Shireen Moosvi, 'Share of the Nobility in the Revenue of Akbar's Empire' 1595-6, *IESHR,* No. 3, 331.
JAMA' BANDĪ:	The work of determining *jama'* [1], *Agrarian System*, p. 261 n.
JAMA'-I RAQAMI:	Term for *Jama'* [2] under Akbar's predecessors and during his early years *Agrarian System,* pp. 243, 302 n, 303-4 nn, 345.
JIHAT:	Cesses, taxes on certain trades, *Agrarian System,* pp. 283 n.
KANKŪT:	Assessment of revenue by applying a crop rate [*rai'*] to area measured before hand, *Agrarian System*, pp. 214, 232, 236, 255, n, 260 n, 276-77, 290.
KALĀNTARĀN:	Literally "big ones"; members belonging to dominant elements, *CEHI*, 248.
KĀRKHĀNA:	Workshop and store establishment. S.M. Jaffar, *Some Cultural Aspects of Muslim Rule in India,* 88; *Economy of the Mughal Empire,* 262.

KARORĪ:	Revenue-collector of the Khāliṣa, the Imperial revenue, to establishment, *Agrarian System*, 275-83.
KHĀLIṢA-I SHARĪFA:	Territories and sources of revenue, reserved to yield revenue, the Imperial treasury, *Agrarian System*, 259.
KHĀNAZĀD:	Lit: those born of persons already slaves of the Emperor, a primary claim on a *manṣab* was thought to vest in the sons and close kinsman [*khānazād*] of those already in service, *Apparatus, XXI.*
KHĀSRĀT-I ZABT:	Paper giving details of area measurement in order to assess revenue thereon, *Agrarian System*, p. 253 & n.
KHARJ-I SADĪR O WĀRID:	Expenses on touring officials or on hospitality to travellers, *Agrarian System*, p. 288.
KHAṢA SHARĪFA:	Emperor's own establishment, *Agrarian System*, p. 328.
KULKARNI:	Counterpart of *Patwari* in the Deccan. *Agrarian System,* p. 166 n.
KOTWAL:	Police and head of town, *Agrarian System*, p. 75 n.
KHURĀK-I DAWWĀB:	Supplies for animals of imperial stables, demanded from *manṣabdārs*, money levy in lieu of such supplies; *Agrarian System*, p. 311 n.
KUROH:	The Perisan form of Sanskrit *Krosa*. The standard imperial Kuroh often called *Kuroh-i Pādshāhi* represented a length of a little over 2½ miles, *Atlas,* XIII.
MAHĀJAN:	Merchant-usurers, professional money-lender. Irfan Habib, 'Usury in Medival India', *Comparative Studies in Society and History,* VI, No.4, July 1964, 394.
MAḤAL/ PARGANA:	The two terms being practically synonymous ordinarily stand for the territorial division within the Mughal empire, [*Atlas, IX*]. *Pargana* is essentially territorial division; *maḥal*, a revenue unit. All *parganas* were maḥals, but the word *maḥal* was also applied to certain specified sources of revenue such as port or market taxes, *Economy of the Mughal Empire* & c., 10.
MAḤAL-I TAN:	Territories from which salary is to be paid by *jāgīr*.
MĀL-I WĀJIBĪ:	The authorised land-revenue, CEHI, I, 242.
MALBA:	Payment from village fund on items other than land revenue, official exactions from villages, 154n, 244 n, land revenue due, see *mal* [land revenue] *Khārāj, Agrarian System*, pp. 153, 209-10, 300n 380n, 400.
MANDAVI:	Trade centre, market. Richards' *Mughal Administration in Golcunda,* 1975, 186.
MANṢAB:	Numerical rank, the number assigned to a man during the Mughal period; basic unit for determining status, pay, and military obligations. *Cf.,* Shireen Moosvi, '*The Evaluation of Manṣab*', *JRAS*, No. 2, 1981, 173; M. Athar Ali, 'Towards an Interpretation of the Mughal Empire', *JRAS*, No. 1978, 40.

MANSHŪR:	A royal receipt and a mandate, Momin, 54.
MAHR:	Wife's dower in Muslim law, *Agrarian System,* p. 192n.
MAWĀS:	MAWAS, Rebellious area, 30, *talab* [rebel [s]], *Agrarian System*, pp. 379 & 399.
MĪRĀB:	Official in-charge of irrigation, from canals and channels, *Agrarian System*, pp. 36, & 96.
MIR BAKHSHI / BAKHSHI-I MAMĀLIK:	In-charge of the awarding *manṣabs* and checking *manṣabdārs* contingents through the *dagh* system and controller of intelligence. *Apparatus*, XXV.
MUCHALKA:	Bond, written undertaking, *Agrarian System*, pp. 164 n, 179.
MUSA'ĀDAT:	Loan advance made to a *manṣabdār*, loan, *Agrarian System*, 269; *Mughal Nobility*, 52; 'Usury in Medieval India', 410.
MUTAFARRIQA 'AMAL:	Assignment of several *jāgīrs* within a single *pargana, Agrarian System*, pp. 326, 32-7n.
MUṬĀLIBA:	Claim of the Imperial exchequer for amounts owed to it by the *jāgīrdārs, Agrarian System*, pp. 267, 269.
MUTAṢADDI:	General designation for official. But specially applied to the customer of the Ports of Cambay and Surat. *Apparatus*, XXV.
MUWĀZNA-I DAH SALA:	DAHSALA, Papers giving details of area and revenue of per ten years [or more or less] *Agrarian System,* pp. 5n, 213, 246n, 259, 305, 306 n, 307, 338 n.
NIṢĀR:	Gifts offered by the nobles to the Emperor, *Mughal Nobility*, 144.
NETAN:	Unit of area [Berar], *Agrarian System*, 6n.
PĀIBĀQĪ:	Lands temporarily in-charge of the Imperial officials pending assignment to *jāgīrdārs*, Athar 'Ali, Review of J.F. Richards' *Mughal Administration*, 1975, 159; cf. *Agrarian System*, 285-9.
PARGANA:	Territory delimited by Mughal administration for revenue and administrative purposes [*Cf., maḥāl*], *Agrarian System*, pp. 2; 300, 332 & 336.
PESHKASH:	Fixed annual tribute; large present or a cash offering, additional to any revenues which the chief might have to pay the court, *Agrarian System*, 181, 184-5, 289.
PHAD:	System of cooperative management of irrigation from canals and streams [Baglāna], *Agrarian System*, p. 33.
RĀHDĀRI:	Tolls and cesses exacted by the various authorities controlling the routes, *Agrarian System*, 67.
ṢADRŪṢ ṢUDŪR:	Central minister in-charge of revenue grants, *Agrarian System*, p. 343.
SARDESH-MUKHĪ:	Claim to 9 [or 10] percent or revenue.
SALĀMI:	Gift offered on salutation by inferior visiting his superior, *Agrarian System*, pp. 176, 288 & n.

SARKĀR:	Administration of government, establishment of a prince or a noble; sub-division of a province, *Agrarian System*, 267, 325 & n.
SARKHAT:	Receipt or memorandum given by a *muqaddam* and *patwari* to peasants, *Agrarian System*, pp. 107, 272.
SATARAHI:	Synonym of *zamīndārī*, from claim of one-seventeenth of the produce. *Agrarian System*. pp. 166. 172 & n, 179-80, 187 & n, 200, 345 n.
SAZĀWAL:	Persons deputed by the central government for the execution of the orders, Z.U. Malik, *Reign of Muḥammad Shāh*, 293.
SELA:	Shella, selaes. High priced cotton stuff, *A'in-i Akbari*, I, 108.
SIHBANDI:	Troops employed by the nobles for a temporary period for collection of land revenue and police duties, *Nigār Nāma-i Munshī*, 93.
SHIKĀR:	Hunt, levy of money or labour to help organise hunt; *Agrarian System*, pp. 289, 289-90 n.
SHIQDĀR:	[Originally officer-in-charge of *shiqq*, large territorial division [14th century] *pargana* level officer-in-charge of revenue collection under the Sūrs, subsequently petty revenue official.
ṢŪBEDĀR:	This and other designations such as *nāzim, hākim, sipahsālār* and *ṣāḥib-i ṣūba* were used for the Governor of *ṣūba, Apparatus*, XXVI.
TAFAWAT-I DĀGH:	Deduction from pay claim, I. Habib, '*Manṣab* Salary Scales Under Jahangir and Shahjahan', *Islamic Culture*, July 1985.
TA'AHHUD:	A pledge given by a prospective official about the amount he would assess to collect.
TAN, TANKHWAH, TANKHWAH-I JĀGĪR:	A *jāgīr* assigned in lieu of the salary due to *manṣabdār, Mughal Nobility*, 75.
ṬALAB:	The annual total pay claim, I. Habib, '*Manṣab* and salary scales under Jahangir and Shahjahan, *Islamic Culture*, July, 1985.
TAKHFĪF:	Abatement in revenue, *Mughal Nobility*, 77.
TAPPA:	A combination of few villages named after the largest of the villages under its jurisdiction; sub *maḥāl*, Yasin's Glossary Br. Mus. Add. 6603 f. 55 [b]; B.R. Grover, 'Raqba Bandi Documents Under Akbar', *IHRC, XXVI*, Pt. II, 59.
TAQĀVI:	[Literally, strength giving], loans made by the government to cultivators, a term used in the Mughal administration for advance for the cattle and for sinking wells, I. Habib in *CEHI*, 65; *The Mughals and the Jogis of Jakhbar*, 97n.
TAQSĪM:	Papers containing records of area and revenue of past years, *Agrarian System,* pp. 243 & n 244n, 246n.
TAṢḤIḤA:	The minister's certificate verifying the horses, arms and armours maintained by a *manṣabdār* bore the signatures of the *Dīwān* and the *Bakhshī*, Momin, 93-9.

TAUFIR:	Excess on specified area of revenue grant, *Agrarian System*, p. 346.
THĀNA:	A military or a police post. A.J. Qaisar, *Medieval India-A Miscellany,* II, 72.
THĀNADĀR:	Officer-in-charge of military or police post, *CEHI*, 244.
TOPK̲H̲ĀNA:	The artillery department which included all fire arms not only but also muskets and rockets whether handled by horsemen or infantry, *Ma'āsir-i 'Ālam-gīrī*, tr. J.N. Sarkar, 329.
WAQĀI':	The news reports of the *waqāi' nigār*, I. Habib, Postal Communication in Mughal India, 65.
WAQĀI' NAWĪS:	News-writer or official entrusted with sending reports of all public business and other news. Usually the office was a subordinate of the *Mīr Bak̲h̲shī.* He appointed his own agents [*gumashtas*], *Apparatus*, XXVI.
WAṬAN JĀGĪR:	The chiefs who obtained *manṣab*, their old dominions were known as their *waṭan, Mughal Nobility*, 79.
WUJŪHĀT:	Taxes other than the land revenue, comprised under *jihāt* and *sair jihāt, Agrarian System,* 283.
YĀDDĀSHT:	A note, memorandum, memorial [Wilson, *Glossary*, 800].
ZAMĪNDĀR:	Persian compound meaning holder of land used for any person with any hereditary claim to a direct share in the peasants' produce, *CEHI,* 244.
ZORTALAB:	[Usually of territory] "force demanding, seditions, not paying revenue unless forcibly compelled to do so = *mawās*", *Agrarian System*, pp. 327n, 379 &n.

Index

B

E

L

M

N

Q

R

T

U

V

W

Y

Z